Selected Papers
of Arnold Goldberg

Selected Papers
of Arnold Goldberg

Arnold Goldberg

IPBOOKS.net
International Psychoanalytic Books

International Psychoanalytic Books (IPBooks),
30-27 33rd Street, #3R
Astoria, NY 11102
Online at: www.IPBooks.net

Interior book design by Maureen Cutajar, gopublished.com

ISBN: 978-0-9985323-0-1

Foreword

While attending the Chicago Institute for Psychoanalysis, I looked forward to being Arnold Goldberg's student in a class for advanced candidates. Given his five decades of practice as a psychoanalyst, teacher, scholar, and always a philosopher, I believed that Goldberg would surely have the certainty that I longed for and his teaching would provide the security of a fixed and definite position.

During one of his classes Goldberg drew a line across the blackboard to illustrate a point. One end of this line represented classical theory, and at the opposite end, was the point of view that considered classical theory as not especially significant. Goldberg asked each of us where we staked our claim on this line. A feeling of relief set in, as this seemed to indicate that I could find a position that was absolute and certain.

My relief would not last, of course, as a careful reading of Goldberg's papers written between 1971 and 2015 tells another story: That while we might locate ourselves on all sorts of lines, the multiplicities of view on transference, conflict, misunderstandings, pluralism, correctness, negotiation, pragmatism, confidentiality, boundaries and apologies, demonstrate that an absolute and fixed position cannot exist.

Later though, I would feel pleased by this understanding, that wherever we place ourselves on Goldberg's line, with every negotiation and each interaction, we are moved from our static position. Goldberg reminds us that each and every negotiation can cause us to remake ourselves, and that "once one can see phenomena in a new light then they will never be the same as before" (1984).

When I approached Goldberg about collecting his papers and organizing them into a book, I asked if he wanted to participate. It should come as no surprise that Goldberg encouraged me to undertake this project and to find my own point of view. He said that I was free to collect and arrange his papers in the way that best suited me. With this in mind, I have ordered the papers chronologically and thematically. Each chapter begins with a brief reflection of how Goldberg's views offer greater understanding of psychoanalytical themes, such as the importance of empathy and the roles of pluralism and pragmatism in determining a course of therapeutic action. I hope the selected works can serve as a valuable reference in finding your point on Goldberg's line, at least until your next professional negotiation changes your perspective once again.

—GM

Table of Contents

CHAPTER ONE

Where I Was From

The publication of Arnold Goldberg's 1975 paper *A Fresh Look at Perverse Behavior* is a significant and marvelous advance in the development of psychoanalytic theory.

In this paper, one of Goldberg's earliest, he frames his own theoretical approach to perverse behavior and in the process expands Heinz Kohut's conceptualization of perversions as disturbances in the narcissistic realm. According to Goldberg, "perverse activities are attempts to supply substitutes in the absence of the self-object, which if lost lead to more regressive states." At the time, this approach was a radical departure from the more widely accepted explanation linking perverse activities to the Oedipus complex, drives and infantile fixations. This was, indeed, a fresh look.

If, in Goldberg's view, perverse behaviors are considered disturbances in the narcissistic realm, this perspective alters the nature of the transference configurations. Disruptions, particularly misunderstandings, in the relationship may result in the use of sexual behavior to manage painful feelings and stem the tide of regression.

This paper includes two vivid clinical examples that well articulate Goldberg's fresh perspective. The first case presents a merger transference where the patient's need to maintain a connection was expressed in dreams of giant electric wires and plugs, of plumbing connections, all related to a plugging into a source of energy and feeling. Separations, misunderstanding, or lack of sensitivity disrupted the patient's connection to the analyst, and as a result, the narcissistic configuration was revealed. Breaks in the self-object tie have a number of consequences, such as overstimulation or rage as a response to the grandiose drive not being properly reflected. The affects that emerge from these breaks may threaten fragmentation and in an effort to cope, the patient may sexualize the experiences. This is the point of therapeutic action, which places disruptions in the self-object connection at the center of the analyst's understanding and explanation.

In the second clinical example, the patient had undergone a previous analysis, where perverse sexual symptoms were believed to be a manifestation of a superego deficit following the birth of his first child, a son. In the second analysis, the perversion was understood as a feeling of longing for union with an idealized and omnipotent figure and that this feeling was sexualized. The patient's recounting of the perverse material to the analyst could be considered a turning point in the analysis, as the patient indicated a capacity to tolerate affects usually handled via sexualization.

This paper introduces to us the concepts of narcissistic transferences, the consequences of disturbances in self-object connections, and the use of sexual symptoms as a solution to the disruptions in the self-system.

A Fresh Look at Perverse Behavior (1975)

Perverse behaviour or deviant behaviour is that which has gone astray. Synonyms, such as wicked and corrupt, clearly indicate the nature of the detour and the need to correct the wayward path. Sexual perversions are felt to be directional errors along the road to sexual maturity and thus signs of persistent infantile fixations or regressions. Although some sexual perversions seem clearly deviant, there are a host of non-genital activities which are considered normal or at least non-pathological as long as they do not represent the main avenue of sexual enjoyment. Indeed if one considers the present socio-cultural climate in evaluating normal sexuality, only the most blatant forms of deviance qualify clearly as pathology. Yet a good number of sexually perverse individuals are manifestly unhappy and are clearly driven by their perversions. It would appear that psychoanalytic investigations of the perversions would yield a rich source of data to define and delineate the nature of this pathology. However, psychoanalysts have not been of uniform opinion as to the aetiology and classification of perverse sexual behaviour.

Anna Freud (1965) says that it is considered a rule that the diagnosis of perversion in an adult signifies that primacy of the genitals has never been established or has not been maintained, i.e. that in the sexual act itself the pre-genital components have not been reduced to the role of merely intro-ductory or contributory factors. When Sigmund Freud noted the reciprocal relationship between neurosis and perversion he indicated that the neurotic suffered because he could not allow himself the expression of perverse impulses while the pervert indulged himself and thereby avoided neurosis. Freud (1905) defined perversion as sexual activities which either extend in an anatomical sense beyond the regions of the body that are designed for sexual union or that linger over the intermediate relations to the sexual object. In 'A Child is Being Beaten' (1919) he clarified the relationship of the perversion to the Oedipus complex. Fenichel (1945) underlined this concept by considering the perversions as equivalent to neurotic symptoms in that they represented escapes or retreats from castration anxiety and could be classified and analysed on that basis. However, the issue of perversion still remains a dilemma. When a given sexual act can be considered a perversion is still in question, since the category runs the gamut from severe manifestations of distorted reality, such as seen in some bizarre fetishists, to behaviour considered within the purview of acceptable sexuality, such as cunnilingus, fellatio and perhaps even infidelity.

Glover (1932) was never happy with the classification of perversion. He commented on the fact that Freud felt that perversions are not formed directly from component impulses but must first have been refracted through an oedipal phase (as Fenichel had insisted in a rigid way). Thus, Glover felt that aetiological differentiation became paralysed. After reviewing the contributions of Sachs that repression was a serial process and thus layering could be seen in perversions and that of Rank who felt that the perversion groups had different systems or localities, Glover advanced a new approach. He felt that perversions show an orderly series of differentiations as regards both aim and completeness of object, but this developmental order runs parallel to the developmental order of psychoses, transitional states, neuroses and social inhibitions. He suggested that perversions assist in preserving the amount of reality sense already achieved by what represents a sacrifice of freedom in adult libidinal function. Thus he postulated a developmental series of anxiety situations which could give rise to either neurotic symptom formation or perversion formation. Perversions were said to patch over flaws in the development of the reality sense.

Kohut (1971) has advanced somewhat this idea of Glover's and introduced a novel way of conceptualizing some perversions. He has proposed that specific circumscribed disturbances in the narcissistic realm are usually the nuclei of these disorders. Based on his outline of stages in the development of narcissism from early autoerotic activity or disparate self-nuclei to a cohesive self which has two basic forms, the grandiose self and the idealized parental imago, he has redefined perverse behaviour in terms of a sexualization of pathological narcissistic constellations.[1] Perverse activities

---

[1] Freud explained the significance and meaning of sexualization in the following quote from the Schreber case (1911): 'People who have not freed themselves completely from the stage of narcissism—who, that is to say, have at that point a fixation which may

4

are attempts to supply substitutes for the absent narcissistically invested self object which if lost permanently lead to more severe regressive states. Perverse sexual activity may thus be said to stem the tide of regression. To clarify this point further it is necessary to emphasize that at moments in all development and at some times in adult functioning, another person serves as psychic structure. To the degree that one is not completely a finished structural entity, we may utilize others as parts of ourselves or as narcissistic objects or as structures in the sense that a functional attribute is assigned to the other. Kohut's position is that such usage of others which persists leads to fixations which represent missing parts of ourselves. These fixations are traced to the emotional non-availability of significant persons during development and a persistent deficit thereafter. The deficit *per se* does not cause the perversion. Perverse activity is *one way* some individuals express this deficit. And certainly not all perverse behaviour is illustrative of this pathology.

Kohut has further clarified the coexistence of perverse behaviour with seemingly realistic ego functioning by his concept of the vertical

---

operate as a disposition to a later illness—are exposed to the danger that some unusually intense wave of libido, finding no other outlet, may lead to a sexualization of their social instincts and so undo the sublimations which they had achieved in the course of their development. This result may be produced by anything that causes the libido to flow backward (i.e. that causes a "regression"): whether, on the one hand, the libido becomes collaterally reinforced owing to some disappointment over a woman, or is directly dammed up owing to a mishap in social relations with other men—both of these being instances of "frustration"; or whether, on the other hand, there is a general intensification of the libido, so that it becomes too powerful to find an outlet along the channels that are already open to it, and consequently bursts through its banks at the weakest spot. Since our analyses show that paranoics *endeavour to protect themselves against any such sexualization of their social instinctual cathexes*, we suppose the weak spot in their development is to be looked for somewhere between the stages of autoerotism, narcissism and homosexuality and that their disposition to illness must be located in that region' (p. 62).

Hartmann (1955) later gave a somewhat more abstract meaning to the term in his discussion of neutralization. The idea of sexualizing a narcissistic constellation is closer to Freud's original description but is in keeping with the later elaboration. However, the concept of aggressivization is not one that Freud specifically entertained and is not considered here.

split. This is a hypothetical structural view of the psyche which pictures the perverse behaviour as residing in a split-off sector of the psyche. In treatment, this area must first be integrated with the central sector of psyche so that the flaw that Glover speaks of can be repaired. We thus are on the threshold of a new and more coherent classification of the perversions by explicitly emphasizing what is implicit in Kohut's formulations. The developmental forms of narcissism can theoretically express themselves in a sexualized manner, and perverse behaviour that may occur can be correlated to the developmental stages of narcissism. Though Kohut warns against directly translating perverse behaviour into structural terms i.e. to match missing structural segments to specific perverse behaviour in order to explain or clarify it, we may one day be able to make some parallel connexions between symptom and stage by considering the usual vicissitudes of instincts and the usual modes of defence and see thereby if some point to point connexion is valid.

This essay will present material from two cases of perverse behaviour in analysis in an attempt to delineate the basic developmental fixation points of narcissistic constellation that are being sexualized. This will necessarily only hint at the generalization suggested for an overall classification of perversions but for this a case book of narcissistic personality disorders is needed. Much of this has already been done in the published work of Kohut. The other point of this essay is to offer an addition or amendation to Kohut's thesis. The role of the affect in perverse activities will be underscored with an attempt to illustrate that such activity offers a sexualization of affect. Perverse behaviour not only stems the tide of regression but allows for mastery of painful affects by an active recreation of a situation which was experienced as overwhelming by the individual. The passive experience of being overcome by painful affects—not merely anxiety but clearly delineated feeling states—is handled by sexualizing the entire situation which then can be tolerated or mastered in this active sexual manner. At times the feelings during the perverse activity are totally sexual but at other times some of the original painful feeling e.g. humiliation or embarrassment become a part of the sexual experience. They are but a reflexion of an earlier situation wherein a disruption or trauma to a fragile narcissistic equilibrium led to a regressive movement which is handled in a peculiar behaviour pattern. In analysis one may reveal the nature of the structural deficit as well as the affective state associated with this fragile narcissistic configuration ad its break-up.

There are two equally valid explanations for sexualization being manifested instead of the more appropriate behaviour or feeling. According to the first, the unavailability of the archaic object does not allow for neutralization and thus we see the more raw and primitive expression of the drive. The process of progressive neutralization would appropriately lead to phase-specific internalization if the object were available. The other explanation concerns the active use of sexualization to handle more painful affects; this is more in the sense of the ego's participation in symptom formation. We note here that even the anticipation of pain is to be avoided by such sexualization.

When we at this point 'explain' the sexualization we do not in any way contribute to an understanding of the choice of neuroses or the cause of perversion. The usual questions remain as to why a particular person manifests a conflict in one way and not in another. No doubt only a total genetic approach can give this kind of an explanation, i.e. an aetiological one, to the study of perversion. The concept of sexualization of affect is a contributory explanation and perhaps it is better stated to say that this explains the meaning of perversion rather than its cause.

CLINICAL MATERIAL

Freud wrote (1927) that cases of fetishism do not often present themselves for analysis and the same may be said for a variety of other perverse behaviour. More often than not a perverse symptom is revealed in the course of analysis and perhaps no analysis is ever without some perverse manifestations if for no other reason than for the relative lack of full genital orgastic activity in neurotic people. Many cases of perversion which are seen in analysis often present themselves under duress and usually after an acute 'discovery' crisis wherein they are sent for help. Fenichel (1945) felt that perverts were different from neurotics in that they liked or received pleasure from their symptoms but were guilty about this fact. That may be an over-simplification since many cases of perversion are extremely anxious during the pervert act while others claim little or no feeling. Likewise, the feeling of shame is often dominant in confessing the deviant behaviour or upon discovery. The profound characterological changes resulting from lifelong perversions which the ego accommodates and champions make it almost impossible to formulate a singular impression.

CLINICAL EXAMPLE 1

The first case is that of a 35-year-old physician referred for analysis after he was discovered by his wife to be masturbating in front of his neighbours' children. He also confessed to masturbating comatose patients in his practice as well as the several dogs kept as pets in the house. This was a reciprocal activity which consisted of masturbating himself, the passive other (child, patient or dog) and sometimes having the animal (only) lick his penis. The patient felt mortified by admitting this activity and his self-condemning manner was prominent throughout the beginning of his analysis.

This was the second analysis for this patient and indeed he was referred by his former analyst to whom he had returned in this moment of crisis. His first analysis ended when he had married. His perversion began after he had been married for several years. His sexual activity with his wife diminished over the several years of his marriage and was almost non-existent at the time of referral. His wife did not complain of this and never insisted on intercourse thereafter.

The patient's past history was that of the oldest child with a younger sister born to a physician father described as a barbiturate addict, and a mother spoken of in a distant and respectful tone. His life was a lonely one but seemed to centre on his erratic and unpredictable father. The patient had a series of homosexual contacts beginning at age nine with a cousin, continuing through high school with a teacher and ending shortly before his marriage. None of these were intense or lasting. He felt that his analysis had been successful and had enabled him to marry. He could not explain his present predicament. It began with solitary masturbation and progressed to the involvement with these passive participants.

The patient had been an obedient child and a good student. He often accompanied his father on house calls but remembered also how he would sit by his bed as father slept off a drinking bout or a drug stupor. He was continually embarrassed by his father because of this but was also proud of him and pleased to be with him. When later he went to medical school and returned to watch his father do surgery he was painfully disillusioned to see how inept his father was. Mother is rarely spoken of and when she is, it is more in the nature of the two of them looking after, waiting for, and worrying about father. The father died a year before this analysis; mother was still alive and well. The father had deteriorated a good deal before his death and was placed in a nursing home.

The patient began analysis as an obedient and dutiful patient. The hours were dull and deadly, and as the initial humiliation dissipated, they were empty and hollow. The perversion slowly disappeared to be replaced by solitary masturbation usually before or after the analytic hours. The early dreams were of fears of a big car overtaking and running down someone. The clear message that seemed to come through was of this patient's struggle over stimulation, his fear of being overstimulated and his need to control his feelings. Rather than a detailed recounting of the analysis, an effort will be made to characterize the primary transference manifestations of this patient. In brief, it was to effect and maintain a connexion. There were dreams of giant electric wires and plugs, of plumbing connexions, of computer terminals and of intricate Rube Goldberg apparatuses—all related to a plugging in to a source of energy and feeling. In the analytic setting the crucial issues revolved around separations, disruptions, misunderstandings, lack of sensitivity, etc. Where originally I had anticipated an intense father transference and then, more specifically, an idealized parental transference, I soon saw the patient as primarily merging with me. That is, I had no discernible separate identity or presence.

Quite in accord with Kohut's description of the merger state the union was essentially a narcissistic one with a feeling of being alive when it was joined, a perverse activity when it was disrupted, and a dead and depressed feeling when a separation extended itself. It is not my intention to repeat

Kohut's descriptions of the analytic work with such patients. Interestingly, the excessive use of machine imagery paralleled the patient's preoccupation with machines as a child and the rare joy accorded to him by his solitary repair of them. The main point to be emphasized is how the perversion represents or expresses the threatened relationship. An example of this occurred when I asked the patient to change an appointment time for my convenience. He reported a masturbatory fantasy of my masturbating him from behind while in turn he masturbated and felt invigorated in pursuit of this fantasy. He then became angry at the very end of the fantasy. The analytic work revealed an empathic deficiency on my part in that I asked casually for a change which was a lot of trouble for him but yet was something he wanted to do. The patient associated to anger at me for charging for an earlier missed appointment wherein he felt I did not realize and appreciate his efforts to come to the analysis. The masturbation reflects a break in the merger. The feeling of vigour represents his wanting to do something for me. The fantasy of my stimulating him represents the request from me which was unusual. The anger represents the rage at the thwarting of the grandiose drive which evidenced his exceptional efforts to come to his hour but these were not being properly reflected. The entire narcissistic configuration is sexualized.

Another example may illustrate more clearly the role of the feelings in the perverse activity. The patient was performing surgery with an assistant when excessive bleeding was noticed. A crisis was felt in the operating room and everyone responded with vigour. The patient soon realized that his assistant had taken charge to become the operator and he found himself an assistant until the crisis was stemmed. Afterwards he retired to his office and masturbated using the cardboard cylinder inside a roll of toilet tissue. When he reported this in analysis he said he felt terribly embarrassed during the surgery, more so during the masturbation and even more so talking of it in analysis. The urge to be a passive member of a unit wherein he is excited or stimulated was reenacted in the surgery. This led to intense shame and humiliation which was of almost traumatic intensity. In order to handle the feelings they were sexualized. The more fearful regression is to a feeling of separateness wherein the self is experienced as dead and empty and suicidal ideation is seen. The dead feeling as well may be sexualized. This was sometimes reported as masturbation or orgasm without any feeling whatsoever. The above incident following the surgery also utilized the image of the cardboard cylinder to reflect a feeling of confinement or containment which he noted in the surgical session. It may be noted that all of these issues were directly paralleled in the analysis which he felt as confining, humiliating and something he wished to be free of, yet could not do without.

Still another vignette may serve to illustrate a transitional state from a sexualized complex interaction to a common psychic state which likewise becomes regressively handled via sexual activity. During the later stages of his analysis the patient reported masturbating with a feeling of confusion: there was no fantasy available to consider and there was no feeling of satisfaction or relaxation following ejaculation. The analytic work concerned itself with the patient's indecision over cancelling an hour to participate in a personally gratifying meeting. He struggled with uncertainty in an alternating and dispassionate way and finally arrived at a feeling of ambivalence. In a startling moment of insight the patient saw that he was having conflicting thoughts about this decision and that he had sexualized his confusion as a handy albeit premature way of mastering his affects.

CLINICAL EXAMPLE 2

The next case will be used to illustrate perverse behaviour which handled a different narcissistic configuration and a different affect and which could be correlated with a situation of childhood.

This patient was a divorced 40-year-old physician, the father of three. He had likewise had a previous analysis. The present as well as the previous treatment were initiated by his being discovered in his perverse behaviour. This took the form of fellatio performed on the patient by female patients whom he stimulated during routine physical examinations. The number and variety of such responses was unusually high and the patient rarely repeated such behaviour with any single patient. I think this does classify as a perversion since this was an episodic activity associated with anxiety and followed by what he described as guilt but which often seemed clearly to be shame. The willing participants were unnamed and unknown and hardly more than vehicles for the act.

The patient's past history was that of a poor boy from a large family of six children raised in a small town in Canada by an extremely cold and religious mother and an alcoholic father. He recalls his mother as being a demanding but unresponsive woman for whom expression of emotion was a sign of weakness. Father became ill when patient was a teenager and stopped working until he died several years before the analysis. The patient was unusually close to a brother who died in an accident when a young man. The patient was markedly moved when discussing this. An outstanding feature of this patient's childhood was an undiagnosed illness which began when he was eight and continued until he was sixteen. He had repeated intense pain in his right femur which occurred for several days and nights and then would subside for an undetermined time. The doctor could find nothing wrong with him and finally accused him of just not wanting to go to school. Thus the patient would endure this pain silently by

himself night after night. He would often awake and sit in his mother's chair and listen to the radio and/or masturbate. Interestingly, no other member of the household was disturbed during the night and the next morning the patient felt unable to tell his parents what he had endured the previous night. Finally at age sixteen his older brother took him to an orthopaedic surgeon who diagnosed a chronic infection of the bone and subsequently operated with complete success.

The patient had begun his first analysis shortly after his perverse behaviour was first discovered. He reported that his deviant activities began after the birth of his first child, a boy. That analysis had concentrated on the perversion as a manifestation of a superego deficit and after some time the activity stopped and analysis terminated. The patient felt much better during his analysis and felt sorry that his symptom returned rather soon after termination. He was hesitant to disappoint his analyst by reporting such an exacerbation.

The present analysis began after his perverse behaviour had been going on for several years. The patient reported it with extreme tension and agitation and at times he was inaudible. Again, the analytic effort will be condensed for purposes of illustration. The patient soon settled into a stable transference wherein he longed to be a part of a strong secure imago. The fellatio behaviour seemed to illustrate the connexion of a weak person to a powerful one. The woman of the behaviour was represented in dreams as an old woman and seemed to be the weak, dependent image of the patient. He struggled to be the strong man with the big penis as well. The perversion diminished to a point of an occasional recurrence which was seen as representing disruptions in the analytic situation. On one occasion the patient's son became ill and needed surgery and the patient cancelled his hour in anticipation of the procedure. An outbreak of his perverse acting out resulted and the dreams and associations revealed his struggle over his wish to ask the analyst to be available in case he was needed. The patient had a tremendous conflict over wanting to call the analyst just to let him know what the surgery revealed. He then recalled his overwhelming longing to tell his parents at the breakfast table that he had been in terrible pain at night but clearly seeing in his mother's face that he had best not complain. He next remembered a tonsillectomy when he was four years old. He was ready to leave the hospital and his father picked him up and carried him out. He had remembered this previously with a feeling of outrage at being treated like a baby when he was old enough to walk out like a big boy. But now, for the first time, he recalled how marvellous he had felt to be held securely in his father's arms and how he had longed for such a union with a powerful person. The perversion was now to be understood as mobilizing this very feeling of longing for union with an idealized and omnipotent figure and that this feeling was rapidly and effectively sexualized. The longing and the structural need became sexualized and in the behaviour one sees not only the sexualization of the idealized parental imago, the sexualization of the grandiose self but the feeling state as well is experienced sexually.

This patient also can be a source of clarification about the precipitating event connected to adult perversions. The oft repeated emphasis on 'meaningful life events' such as the birth of a first child in order to explain the onset of neuroses is a phenomenological effort commonly given significance in non-depth psychologies. Interestingly, this patient after long analytic work revealed a combination of situations involved in the outbreak of his perversion of which his son's birth was rather a minor factor. In particular he was about to embark on a certain career line which would necessitate his being the centre of the stage for long periods of time. His agitation and excitement became almost unbearable for him and were partially handled through his perverse activity but more adequately solved when, during his first analysis, he chose to pursue a different speciality. Only during his re-analyses did he re-experience those upsetting feelings and decide to begin again on his original ambition. The birth of his son did contribute to the problem by making the patient's wife less available as an object to absorb some of his exhibitionistic fantasies, but this patient's problems were narcissistic and he needed self-objects to handle his tension. This is in distinction to conceptualizing some competitive or hostile feelings to a rival son.

DISCUSSION

In 'Inhibitions, Symptoms and Anxiety', Freud (1926) developed his new theory of anxiety as a state created by the ego in response to an awareness of danger. In a somewhat anthropomorphized version it is as if the ego scans the oncoming id urges and pushes the button when a dangerous one looms over the horizon. What was originally passively endured by the psyche becomes transformed into an active production albeit now in a manageable dosage and now in order to serve to protect against old dangers and pains. So it was to be with affects as well. The original state of affects were near-traumatic moments of the infantile psyche. As growth and development occurred the mature ego was seen to produce feelings to correspond to these early traumatic states but these were now to be enjoyed or experienced by an ego which was in the driver's seat.

It seems logical that an early form of active stimulation of the child is sexual self-stimulation and by reason of habit and immaturity this is resorted to for a variety of soothing and comforting experiences. In perversions the sexual activity is singularly significant for handling overwhelming feelings as well. Because of insufficient structuralization and neutralization, the psyche is not able to master and discharge the many feelings which when aroused become experienced as traumatic and, to aid in its mastery, sexualization is resorted to. Rapaport (1953) speaks of sexualization of anxiety and Kohut (1971) notes the sexual feeling of triumph in perversions. It seems feasible to include a wealth of feeling states in this list ranging from shame and humiliation to longing to even quite positive feelings such as joy and excitement. Any of these are capable of inducing sexualization and of being expressed this way literally.

It has been said that psychoanalysis does not have an adequate theory of affects. The attempt by Rapaport to delineate one was based on drives which by dint of channels, valves etc. became transformed into affects. Our hoped for theory of affects must incorporate *what* affects are associated with *what activity* and *how the psyche does the experiencing.* Kohut's contributions in the particular area of conceptualizing object relationships as sometimes substitutes for structural deficiency may allow us to begin to map out what structures (in the psychoanalytic sense) really do make up the psyche. Seeing perversions as sexual displays of missing structure is like a new tool for observing the psychology of man. Adding the feeling states which are sexualized as well, might one day lead to a comprehensive theory of psychoanalytic behaviour and associated affects.

The concept of the vertical split may be of help in both our therapeutic work as well as a broadening clinical theory. The split-off area of the psyche has been described by Kohut as analagous to the mechanism of disavowal which Freud spoke of in regard to the fetishist. Not only do the two parts of the psyche not communicate with one another so that one does not know what the other is doing, but the feeling states are clearly different. Kohut emphasizes that the first work of analysis is to address the reality ego in order to heal the split or integrate the ego. Perhaps the unbridled behaviour of the grandiose, split-off sector serves the function of handling the painful affects which the reality ego cannot tolerate. Patients often clearly comprehend interpretations directed to the avoided affects which they discharge via perverse activity. Interpretations must, of course, be given in a total context but I believe attention directed to the feeling states is most helpful. The insights gained by patients in this respect seem to aid uniquely the integration of the ego.

Although it may be going too far to say that psychoanalysis has as its sole aim the communication of affect (Modell, 1973), it can be considered that the expression with empathic participation of appropriate affect is one goal of analysis. The work of analysis that precedes such expression is either analysis of resistance or insights which aid the ego to tolerate the affect. The sexual acting out of the patients described above may be thought of as defence transference or work prior to or involving disruption of the stable equilibrium of a narcissistic transference. Kohut speaks of the moments when the patient can tell you of his perverse fantasies and activities as a turning point in the analysis. This may also be the point when the patient can tolerate the associated affects that go with the perversion. The experience with the above patients manifested a difference in the telling of the perverse activity from the early descriptions to the later, more total emotional experience. The latter probably reflected a more integrated self involvement, a more unified ego tolerance and the associated diminution of the need for sexualizing the affects. The efforts of analysis to prevent or alter perverse activity are effective only so long as the analyst serves as the inhibiting structure. Perversions then are never incorporated into the psyche but utilize other ways of disguise or defence. The patient who had an analysis of his perversion based on a pleasure seeking activity not properly handled by his superego, could clearly differentiate the pleasure of sexual activity from the driven pain of perverse activity. The patient who masturbated in front of his children rarely conceived of anything approaching pleasure in these pursuits. Each of these patients felt a different kind of pleasure in pursuing activity which was not sexualized and to which more appropriate affect could be associated.

Classification in psychoanalysis can never be based on phenomena alone. No set of behavioural criteria reflect properly a depth psychological investigation of mental processes although some statistical correlations are often helpful. Perverse behaviour seen as sexualization of narcissistic configuration and the associated affects offers hope for a psychoanalytic classification of disorders which have never been happy members of our diagnostic categories.

SUMMARY

A review of psychoanalytic thinking on perversions is offered and brought up to date with an outline of Kohut's concept of perversions representing sexualization of narcissistic configurations. An emphasis is made on the sexualization of the affects to underscore the structural defect in perverse behaviour. Broad constructions directed to the disavowal of feelings are considered most meaningful in analytic treatment of individuals suffering from sexual perversions.

REFERENCES

Fenichel, O. (1945). *The Psychoanalytic Theory of Neuroses.* New York: Norton.

Freud, A. (1965). *Normality and Pathology in Childhood.* New York: International Universities Press.

Freud, S. (1905). Three essays on the theory of sexuality *Standard Edition* 7.

——1911 Psycho-analytic notes on an autobiographical account of a case of paranoia (dementia paranoides) *Standard Edition* 12.

—— (1919). A 'child is being beaten': A contribution to the study of the origin of sexual perversions. *Standard Edition* 17.

—— (1926). Inhibitions, symptoms and anxiety. *Standard Edition* 20.

—— (1927). Fetishism. *Standard Edition* 21.

Glover, E. (1932). A psycho-analytic approach to the classification of mental disorder. In: *On the Early Development of Mind.* New York: International University Press, 1956.

Hartmann, H. (1955). Notes on the theory of sublimation In *Essays on Ego Psychology* New York: International University Press, 1964.

Kohut, H. (1971). *The Analysis of the Self* . New York: International Universities Press.

Modell, A.H. (1973). Affects and psychoanalytic knowledge. *The Annual of Psychoanalysis* vol. 1. New York: Quadrangle Books.

Rapaport, D. (1953). Some metapsychological considerations regarding activity and passivity In *Collected Papers* New York: Basic Books, 1967.

Some Countertransference Phenomena
in the Analysis of Perversions (1977)

One might consider Goldberg's paper, *Some Countertransference Phenomena in the Analysis of Perversions* (1977), as an accompaniment to the earlier paper, *A Fresh Look at Perverse Behavior* (1975), because the self-object transferences have their own countertransference responses. Goldberg demonstrates the way that the developmental lines of the grandiose self and the idealized parental imago are re-enacted in the analytic setting as narcissistic transferences. The question arises: What are the countertransference reactions to the narcissistic transferences?

Goldberg states that countertransference reactions fall within two broad categories: general and specific.

The general countertransference reactions are related to the power of the patient's perverse behavior to intimidate the analyst. This reaction is not simply because the perverse behavior might result in legal or criminal action. When the perverse behavior is an event that takes place outside of the analysis and the conflict has yet to enter the transference, this might lead to our countertransference reaction to overcome and control the behavior. Furthermore, the symptoms cannot be construed as a message or communication, which can be deciphered like a dream. Instead the behaviors are considered "intensely personal and individual acts of restoration which have no communicative significance." The analyst's more general countertransference reaction is an indication that the perverse symptoms have yet to join the analysis. It is when "the perverse behavior becomes an indicator of things gone wrong; of feelings not confronted or experienced; of empathic failure; of the analytic work running badly that the analyst becomes part of the symptom complex and the perverse behavior joins in the analysis." In other words, when the patient's symptoms are determined to be a reaction to the disruptions in the self-object tie, the countertransference reactions are considered to be specific reactions.

In these early papers Goldberg introduces us to themes that will unfold over the next many decades in his writings. These themes of understanding and misunderstanding, disruptions, of things gone wrong, of affects turned sideways, of restoration, will be returned to again and again, ever deepening our understanding.

—GM

INTRODUCTION

When Sigmund Freud (1910) initially formulated the concept of countertransference he noted: "We have become aware of the 'counter-transference, which arises in him [the analyst] as a result of the patient's influence on his unconscious feelings, and we are almost inclined to insist that he shall recognize this counter-transference in himself and overcome it" (pp. 144-145).

Later he advocated an emotional coldness on the part of the analyst, for his own protection and for the benefit of the patient. This was especially necessary when the patient had fallen in love with the analyst. Indeed, Freud properly emphasized the libidinal components of the transference more and urged the analyst not to look upon the love of the patient as a conquest and not to fall in love with the patient(s) in turn, thus allowing his own impulses to emerge unchecked.

Fenichel (1945), in reviewing the problems of the countertransference, felt that the more dangerous impulses of the analyst had to do with *narcissistic* rather than libidinal components. It seemed more difficult for the analyst to check and/or comprehend impulses dealing with his own personal regard or esteem than those that dealt with his feelings, be they loving or hostile, toward his analytic patient. The complete literature on this facet of analysis is rich and complex, and will not be reviewed here; rather we will turn directly to the narcissistic components.

One major step in clarifying the many questions about these and other narcissistic issues was accomplished by Kohut (1971), who pointed out that the narcissistic object is experienced as a part of the self. To achieve this seemingly simple definition, a number of steps were required:

1. A redefinition of libido was in order—one that moved from a consideration of cathexis as "charge" or investment of energy to one that emphasized its purely psychological aspect. One cathects

that in which one is interested. Since the quality of the libido becomes defined by the nature of the experience, if we experience another as a part of ourselves, we justifiably can claim that narcissistic libido is thereby employed.

2. A working separation of the developmental lines of narcissism and object libido was suggested. This merely means that operationally we can concentrate on the growth of the self as distinct from that of objects which we love and/or hate. Certainly it does not mean that narcissism and object love are not intricately related; rather, it may be profitable to clinically trace singular lines of development. The separateness of narcissistic development is offered for one's use clinically; it cannot or should not be dictated or be a subject of legislative inquiry as some have suggested. With that proviso in mind, it may be helpful to concentrate on a pure culture of narcissistic problems in tracing self-development from early infancy to adulthood. This effort enabled Kohut (1971) to describe particular way stations in such development: the Grandiose Self and the Idealized Parental Imago.

    Of course, this places the self in the center of our clinical inquiry and thereby allows descriptions of what Kohut delineated as specific narcissistic transferences or transferences that correspond to the points in development wherein these forms of narcissism became dominant and subsequently are re-enacted in the analytic setting.

3. Therefore, the delineation of specific narcissistic transferences in analysis confronts us with the analyst's counter-reactions to those transferences; also, it opens up a consideration of the analyst's narcissistic problems quite independent of the particulars of the patient's presentation.

To return to the concept of the narcissistic object or self-object, we have emphasized that it is experienced as a functional unity with one's self; this is something which is readily agreed upon to be a common enough occurrence, both within and outside of analysis, both in early life and throughout adulthood—and it is always relevant to an inquiry concerning countertransference.

One arena where much may be gained from concentrating on the narcissistic issues of the countertransferences is in the analysis of perverse behavior. In particular, Kohut has described such behavior as rather prevalent in narcissistic personality disorders, especially when a relatively stable narcissistic transference is disrupted and a regression begins to take place. The acting out of the perversion is seen as an attempt to halt the regression by a sexual display or substitutions of the sought-for narcissistic object.

It is uncertain as to whether anything specific can be delineated as to countertransference reactions in the psychoanalyses of patients with perverse behavior. Whether such reactions fall within the broader category of acting-out behavior of any kind or whether they are only peculiar to the analyst, without particular relevance to this kind of patient, remains open to question. Bearing in mind these qualifications, it might be beneficial to investigate some of these reactions in detail. Here, too, we must neglect the rich discussions in the literature.

CLINICAL MATERIAL

My own curiosity about reactions of the analyst to perverse symptomatology occurred after I had been aware for a short time that I was feeling differently about a specific patient who was capable of acting out perverse symptoms. This patient told me of a dream in which an expert was teaching him how to cast a fishing rod. Once before, he had been adept at this form of casting (this, too, being part of the dream) but had given it up for the simpler method of using a spinning rod. Now he was relearning this technique and felt rather good about it; he was not as good as his teacher, but he was getting there.

His first association was of learning again how to relate to his wife, from whom he had felt estranged for many months, during which time they did not have sexual intercourse. He felt analysis was helping him to slowly re-engage himself to his wife. Next he recalled that his father had been an expert fisherman and that father and son had gone on many fishing excursions together. This brought him back to the memory of needing his father to somehow handle his mother. Many hours earlier he had told of insisting, as a boy, that his father return home from a hospitalization to intercede in the incessant bickering between himself and his mother. He recalled his father as a rather strong and admirable person who had fallen from grace at an uncertain period in the patient's development. The father had become sickly and alcoholic, and the period of age twelve to sixteen seemed bereft of memories of him. Before then, the father was something; after that, he was not very much. In the analysis, we had reworked the loss of this relationship to an idealized parent, and we had connected the near-disintegrating experience of that loss to repeated adult experiences which manifested themselves in perverse behavior (the exact type of which is not relevant at this point).

But it is the analyst's participation in the endeavor that interests us here: what is significant is my changed attitude toward this patient—my lack of worry or anxiety about his acting out. Clearly in the dream he represented the fact that he was learning how to take care of himself; to literally and figuratively use his own penis; to manage for himself and, indeed, to analyze himself. One can also see his wish to be admired for his new accomplishments, and for some time now he participated more and more in the analysis, in the sense of actively doing most of the work. But only a few weeks earlier he had reported an episode of perverse behavior, and I had reacted differently: I realized now that it no longer troubled me.

To recall the beginning of this and similar analyses of such patients is an exercise best attempted when the phase is some time past. In describing some of the analyst's reactions to this very broad category of patients, I shall use the term countertransference to refer to the entire gamut of reactions and responses of the analyst, whether they be to specific unconscious images or fantasies of the patient by the analyst or to diffuse behavior patterns discerned by the analyst in himself.

The considerations of countertransference phenomena will be of two types: general and specific. The former is concerned with those reactions which are not determined by particular transference situations but which more properly relate to acting out as it occurs in any analysis, more often *before* a stable transference is achieved. The latter type includes reactions to specific narcissistic transferences.

GENERAL REACTIONS

The above-mentioned patient began his analysis in a routine manner but soon provoked strong feelings of impatience and restlessness within myself. Initially, I had been eager to begin this analysis of a man who ostensibly suffered over his perverse behavior. I was anticipating new insights concerning such behavior and was eager for them, perhaps even ambitiously so. However, the patient was slow to talk, difficult to hear, and reluctant to participate. He spoke haltingly, having to clear his throat endlessly, and I restrained myself from urging him to speak up and get on with it. During this period, the explanation offered to myself for this resistance involved the patient's apprehension over self-exposure meeting the eagerness of his analyst. I did not appreciate the patient's need to over-control his feelings. But the frustration did not abate. Only much later was it clear that this patient shared with other such patients a capacity for intimidating the analyst. The acting out of the perverse symptom not only was an event outside of the analysis, but the legal or criminal action that it could cause threatened to destroy the analysis. Of course, any patient can end an analysis at any time; often his doing so is felt to be an unwitting or unconscious act. However, the full force of a disclaimer of responsibility by a patient is felt nowhere more keenly than in perverse behavior. The patient is intimidated, also. In this case entire hours were devoted to self-condemnation and chastisement over an acting-out episode which almost led to discovery and legal intervention.[2]

The existence of such a split-off part of the personality or extra-analytic intrusive presence tends to intimidate and threaten the analyst's feelings of control and dominance over the analysis. Undoubtedly, it constitutes a basic narcissistic threat to the analyst, who has begun to feel the analysis as a personal and proud possession which is experienced as

---

[2] One particular case of perversion had been referred for analysis by a general psychiatrist, who subsequently acted as a sort of liaison between the patient and his lawyer and other authorities who wanted reassurance that measures were being taken to correct his behavior and that he was "safe" for continued employment. In this instance, I never became involved with third parties, and the analysis was not hampered by such complications.

contiguous with the self and valued as part of the self. I was often forced to restrain myself from getting the patient to be more of a classical analytic patient who would talk about his conflicts rather than make our job so difficult by these actions, which only seemed to upset our work. This is a form of the general countertransference reaction noted above.

The tendency to blame the patient for misbehavior runs parallel with the tendency likewise to forgive him. The analyst who somehow allows such judgmental feelings to intrude upon an analysis often is struggling with personal problems of values as well as of ambition. Kohut speaks of the situation in the analysis of narcissistic personality disorders wherein the analysand sees the analyst as the embodiment of idealized perfection. This may lead to the analyst's need for a defense against his own unconscious grandiose desires which cause him to either reject or bask in the patient's idealization. Although both responses can be seen as nonanalytic stances, a common solution to the quandary of where to position one's self in terms of the patient's misbehavior is to treat it as a communication. A predominant theme in psychoanalysis has been the idea that symptoms really are communications which can be deciphered. Like dreams, they are seen as mental products capable of being understood and interpreted and, in the case of pathological material, done away with or resolved. My own impression is that as valuable and useful as it may be clinically to consider a perverse act as a message or communication, it is clearly not that, in fact. Patients simply do not become involved in perverse behavior in order to tell the analyst something that they otherwise cannot communicate. Such may seem to be the case, and it may be helpful to attempt to decipher the act as if it were a coded message, but perversions do not have that intent or meaning. They do not take place in a community of signals and symbols; rather, they are intensely personal and individual acts of restoration which have no communicative significance, except in those rare cases where they are consciously and purposefully employed in this regard.

An example of the question as to whether the perverse symptoms were to be construed as communication or otherwise was observed in one analysis when the patient handled a particularly stressful event in contrast to an earlier occasion. I was to be away and the patient compared his feelings about this separation to an earlier period in the analysis when he simply acted out repeatedly and his activities seemed to have no connection to my impending absence. I noted this to be a marked improvement in his capacity to tolerate the analytic disruptions. Shortly afterward, however, he became engaged in an unusually high incidence of perverse actions which seemed almost out of control. Now we did talk about this as if he were telling me that he was not yet well enough to terminate. But his actions were also seen as a series of regressive moves related to termination as a loss of the sustaining narcissistic object. The latter seems to be the more cogent explanation, since the perversion as message implies a certain willfulness to the patient that he can hardly claim to his credit. This patient's actions also related to a specific constellation dealing with parental ambition. Over and over he experienced any improvement as an urgent spur to "get it done with." After further analytic work he recalled how his parents would respond to his achievements by a vigorous mobilization from which they excluded themselves, however. For example, when an awards dinner was scheduled, these rather poor people would manage to gather enough money to send their son to the affair, but never attended themselves. The patient's initial feeling that his parents did not really care about him was modified: now he knew that they were quite ambitious for him, and he felt inexplicably alone. His parents' ambition was peculiarly tied to his own abandonment, and, as he rose to become the only professional person in the family, he also became more and more alienated from them. Quite in contrast to a child who grows closer to a father as he replaces him, this boy became more of a stranger. In his analysis, improvement therefore was sensed to be a reflection of the analyst's ambition (which it was); this signaled both a general and specific reaction (in a different sense than our earlier classification): the former to the loss of the sustaining self-object; the latter to the particulars of this person's development. The result was the recrudescence of perverse behavior.

The patients I have seen in analyses do not understand their perversions, nor do they utilize them in a network of social relationships, except as any symptom may take on a *secondary* meaning or value.

Rather, they, too, look upon them frequently as foreign bodies to be controlled or done away with or ignored. To be sure, perverse behavior seems to be a mode of expression that predominates during certain periods, but the intent is not the same throughout the periods of prevalence and of absence. Nor is it true that if the patient could tell the analyst something or other, the action thereby would be made unnecessary. The reason for stressing this point is that perverse behavior is not a road to the unconscious, as are dreams, but is often considered with displeasure and some degree of annoyance by both analyst and patient.

However, often a subtle shift soon takes place between patient and analyst as to where the aforementioned blame or responsibility is to be placed, innocently or otherwise. Soon the perverse behavior becomes an indicator of things gone wrong; of feelings not confronted and experienced; of empathic failure; of the analytic work running badly.

It seems to be the case that the view of perverse behavior changes: rather than being felt as delaying or preventing the patient from analyzing, it seems to join in the analysis. Perhaps, to use an analogy, the unwelcome guest, unfortunately, *was* invited.

SPECIFIC REACTIONS

My limited experience with perversions has indicated that they do not change markedly in form during analysis. To be sure, many patients who do not initially come to analysis for relief of this problem often show some such problem during analysis; we are reminded that Freud felt that fetishism was near universal. However, one or more kinds of behavior seem to be fairly fixed for each patient. When the analyst thereby becomes part of the symptom complex, it is only that he becomes the precipitant for the extra-analytic action or a cogent member of a fantasy that accompanies such behavior.

The first example of perverse behavior joining in the analysis illustrates a form of transference which is in line with Kohut's more detailed descriptions. Here we enter the area of specific reactions, and again it is those of the analyst on which we focus. A patient who had a symptom of having dogs lick his penis reported an episode of this sometime well into the analysis. He also had masturbated earlier that day with a fantasy of his masturbating me. It seemed to be related to his telling me in great detail of a recent meeting where he handled people and issues with a good deal of alacrity and ability, and I had chosen to interpret this as an avoidance of his apprehension about an approaching missed session. In looking back to this hour, it seemed that I felt a reluctance to enjoy or share his excitement. Somewhere I had thought that my job was not so much to nod and smile as to explain; and I partially resented his implied insistence that I confirm his good feeling. This reminded me of Winnicott's (1958) description of people who "wet blanket" or manage to deflate the enthusiasm of others. My effort at interpretation was really aimed at diminishing his own state of vigor and excitement, and stemmed from an effort to keep myself from these feelings and/or to compete with him for center stage.

Now in the act of perversion the patient is exhibiting himself to dogs and eliciting an erotic response from them. Although he is fond of these animals, who usually are quite friendly, it is clear that the act carries the stamp of humiliation and degradation. He is quite ashamed of wanting any attention for himself and, indeed, was raised in a family where only his father was entitled to attention of any kind, be it praise or worry. The countertransference reaction to his demand had been based upon an old competition for precedence within the family. This clearly seems to be in the realm of those narcissistic transferences of the grandiose self which require mirroring or confirmation, and which may be met by a reluctance on the part of the analyst who needs similar forms of gratification. Again, in this regard perverse behavior is not so peculiar in itself, but it is a rather clear barometer of the state of transference, and within the behavior one may see a clearer meaning of the act, even though it is never brought about *de novo* by the analysis.

The patient recalled his mother instructing him to telephone his father, a physician, to find out what time he would return home. He remembers doing this as a very young boy and has vivid recollections of how painful it had been to wait for him. Finally, the car would pull into the driveway and father would sound the horn, and the boy would rush out to greet him. In a flash he could tell if his father was able to respond to him or if he was so beset by personal thoughts, fatigue, or depression that he would withdraw immediately and begin to drink shortly afterward. Therefore, via this pantomimed act, he would deal with the pain of eagerness and enthusiasm that had nowhere to go.

An example of another form of specific transference reaction was presented by a patient who had formed an idealizing transference. His perverse activity was varied and not significant in terms of this vignette; however, it did run in erratic spurts and sometimes barely seemed to be an issue. One time, however, it had a particularly persistent and unyielding quality; this incident, too, was connected to a series of missed appointments—this time necessitated by an annual analytic meeting. When the meeting was mentioned, the patient immediately connected it to a time one year previously when *he* had been away. When I casually mentioned that my meeting occurred around the same time every year, he wondered aloud if I had charged him for the missed hours *even though* I, too, had been away. Although I clearly knew that I could not and would not do such a thing, I found myself quite frightened that I *had* done so. I was very anxious that I would be caught in a sort of illicit behavior, and although the apprehension was quite irrational, I could not rest until I had looked up the bills to reassure myself.

In retrospect, I saw that I secretly felt unreasonably idealized by my patient and, likewise thought that the values assigned to me were not mine. When the patient wondered if I would be honest, as he knew I would be, I later felt an added sense of burden and increased care that I dare not misbehave in the future. It still is not clear to me whether the concern about acting out in this case was a particular kind of counter-reaction in this particular kind of patient. Nor can one say if the mere (although at times severe) discomfort of being idealized by a patient is the usual countertransference reaction in this variety of transference. For some reason, however, it does seem that action appears to be more of an issue in the over-all countertransference reactions of perverse behavior.

I would like to illustrate an example of countertransference reaction which I felt enabled me to gain some increased insight into the patient first described. As noted at the beginning of this essay, the patient was struggling to re-establish a sexual relationship with his wife. He accompanied his daughter and her girl friend on a weekend of skiing and, due to poor weather conditions, failed to return in time for his Monday analytic session. The following day he recounted the weekend with great shame and mortification as he described his acting out with his daughter's friend. I told him that I thought it would be more profitable for us to analyze the reasons for his behavior than for him to indulge in self-chastisement. He clearly felt criticized by this comment, but the hour proceeded with some mutual agreement that the missed session may have contributed to the acting out. I felt uneasy when he left, as if I had been too harsh; my uneasiness increased when he failed to appear for the next session. I looked forward to the last day of that week, hoping to see if matters could be clarified, but he again failed to appear. I telephoned to ask what had happened; he had overslept; things were all right; he would see me Monday.

He arrived on Monday, stating that he had felt quite anxious since our last meeting, had acted out his "symptom" (that of fellatio with anonymous patients in his practice), and was extremely tense with his wife and daughter. He described a dream: There has been an accident; two people had been killed, and the traffic was obstructed. The patient left his car to get around the obstruction but was concerned as to how to proceed without his car. He met a man in a wheelchair who was very bitter and unhappy, and the patient encouraged him. He asked a man if he could use a telephone but was refused permission to do so. When he did get to a telephone, he was unable to get through to the man he wished to contact. Finally, he saw his analyst who told him to eat more and get new shoes. The patient associated my comment about his inadequate diet to my telephone call (this, by the way, was the countertransference phenomenon which I felt to be significant). He told me that he was extremely apprehensive about getting back together with his wife; he had great fears that she would reject him or be critical of him, and that he would act out. He returned to the hour when he felt I had criticized him for not being more analytic, saying that I did not understand how he felt surrounded by temptation which he could not resist if he remained at odds with his wife. He so wished I could see how tense his relationship *was* with his wife. It soon became clear that he did not want anything done; rather, he wanted his suffering to be recognized.

His comments reverberated with memories of a childhood of pain, when his parents could do nothing for him and avoided any discussion of the pain, whereas, untruth, he wanted them to acknowledge what he was enduring. I pointed out that he wanted me to say: "I know what you are going through"; he then recalled wanting these words from his father, especially in relation to a cold and critical mother. But father had responded to the wrong thing, just as I had commented upon his diet in the dream. He had wanted to talk to his father about his mother, but his father was not there. Then he recalled the awful feeling of loneliness when no one was there and he would resort to masturbation or simply live with a feeling of despair. At this point of failure of his idealized parent, in this case a solicitous but misunderstanding one, he had resorted to various methods of self-stimulation.

In retrospect, I felt that my action (which had resulted from unanalyzed guilt or shame at being too harsh with him) in telephoning had enabled me to see what I had missed. The dream was of two missed appointments; an effort to re-establish an empathic union; to reinvestigate his pathetic self (and his unhappy father), though he was repeatedly frustrated at getting his point across. At the end of the dream he sees his well-meaning but irrelevant analyst. This provoked the patient to return again to a period in his early adolescence when he had no memory of his father. I suggested that the father was depressed at the time, and the patient responded to this immediately. He spoke of his father's needing him then, and he said: "I have no memory of him because during that time I had no self of my own."

Essentially, the countertransference reaction was a narcissistic one which enabled me to see the narcissistic pathology of the idealized and disillusioning father. The more general relation of this sequence of developmental issues to later perverse pathology seems to be a fertile subject for future inquiry. A need remains for more pinpointing of specific forms of these disorders, and especially, to separate out the crucial and significant factors. Not all cases of this sequence develop perverse symptomatology, nor are all of the forms of the pathology clinically similar. Undoubtedly, specific developmental problems combine in particular was with adventitious environmental phenomena, as when the lonely and abandoned child "discovers" the fetishistic object.

Another not uncommon countertransference phenomenon witnessed in the analysis of patients with perverse behavior is a supposed identification with the victim, wherein the analyst feels and reacts like the companion in the perverse act. As dominant as this may seem to be portrayed in analysis, it does not often become an action and so usually can be handled via interpretation of fantasies and dreams. Sometimes, however, the analyst does participate unwittingly in the behavior, and here, too, the narcissistic elements may need underscoring. One example that comes to mind is that of an analytic hour which was only to be thought of as frustrating with no possible way to bring it together or make sense of it. The patient told of having spent the entire previous night trying but failing to have intercourse with a woman who was one of many such individuals, conquered routinely and easily. This patient engaged in other perverse behavior as well, but his indiscriminate promiscuity might also qualify for this appellation. The puzzling part of his story related to his perseverance, a rare quality of his. Suddenly this connected to his frustration in another area of his life, i.e., his attempts to complete a business venture and the extreme reluctance of his business partner to consummate the plan and allow the patient to get his own work started. Now the analyst knew that the business frustration was being sexualized in the night's misadventure and, subsequently, relived in the transference wherein the analyst felt the torment of the patient. In truth, this was not so much an engagement of two individuals as it was a situation in which the patient induced the experience in the analyst who, like the sexual object, really was experienced as a unity with the patient. The connection to a childhood experience of prolonged frustration without a satisfactory closure was achieved next, and the role of the frustrating parent was delineated. Again, the issue was primarily and developmentally a narcissistic one.

In order to pursue this more general topic of these reactions, it is necessary once again to gloss over the enormous literature on the treatment of acting-out patients and the propensity of the therapist to join in the action. As a general rule, this has not been a major issue in these cases, save for minor events more likely to be considered as acting in the analysis proper (as above, in the telephone episode). However, the most glaring impression one can gather from these patients is that the perverse behavior substitutes for a different kind of life with different life experiences. In another paper (1975), I detailed a thesis that such sexualization of behavior was a simultaneous sexualization and avoidance of painful affects. As Kohut has explained, the sexualization of the narcissistic configuration, i.e., the psychological and structural meaning of the analyst to the patient, is painted and lived in sexual terms; so, too, are the relevant affects reduced to some kind of erotic experience. Although Kohut clearly states that these are stopgap measures to prevent further regression, it is no doubt clear that they become habitual, as well. My own impression is that the establishment of a narcissistic transference and an ensuing narcissistic equilibrium is particularly difficult in some of these patients who have too long used substitute methods of experiencing life. These narcissistic configurations are exquisitely painful for the patient to endure, and they seem quite sensitive to anticipating the painful feelings most keenly associated with disruptions and disappointments. They then shift to the other arena of living, i.e., the acting out of the perversion. Undoubtedly, such behavior can clearly be seen as developmentally earlier in origin and thus should be classified as a regressive move, but it also can be seen as a predominant parallel or alternative way of behaving. Acting is not replaced by thinking, although it *is* succeeded by it. Rather, both modes coexist, and treatment tries to shift the arena to contemplation instead of action.

The most striking and clear shift in the analytic work with such patients is seen in the change from acting out to the presence of significant emotions within the analysis. Patients who were seemingly oblivious of anxiety, depression, enthusiasm., or whatever, begin to announce how they feel about things, people, and events. For the analyst, this may or may not be a welcome transformation. No matter how much one may look for the re-experiencing of painful affects in the transference, they may be seen as potentially disruptive and alien due to the long-standing vulnerability of the self to overstimulation. Since the analyses of narcissistic disorders concentrate so significantly on the self-experiences, resistance by the analyst to the reliving of affects seems clear-cut. When one first sees a patient with a long-standing perversion move to thinking about a coming event which is fraught with anxiety, it seems like the most catastrophic anxiety possible. On the other hand, we also feel a certain welcome since now we are back in a familiar environment.

For the analyst, thinking and contemplating and talking are everything, and such patients thus are peculiarly difficult and puzzling. It may well be that the supposed infrequency of such patients to seek treatment is a misalliance of sorts. The patient views a part of himself as alien and the analyst tries to treat that part. Kohut says that we always address the reality ego in regard to the split-off part of the ego or self. Perhaps another way of looking at it is that the patient has alternate ways of behaving, and the verbal and self-object-related one is potentially much more upsetting.

One of the above patients told of the time a previous analyst had advised him to masturbate whenever he felt the urge to act out his perverse behavior, supposedly in order to drain off the urgency of the need. One can see the analyst's position: he must have felt apprehensive about the patient's behavior and thereby rationalized his advice with some theoretical sleight of hand.

To be sure, these are difficult patients who frighten easily and threaten us, particularly in the narcissistic sphere of our own lives. All the more so because they are predominantly living their conflicts in a different arena of life—one that we feel is unfamiliar to us and must be overcome and controlled. It is really a quite unsatisfactory substitute for the emotional richness of the option we can offer.

Discussion

The major conclusions to be reached in regard to the countertransference phenomena in the analysis of perversions fall into two broad areas. The first has to do with the fact that perverse behavior is action and not thought; that the analyst works to change the arena of consideration from the former to the latter. The analyst's reactions to this task are those dealing with his narcissistic rage at the frustration of this difficult task. Into this particular category fall the problems of treating perversions as coded messages, in addition to those involving participation by the analyst inside or outside of the analysis. The entire gamut of responses to a symptom not readily incorporated into analytic work brings out and emphasizes the issue of perverse symptomatology as having a unique status in psychoanalysis.

The second broad group of reactions that we have noted are those related to the various particular narcissistic transferences which arise in these analyses. These are carefully listed and described in Kohut's work, and now we would merely support the thesis that the perversions studied were disorders of narcissism. The evidence is abundant that, for the most part, the establishment of a narcissistic transference does away with the acting out, until and unless a disruption occurs in the transference. These disruptions are not necessarily technical errors, although they may be seen as such since any failure of empathy could qualify for this appellation; rather, they herald a situation of disequilibrium wherein the existing psychic structure is unable to tolerate the feelings of the moment. Not all empathic breaks lead to perverse acting out; not all instances of proper empathy do away with such symptoms. However, as analysis proceeds, more and more does the symptom join in the analysis.

These conclusions do suggest a major change in the analysis of perverse behavior, and point to a drastic reconsideration of the classical analytic picture of this diagnostic category. First, the faulty resolution of the oedipal conflict, with subsequent regression to more direct and infantile modes of sexual gratification, does not seem to be a satisfactory explanation for much of our case material. Second, the bulk of perversions may be related to narcissistic disorders. However, it may well be a countertransference problem of sorts if psychoanalysts fail to exercise all of their options in attempting to clarify and explain data that heretofore has escaped our complete comprehension. Countertransference may occur both in our consulting rooms as well as in our scientific discussions; as analysts, it is but another task for scrutiny.

REFERENCES

Fenichel, O. (1945), *The Psychoanalytic Theory of Neuroses*. New York: Norton.

Freud, S. (1910), The future prospects of psychoanalytic therapy. *Standard Edition* 11:139–151.

Goldberg, A. (1975). A Fresh Look at Perverse Behaviour. *International Journal of Psycho-Analysis* 56:335–342.

Kohut, H. (1971). *The Analysis of the Self*. New York: International Universities Press.

Winnicott, D.W. (1958), *Collected Papers*. New York: Basic Books.

CHAPTER TWO

Disorders in the Self-System

In a series of papers, beginning with *On Waiting* (1971), then *The Wishy-Washy Personality* (1986) and *Disorders of Continuity* (1990), Goldberg addresses a particular quality of the self, that of a feeling of sameness through time and space.

The intent of Goldberg's essay *On Waiting* (1971) is to examine an experience that we all share, that of waiting. His approach is to understand the frustrations that result from waiting not as aggressive reactions to drive tensions, but as disruptions to the self-system. The system of the self includes a variety of self-experiences such as self-esteem, self-cohesiveness, and humiliation, which are affected by the experience of waiting.

The impatience, or perhaps narcissistic rage, that some of us experience when we must wait can be understood as an injury to our omnipotence thereby disrupting an ongoing feeling of continuity of the self.

Goldberg's paper *On Waiting* illuminates a sequence of disruption wherein a patient continually arrived late for session, in part to avoid the experience of waiting. Goldberg understands this tendency as the patient's need to have complete control over when he began the session. When the patient was a child, his father would unpredictably and inexplicably turn off his attention, and as a result, the patient's self-continuity or feeling of sameness was destroyed. He felt shattered and disrupted and he then reacted with narcissistic rage. To be in control of the session start time was meant to turn a passive experience into an active one, and to avoid disruptions and break-ups in the continuity of the self. Waiting, then, is understood as yet another experience that may have consequences to the integrity of the self, resulting in disorders in the self-system.

—GM

On Waiting (1971)

The intent of this essay is to examine the experience of waiting or the subjective sense of time passage by the psychoanalytic method. Much of this is an articulation of some newer analytic considerations about narcissism and the self-system. A subsidiary theme will be to extend the concept in an attempt to generalize to parallel processes in other disciplines or areas of study. The problem of continuity in science is a yet unsolved one and no doubt we insist upon processes of continuity where none exist. Many attempts to supposedly bridge or connect disciplines fail because of this. However, the issue of generalizing about areas of scientific study remains valid if we concentrate on phenomena that are called isomorphic by Bertalanffy (1968), i.e. those that belong to a unitary theory with unifying principles and thus have a similarity in form. Such phenomena as organization, differentiation and goal-directedness are of importance in all biological, behavioural and social phenomena. Certain other isomorphic concepts may be familiar as, for example, excitability, reaction time, changeability, etc. These are not discipline-specific and perhaps can lend themselves to study via one method such as psychoanalysis and still allow for generalizing to and from other disciplines. The particular example of this investigation will be of waiting or the sense of passage of time.

Susanne K. Langer (1967) says:

> Waiting is not necessarily behavioural; it occurs in organic activities, too, and in cytological processes, and may well be the basis of the much discussed mystery of 'timing'. The actualization of an impulse does not necessarily collapse the moment it is not implemented. It may be suspended until the means of the continuance arrives, whereupon the act expands and accelerates again.

This, then, is one example of a line of continuity which transcends our common divisions, i.e. an example of a non-discipline restrictive phenomenon.

To return to Langer:

The speeding and slowing of rhythms, such as breathing under different conditions of oxygen supply and of carbon dioxide concentration in the lungs, illustrate the automatic self-adjustment of vital acts, within fateful limits to others which complete their promoting situation. Entire suspension in mid-career is an extreme form; ordinarily waiting for concomitant acts to develop and furnish substrates or means from moment to moment is an easy and continual practice, a characteristic of acts. In higher forms where mental processes become prominent, it is one of the constant modifiers of their psychical phases, and sometimes a keenly felt act in its own right.

To examine some psychoanalytic data along this axis may aid us in evaluating continual or similar processes or acts from biological to social and even to subject them to philosophical appraisal. In the psychoanalytic sphere, by using the psychoanalytic method, we can tease apart one function along a longitudinal axis and concentrate on one or another phenomenon. Concepts such as self-starting, the capacity to wait, the role of waiting in creativity, etc. are all to be considered. The purpose of this essay is to stimulate and provide such an overview; to serve as an illustration of categories which do more than bridge. Perhaps then we can consider those phenomena that unify biology, psychology and sociology as other kinds of arbitrary categories than those usually adhered to and which may thus expand our perceptions or allow for different perceptions.

THE PSYCHOANALYTIC ASPECT OF WAITING

All of us wait. Some tolerate it well and some poorly. It is sometimes considered a virtue and sometimes a necessary evil. In countries such as England it is quite common for people to line up to wait in an orderly and dignified manner for a bus or a service; but, on occasion, in the United States we push and shove and cannot wait for what we want. We do feel we have to learn to wait, that it is something that comes with time and perhaps maturity; however, there is, in all of us, a lurking antagonism to waiting. We bear waiting, but we probably rarely try to understand it.

Consider for a moment an example of a particular patient in analysis. This patient came initially for treatment with complaints of emptiness and meaninglessness, of an inability to maintain a close relationship with his wife and a variety of indicators of a narcissistic personality disorder. In the second year of treatment the patient had been away from analysis for the summer and had attempted unsuccessfully during that time to write a book which he had been carrying around in his head. He returned to analysis in the autumn and remembered an event which occurred when he was 8 years old and was about to perform in a piano recital. He recalled with much pain and vividness the moment when he came on to the stage and inexplicably could not get started. He looked imploringly at his piano teacher to start him off but she was unable or unwilling to aid, and he ran off the stage humiliated and embarrassed. With the recall of this memory and the resumption of his analysis he felt an exciting self-experience and began to write his book which he finished in a week. He got started!

There are multiple ways of looking at this phenomenon such as the patient achieving an identity as an author, the patient freeing hitherto unavailable psychological energy, the patient achieving a cohesive self-system, etc. One additional way is to examine the problem of self-starting or self-initiation along an axis of waiting, i.e. to consider the problem of 'suspension of an act until the means of continuance arrives'.

LITERATURE REVIEW

Waiting as such is not usually considered in the psychoanalytic literature, but associated phenomena such as timing and the sense of time, impatience and urgency are focal concepts. No attempt will be made to encompass the enormous literature about the broad category of time here, but some relevant references to the theme will suffice.[1]

---

[1] An excellent overview of the problem of temporal experience is given by Ornstein

Freud (1925) made his major reference to the sense of time in his 'A Note Upon the Mystic Writing-Pad' paper, wherein he connected the discontinuous method of functioning of the system *Pcpt.-Cs.* with the origin of the concept of time.

Federn comments upon the sense of time in his discussion of *déjà vu* and in a seemingly minor modification of Freud likens the 'estrangement of time' feeling to an emerging experience being alternately charged with narcissistic cathexis and then being deprived of it.

Although our current understanding of narcissism owes much indebtedness to Kohut (1968), I think he would agree that our debt to Federn (1952) is not fully recognized. In his discussion of depersonalization and estrangement, Federn describes the loss of libidinal cathexis of the ego core (in the former) and the ego boundaries (in the latter). Today we might translate these as losses of self-cathexis. Federn notes the breakdown in the feeling of unity in regard to continuity, as well as contiguity and causality. Insufficient continuity manifests itself in the inaccurate feeling for time: past, present, and future. The passing of the moment is vague and there is an uncertainty as to the historical sequence of memory. In brief Federn assigned the organization of time to the self system.

Anna Freud states (1965) that as the child develops, the emergence of a time sense is a pointer to bygone conflicts with anal strivings.

Piaget (1954) has shown the development of the sense of time to be related to the child's recognition of action as his own.

Edith Jacobson (1964) notes that the child's experience of his self as a composite and coherent identity profits from the sense of time rendered by the superego.

Fenichel (1945) connects the intolerance for tension and waiting to the organization of the infantile personality. People who cannot wait are unable to judge reality, and those who cannot endure pain or frustration are likened to 'addicts without drugs' and have never developed the ego

---

(1969, chap. 1). The remainder of the book is devoted to a cognitive theory of time experience and is perfectly compatible with psychoanalysis but limited in its restriction to one aspect of psychic functioning.

forces necessary to handle the id. Fenichel notes that oral fixations and early trauma play a significant role as to the causes of this intolerance.

His feeling is echoed by Rapaport (1960) and Hartmann (1964), who concentrate on the ego's capacity for delay as an indicator of ego strength. Rapaport's imagery is of channels of discharge and sluice valves to regulate the outflow.

Hartmann notes that the ego promotes detours and introduces the factor of growing independence from the immediate impact of present stimuli. Internalization includes both the danger signals and other functions in the nature of anticipation.

Glover (1956), commenting in a different vein from Rapaport about this concept, said:

> Psychic feeling of disruption is thus a typical and early tension affect, which in the course of development may become fixed in different forms ('canallized' by association with phantasy systems) according to the experiences and unconscious ideations of different developmental periods.

It appears that Glover has taken the phenomenon of disruption or bursting or impatience and connected it to the quality of an experience. Thus one can have the 'can't wait' feeling at oral, anal and phallic levels, or indeed it may be ascribed to multiple aspects of psychic functioning.

Waiting is considered an essential element of analytic treatment. Freud emphasizes the patience of the analyst in relation to the timelessness of the unconscious. In his discussion of the Wolf Man, Freud (1918) stressed his own waiting until the attachment to himself had become strong enough to announce the end of treatment. In his advice on the giving of interpretations the analyst is to wait until the patient is almost there himself and needs but one more step to the correct solution. Likewise patients wait for the analyst to make sense of their productions and develop an inner timing of expectations from their particular analyst.

The Developmental Continuum of Waiting

Waiting is an act of suspension. Langer (1967) states:

The principle of waiting is clearly exemplified in the conjoint actions of multi-enzyme systems, in which not the fastest but the slowest catalyst involved in a transformation is the 'pace-maker', since chemical reactions are not driven by successive impulses, but require their own exact times, so that complex cycles are possible only if the faster reactions can be suspended until the slowest is completed.

She further quotes Ephraim Racher as saying: 'When a steady state is established the rate of the overall process is governed by the rate of the slowest reaction. Then each step proceeds at the same rate.'

In parallel fashion we may hypothesize that the development of the psyche involves multiple repeated suspensions to allow the slower reactions to be integrated and that the inability or incapacity to wait can indicate both the very issue of change and its resulting (temporary) lack of integration as well as indicating (at times) primitiveness and its absence of integration.

The infant who cannot wait to be fed and literally cries until the food reaches his stomach is considered the prototype of impatience. However, the infant may be considered as multiple non-integrated aspects of psychic functioning which discharge at different rates and at different times. The slowest part of the system that the hungry infant's psyche cannot wait for, the slowest reaction that governs the rate of the entire system, is the mother who has to prepare the food. In this system the pacemaker is outside of the psyche and not properly a psychoanalytic model of impatience but rather a two-party social phenomenon.

Freud (1926) postulated the hallucinated breast as the intrapsychic component which completes the wait. The transaction from hallucination to fantasy to thinking or purposeful action were seen as the evolving steps in this continuum. However, the hallucination or the thought never satisfies the drive; there is no true gratification and yet there is a decrease of impatience. Though this concept has been employed to explain the growing capacity to wait based on the growing capacity of the ego to delay or modify the drives, there remains an element of the unexplained as to why a fantasy of gratification should have some of the effects of gratification. On some occasions the fantasy serves to stimulate the drive and this in turn may lead to urgency and impatience.

The observation of infants and children reveals that often the sight of the mother preparing the food allows for waiting. The growing child experiences the feeling of omnipotence and control which in effect is the precursor of his own capacity to gratify himself. As the child sees the mother prepare food he experiences his own fantasied or imagined control over food preparation. The developing capacity to wait seems to echo and parallel the feeling of magical control over the environment and this is quite independent of the direct drive gratification.

To put it another way there is both an object-for-gratification aspect and a self-image aspect to the capacity to wait. Impatience is both the lack of the object and the instability of the self. Therefore the capacity to hallucinate or later to fantasy the gratification completes the system and allows for a modicum of patience. It does not gratify the drive but the momentary expansion of the self is sufficient to calm the impatience.

As another analytic example may illustrate: the above-mentioned patient with a narcissistic personality disorder was chronically late for his sessions. His lateness was not a hostile act against the analyst as a separate object but rather a manifestation of the patient's intolerance of being early and having to wait to enter the office. He came late in order to have complete control over when the hour would begin. His major anxiety became clear over the ending of the hour which was beyond his control and indicated a rage reaction to this frustrated wish to control the hour. The genetic origin of this particular phenomenon related to the patient's puzzled relationship to a father who inexplicably and unpredictably 'turned off' in his attention to the patient. The patient felt shattered and disrupted, his self-continuity or feeling of sameness was destroyed and he reacted with narcissistic rage.

He said that he felt terrible because he was 'dismissed' arbitrarily by his troubled and preoccupied father. Thus in analysis he tried to change the passive experience into one of active control. It is suggested that the impatience that we see in children and some adults is an aggressive reaction to an injury to their omnipotence (which oscillates with their helplessness) and of their self-image and not the same as their frustration over drive tension. This reaction is one of narcissistic rage to the disruption of the feeling of continuity of the self or self-sameness (a particular ego function). Indeed in the development of the child there occurs a variety of self-experiences such as self-esteem, self-cohesiveness, humiliation, etc. The growing capacity to feel the same (relatively) from one moment to the next and over a period of time is this feeling of self-continuity and this appears to be the narcissistic component to the capacity to wait while the rage reaction is the response to disruption of this experience.

Thus we may consider the development of the act of starting as reflecting a newly integrated self-experience. Impatience is an early omnipotent reaction to missing parts experienced as outside of the self. The capacity to wait probably utilizes an aspect of self-control which is not so much an ability to dampen drives as it is a sense of self-sameness or self-continuity which protects against the vulnerability of disruption.

Another patient with the symptom of premature ejaculation seemed typical of sufferers from this disorder in that he complained of some anxiety but mainly of shame and humiliation. He was frightened and embarrassed over the fact that he could not control his ejaculation, that it was an experience which he passively endured and which literally would not wait for him. Disorders of ejaculation reflect a developmental continuum of starting, impatience and capacity to wait. One needs an intact self to get started as well as to wait. The latter, however, implies an anticipation of future intactness and allows for suspension of the completed act. The phenomenon of impatience reflects a vulnerable self and/or an early grandiose self which defend against the vulnerability by a premature closure.

This consideration should be clearly distinguished in its defensive nature. Another patient had trouble getting started in almost every hour. He painfully searched his mind for something to say and could only think of the fact that he seemed to have nothing to say. If the analyst would get him started or if somehow he could work the analyst to talk, then in his opinion he would feel relieved and it would be a good hour. In truth, however, he required more than a start because he did not want to be left on his own at all. For this patient the use of the external object was defensive to keep him from introspection and self-examination.

There was little rage or humiliation accompanying his manoeuvres and his feeling of self-continuity was intact.

For some patients the examination of the resistance to waiting reveals an unconscious meaning which may be surprising. One patient, having to wait for his hour to begin because the analyst was late, had a dream the following night of travelling through the country and taking a side trip through an area of devastation. He felt despondent and depressed at this sight but had a peculiar yearning to return to this place and perhaps undo the stark, barren, unhappy sight. His associations led him to that period of his life when he felt ignored and abandoned by his parents and resorted to long and lonely played out fantasies in a secret hill that was his very own. For this patient the avoidance of waiting was an avoidance of experiencing the painful affects which he had hoped were left behind in his childhood.

On occasion the issue of waiting appears in a dream. The following illustrates this: 'I was going to a party given by an important man—there were lots of wealthy people—I had to wait for the elevator. ...' The associations to the dream had to do with the bill and the patient's wish to pay it immediately versus not to pay at all; but his wish was subject to an insurance payment. Also the patient planned to leave for an extended summer vacation with which analysis would interfere and this troubled him. The wait in the dream refers to a self-cautioning mechanism helping him to handle the urgency of so many decisions and conflicts. This patient's dream had occurred over the weekend and showed the preconscious concern with keeping the self intact by keeping it in suspension until analysis resumed. However, the further analytic work clarified that the important man was the early grandiosity of the patient which was soon to arrive on the scene. The patient's struggle over paying and leaving was resistance to re-experiencing this early grandiosity. This nicely demonstrates the rule that the overall process is governed by the rate of the slowest reaction.

One routine in analytic practice is to allow the patient to begin the hour, to choose the topic for the day. This was a technical point developed by Freud over a period of time and not fully evidenced until he wrote his paper on the Rat Man. The unspoken rule is to allow the patient to start so that he introspects and concentrates on the intrapsychic as a closed system rather than a two-party system as in a conversation.

In analysis of the relatively silent or unproductive patients, the analyst often feels impatient and sometimes gets angry. He distracts or amuses himself with formulations about the paucity of material or else diverts himself with a variety of fantasies. He may go so far as to discharge his feelings by way of an interpretation or to sometimes try encouraging or prodding or chastising the patient. My own understanding of this series of phenomena does not involve that of some frustrated libidinal drive discharge but rather of a reaction to the helplessness in myself evoked by these patients. The reaction is a modicum of narcissistic rage due to the threatened loss of control of the situation. The developing patience of the analyst seems to correlate with the growing wisdom and maturity of the analyst and this is expressed sometimes as 'a firming of the identity of the analyst' but more properly as the more secure function of self-continuity or self-control.

As development proceeds one can correlate the oral urgency and inability to wait, the anal-sadistic use of delay as a hostile act and the genital accumulation of control to orgastic discharge. The genital orgasm represents a turning point in waiting because there now occurs an exquisite pleasure in the waiting. This parallels the development of self-cohesiveness and self-control, so that what was previously a passive experiencing of the discharge is now a controllable and active handling of it. Waiting becomes a pleasurable phenomenon.

One sees the manifestation of waiting as pleasure in the variety of experiences which involve the building up of tensions, the lengthening and drawing out of the tensions and the careful regulation to the point of discharge.

THE ANGUISH OF WAITING

For some people waiting is intolerable. Even brief periods of waiting cause discomfort and prolonged waits are unbearable. They 'climb the walls' or 'crawl out of their skins' or are 'about to burst'. The end of waiting is not a pleasure but a relief and though they may somewhat masochistically get involved in waiting episodes, they experience such periods with anxiety and dread. There is another and different quality added to that of the building up of drive tension. Based on the model of development it would appear that this torment is related to an external source needed to afford relief. The person not only depends on someone else but is literally at the mercy of another. What is a potentially sado-masochistic relationship of one person teasing or tormenting another becomes extended to an uncertain or unknown end to the tension which end is entirely beyond the control or the limits of the individual. The feeling of self-continuity is destroyed temporarily and the end of waiting restores a feeling of wholeness and with this comes relief.

When I was young I attended school some distance from home and had to be driven to school and home again. Often my father was busy working when school ended and I would have to wait for him outside on the corner. I was sure I waited hours and hours, and years later I would complain to my analyst of my father's lack of concern for his cold and usually hungry child. The reluctant truth was probably closer to 20 minutes but the time of waiting for children is often unbearable. I had heard that time passage is longer for those who have lots of time ahead of them as do children and faster for those who see the end as nearer. I suspect the reasons are more related to feelings of relative helplessness and lack of modification of the grandiose self. Anna Freud (1965) complements this by noting the evaluation of time at various age levels. This depends on the subjective inner relations of either id or ego dominance over the child's functioning. Marie Bonaparte quotes Freud as saying that the sense we have of the passing of time originates in our inner perception of the passing of our own life. When consciousness awakens within us, we perceive the internal flow and then project it into the outside world.

No doubt the variable estimates of how long one has waited or how long a given period of time is judged to be has no unitary explanation. Phenomena such as novelty or pleasure versus boredom play a significant role. Ornstein (1969) explains the process as one involving coding and storage of stimuli and thus feels that more organized or coded experiences are felt to be shorter. An additional factor in terms of enjoying an experience may be the relative lack of self-cathexis due to hyper-cathexis of the activity and thus time is felt to have passed quickly.

THE BENEFITS OF WAITING

Shakespeare has Iago say:

> How poor are they that have not patience
> What wound did ever heal but by degrees
> Thou know'st we work by wit and not by witchcraft
> And wit depends on dilatory time.

This quotation serves well as an analytic credo because the mainstay of analytic insight is the slow accumulation of fact and connexion. Waiting involves a process which is allowed to finish, is seen to its end. Certainly we allow for our own arbitrary choices of beginnings and ends, but within any enormous or infinite process there are sub-cycles or processes with limiting boundaries. Wounds take time to heal, children take time to grow and knowledge takes time to accumulate. There is no doubt that the very quality of the passage of time has a salutary effect on these processes. Such principles as organizing, integrating and maturing are those involving slow gathering together, arranging and hierarchical regulation. Children learn by the organizing of words into sentences, into integrative jumps of conceptual thinking. Emerging nations develop by fits and starts, by integrative jumps and by a kind of maturational process peculiar to themselves but certainly requiring time. Mature nations often take longer to make decisions or to respond to provocations and hopefully have more positive qualities such as patience. In the psychotherapeutic experience of many, waiting to get treatment, such as waiting lists of clinics, reveals that many patients get better while waiting. In one study (Goldberg & Rubin, 1964) patients who were left alone after long periods of emotional disturbance seemingly had spontaneous recoveries. Perhaps some process which was being observed in midstream and showing phenomena interpreted as pathology was allowed to proceed to completion and the disturbance or epiphenomenon receded. Or perhaps the introduction of a waiting period into the process changed something. The latter aspect would relate to the above-mentioned ideas, such as the person taking over for himself and exerting self-control over his fate. To be sure, there are numerous other psychological reasons for these incidents of supposed self-cure.

In psychoanalysis the waiting phenomenon has been examined via the concept of working through. The essence of this is the model of mourning and involves the piecemeal digestion or assimilation of painful or unmanageable tensions or affects. Reducing the unmanageable or unwieldy to size allows for gradual integration over a time period. The capacity to do this is expanded to an idea of maturity or health wherein the psychic apparatus is geared to regulate drive tension and gratification so that piecemeal handling of excitation is standard and pleasure is maximized. The introduction of something new, whether it is a repressed memory or an id impulse, often is traumatic not only because of its ideational content and quota of painful affect (on the basis of quantity), but also because of its inherent disruptive quality. Working through takes time because of the need for integration and this should be separated from the new being painful or unmanageable. Sometimes previously repressed material which is not completely assimilated into what we call consciousness is not re-repressed but is seemingly held in limbo waiting until a place is found for it.

The well-known and poorly tolerated (by others) impatience of adolescence is often ascribed to the pressure of the newly reinforced drives. However, it should also be seen as reflecting the overall concept of change which manifests itself as impatience because of the disruption of the system. Urgency is not always a signal to respond; it can also be a sign of new arranging or order.

SOME ASPECTS OF APPLIED PSYCHOANALYSIS OF WAITING

Waiting and patience are such ubiquitous themes in art, music and literature that no survey could be exhaustive. We are all familiar with the build-up of tension of musical themes as we wait for the release that never comes. The fadeout in motion pictures has taught us all that we need not wait and time has passed in that brief black space. In the theatre Beckett has beautifully demonstrated the dilemma of man in *Waiting for Godot*. This play and its sequel, *Endgame*, illustrate (for some in a slow, boring and unending manner) the issue of man as he waits for his meaning or his fate or his death. No attempt will be made to explain the play, but one cannot help but experience the issue of waiting, as it can stand for or symbolize so many things. The issues presented are

> Temporality and evanescence; the tragic difficulty of becoming aware of one's own self in the merciless process of renovation and destruction that occurs with change in time; of the difficulty of communication between human beings; of the unending quest for reality in a world in which everything is uncertain and the borderline between dream and reality is ever shifting; of the tragic nature of all love relationship and the self-deception of friendship and so on.

The artist, in his own creative manner, articulates so much by utilizing a particular theme of waiting. But Beckett has said: 'I take no sides. I am interested in the shape of ideas. It is the shape that matters.' And his play is a form that allows a variety of contents to fill it and be drawn out.

Another illustration that may be of interest is that of the person in confinement. The prisoner waits to be released or else resigns himself to a life of incarceration. The initial anxiety of waiting for release subsides and then returns as the date approaches. This is equally true of the confinement of pregnancy. The serenity of the pregnant woman (sometimes used to explain the Mona Lisa mystery) is that of the woman who waits in a beautiful and controlled manner when she feels her self-continuity and self-control are heightened. She knows when and how long she must wait, and anxiety only returns with the indefiniteness of the final hours. Women with a shaky feeling of self-continuity are more terrified than pacified by pregnancy, which is but another threat to holding themselves together.

The act of creation *per se*, either in a work of art or in a pregnancy, consists of organization and arrangement over a time period, with waiting playing a unique role. Some artists speak of waiting for inspiration as though some unconscious spark or impetus allows a percolating process to pursue its fulfilment.[2] Psychoanalytic investigations of creativity which do not pursue the supposed peculiar dynamics of the artist often stress the unique organization or integrative qualities involved in the work of art. The artist, just as the pregnant woman, is a self-contained unit that waits for the ingredients to gel or to come alive. The peculiar serenity or self-fulfillment of the creative person perhaps relates to the function of self-continuity that creativity seems to reinforce.

Another intriguing approach to examining the waiting phenomenon concerns itself with drugs; in particular marijuana. One striking effect of marijuana intoxication is that of time distortion, more particularly that of time delay. Events take a very long time to happen. Indeed the so-called or supposed intensification of perceptions may be more properly (or partially) due to the lengthened time that one seems to be experiencing perceptions. Some people luxuriate in the atmosphere of slowness and delay and almost timelessness. For others the experience is frightening or boring and they cannot wait for it to end. One striking fear shared by people who have had a bad experience with marijuana is that they remain in its grips until it wears off and there is no good antidote or neutralizer to it. I am not familiar enough with analytic material of marijuana users to in any way correlate this effect with psychopathology, but I feel that a different orientation to drug effects (rather than a listing of disrupted ego functions) might have more profitable results.

DISCUSSION

A useful concept to employ in order to comprehend the issue of waiting

---

[2] When Freud (1910) wrote of Leonardo he said: 'The slowness with which Leonardo worked was proverbial. He painted at the Last Supper in the Convent of Santa Maria delle Grazie in Milan, after the most thorough preparatory studies, for three whole years ... Leonardo often used to climb up the scaffolding early in the morning and remain there till twilight never once laying his brush aside, and with no thought of eating or drinking. Then days would pass without his putting his hand to it. Sometimes he would remain for hours in front of the painting, merely examining it in his mind.'

is to consider the self or the self-system as an organizer (Grinker, 1957). A variety of experiences are brought together and arranged as part of the system self, and this can be thought as operating in relation to other systems. The concept of ego as system can be considered as hierarchically at a different level, or one can use other abstractions to conceptualize a multiplicity of systems. The thesis presented here is that the sense of time passage is a quality or function of the self-system.

The phenomenon of anniversary reactions can be used to illustrate the employment of this thesis. Pollock (1971) and others have surveyed and reported on the ubiquity of these time-bound reactions. Recently Seitz (1971) likened anniversary reactions to a computer programming which is set off at regular intervals via some unconscious stimulus. In the development of the anniversary reaction there first occurs an external event which has some traumatic qualities for the psyche. A passive and unprepared psyche endures something for which it is not prepared. The psyche then actively takes it (the experience of the event) and makes it its own and periodically re-experiences it either as a form of mastery or as evidence of a repetition compulsion. Peculiar to anniversary reactions is the capacity to wait until the appropriate time for discharge or expression. However, what has happened is that the external event which was passively endured becomes organized on a time axis and becomes one's own. Pollock has likened the process to that which underlies some forms of learning and basically it involves stamping something as part of oneself. This internalization process is organized and regulated and follows the rules laid down for multi-enzyme conjoint systems, i.e. the slowest catalyst involved is the pacemaker.

One can conceptualize the self as regulating or organizing a variety of pacemakers in terms of starting and waiting. The principle of waiting involves arranging a multitude of ingredients and holding them in suspension until the slowest reaction can be integrated. Psychologically, there is a development of this principle from an incapacity to wait to a fragile and vulnerable organization which controls drives and external stimuli to a firm self-system which has continuity and can experience pleasure in waiting.

Some speculations concerning the more complex area of time in a psychological sense offer themselves via this kind of systems approach. The psychological meaning of time involves consideration of areas such as beginnings and endings, time experience, rhythm and a host of other phenomena which connect to and derive from this concept. I suspect that time is undefinable and almost idiosyncratic because it is a complex individual regulating system which functions silently at times, expands and contracts as issues and events present themselves and interdigitates with other psychic systems. Thus it has no meaning or boundaries but is a variable function. For example, punctuality and worry over time might express interrelationships with the superego system. Impulsivity, so characteristic of hysterics, is more clearly an example of what is often described as an id eruption in conflict with an ego and/or superego restraint—a different systems interaction. I have tried to demonstrate above the experiencing of time passage as primarily involving the self-system. The connexion of biological rhythms and psychological 'timing' is obvious as well. There can be a multitude of systems or organizers and one need not confine ordering data according to the common structural categories. The difficulty to be avoided is to insist on certain systems activity where there is no relevance. For example, in all likelihood the issue of time, as well as that of the self, has no real meaning in regard to certain types of abstract thinking. Perhaps the supposed 'timelessness' of the unconscious is another misnomer and one might be more accurate in saying that these kinds of experiences have no relevance to time. Hopefully psychoanalysis can profit from reordering and rearranging some concepts without departing from the use of the basic psychoanalytic method. Perhaps we can expand from careful examination of processes with psychoanalytic tools to more unitary processes which go beyond psychoanalysis but are part of the open system that is man. I hope that the similarities elucidated here are not superficial in the sense of analogies that are scientifically worthless (von Bertalanffy). Rather this can be part of a search for logical homologies which implies more than metaphor but a formal correspondence founded in reality.

REFERENCES

Bertalanffy, L. Von (1968). *General Systems Theory.* New York: Braziller.

Federn, P. (1952). *Ego Psychology and the Psychosis.* New York: Basic Books.

Fenichel, O. (1945). *The Psychoanalytic Theory of Neurosis.* New York: Norton.

Freud, A. (1965). *Normality and Pathology in Childhood.* New York:: International Universities Press.

Freud, S. (1910). Leonardo da Vinci and a memory of his childhood. *Standard Edition* 11.

——— (1918). From the history of an infantile neurosis. *Standard Edition* 17.

——— (1925). A note upon the 'mystic writing-pad.' *Standard Edition* 19.

——— (1926). Inhibitions, symptoms and anxiety. *Standard Edition* 20.

Glover, E. (1956). *On the Early Development of Mind.* New York: International Universities Press.

Goldberg, A. & Rubin, B. (1964). Recovery of patients during periods of supposed neglect. *British Journal of Medical Psychology* 37: 265–272

Grinker, R. R., Sr (1957). On identification. *International Journal of Psycho-Analysis* 38:379–390.

Hartmann, H. (1964). *Essays on Ego Psychology.* New York: International Universities Press.

Jacobson, E. (1964). *The Self and the Object World.* New York: International Universities Press.

Kohut, H. (1968). The psychoanalytic treatment of narcissistic personality disorders: outline of a systematic approach. *Psychoanalytic Study of the Child* 23.

Langer, S. K. (1967). *Mind: An Essay on Human Feeling.* Baltimore: Johns Hopkins Press.

Ornstein, R. O. (1969). *On the Experience of Time.* Harmondsworth, Middlesex, and Baltimore: Penguin Books.

Piaget, J. (1954). *The Construction of Reality in the Child.* New York: Basic Books.

Pollock, G. (1971). On time and anniversaries In *The Unconscious Today,* ed. M. Kanzer. New York: International Universities Press. (In press.)

Rapaport, D. (1960). The structure of psychoanalytic theory. *Psychology Issues Monograph* no. 2 monograph 6.

Seitz, P. (1971). ESP and anniversary reactions. (Unpublished manuscript.)

The Wishy-Washy Personality (1986)

This theme of the continuity of the self is taken up again in *The Wishy-Washy Personality (1986)* (what a title!). Here, Goldberg addresses a particular deficit in the structural integrity of the self, one that accounts for an inability to feel strongly about a choice. How do we explain this inability? It seems that choice always involves change from one state of the self to another and likewise demands some reorganization of the self as it moves from the first stage to the second. In childhood these transitions require a continual supporting relationship. The loss of an available caretaker over the change sequence can create anxiety in the child. With this anxiety, change can be frightening and potentially disorganizing, and the child will seek out stability and safety. According to Goldberg, "One can move freely from one point in time or space to another as long as there is the security of some stable and unchanging self-experience. Developmentally this may be offered by a sense of being able to return to touch base for refueling or reassurance or comforting. Soon the next step becomes a source of comfort and reassurance and one may pass into it by something akin to a mourning process for what is left behind." Here there is an emphasis on the development and organization of the self as linked to the nature of the self-object connection, and a structure that is distinct and different from the ego.

—GM

INTRODUCTION

This essay is intended to develop further and explicate a characterology of psychoanalytic self psychology. As with all character studies it should be seen as highlighting traits that are ubiquitous to some degree in the entire population, while outstanding in some few individuals. It is thus to be considered as a lifelong pattern of behavior which in turn is tied to normal development. This linkage should not be seen as connecting a specific time of occurrence, but rather as one denoting a certain enduring quality of relationships. We may see the self through life as having qualities of coherence, firmness, harmony, continuity, etc. This last point, that of a feeling of sameness through time and space, will be focused upon as crucial to the emergence of the particular character to be considered here. In a previous paper on the misfit, the developmental difficulty of that pattern was noted to be a failure to achieve a necessary transition from one stage to the next because of the lack of sustaining selfobjects at the succeeding stage. The present cohort of patients is differentiated on the basis of the failed sense of stability which would allow such a transit to be even considered. In a simplified way this would translate to the wishy-washy person showing a defect earlier than the misfit, but such a simplification should not be read as being time-bound, e.g., the first at 13 months and the next at 21 or as reflecting severity of pathology. Since we see that people need stability and responsiveness throughout life, we should be able to highlight a character disorder that reflects the problematic state of these needs. The one that is selected here for examination is that of self-continuity. Once again it is necessary to examine this sort of organization primarily in terms of the emerging transference manifestations and not at all in a phenomenological or descriptive sense of social relationships, although these may conform to what is ultimately to be the prevalent transference. It is probably also necessary to present a disclaimer to the effect that even though one links a developmental problem to later adult psychopathology, it is not always the case that such problems inevitably lead to such pathology nor need it be true that the later pathology is always a product of the earlier difficulty, i.e., the linkage is not a rigid one.

DEFINITION

Not surprisingly the term wishy-washy is listed in Webster's New World Dictionary and is an accepted phrase in our language. One could, of course, substitute a more scientific sounding word or phrase, but this one is unusually evocative. It suggests an unesteemed individual, and in turn one can often conjure up an image of such a person. In more cases than not, it is a woman who is surrounded by a network of similar words such as weak, insipid and flighty. Still, although such a vulgar phrase may hardly seem to be a fit topic for scientific inquiry, perhaps a case can be made for a more sturdy definition: one based upon psychoanalytic evidence and principles. As such it will be enlisted in the category of character disorders and will be considered as an "habitual mode of adjustment of the ego to the external world, the id and the superego" or else as a pervasive subjective feeling concerned with adaptation (Goldberg, 1983). The person possessed of a wishy-washy personality is seen in a particular manner in relation to the world and to himself or herself; such persons have a corresponding feeling about themselves and what they are, as well. It is, of course, the emergence of this form of appearance or adaptation in a psychoanalysis that allows us to consider it as representative of some particular significance and to differentiate it from the superficial evidences of this in ordinary social intercourse.

It is a rare person who has not had some experience that might correspond to this phenomenon, and who cannot thereby easily identify it as an issue which may seem to dominate the life of some people. It is likewise a personality pattern that need not be associated with any sort of subjective discomfort or distress while on the contrary often leading to a medley of negative feelings in others. A common feature of the problem is this lack of awareness of it to the bearer and the relative ease with which it is rationalized with terms such as easy-going or flexible. In the course of analytic treatment the basis of being wishy-washy may thus be experienced with a good deal of sadness and despair as the patient discovers what may be a profound deficit in his make-up. Indeed the thesis of this essay is that the malady is a reflection of a deficient structural organization that may be more prevalent than is ordinarily noted.

Though some might espouse a way of life that allows for contentment by suspending judgment and thereby freeing oneself from the problems and anxieties of searching for the truth or the right way of living, it is more the case that the wishy-washy personality has not opted for the way of skepticism but rather is robbed of that very sort of peace that a true skeptic may achieve (Stroud, 1984).

DIFFERENTIAL DIAGNOSIS AND INDECISIVENESS

The indecisive person is thought of as torn between one or another courses of life or ways to act or sets of beliefs. He is pictured as standing at the crossroads of a bifurcating road and so unable to commit himself to the one or the other presented path. Every step down one lane causes anxiety about forsaking the other. The neurotic counterpart for indecision is the obsessive-compulsive who must undo everything that is done, who begs others to decide for him and then rebels at the decision, and who is poised at indecision as a solution to the conflict below. Wishy-washy people, on the other hand, are not particularly concerned about going down one path rather than the other, they have no real regrets about the choice of one thereupon precluding the other, and they are more often relieved at a decision being made; by themselves or anyone else. Their problem lies in the fact that they do not or say not that they really care. They may or may not be relieved by a decision being reached, but they are lacking in the feeling of true satisfaction in having arrived at one. Nor do they evidence much regret at having missed out on the alternative, since decisions and choices and options do not offer a field of concern and interest for them. At times they do regret the lack of enthusiasm that they see manifest in others over these issues, but they often mask this in terms of a rationalization about not having the same degree of concern about some things that others seem to possess.

The ability to see both sides of a question is often the hallmark of an even-handed person and is at times associated with growing maturity and wisdom. This posture is linked as well to indecision but has been lifted away from the intrapsychic conflict of the obsessional individual to a more conscious deliberation involving the relative weights of one choice versus another. But wishy-washiness is overwhelmingly lacking in the capacity to consider one thing and then move on to contemplate the other, since the necessary firmness to take a stand seems nowhere present. If anything there is a puzzlement and bewilderment on their part as to the effort expended to evaluate positions, since it seems of little moment if one decides one way rather than another. True ambivalence is filled with regrets, and the wishy-washy person has little of that.

To be wishy-washy is not so much to be unable to be decisive as it is to be unable to care about the problem. Something is missing or lacking that allows for the struggle to take place and this deficit so permeates the personality that one is more readily characterized as vapid and shallow than as locked in uncertainty. They lack the solid state on which one plants one's feet as contemplation over choice proceeds.

AND COMPLIANCE

The compliant person is a master of agreement and conformity and is noteworthy as to the ease in which they adapt to situations and to others. Though seen as weak at some times and by some others, they primarily fit themselves into situations and do so with a minimum of discomfort and distress. Such an attribute is thought of as revealing a flexibility of personality and thereby a lack of rigidity and stubbornness. It is also felt to complement the more dominant and perhaps more rigid other person who cannot so bend to meet the demands of people and the world. On occasion, compliance is seen as a nuisance in its eagerness to still dissension and debate, and it may thus reveal a defensive posture against stirring up heat and discord. As such it can reveal a fear of anger and discontent and a protective facade against the pain of such affects. No doubt much compliance is of this nature, but in this light it retains the elements of a developed organization which is goal-directed and in the service of maintaining a personality. There is nothing to this that suggests that the person is best by anxiety over what to do or by resentment at having so chosen or at being forced to do something. Regardless of the defensive nature of compliance and its subsequent hidden hostile intent, it is often only a problem in the area between personalities, i.e., one wanting with some degree of intensity, and the other going along with some pleasure in agreement.

Aside from the compliance of hostility and hidden resentment, there does exist one that reflects genuine ease of adjustment and conformity. There are people who have a non-conflictual life of fitting-in with a minimum of strain or struggle, and it seems apparent to all that this can be accomplished with no evidence of uncertainty or wishy-washiness. Thus compliant people need not be and usually are not wishy-washy.

AND PASSIVITY

The passive position, whether or not associated with femininity, is defined in opposition to that of aggression. It is receptive rather than direct and reactive rather than initiating. It usually has little earmarks of indecision as long as someone else takes the lead or dictates the direction. It is undoubtedly seen from outside as a posture of compliance but seems to restrict its evidence of this to a modicum reflecting passivity, i.e., one could imagine a compliant, yet aggressive individual.

Just as with compliance, the passive person may appear to be indecisive, but really he or she only is waiting to be told and directed. There is no necessary conflict about doing, as long as it is in the favored passive mode. And though passivity may be defensive or otherwise, it need not be evidence of a weak and vapid structure. Passivity as well is often looked upon as an admirable and positive way to live, but this is never true of wishy-washiness which always has negative connotations.

PHENOMENOLOGY

A description of the wishy-washy person must focus on the peculiar status of concern or care in their lives. To do something or to be something or someone need not be simply a matter of indifference to such a person, but rather one avenue seems to have no inherent advantage over the other. This circumstance leads such people to say that they care not, when in truth, they more likely cannot care. Thus they are neither carefree or careless, both words which reflect a capacity that may or may not be exercised. They wish, sometimes openly and often secretly, that things matter more. Such a longing often reveals itself in treatment, and the facade of ease gives way to puzzlement over how others can feel so committed to things. When change does occur it may be a wrenching experience which disturbs the people around as well as the wishy-washy person per se. It leads to a realignment of relationships with strong fears of being disliked by those who counted on you to be flexible and undemanding. No doubt there exist degrees of wishy-washiness, and it may dominate a personality or else reign in but one segment of behavior. Our clinical material should therefore demonstrate and describe a person who felt that it was a pervasive feature as well as one who had it as a sometimes thing. The developmental issues which will be touched upon should therefore reflect the sort of problem that can be seen as varying in its import. One of the patients to be presented felt it a major aspect of functioning while another is said to manifest it alongside another characterological problem; and one could correlate these differences to the different transference reconstructions.

DEVELOPMENT

Though children are often described as stubborn or obedient, difficult or easy-going, determined or easily persuaded it is rare to hear of anyone characterizing a child as wishy-washy. That term seems reserved for an age possessed of the ability to know enough about oneself to be sure of what one wants, an age that corresponds perhaps to an Eriksonian achievement of identity though certainly the etiology of the difficulty is not of that period. Since this is so much a social concept it remains to be seen if there can be a corresponding psychoanalytic explanation to the state of knowing what one is and what one wants. It would, however, be a banality to merely say that the developmental step that is necessary is essentially that which corresponds to a firm self or sense of self. To be sure firmness is the basic requirement or essential ingredient that combats wishy-washiness, but the infirm self can be seen to manifest any variety of difficulty and pathology. The question to be addressed is that of a particular deficit in the structural integrity of the self; one that accounts for an inability to feel strongly about a choice.

At the risk of speculation there may be some general ideas which could be suggested as indicative of the source of the problem which, in turn, might be studied for verification in a clinical setting. One is that of movement or transition. It seems that choice always involves change from one state to another and likewise demands some reorganization of the self as it moves from the first stage to the second. Children need a continual supporting relationship in order to effect such transitions and will have maximum anxiety if the caretaker or selfobject is unavailable or lost to them over the change sequence. Such anxiety tends to make change frightening and lends safety to staying as is. Thus one scarcely invests interest in what may lie ahead, since any aspect of stepping forward is frightening and potentially disorganizing. Since this is a general delineation of development that could well fall into the catch-all of separation-individuation, it needs a better detailing to say see if we can say just what is required to enable one to invest in something new: without fear and with interest and enthusiasm.

To pursue the problem of firmness and transition, we can isolate the subjective feeling of sameness or continuity over time as one essential complex emotion that merits attention. One can move freely from one point in time or space to another as long as there is the security of some stable and unchanging self experience. Developmentally this may be offered by a sense of being able to return to touch base for refueling or reassurance or comforting. Soon the next step becomes a source of comfort and reassurance, and one may pass into it by something akin to a mourning process for what is left behind. There is a developmental push to new stages of growth and achievement which, although initially frightening, are likewise gratifying and fulfilling. The self is thus expanded at developmental progress and at any point one is capable of a view that looks backward and forward and which, of itself, assures the feeling of continuity through time and space.

No doubt the sense of sameness is a continual developmental accomplishment, but probably there are points in life when it begins, is fostered and needs maximum nurturance. To ascertain these nodal moments, psychoanalysis must turn to a reconstructive approach that reflects best just why and when the disorder comes about.

CLINICAL MATERIAL

Much has been said about the value of single case generalizations (Edelson, 1984), but the one that follows is primarily illustrative. A brief mention of similar cases will be attempted for contrast, and, furthermore, one assumes a host of such cases in any clinical practice.

CASE REPORT

This is a case of a middle-aged woman who entered analysis for extreme hypochondriacal preoccupation of near disabling proportions. Her analysis was not especially noteworthy except for the material to be focused upon in terms of the topic of this essay. After several years of work she reported a dream as follows:

> She was walking down the street and saw her friend Sylvia. She was unable to see Sylvia's face however either because of fog or a cloud or hair obstructing it. She tried to push whatever it was away so that she could get a clearer glimpse of it but did not seem satisfied that she had accomplished this. She awoke frustrated from her efforts at getting a clear view of Sylvia.

Sylvia is a good and dear friend of the patient's, and, as she thought and talked about her, she centered on the fact that Sylvia was an uncomplicated person. This was meant in the sense that Sylvia knew what she wanted and just did it; not beating around the bush and waffling. The patient recognized how much she wanted to be like this, but came to realize that this had long been lacking in her life. She usually did not know what she wanted to do or to be. For instance, this weekend her husband was to be away on business, and she was free to do whatever she pleased. Whenever this happened she would plan her time down to the minute; although it seemed that her plans need not concern events and activities that especially pleased her, but rather that they cover a total schedule of her time. She did not concern herself with whether she wanted to do one thing or another, but rather that all the time was accounted for. In fact she was married to a man who was a model of discipline, time allocation and duty; and she was content to go along with him on whatever he had planned. But she never particularly liked what they did together; nor was it the case that she was particularly displeased. She just went along. She felt that the dream was an indication of her wish to find herself as a more determined or certain person.

In the patient's work as a poet, she began by first constructing some form of solid structure which she would later freely fill in. She likened this to her planning her weekend and to having a husband who planned everything. Left with too much uncertainty she felt unable to perform creatively until a minimum decisive step had been made.

The dream coincided with two events in her life. The first had to do with a reading of her poetry that had been scheduled. She was asked to share the podium with another poet and friend, and she had agreed, or perhaps it might be better to say, acquiesced. She did this readily, but only later had misgivings about it. These increased in frequency and intensity until the patient had a fantasy while riding on the expressway. She thought of seeing a horse belonging to Louis XIV from the rear, quickly identified this is a horse's ass, and soon thereafter decided that this was her image of herself for agreeing to share the program. This led to a decision on her part to recant her agreement and flooded her with apprehension about what would be thought of her along with an accompanying positive feeling of pride in having made this decision. She announced that she had to have the program to herself in spite of feeling that she would be exposed as selfish and fearful of competition. The uniqueness of this experience of clearly knowing what she wanted was literally overwhelming.

The correlative events in the analysis were those surrounding her missing a single session to join her husband for a long weekend. Separations were always difficult for her, and although this was no different in its potential fearfulness, it was of some distinction in her planning for it. In the history of this particular analysis there had been a sequence of negotiations about missing sessions. The analysis had begun with a fairly clear contract that the patient was responsible for all of her sessions and would therefore pay for any she missed, for whatever reasons. She had no questions about this point, although admittedly she was a patient who rarely took issue with things of any kind. During one long vacation her husband had protested mightily about paying for missed hours, and so the patient asked if we might renegotiate the agreement to something like a friend of hers had with her analyst, who tried to fill hours that were vacated and so relieved her partially of responsibility for all of them. The issue of missing hours and payment was subjected to long and repeated scrutiny in the analysis until I felt that there was little more to be gained from this work. The pressure from her husband for a change remained intense. I agreed to the change, and during the patient's next absence she was beside herself with anxiety about the hours that were taken away from her while she was away. She had to feel and know that her hours remained hers. We tried to connect this to her childhood feelings concerning the birth of a brother at age 4. He turned out to be a very sickly child who required the concentrated attention of their parents until he died when he was eight years old. For some reason the patient felt this explanation was unsatisfactory inasmuch as she was already in school when her brother became ill, and she could recall no feelings of being usurped. Rather her fearfulness about losing her hours seemed more clearly evidenced in a general fantasy of hers about dropping from sight in terms of me and my memory. She once noted that I turned away from her as soon as her hour ended to tend to some papers on my desk. She elaborated this fantasy that I wanted to be rid of her or perhaps that I forgot her as soon as she was gone. She wanted to keep her hours even while she was away in order to stay alive in my mind, to not be forgotten, to establish a continuity of presence. She had decided on this shortly before the time of the poetry reading and the decision that *that* had prompted in her.

I privately compared this fantasy and fear of my turning away from her to another case in the literature (Goldberg, 1978), that of a man described as a procrastinator who also was a voyeur. He, too, showed severe separation anxiety, and related it to wanting to be retained in the mind's eye of the analyst. His case report detailed how he drew a picture of the analyst's face during a weekend separation and painted miniatures of himself where the eyes, nose and mouth of the analyst should be (p. 272). The reconstructive work in this analysis had to do with an exhausted mother who was unable to fully respond to her son. It was felt that this was never an absolute absence, but rather that her limited energies did not allow her to respond in accordance with the timetable of the child's needs. A minor note in the case report indicates that the symptom of procrastination disappeared as the analysis progressed.

The patient is described as always studying his mother's face which was inscrutable: like a mask. He said that no matter what her mood she showed but one face. He also said that thinking of her face gave him the creeps. In contrast to the first patient whose mother seemingly had no steady, even if inappropriate, gaze, this man felt an irritating sameness to his mother's mood and expression. The patient was disturbed over the inappropriateness of the responsiveness of his mother and longed for something else. This is in contrast to the patient who said that her mother had no particular feeling about anything, and who therefore had nothing for her to scrutinize.

My own patient did not have an exhausted mother as much as she had an elusive one. There was no evidence of depression in the mother but rather a sort of restlessness or flightiness or preoccupation, much as the analyst who wants to be rid of the patient in order to get on with other things of real interest to him.

With this patient as with most of the others with similar problems, after a decision was reached, there occurred a period of relative tranquility. As a rule this is often short-lived and ushers in a new state of severe anxiety. This latter phenomenon is found to be due to the feeling of total abandonment and aloneness as one marches down a chosen path. The patient soon reported a dream:

> I am in G's department store and feel good but want to go home. A phone call informs me that I must go through a pass to get home. The pass is surrounded by trees and a ravine. There are horseback riders on the path but the horses are under control and I am not afraid. But soon the horses get larger and riderless and I am afraid. Suddenly a tiger leaps out and I wave a white towel and awake in terror.

The associations to the dream were to a feared attack by a critic of her work. G's store was probably the comfort of the analysis when she had reached a decision. She realized then that she wanted to go home, and the phone was a warning. The pass was like one that she used to go to the beach as a child. Now she recalled all the fears that she had as a child: of shots by the doctor, of all the people throughout her life who had power over her. That was the whole thing: that she really did not have control, people were unpredictable, and she was not in control of her life. She then turned to the analysis and saw the dream as approaching termination with the conviction that it would be done to her rather than being under her control.

The conceptualization of this patient's difficulty in not having a sense of sameness and solidity through time can be illustrated in many ways. Mahler might see it in terms of separation-individuation, wherein the child becomes anxious when she feels too distant from the parental figure and so must repeatedly return to refueling. Others might visualize it in terms of some needed introjection of "holding objects" which allow for more autonomous function. I (Goldberg, 1983) had suggested using a metaphor of

ownership to picture the sense of something being owned and therefore under one's control. Such a metaphor removes the boundary between persons as psychological entities and allows an idea of shared ownership, i.e., something had by both mother and child without the usual connotations of the transitional objects seen as "things" such as blankets. The idea of the child, the image of the child shared by mother and child is then illustrated in a new form of representation. Just as ownership is seen as an issue over the analytic hours, it is likewise one of the same form about one's person.

Let me illustrate this point of ownership with another clinical example of the patient previously mentioned. She had gone to a lecture on poetry given by an eminent poet and had sat enthralled and elated by what he had to say. Some of it was difficult to comprehend, but much of it was especially meaningful to her because it so resonated with her own feelings and convictions about the subject matter. The audience was a mixed one and afterwards several friends who were not very learned about the subject approached to ask her questions since the lecturer was surrounded by other interested inquirers. She felt bewildered and unable to clearly articulate her thoughts, and as the next day approached, she felt more and more uncertain as to whether or not she had really understood the man. Her husband was irritated at the lecturer for giving so erudite a talk and demanded that the patient, his wife, translate it for him. She got dizzy and begged off. When she came for her analytic hour she was able to describe the lecture and its content fairly coherently but saw her position erode as she described the events of the previous evening. She likened this to a difficulty in school which likewise made her always feel uncertain and unsure of her position and knowledge. In her words, she said how hard it was for her to own something, some fact or idea, as her very own. She so quickly lost the base of certainty that she stood on because the other person could not reinforce the sense of sureness; often because of an innocent ignorance of their own. Her wishy-washiness was reflected in this form of easy erosion of the sense of conviction that seemed, in itself, so unsettling to her because it intensified a sense of abandonment.

The essay on utilizing new metaphors also suggested a change in our concepts of representation which, at a minimum, are problematic (Boesky, 1983). A static picture or image or idea of the self cannot do justice to this issue of the self in transit. The above dream is a representation of movement and thus serves to deliver a picture of sequences and development over time. In the creative activity of the patient she moved as well from static or cross-sectional icons to those that moved through space as well as through time. The act of creating is one that makes a claim for mastery, control and ownership and also delivers a presentation to another person to share. This may also be the attempted solution of the child's to the inability of the mother to retain the child in her mind. We shall later note how the creative product aids in a solution of the problem.

The "representation" that we are outlining is not seen as residing in the head of the patient since we must momentarily dispense with the simplistic notion that unarguably every thought does indeed sit somewhere in the brain. Rather we see this representation as necessarily shared between mother and child, and so the child must feel he or she exists in a shared or mutually constructed reality of mother and child. The child is seen as one in his or her eyes as well as in the mother's eyes, and this is carried on as he feels carried by others in the same manner. Co-existence is a different kind of representation than that of a singular image of oneself.

With the patient's decision to have her hours remain hers while she was gone, she seemed able to leave on trips with less anxiety and even soon thereafter to contemplate a termination: something that had previously filled her with dread. She ceased to feel so uncertain about what she wanted to do and to be and feared that she would be seen as obnoxious and a pest by family and friends. Knowing what one wanted seemed such a new and different sensation that she felt it as nothing that she had known before. It may be noteworthy that the patient did not have much trouble or conflict about making decisions since as noted above, she was not ever an indecisive person, and, with her newfound sense of certainty, she merely enjoyed the state of deciding. In a sense she felt confirmed about herself in a way that had been previously unknown to her. Whatever had been lacking in development before now seemed to be behind her.

There still seems to be a need to unpack this very large and cumbersome term of responsiveness or mirroring to see if there could be a more specific defect in the relationship between parent and child that on occasion led to this characterologic picture of wishy-washiness.

SPECULATION

Adler and Buie (1979) have described the difficulty of borderline patients in their maintaining an image or memory of the therapist in their mind over periods of absence or expectable separations. Such patients seem unable to conjure up a picture of the missing person and, in this manner, to effectively think about and thereby to use that thought or image for comfort, soothing or planning. They lack a developmental achievement of what Piaget has called evocative memory and this cognitive deficit is responsible for the unstable, erratic, emotionally labile personality and the ensuing overall difficulty in treating such patients. They provoke uncertain and unpredictable reactions in therapists who are troubled by the intensity as well as the irregularity of the patient's affective stance. Therapists often behave in an indecisive manner in dealing with borderlines, and/or they usually attempt to become a stable and reliable selfobject to patients. Phrases such as the patient having an "insufficient internalization of holding objects" are said to describe the central defect which the therapist aims to ameliorate and/or correct. It is important at this point as an aside to emphasize and clarify the fact that the patient described above is not to be considered as borderline.

One maneuver sometimes used in the treatment of borderlines is to allow them to phone over weekends or to carry a picture of the therapist in order to handle periods of separation. In marked contrast to this, my patient gave me a picture (actually a number of pictures ranging from photographs to portraits) in order to have me remember her. Her fantasies about the picture(s) had to do with whether I would display them in such a way that they would be readily visible or else they would be secreted away and so hidden from sight. Essentially the transference seemed to disclose a relationship to someone who seemingly suffered from the defect that Adler and Buie had described, i.e., a borderline personality disorder with a failure of evocative memory. It was not one that represented the exhausted and depressed mother who potentially participated in the formation of a child who later developed mixed procrastination and perversion; inasmuch as we do see perverse symptomatology arising from the spasmodic unavailability of the parent. Rather we see the disclosure of a chronic failure of the parent to respond in a manner that should be a routine part of any interaction: that one is being treated as the same person from day to day. The issue of feeling that one will not remain remembered emerged in the transference with the patient's conviction that I was always sitting on the edge of my chair waiting to be rid of her. She had a variety of fantasies that turned on my wishing to wash my hands of her, to forget her. The counter-transference reaction was probably one that echoed this, since she was a woman in her fifties who claimed that life was over for her. I felt it painful to myself struggle with the fact that I would also be forgotten one day, as indeed all of our wishes for immortality resonate with this early wish that the world not lose sight of us.

A recent paper by Robert and Edna Furman (1984) discusses a certain form of child-parent interaction that they call intermittent decathexis. Such parents seemingly become so self-absorbed that they periodically lose contact with their offspring. The children of these circumstances are said to identify with the use of this primitive defense mechanism, to develop a false self caused by continuous decathexis of parts of the child's personality rather than intermittent total parental decathexis, and a lasting lability of their own cathectic investments. It is interesting to compare such non-analytic data with analytic reconstructive material inasmuch as it has such a ring of truth yet often is lacking in some individual details. The clinical experience reported here does not confirm the identification with the parents or some of the material about the parental cathexis. This is not to deny that very correct and cogent observation that parental interest is a sine qua non for a child's development. But something is certainly missing in ascribing it to investment of energy and saying that such investment "determines the harmonious functioning of the personality." We probably need to concentrate more on the particular nature of the interactions.

The male voyeur told of giving his mother some pottery he had made, but she soon thereafter gave it away. The gift of the child is an effort to have some place in the mother's life, and here the mother was unable to provide that niche for her son, and he was disappointed. The female patient told of never knowing what mother wanted while feeling her father was someone who had only one correct response for anything, i.e., nothing could be negotiated, if you hit it right you were lucky and more often than not you were wrong. She did not offer gifts for remembering until she had progressed somewhat in analysis, since she did not feel secure enough to make a try. Interestingly the male patient gave a picture to his analyst as well: that of someone watching someone else.

It takes no great leap of imagination to speculate that a profound uncertainty about one's sameness or continuity from one time to the next time would be etiological in the formation of a personality of uncertainty, indecisiveness and wishy-washiness. Perhaps the steady recognition of this patient by her mother was what was missing in her growth. Such recognition is a shared ownership and a shared communication. It is represented over time and space in dreams, enactments and creative work.

DISCUSSION

The need remains to better delineate just what terms such as "mirroring" mean at different developmental levels in a child's growth. In particular we should try to know what different forms of pathology can result from failures of such needs, and especially to clarify that a host of factors such as timing, consistency, intensity and substitution of one parent for another play crucial roles in the emergence of such pathology. To be sure one may posit something like a "failure of mirroring" and insist that it was a lifelong problem, or that it was responsible for all manner of difficulties. But this seems too close to the problem that all psychoanalysis has had with reducing every instance of pathology to oedipal struggles and then insisting that it is indeed such a multivariete phenomenon that it is capable of covering all pathology. There is a certain poverty of explanation in saying that a neurosis comes from a conflict between instinctual drives, superego prohibitions and ego strengths just as there is in stating that all trouble is due to emphatic failures from a selfobject relationship. These are but general pointers to particular forms of disordered development that should be re-evoked as specific transference configurations. It likewise seems unsatisfactory to label parents as narcissistic or depressed or even borderline since these appellations need carry no specific form of behavior except in the most general sense. Certainly we need generalizations to categorize our clinical data, but for a true developmental psychology we must aim to place our findings on an axis of development and deviations thereof.

Patients who are wishy-washy or whose wishy-washiness is revealed in treatment suffer from not knowing where or how to move forward because of a lack of the necessary structure to ensure self-continuity. This deficit may arise from a failure to achieve temporal continuity in the child's development by way of parental recognition and responsiveness. In the transference this is manifested by a feeling of being forgotten between hours, of losing one's hours or of having to terminate before they are ready. The analyst is experienced as one who cannot hold on to a permanent image of the patient, such as has been attributed to borderline patients. This may well reveal that the patient's mother was such a borderline personality or at least she suffered from this sort of cognitive defect. Wishy-washiness disappears as the patient creates a temporal bridge in the analysis: one that allows for continued existence over periods of time by way of the analyst's memory, i.e., the patient is alive in the mind of the analyst.

CONCLUSION

As we move from concepts of people as independent units in time and space to those of selves composed of sets of relationships (Goldberg, 1978) we need different metaphors to describe our clinical material just as we needed different theories (Kohut, 1971) to explain it. People seen in networks of relationships can also be seen to manifest certain forms of pathology only revealed vis a vis these matrices (Goldberg, 1983). One such form of pathology is that of the wishy-washy personality. This individual is unable to choose a course of action or to care about such a course because of a defect in the structure needed for such transit. The defect lies not within the subject but is one of a shared concept between the self and selfobject, and possibly has to do with a failure of the maternal caretaker to hold the child in her mind, much as the borderline patient fails to manifest evocative memory. The metaphor of shared ownership seems best able to deliver this deficit which may be healed in treatment by devices which serve to allow transit in time and space.

A revisiting of much non-oedipal pathology in terms of the varied construction of networks of relationships might widen our considerations of psychopathology and might as well better differentiate what has heretofore been but large and amorphous forms of equally obscure categories of developmental failure that are responsible for these problems.

REFERENCES

Adler, G. and Buie, D. H. (1979). Aloneness and borderline psychopathology: The possible relevance of child development issues. *International Journal of Psychoanalysis* 60:83-96.

Boesky, D. (1983). The problem of mental representation in self and object theory. *Psychoanal. Quarterly* 52:564-583.

Edelson, M. (1984). *Hypothesis and Evidence in Psychoanalysis* Chicago and London: University of Chicago Press.

Furman, R. & Furman, E. (1984). Intermittent decathexis — A type of parental dysfunction *International Journal of Psychoanalysis* 65:423-434.

Goldberg, A. (1983). On the nature of the misfit. In: *The Future of Psychoanalysis* ed. A. Goldberg. New York: International Universities Press.

Goldberg, A. (1983). Self psychology and alternatives perspectives on internalization In *Reflections on Self Psychology* eds. J. Lichtenberg and S. Kaplan. Hillsdale, New Jersey: The Analytic Press.

Goldberg, A. (ed.) (1978). *The Psychology of the Self: A Casebook* New York: International Universities Press.

Kohut, H. (1971). *The Analysis of the Self* New York: International Universities Press.

Stroud, B. (1984). *The Significance of Philosophical Skepticism* Oxford: Clarendon Press.

Disorders of Continuity (1990)

In Goldberg's paper, *Disorders of Continuity* (1990*),* he once more takes up the topic of the self as including the properties of continuity through time and space, with disorders of continuity indicating a form of structural pathology, "manifested in problems of initiating, interrupting and terminating all manner of behavior." Again, Goldberg focuses on those transference aspects that allow us to infer something about this sense of continuity. "With patients who evidence disorders of continuity, the transference revolves around issues of form (e.g. predictability vs. unpredictability; regularity vs. irregularity) rather than issues of content. No matter how regular and reliable the analyst may be, the major issue for the patient is the anticipation of disruption." Disruptions, such as a break in the regularity of the analytic meetings, might be disorganizing to the self. Interpreting the meaning of these disruptions and un-mastered separations can serve as therapeutic actions that lead to structure formation.

—GM

*　　*　　*

This article begins by delineating the concept of the self as a psychic structure: one, which has the property of continuity through time and space. The use of the concept of psychic structure and representation is explicated and defended. Disorders of continuity are characterized as reflecting certain forms of structural pathology and as being manifested in problems of initiating, interrupting, and terminating all manner of behavior. These phenomena become reenacted in the transference phenomena emergent in the analyses of these disorders of continuity. Interpretations are more effectively directed toward the formal components of the structure rather than toward the unconscious contents. Perversion is considered as one form of these disorders, and clinical illustrations are used to demonstrate this problem. The developmental perspective is linked to the activity of interpretation by way of two issues related to continuity: planning ahead and looking backward. These capabilities are part and parcel of normal development. Their absence reflects disorders of continuity, and their place in the interpretive work of analysis allows a structural change that re-establishes this property.

INTRODUCTION

Despite the interplay of form and content in psychoanalytic discourse, analysts have traditionally pried apart these two dimensions of mental experience, giving prominence, in an alternating fashion, to one dimension or the other. Freud was primarily interested in the content of unconscious material capable of achieving consciousness, and this view is still championed by analysts who concern themselves with the nature of the unconscious fantasies that underlie neurotic symptomatology (Arlow, 1969). The ego psychologists (Hartmann, 1958) focused more on the manner in which the psyche deals with unconscious demands and environmental conditions. Waelder's (1936) principle of multiple function, on the other hand, directed attention more to the how of psychic function. An adequate psychoanalytic nosology must obviously attend to both form and content in a substantive way, that is, it must go beyond a simple categorization of psychopathology in terms of a "conflict" and/or "structural deficit." In order to explain the origin of so-called deficits, whether in interaction with, or in contrast to, issues of conflict, we must study and describe the putative structures themselves. Toward this goal, this article examines the self as a structure capable of accounting for the transference phenomena of discontinuity in certain forms of psychopathology. By way of explaining what such discontinuity entails, and how it gains clinical expression, an effort is made to elicit the form, that is, the structure of the self, along with the way in which this structure becomes a source of psychopathology.

THE STUDIED STRUCTURE

The issue of whether or not the structures of the mind (e.g., the components of the psychic apparatus) can be, or ought to be, comprehended in a manner isomorphic with our understanding of the structure of the brain continues to divide psychoanalysts. The latter is material, some say, whereas the former is ethereal or at least unverifiable. Analysts seem to enjoy a spectrum of opinion ranging from the position that structures are convenient fictions that facilitate easy categorization, to the position that they are concrete elements in the mind with more-or-less definable origins, modes of action and predictable effects (Waelder, 1962). With more recent efforts to bring neurophysiology into closer proximity with psychoanalysis, some (Schwartz, 1987) have given way to the temptation to speak of "neurons or the couch" and of representations that approximate "things" in the brain.

The ultimate reconciliation of neurophysiology and psychology would perhaps lead to what some philosophers (Churchland, 1986) call "eliminative materialism"—that hoped-for, but still elusive, state in which all psychological concepts would be reducible to, and therefore replaceable by, complex neurological explanations. Until that time arrives, these philosophers aver, we may feel free to use psychological concepts as temporary gathering places for observable psychological functions. It follows from this viewpoint that psychoanalytic structures will at some point be translatable into neurophysiology, or else will stand revealed as "purely abstract" concepts (Freud, 1933) that should be discarded.

That the envisioning of such a future crossroads is not an idle issue becomes clear when analysts attempt to speak of structural deficits, structural changes, and structural theory; for it is at such junctures of theorizing that they seem unsure whether they may impute to such structures a status equal, say, to that of the hypothalamus, or at least to some neuronal circuit that tells "when, how fast, and in association with what other active neurons [do] cells of a particular function fire" (Schwartz, 1987, p. 499). An understanding of the place of structure in psychoanalysis suffers not only from vagueness of definition but from visual inaccessibility: Psychoanalytic structures seem invisible. If, following Bertalanffy (1968), who held that biology simply designates as structures processes of long duration, we let our understanding of function subtend our use of the word "structure," we arrive at the possibility of a bridge between psychology and neurophysiology. An object is studied by way of its morphology or appearance, which is tantamount to its structure and physiology, which, in turn, is tantamount to its function. For those concepts that defy visual or any other sensory scrutiny, however, we may justifiably conflate structure and function and claim, heuristically, that functions that endure over time are psychoanalytic structures. Thus can we begin to examine any set of functions for its structural properties; continuity is one such property.

REVIEW OF LITERATURE

This review of the concept of structure in psychoanalysis is deliberately limited; my intent is only to justify the application of the concept to psychoanalysis, not to survey the range of meanings that have been imputed to it. For a more complete review, the reader may consult Seitz (1968) for the literature up to 1963 and Levey (1985) for contributions thereafter.

Freud (1900) allowed that the only worthwhile addition to his theory of dreams was offered by Silberer, who noted that periods of regression approximating sleep evinced a particular form of imagery (i.e., anagogic imagery) that seemed to stand for particular mental states. Silberer demonstrated that observation plays a part in the formation of dreams, but he also hinted that one may "observe" things that are not mental contents (e.g., thoughts), but rather are states, such as fatigue or willingness. Thus, one may discern a wish to remain in a twilight state rather than being fully awake in a dream scene of stepping across a brook with one foot and then immediately drawing it back. Such images, for Silberer, were functional phenomena or pictorializations of states rather than of objects. Freud, while applauding Silberer's discovery, denied that dreams could be classified as either anagogic or psychoanalytic. In retrospect, it seems that Silberer's discussion of functional phenomena referred mainly to narcissistic states.

Seitz (1968) hypothesized that periods of narcissistic regression allow one to study structure in the form of concrete imagery. He presented analytic cases in which structures, substructures, apparatuses, and mechanisms were represented in dreams and other imagery. He carefully distinguished the idea that such images represented actual and accurate perceptions of endopsychic structures from the possibility that they were merely dreamer's own theories and speculations about his or her mind and its disordered functioning. Seitz opted for the former: He felt that his evidence showed that the images in question were disguised perceptions of the dreamer's own mental functions and structures, and that they resulted from reactivated childhood conflicts associated with the incomplete development of such functions and structures. Most of Seitz's imagic material seemed to pertain to what he called the regulatory apparatuses of the ego. A dream of broken shoestrings reflected the need to hold things together; a dream of a blown fuse represented an emotional overload.

Kohut's (1971) self-state dreams seem a natural continuation of this idea that dream imagery illustrates a state rather than an object. For Kohut, self-state dreams reveal not only content but form, so that a building that is rickety and weakened is a statement about a like feeling about oneself. His observations do not deny the content meaning of such dreams; rather, they direct analytic attention to the other, that is, the structural, meaning. For Kohut, as for Seitz, the structure that is imaged is considered to be an accurate endopsychic perception.

But do we have a right to claim that psychic structures "exist" in the same way as the observable, material structures of the neurosciences? After all, if a patient dreams of a rusty mainspring of his watch (Seitz, 1968) than regulates the rate of discharge by holding, storing and retaining force, we are not thereby actually claiming that such a structure truly exists. But if by the same token, such a dream goes on to indicate that the mainspring has been cleaned and that the watch is now functioning well, may we not then say that, for the dreamer, things are indeed "working better?" How can one tease apart what is "seen" in the mind's eye from what "exists" in the mind?

There is an old idea in neurophysiology, which has by now become a joke, about the "grandmother neuron." It derives from the simple notion that a single percept or idea has a particular anatomical site in the brain where it is registered, stored, and retrieved whenever an occasion demands it. Its connections to related memories or significant issues in one's mental life likewise correspond to analogous anatomical connections within the brain. The idea of one's grandmother is thus anatomically reducible to a particular neuron. To elaborate or extend this concept to neuronal nets or patterns that more adequately encompass the essence of grandmother is essentially an effort to obscure the basic untenability of such analogical reasoning. It now seems to be the case that local representation, that is, the notion that a particular place in the brain "stands for" a particular idea or percept, is giving way to distributive representation, that is, the notion that large areas of the cortex respond at different times to different inputs. There is no need at this juncture to delve further into the challenge presented by the ideas of parallel distributive processing, the name given to this new theory of brain functioning. I simply want to underscore the fact that a structure of the brain does not correspond to what we may see through a microscope any more or less than a psychic structure is what we may discern in a dream. To wit, brain structures are not more easily circumscribable than ego structures. This insight, in turn, leads us to tease apart just how structure differs from representation, another old, familiar, and persistently vague term.

STRUCTURE AND REPRESENTATION

The structures of the mind are categories that reflect slowly changing and/or enduring functions. They become the mainsprings of our theory as we utilize them to gather data that fit into meaningful patterns. There is a necessary to and fro between data gathering and ideas about structure formation insofar as any theory, owing to its inherent limitations, must be modifiable to allow new concepts and categories to incorporate new data. The structures of psychoanalysis are therefore categories of observation: They range from the microstructures attributed to a particular function (e.g., a defense) to the macrostructures (e.g., the superego) that encompass a family of functions.

Analytic discourse becomes very confusing when we speak of representations as in some way equivalent to structures. This spurious equivalence leads us to impute all sorts of abilities and capacities to representations (Boesky, 1983) and even to liken them to actors on a mental stage (Sandler & Rosenblatt, 1962). In analogy to the complex inner workings of any computer or intelligence machine that now and then aids us in visualizing brain function, a representation may be better thought of as a "printout" of whatever is going on inside the mind. As a computer proceeds through a series of computations, an operator can "ask" it to display on a screen or print out on paper the results of its efforts, including a partial print of its processing up to a certain point. Such a display or printout is not taken to be equivalent to the computer's internal processing; rather, it is only taken to "represent" that processing. Printouts thus tell us nothing about the reality of machine-generated operations. As representations, they only "stand in" for those operations.

Newer ideas of brain function challenge the notion of representations as internal images. The very idea of a representation derives from the belief that the world is composed of things of all sorts that are mirrored in the mind, stored in appropriate categories, and called up when need-ed (Skarda & Freeman, 1987). This perspective, championed by many analysts, has been urged upon analysis as being most compatible with neurophysiology (Schwartz, 1987). In truth, it may well be the case that "the concept of representation (e.g., symbols, schemata, codes, maps) is unnecessary as the keystone for explaining the brain and behavior" (Skarda & Freeman, 1987, p. 184). We may of course retain the concept in the original sense of "representing" something to the mind's eye, but, in so doing, we must no longer attribute all manner of influence to so-called self and object representations. To repeat: Such re-presentations are but stand-ins, clues to the complex workings of neurological and/or psychoanalytic structures. Structures per se are complex configurations that are only fleetingly and imperfectly revealed to us via representa-tional stand-ins. The ways of revealing the representations, gain expression in fantasies, dreams, and behavior such representations serve as indicators, however incompletely, of underlying functional activity considered as structure. It is to one such structure vital to psychoanalyt-ic theory that we now turn: the self.

THE SELF AS STRUCTURE

In contrast to Grossman (1982), who considered the self to be an indi-vidual fantasy determined by the structure of the ego, many analysts have made a strong theoretical claim for the self as a bona fide structure, albeit of a status different from that of the ego. Thus, whereas Jacobson (1964) cautioned us not to use the term *self* as a psychological construct, Kohut (1971) considered it to be a valid collective for the structure that underlies the memory traces of self-representations. He claimed, further, that the self is continuous in time and space, and that this temporal and spatial organization gains expression in the different forms of an analytic transference. It is to the particular quality of continuity in time that attention is now to be directed.

The hierarchical model of mental functioning proposed in *Models of the Mind* (Gedo & Goldberg, 1973) is partially filled in along the time axis suggested by the model. More specifically, an attempt is made to conceptualize the self as a theoretical construct along a time axis and thereby to focus on certain disorders in the attainment of a sense of continuity that correlate with certain transference manifestations. The model of development in *Models of the Mind* suggested that different psychic models be employed to address different developmental issues. Granting this premise, it is still possible and potentially desirable to propose a conceptual vehicle that will gather together psychopathology that seems best located along the longitudinal axis of temporal disorders.

THE SENSE OF CONTINUITY AS A DEVELOPMENTAL ISSUE

The developmental way of looking at psychopathology owes much to Anna Freud (1965), who commended a metapsychological profile of patients organized in the analyst's mind out of the bulk of material collected during diagnostic interviews. Each of Anna Freud's profile items is assessed along a developmental or time axis. This "developmental line" approach was filled out in the hierarchical model presented in *Models of the Mind*. If one concentrates solely on the time axis per se, one can see disorders that reflect temporal problems: those of initiating, of sustaining, and of ending. We learn from patients that they have difficulty in beginning new activities, in seeing themselves as the same person over time (and/or knowing themselves to be "held together" over time), and in terminating any relationship, especially that with the analyst. In psychoanalysis we see continuity problems reenacted in the transference via difficulties about beginning an analysis or starting an hour, severe disorganization when analytic hours and the transference in particular are disrupted, and anxious preoccupation with the inevitable ending of the analysis. (In certain cases, such preoccupation looms heavily over the analysis from its very inception.) This is not to say that particular unconscious conflicts will not mobilize similar temporal issues. Indeed, one problem in assessing a developmental profile is this very issue of differentiating form from content; one must determine, for example, when purely psychoeconomic issues dominate over and against the particulars of a conflict.

One common form of an analytic disruption that does not represent a problem in continuity corresponds to Anna Freud's suggestion that missing parts of a developmental sequence are due to repression whereas exaggerated parts are due to reaction formation. Thus there can be a smooth flow of a developmental history with a missing segment that but adds to the story. For example, a man in analysis wanted to take a brief vacation to settle some business affairs. A series of violent dreams followed this plan, and the interpretive process illuminated a potential, albeit unconscious, struggle with the analyst. This discovery in turn revealed the analysand's deep longing to be victimized by the analyst by being charged for the missed hours (an event that had never occurred in the analysis) alongside a deeper wish to be missed by the analyst. The homosexual material that subsequently emerged connected to many men in the analysand's life, ultimately leading to heretofore repressed material regarding his father. This patient had always been heterosexually oriented and, prior to the analysis, was out of touch with this newly uncovered material. Here, then, is a case of an analytic disruption that betrayed no signs of a self-structure deficient in its temporal organization. This man had a sure sense of himself through time; the need to fill in a missing piece of his history was not reflective of the types of pathology under consideration.

Elsewhere I have discussed patients who struggled over beginnings as well as patients for whom transition points were disorganizing and termination was terrifying (Goldberg, 1988). For all such patients the transference seemed to consign the analyst to the status of a selfobject in Kohut's sense, that is, the analyst assumed a functional role for the analysand's self by participating in the filling in, or making good of, a deficiency of the self. For these patients, who form a stable self/selfobject relationship with the analyst, the transference, much like Winnicott's holding environment, is the scaffolding for and of the person. It is in the form and structure of the transference that we see problems of continuity and discontinuity emerge, and it is in the interpretation of the moments of discontinuity that the bulk of the analytic work seems to take place. To illustrate such phenomena of discontinuity, we employ a concept of a self-structure that is continuous through time and space and is represented as such in the analysis.

Consider, for example, the dream of a designer that consisted of connecting bridges in a city. He said that these bridges were well-conceived structures designed by an able architect, and that the city had spent a good deal of money to have them designed and built. Shortly after reporting the dream, he observed that he felt that things in his own life were now coming together, and he recently felt able to steer a course midway between feelings of elation and despair. I think these remarks do in fact refer to a state of relative structural integrity brought about by the transference in its formal components. It probably is of little moment whether one characterizes this subjective sense of integrity as an intact ego or a stable self. In the cases that follow, the disorder of discontinuity does seem most felicitously explained as a self-disorder.

CLINICAL ILLUSTRATIONS

This case concerns a homosexual man who entered analysis because of a feeling that his homosexual behavior was getting out of control. He had no desire to change his sexual orientation, believing himself to be a very committed homosexual with no interest in heterosexuality. On the other hand he did live a dual life, because his sexual orientation was unknown in his work circle, and his homosexual friends and lovers rarely became part of his work-related social life. His sexual activity was usually restricted to a single lover, although both partners had recourse to promiscuity as a parallel life style. Thus, the patient has had multiple one-night stands and engaged in a variety of sado-masochistic behaviors. The fear of acquired immune deficiency syndrome (AIDS) added to his wish to gain control of his sexual life.

One of the diagnostic dilemmas surrounding homosexuality is that the psychodynamics of homosexual behavior need bear little relationship to the overall pathological picture of the homosexual patient. As Socarides (1960) pointed out, there appears to be no clear correlation between sexual behavior and psychiatric diagnosis. Even in psychoanalytic circles, there remains considerable uncertainty as to the analyzability of homosexuality; some analysts consider a change in sexual behavior to be out of the question whereas others insist that such change is a proper goal of analysis. Although most cases of male homosexuality evince a familiar form of dynamic conflict involving, to varying degrees, longing for the father and fear of the maternal sexual organs, it remains a fact that the uncovering of unconscious fantasies may have little relevance either to nonsexual symptomatology of anxiety and depression or to the issues of sexual preference. Given these realities along with the clinical futility of simply invoking biological considerations, it may be useful for the analyst to concern himself or herself less with the content of dynamics and more with the form and stability of underlying structure. Indeed, it may be the case that many problems of perverse behavior can be profitably reexamined as disorders of continuity.

The patient in question rather quickly settled into a stable idealizing transference. This transference manifested itself not only as an overvaluation of the analyst's wisdom and virtue but also as a reliance on the analysis for steadiness, regulation, and comfort. We soon noted that any sort of disruption in the regular sequence of analytic hours called forth sexual behavior, often involving the subjugation of a partner and/or a like submission on the part of the patient. Although this perverse behavior was often followed by considerable shame and guilt and all manner of pledges to abstain, it soon became clear that a period of anxiety preceded the acting out, and that this anxiety regularly anticipated a disruption in the analysis. Initially these disruptions were weekend separations, but they came to include holidays, vacations, planned changes in the schedule, and analytic misunderstandings and mistakes. Long before a holiday or a vacation, the patient would begin to report dreams about missing pieces, and after an analytic failure, he would report other dreams involving his being bruised or injured. The regular sequencing of analytic hours and the reliable presence of the analyst, on the other hand, became a strengthening process that allowed a complete cessation of homosexual activity along with the emergence of a wish to become heterosexual.

Almost all of the material concerning interruption and disruption related to the patient's father. The parents had divorced when the patient was 7, and the father had visited sporadically until the patient was in fifth grade and about 11 years old. Scheduled visits took place away from the school, but the patient persistently wished that his father would pick him up at school; he was often disappointed as he waited at the school gate for the father's car that never appeared. At other times it seemed that he managed to avoid meeting his father by slipping away, although such memories were only recovered in the analysis. Between the fifth and the eighth grade, the paternal visits became more erratic and unpredictable; they stopped altogether when the patient began high school. Although it was only in high school that the patient did not see his father at all, he recalled telling his friends in the eighth grade that his father was dead. He felt then that a dead father was better than a divorced one, and, in analysis, he insisted that the father knew about this concocted story of his (i.e., the father's) demise. Suddenly, when the patient began college, the father telephoned, wanting to see him. The patient refused a meeting and some years later learned of his father's death. He attended the funeral with a brother. The father had been ill, out of work, and alone when his life ended.

At one point in the analysis there was a change of appointment times and a series of missed phone calls that resulted in the patient's missing an hour. There followed an aborted sexual escapade and a dream of a movie being harried and disrupted by a bouncing ball. The patient associated to his father's visits and the conflict with his mother that ensued on such occasions. He recalled a time when a school chum told him that his father had stopped by for him but missed him. This incident proved one of the first occasions for the perverse solitary sexual activity that predated his homosexual practices. As treatment progressed, analytic events could be increasingly placed into the history of the patient's relationship with the father; to the same degree, the analysis seemed increasingly to be a filling out of that dimension of the patient's life characterized by irregularity and unpredictability.

For those who speak of the patient constructing a narrative of his or her life in analysis (Schafer, 1975), it seems necessary to underscore that the construction of this narrative derives from the transference. A narrative is essentially a work of continuity, that is, a coherent story that begins, spans time, and ends. As analysts, we not only facilitate the filling in of the missing parts of a life but also provide the vehicle whereby the plot can be expressed. As another of my patients expressed it: "I need you to hold me in your mind from one hour to the next so that I do not lose my self."

As the homosexual patient under discussion improved in the analysis, he was forced for a time to cut down from 4 to 3 hr per week. During this period he began to dream in threes; previous dreams had not only contained various groupings of four but were occasionally reported as four separate dreams. The patient used the imagery of ships, trains, and cars with missing parts as he worked through the issue of getting to places. He likewise dreamed of repaired vehicles and occasionally of endless journeys. The nature of the analyst's connection to the patient seems to call forth newer ideas in neurophysiology about parallel distributive processing. These ideas, very briefly, hold that the stimuli or external input to the brain turn on units that over time settle into stable patterns. Various parts of the network can be on or off at any time, and this property of the network allows memories and fragments of experience to achieve completion. This new way of conceptualizing brain function suggests that the brain is involved not in pattern matching but in pattern completion. Although the relevance of this new perspective to psychoanalysis remains to be determined, one possible way of understanding this patient is to see him using the analysis as an effort to complete himself. This effort at completion can be construed developmentally or neurophysiologically but also psychologically, as the filling in of a deficient structure.

A second patient in analysis because of perverse activity developed a transference that focused on a paternal imago in response to feelings of excitement. The patient claimed that his urgent impulses to act out sexually were events beyond his control. He had many dreams relating to excitement and control, and we reconstructed a series of childhood events that were telescoped into a single, lengthy period during which he had to hide the severe pain of a chronic, undiagnosed osteomyelitis from his mother. A doctor had chastised him for complaining without cause, and thus, from ages 8 to 19 (when he was successfully treated), the patient learned not to express his emotions. These emotions did gain expression in his perverse behavior, and as a result, he strove to rationalize as beyond his control any and all activities he felt driven to do.

Midway in his analysis he dreamt of climbing a ladder with one man on top and one man supporting him from below. He connected this lower man to a feeling of being with a brother, a close companion who had died when the patient was 13. He connected the upper man to his father, who had become severely depressed after the brother's death. As we reconstructed a development that seemed to go askew at around the time of the patient's illness, we discerned the earlier origin of his derailment in the relationship with his very unresponsive mother. He proceeded to develop a stable transference and dreamt the following upon anticipating my return from a vacation: "The water is rising and [he fears] the dam will break." He became increasingly able to control his excitement but remained fearful that any such excitement would be condemned by others and could therefore not be expressed.

As the analysis proceeded he connected the emotional side of his life to a series of memories of being with his father until the latter's depression. The patient regained contact with a variety of feelings that seemed gone for many years. He began to see himself in a continuum that supplanted, and brought together, the disparate selves that preceded and followed his bone disease. Although one may explain the dynamics of the case in various ways, there is no doubt that the analysis resulted in the resolution of his sporadic perverse behavior and a smoother and readier access to his feelings. The narrative that we constructed derived sequential continuity from a selfobject transference worked through in the analysis; this transference was illustrated both in the imagery of the patient's dreams and in the manifest structure of the transference.

DISCUSSION

What does it mean to say that one's self is continuous in time and space? What can we say about the possibility of achieving this condition through psychoanalytic treatment? Continuity, thus understood, does not mean that one simply remembers the events of one's life in sequence: Memory per se is essential neither to the seemingly intact self of healthy persons nor to the defective self of patients who, even after analysis, are frequently quite amnesic about much of their childhood. An intact self does seem to have certain attributes that persist over time but, in certain instances, undergo explainable transformations into other attributes. Thus Johnny is the same person at age 4 as he is at age 44, and not because of anything revealed to the observer but because of the special sense of continuity and sameness that both Johnny and those who know him may possess. Not surprisingly this question of just how we come to perceive continuity and sameness has occupied philosophers (e.g., Rorty, 1976) for many years; it has recently re-emerged as a topic of philosophical inquiry drawing on, for example, split brain research.

For psychoanalysis, current speculation can best be stilled by focusing on those transference aspects that let us infer something about this sense of continuity. From a developmental perspective, one may say that every disorder is a disorder of continuity; yet we must delineate a specific "form" that speaks to more than the truism that development has not unfolded in an optimally productive and constructive way. To speak of "arrested development" is not to capture the sense of discontinuity, not only because such "arrest" does not happen in any real sense (i.e., cognitive development seems to escape the arrest), but also because the postulation of an arrest merely repeats a banal truth: that development has not proceeded ideally. As an example of such explanatory vacuity, consider a recent article (Maroda, 1987) in which it is claimed that patients with narcissistic personality disorders are "lost in time" (p. 279), this being laid at the feet of their "history of immaturity."

It is perhaps necessary to underscore the fact that the preceding clinical vignettes about disorders of continuity should not be collected together under the umbrella of pathology due to empathic failure and cure resulting from the provision of good and sufficient empathy. Without in any way diminishing the import of this point of view, it is as incomplete a description as blaming pathology on immaturity. Psychoanalysis calls for a careful scrutiny of each and every structural malformation as well as an interpretation directed to the genetic roots of the malformation. People may indeed feel better in an empathic environment and/or without the burden of interpretive work, but this fact is essentially irrelevant to a psychoanalytic explanation of cure.

With patients who evidence disorders of continuity, the transference revolves around issues of form (e.g., predictability vs. unpredictability; regularity vs. irregularity) rather than issues of content. No matter how regular and reliable the analyst may be, the major issue for the patient is the anticipation of disruption. To explicate more fully their anxiety over the inevitable breakdown of the regularity optimally inhering in the analysis, we turn to two sides of the continuity issue: planning ahead and looking backward.

Planning Ahead

The aforementioned patient who was victimized by erratic visits from his father relived in the transference one graphic source of his problem. This patient's gross display is probably mirrored in similar but subtler ways in other patients. One of the peculiarities of his reconstructed history was that the father who visited regularly during the patient's grade school years abruptly stopped visiting when his son began high school. After a week of analysis in which there was a missed hour and an attempt at rescheduling, the patient explained to me that it had always been clear to him why the visits stopped. The high school was a larger building with several entrances and exits. If one was to meet someone at school's end, an appointment had to be made, that is, a time and a door had to be agreed upon. The grade school, on the other hand, had but one exit from which everyone departed at the same time, so father could come on any day he chose. He would not, on the other hand, commit himself to meeting his son on a particular day at a particular time and place, and so the visits ceased. Thus, the patient had to endure the sporadic and unpredictable father or have no father at all. The father seemed incapable of giving over control of his visits to the son via planned rendezvous that accommodated the latter's schedule.

For this patient, the capacity to plan ahead that is predicated on a reliable and predictable selfobject could not develop. In the absence of such development and the structuralization it entails, the patient failed to acquire the secure feeling that he would be the same next week as he was today. His daily existence was too much at the mercy of an erratic other, so that he was obliged to be constantly vigilant about potential, even if occasionally pleasant, disruptions. The visits of his father, being unplanned, were painful to anticipate and periodically disorganizing. The patient's need to control these visits was an effort at self-control. People who enjoy surprises, in contrast, have a secure sense of self.

LOOKING BACKWARD

The feeling of continuity extends from past to future and back again. It is achieved and maintained by reminiscences. Certain individuals and families routinely discuss events that have transpired and so encourage the process. For the patient under consideration, visits with father were kept not only from his mother, who remained bitter toward her ex-husband, but also from his siblings, who were all older and ridiculed his anticipation of seeing their father. Only the patient, the youngest sibling, kept up regular contact with his father, albeit with no one to tell about the visits. This circumstance heightened his sense of the unplanned meetings as exciting, shameful, and beyond his control—much like his perverse activity of adulthood and his occasional experience of the analysis. Thus was he prevented from establishing that sense of sameness through time that becomes an essential ingredient of self-structure. He went through life with a feeling of discontinuity that gained vivid expression in the transference.

Interpretations in analyses of disorders of continuity are directed to these two capabilities inhering in viable self-structure: planning ahead and looking backward. The patient's vigilance about an impending break is seen as a potential discontinuity in the transference; the interpretation of such vigilance, including reconstructions bearing on its genetic roots, promotes a mastery that can lead to developmental changes. The patient's fragmentation over empathic breaks or unmastered separations is retrospectively interpreted in the manner Kohut (1984) suggested; these interpretations lead to structure formation. The temporal swings, the back-and-forth undulations that typify the form of the transference, provide the basis for interpretive work, and analysis cannot succeed without addressing this dimension of transference.

CONCLUSION

Structure in psychoanalysis, understood to be a category of enduring function, has the same epistemological status as structure in neurophysiology As difficult as this equivalence may seem to the scientist intent on finding structure in clearly definable and discernible "things," we now realize that the theory of the observing scientist as well as that pertaining to the observable object predetermines what is seen. Thus, although the imagery of analytic patients who "see" mental structures is surely a product of their own theory of mind and its workings, this fact need not disqualify such imagery as valid perception. We assume that a classical psychoanalyst may be able to see a superego and tell us what it looks like. Within the constraints of an acceptable theory, that is, we are able to see structures allowable by our theoretical vision, whether such structures are endopsychic or exteroceptive. Things are never out there waiting to be delivered to the mind's eye; rather, things derive from our preconceptions.

Psychoanalytic self-psychology posits a self-concept and takes the self to be an observable structure. The self is held to be represented in many ways, because a representation is no more than a temporary time slice of a complex configuration. The enduring qualities of the self are its continuity in time and space; it is likewise the repository of enduring self-related functions such as self-esteem, self-control, and so forth. Because all material about the self of psychoanalysis derives from the psychoanalytic situation, it seems reasonable to derive a psychoanalytic nosology (Kohut & Wolf,

1978) from the various transference manifestations that act upon, and gain expression through, the self. One variation of this approach is to focus on the form of the transference as it impinges on the self; here one may discern and appreciate the significance of disorders of continuity. Such disorders gain expression in the beginning, middle, and end phases of analysis as difficulties in initiating, in tolerating transitions, and in terminating. Patients experience the transference in terms of past and future physical and emotional disruptions; these disruptions can be correlated to reconstructed parental imagos of unreliable and unpredictable selfobjects. Perverse behavior seems to be especially related to discontinuity disorders, and psychoanalytic treatment can have a dramatic ameliorative impact on such behavior by interpreting the meaning of the various disruptions through which discontinuity is experienced. Whatever stability is achieved by way of the analytic transference is evanescent without genetic reconstruction. The successful resolution of analyses of patients with discontinuity disorders is betokened by an emergent narrative carried by the newly continuous self-structure.

REFERENCES

Arlow, J. A. (1969). Unconscious Fantasy and Disturbances of Conscious Experience. *Psychoanalytic Quarterly* 38:1–27.

Bertalanffy, L. (1968). *General systems theory.* New York: Bragaller.

Boesky, D. (1983). The problem of mental representation in self and object theory *Psychoanalytic Quarterly* 52:562–583.

Churchland, P. (1986). *Neurophilosophy.* Cambridge, MA & London: MIT Press.

Freud, A. (1965). *Normality And Pathology In Childhood.* New York: International Universities Press.

Freud, S. (1900). The interpretation of dreams. *Standard Edition* 5, 503–506.

—— (1933). New introductory lectures (lecture XXXI). *Standard Edition* 22, 57–80.

Gedo, J., & Goldberg, A. (1973). *Models Of The Mind.* Chicago: University of Chicago Press.

Goldberg, A. (1988). *A Fresh Look At Psychoanalysis*. Hillsdale, NJ: The Analytic Press.

Grossman, W. I. (1982). The Self as Fantasy: Fantasy as Theory. *Journal of the American Psychoanalytic Association* 30:919–937.

Hartmann, H. (1958). *Ego Psychology And The Problem Of Adaptation*. New York: International Universities Press.

Jacobson, E. (1964). *The Self And The Object World*. New York: International Universities Press.

Kohut, H. (1971). *The Analysis Of The Self*. New York: International Universities Press.

—— (1984). *How Does Analysis Cure?* Chicago & London: University of Chicago Press.

Kramer, M. K. (1959). On the continuation of the analytic process after psycho-analysis (A self-observation). *International Journal of Psych-Analysis* 40:17–25.

Levey, M. (1985). The concept of structure in psychoanalysis. *Annual of Psychoanalysis* 12–13, 137–153. New York: International Universities Press.

Maroda, K. J. (1987). The fate of the narcissistic personality. *Psychoanalytic Psychology* 4:279–290.

Rorty, A. O. (Ed.). (1976). *The Identity Of Persons*. Berkeley: University of California Press.

Sandler, J. and Rosenblatt, B. (1962). The Concept Of The Representational World. *Psychoanalytic Study of the Child* 17:128–145.

Schafer, R. (1975). Psychoanalysis without psychodynamics. *International Journal of Psycho-Analysis* 56:41–55.

Schwartz, A. (1987). Reification revisited: Some neurobiologically-filtered views of "psychicstructure" and "conflict." *Journal of the American Psychoanalytic Association* 35 (Supp., 1988), 359–385.

Seitz, P. F. (1968). Representations of adaptive and defense mechanisms in the concrete imagery of dreams. *Bulletin of the Philadelphia Association for Psychoanalysis*, 18, 91–95.

Skarda, C., & Freeman, W. (1987). How brains make chaos in order to make sense of the world. *Behavioral and Brain Sciences*, 10, 161–195.

Socarides, C. (1960). Theoretical and clinical aspects of overt male homosexuality (Panel) *Journal of the American Psychoanalytic Association* 8:520–556.

Waelder, R. (1936). The Principle of Multiple Function: Observations on Over-Determination. *Psychoanal Quarterly* 5:45–62.

(1962). Psychoanalysis, Scientific Method, and Philosophy. *Journal of the American Psychoanalytic Association* 10:617–637.

CHAPTER THREE

Empathy

While the role of empathy supposes a proper place in the psycho-analytic treatment of patients, Goldberg declares its scientific standing in *On the Scientific Status of Empathy* (1983). As with any scientific investigation, this process involves the gathering of data, which, in this case, involves the inner life of another through vicarious introspection. Here introspection means "no more or less than examining the private or inner or personal i.e. subjective experiences of the individual."

One of the distinguishing elements of Goldberg's thinking is the joining of philosophy with psychoanalysis. This joining can be traced to many of his early papers, perhaps most clearly in this paper *On the Scientific Status of Empathy*. According to philosopher Wilhelm Dilthey, Goldberg reminds us, two people may reach understanding through the act of *verstehen*. Goldberg understands *verstehen* as "a sympathetic insight into another person which allows one to build up a picture of that person's mental life and thus to understand how and what was his experience." In Goldberg's view, a merger experience would be vital for accomplishing this understanding, and he further states, "It would appear likely that the ordinary communication between individuals is an effort to achieve shared meanings. Some of this involves direct observables and some involves elements of sensitivity to another's inner states and feelings." Goldberg is careful to distinguish between the sustained, prolonged empathic immersion in another's psychic life that characterizes psychoanalysis and the more common occurrence of momentarily stepping inside another's shoes. Slick car salesmen might be able to step inside our shoes long enough to sell us a car, Goldberg warns, but it is something else to stay with another's feelings and inner life in a sustained way in the psychoanalytic process.

Empathy might provide the data, but it is theory that guides us in ordering the data, and here Goldberg maintains, "We must know what to look and listen for in order to complete the marriage of method and theory." Thus, psychoanalysis employs empathy and a guiding theory to determine personal meanings. Here Goldberg distinguishes himself from Kohut, who maintained that empathy was sufficiently curative.

Goldberg concludes that the scientific status of empathy "is both reasonable and justified as long as scientists treat it as they do any means of data gathering. That is to say as long as we are objective, are able to use a variety of theories to guide us and remain alert to the effects of our own observations."

—GM

On the Scientific Status of Empathy (1983)

INTRODUCTION

In a cursory review of the literature on empathy, and especially on the role of empathy in psychoanalysis, one seems to see a division into two camps. One view is that as desirable as empathy may be in the diagnosis and treatment of patients in analysis, it is a relatively rare phenomenon. It is unusual for one person to be truly empathic with another. Furthermore, it is an unreliable procedure fraught with the dangers of error due to deception and countertransference; the achievement of true and reliable empathic connections can be realized only after sustained effort and repeated failures. This camp also tends to contrast empathy with an equally controversial and misunderstood word: inference. It states that inferences are nonempathic conclusions based upon or derived from observations of overt behavior and/or preconceived formulations. When one cannot be empathic, one then relies on inference. However, it is certainly not the case that all those who adjure empathy are as enthusiastic about the use of what is attributed to inference. Some may also ally empathy with inference Buie, (1981) and thereupon denigrate empathy even further, saying that inference is not the same as direct observation and thus is unreliable. Thus both empathy and inference are considered, together or apart; and the one or the other is surely a problem.

The other camp takes an equally severe but quite contrasting position: that empathy is a common and universal mode of communication between people. Just as direct observation allows us to understand others by drawing conclusions from overt behavior, so too does vicarious introspection allow an equal gathering up of data and the reaching of conclusions. So too do *both* direct observation and empathy run the risk of mistaken conclusions by deception on the part of what is observed or on the part of the observer. This view says that there are two ways of knowing: direct, outward, public observation or extraception, and inward, private observation or introspection. The combination of introspection and putting oneself in another's place is empathy.

Before sharpening the contrast between these positions it may be necessary to recall that the accuracy of direct observation depends upon a theory of observation—i.e., one does not see anything unless one already knows what to look for. And usually we infer beyond the immediately sensed. Some say that noninferential observation does exist, especially when we see the familiar. But to infer, as we shall describe later, means only to think logically; and it hardly seems necessary to divide observation into that which is real or true and visible and that which is but merely inferred and thus less likely. Students who look into microscopes for the first time usually see nothing until they are given a theory *and* a set of logical steps to follow. It is also necessary to recall that the data of sensation are not of themselves equivalent to perception since the latter demands some conceptual equipment if something meaningful is to be constructed. Tables are not presented to the mind. The retina and the brain make tables from sensory impressions. The work on visual illusions seems to substantiate this position Brown, (1977). Thus all direct observation is theory laden and logically dictated.

Further study of mental and physical observation has led most philosophers of science to conclude that there is also no inherent advantage of one over the other; rather, they are two different kinds of observation Sellars, (1963). This is not to say that physical and mental sciences are necessarily the same in terms of other forms of scientific investigation such as the determining of evidence and questions of validity and predictability. Rather, we seek only to disabuse the reader of the notion that mental phenomena or introspective data have a special status of being nonscientific because they are private. Thus it seems to be the task of psychoanalysts to determine how they secure the private data of the mind and whether they differentiate this data from the more public observable behavior of the person. The question to be answered, therefore, is how, if empathy is rare, do we ever learn about someone else, and if empathy is ubiquitous, what makes it such an achievement for psychoanalysts?

This essay will not attempt a review of the literature on the role of empathy in psychoanalysis but rather will direct its effort to delineating the position that it can be defined and can enjoy a scientific place in the field.

EMPATHY AND PERSONAL MEANING

It is a long-standing and perhaps also a permanently insoluble problem as to whether one person can determine just how another one feels. Calling this "the question of other minds," philosophers usually come to a halt when they confront the dilemma of whether one can ever reliably say that the experience of redness or the taste of a lemon is the same for you as it is for me. Psychoanalysts live and work with the very clear conviction of being able to penetrate and know another person's mind; yet they often bear the burden of the philosophical conclusion that one never really knows. It is only a guess based on analogy; and there is certainly no way to prove one is right. The problem of this penetration is made more complex when one confronts the fact that while others may tell us how they feel, we can never be sure of their sincerity. For certain groups of persons, in fact, we must depend on avenues of information that are outside of verbal language; foreigners and infants, for example, are for all practical purposes mute.

One of the earliest writers to tackle the problem that ultimately confronts all psychologists who wish to understand another person was Wilhelm Dilthey, who proposed that the act of *verstehen* was a sympathetic insight into another person which allowed one to build up a picture of that person's life and thus to understand how and what was his or her experience. He often stands as the model of the dilemma of psychoanalytic data. His stand was strongly opposed by those who felt it was unscientific Hartmann, (1927). Other philosophers, psychologists, and sociologists have long debated the process of such understanding. Although it is considered the basis of all human communication, some say it has no place as a scientific enterprise since it never can claim the status of certainty. But, as Wittgenstein (1950) has said: "perfect certainty is only a matter of attitude" (p. 52e).

At the outset, it should be clear that the whole problem of the comprehension of another person's mental life commits one to a position of "mentalism" or the belief that there are, indeed, personal or subjective states of mind that are ascertainable. This view is in sharp contrast to the opposing stand of the behaviorists who would deny any scientific status to such inner and thus unobservable sources of data. The *form* of the inner life remains open, but the posture of commitment is a primary one.

Secondly, it follows that concentration on these inner or personal or subjective experiences is necessarily subsumed under the broad category of introspection which means no more or less than examining the private or inner or personal, i.e., subjective experiences of an individual. Unfortunately, such an introspective posture becomes confused with another use of the word "subjective"—biased or swayed by personal feelings. Introspection stands primarily in opposition to extraspection, which is a perception of the external world. As such, introspection must be "objective" or free from bias as well as concerned with nonexternal phenomena. It is in no way subordinate to or at odds with any form of scientific study. It is a matter of direction. Mental phenomena observable by way of introspection into one's *own* mind are equally obtainable by way of vicarious introspection into another's mind. The "data" of one's mind are just as available as the data of the physical world.

But we may often feel on shaky grounds about knowing exactly how someone else feels. The gathering up of all the cues given by one person to another plus the information told to us by the other person allow for a shared meaning to be formed. Such a sharing is a union of meaning. Though it is certainly true that most explanation of such empathic communication is based on some form of a merger experience, it is certainly not true that this is an illusion Buie, (1981). Mergers are not the physical melting of one body into another but are the characteristic state of minds that share meanings. The infant is merged with the mother when they participate in a shared experience; the teacher is merged with the student in an equally intense but significantly more mature form of this relationship. One cognitively knows the boundaries of one's physical body without confusing such knowledge with one's mental boundaries which may remain open. Indeed all open-system thinking commits one to erasing the concept of sharp and closed boundaries and permitting a free exchange of information. A boundary is drawn by a lack of such exchange and not by one's skin.

The very felicitous combination of introspection with vicarious or substitute experience that was introduced by Kohut (1971) allowed him to establish a working definition for empathy which therefore is no more than a method for finding out about another person's inner life. It must, of necessity, include all of the safeguards of any scientific investigation: it must be as nonsubjective (in the biased sense) as possible, and it must be considered as a form of data that is as much in need of verifiability or falsification or whatever as we would expect any other piece of evidence to be. The question of "observer contribution" is no more relevant for empathically gathered data than it is for so-called objective descriptions that are equally laden with the contributions of the observer. It seems most likely, therefore, that questions about empathy as a valid source of information about another person's mental life are often confused or illfounded. Unless we believe in pure behavioral manifestations (including a variety of physiological responses) as the sole source of knowledge of another's mind, we are forced to examine both introspective reports of the person and/or our assessment of the person's mental states by way of our substitute introspection.

It may be true that psychoanalysts divide over whether we use the data of self-reports Ricoeur, (1977) or of empathy Kohut, (1971). It is not true that we are not all introspectionists Brenner, (1968), 1980 I suspect that the former division is also not a real one. Any patient who reports that he feels angry is naturally looked upon as presenting a statement that is only a pointer. We always attempt to determine just what is behind that report as well as what it is a part of; the essential question is: what is the meaning of such a report? The variety of externally observable phenomena such as voice tone, facial configuration, preceding and subsequent comments, etc., are all collected into a total complexity that is taken in via empathy. That the empathy may be missing, defective, misplaced, or excessive is not the question that is now presented. *Any* kind of perception is subjected to those problems and thus demands constant scrutiny if objectivity is to be maintained.

The next problem to consider is the source of confusion about the form of our data; here empathy is contrasted with inference or, even worse, with theory. The first of that couple, inference, is the easiest and simplest to clarify since all thinking involves inferences that are no more than probable deductions from observable, i.e., introspective *or* extraceptive facts. Whenever we cannot directly perceive something, we make an inference. On a hot day, we assume that people tend to go swimming; a sad face suggests a misfortune. These are both inferences, though one can be checked by looking and the other by asking. Since we cannot see everything, we, of necessity, infer many things. Some inferences apply to vicarious introspection and some to extraspection. But inferences, patterns, and theories are indispensable to all forms of thinking and hardly need to be considered in opposition to any. It is the use of a theory without the data that is to be avoided.

The fact is that most of science is based on inference; there are very few things that can be directly perceived. The path of an electron or any subatomic particle is inferred from the tiny markings resulting from a high-energy accelerator. Chemical reactions that result in new compounds are derived by a process of inference. The claim of verifiability by direct perception enjoyed only a brief heyday in the philosophy of science before it was seen that this was not only an unreasonable, but an unnecessary requirement. To be sure, there are sciences such as anatomy which lend themselves to a realistic attitude, whereas others such as physics employ concepts such as force and energy that can never be "perceived." Especially in the historical sciences do we lean heavily on inference and implication. However, these should not be casually grouped with the use of erroneous conclusions that do not fit the data. Inference is not the same as presumption. It is a result of reasoning and not an alternative to observation.

If a patient is silent we are faced with the dilemma of either attaining an empathic position by other than verbal means or else relying on a theory without sufficient data. Again we do not *infer* the meaning of the silence since we lack the data to proceed. We may choose to *guess* at the meaning of the silence by way of one or another theory, but our job is to gather correct data and only then to make inferences.

EMPATHY AND THEORY

It is sometimes difficult to realize the simple fact that a child who recognizes a toy is operating within and with a theory of observation. It may be easier for us to think of this supposed theory as a series of conjectures or hunches that become confirmed or discarded on the basis of trial and error. Children around one year of age, as they begin exercising their new capacity to recognize, may call all four-legged animals "dogs." As they learn more about more animals and their particular differences, they modify their "all animals are dogs" *theory* to engage and consider a wider variety of domestic and wild beasts. That such growth and elaboration of observational theories are the foundation of all knowledge is a position that was best detailed as the "conjectures or refutations" of Karl Popper (1963). His point, though it hardly began with him, was that the theory *precedes* the observation and is verified or changed as observations proceed.

The central position of empathy in psychoanalysis in no way deviates from this process. Empathy is first and foremost a method of observation and thus is guided by a theory that directs it. There can be little doubt that sophisticated and/or easy-to-articulate theories are not readily available to most of those people who nevertheless may be quite capable of empathic contact. That may be the reason why one is tempted to think that a pure observation precedes the construction of theories. Perhaps a change to the words "conjecture" or "hunch," or even "guess," might facilitate the idea that the earliest forms of empathic observation depend on primitive feeling states that one builds upon and then modifies as one grows. The impetus for a merger of mother and child in order to achieve a unity *presupposes* some glimmer of an idea of such unity: i.e., a theory.

If one contrasts "assessment made from psychodynamic formulation with empathic assessment" Buie, (1981), then one is essentially comparing an assessment made from a theory that is not filled in by data with data that are not supported by a theory. Each approach is in error. Let me illustrate by a dynamic formulation of depression based on loss and the concomitant grief reaction. If we use this theory to make an assessment of a patient we then fill it in with our empathic observation of him or her. Is the patient sad? Does he or she speak about the loss? Express ambivalent feelings about the lost object?, etc., etc. The theory guides, but does not determine, our perceptions which are fundamentally empathic, i.e., introspective ones. Even the observation of motoric behavior, speech patterns, vegetative signs are part and parcel of the building up of this inner or personal picture of the depressed and possibly suicidal person. To reach a conclusion on the theory alone is but bad science since it is an example of a form of premature closure.

On the other hand, let us see if a careful empathic assessment sans theory is more fruitful. We should seek a sensitive and completely uncommitted observer to assess the depressions of our sample patient. Since we recognize the impossibility of obtaining a person free from all preconceived ideas, we might concede that our observer should have a minimum of bias. But such an experiment need not even be attempted since our own knowledge of psychoanalytic history shows that before Freud the existence of ambivalence in grief was simply not seen as such. Uninformed observers do not know what to look for, no matter how "empathic" they may be. Of course here we have an example of naïve empathy which can take its place with the naïve realism of direct observation. Those who say that tables are tables and not swarms of electrons are right, but naïve. Those who say that this depressed person is just sad at the loss are also correct, but lacking in the theoretical underpinnings that flesh out our observations. No assessment of another person is full without the combination of data gathering guided by theoretical preconceptions aided by inference. To pit these aspects of science against one another is unfair, unwise, and untrue.

As more elaborate and complex mental states emerge, one's empathy or capacity to think oneself into the mind of another becomes a result of an even more elaborate and complex set of conjectures. This growth of the guiding theory is fundamental to all of our contacts with the world which require the continual modification of and/or refutation of those things which we may "take for granted." That is why an analyst who is empathic may or may not be forced to modify a theory which sees others only as separate objects into one which includes using others as selfobjects. The gap between such an observation and the articulation of the theory employed in the observation may, of course, be a matter of years. The implicit knowledge of such use is there long before it is "known." It arrives from trial and error, is used and found useful, and then can be told to others.

If everyone is capable of both extraspection and introspection, we can readily see that these forms of observation are both trainable and communicable. One cannot tell someone to go out and observe without telling him what to look for; nor can one instruct someone else to be empathic without a similar sort of guide. Thus when we say that an analyst must be a good listener and/or must be empathic we do little more than outline the basic equipment needed. It takes a lot more than a microscope to make a histologist. The mere capacity to be empathic is simply not equal to the special kind of listening and introspection that psychoanalysis requires. The argument against the universal deployment of empathy would restrict it to those rare moments of mutual resonance that only a few gifted individuals achieve in the course of life and then usually in a psychoanalytic setting. It seems crass to think that the ordinary transactions of life involve this special ability, but it also seems hard to think otherwise. It would appear quite likely that any and all communication between individuals is an effort to achieve shared meanings. Some of this involves direct observables, and some involves elements of sensitivity to another's inner states and feelings.

Although there is no doubt that some people tend to be extraordinarily restrictive in allowing themselves to be caught up in empathic assessments, it is hard to get through a day without them. The bulk of human interaction— from buying a newspaper from an irritable vendor, to enjoying lunch with a colleague describing his pleasant vacation, to hearing from your child about his school successes—depend upon an inner, subjective sense of knowing what someone else means by sharing this knowledge with them: however momentary, no matter what the degree of self-reflection, and however comfortable or uncomfortable. This is what a psychology based on mentalism as opposed to behaviorism is all about. We do not feel the vendor is irritable only because of his behavior: angry gestures in strange cultures or people acting angry who are not so inclined are obvious refutations of this position. Our delight in our colleague's vacation and our pride in our child's exploits are part and parcel of normal mental life, and our experience based on such communication is an empathic one.

No doubt we can be dead wrong in our empathy. Our friend may have had a lousy vacation and is covering it up; our child may hate to shine. It is equally true that some customers, friends, and parents could be much better attuned to the inner life of vendor, friend, and child. But just as good and accurate direct observation requires both theory and training, so does accurate empathic observation. Though one is probably never in absolute perfect harmony with another after the first few weeks of life, nevertheless there is an asymptotic curve toward such an achievement.

It is sometimes suggested that the "true empathic method" requires one to suspend all preconceptions and formulas in order to achieve an immersion in a patient's experience which is totally unique to that individual. Such an approach requires resisting all efforts to prejudge or suggest anything to the patient; the analyst must not lend his ideas to direct or influence him. It is, of course, difficult to ascertain just what the analyst *could* say other than repeating the words of the patient, but, more than that, this approach confuses the logic of discovery with the logic of investigation. If none of your theories seems to make sense of the data and you correctly resist forcing the data to fit, then you are embarked on a creative effort to discover something new. Such an adventure happens but once or twice in a hundred or more years, and the field of psychoanalysis is excellent proof of its uniqueness. Just how a creative act or a new discovery is accomplished, of course, merits a separate research of its own into what is appropriately called the logic of discovery. But the vast majority of scientific work consists of applying theories that are known and accepted to advance and/or rediscover the known. Psychoanalysis especially rediscovers its truths in each patient, no matter how much individual variability we may find. If each patient were totally unique, then not only would our field be more art than science, but the essential ingredient of communicability to future generations of analysts would be irrelevant. Though we must remain open to the logic and possibility of discovery we must not confuse this with the ordinary practice of psychoanalysis.

It is important to add one other factor to the psychoanalyst's capacity to use a theory to determine the personal meanings of another person. That is the ability to sustain one's empathy. The vast majority of day-to-day interactions between persons rely on a minimum of empathic contact in order to gather enough data to react. Most of our relationships are posited on organizing a response of one form or another, and we are geared less to immersing ourselves in another's psyche and more to action of some sort.

One clinical example of this phenomenon occurred after a diagnostic case conference at which a psychiatric resident presented the initial interview of a schizophrenic girl. The conference was geared to examining the moment-to-moment emotional state of the patient who was frightened, suspicious, unsure of her boundaries, and wary of the therapist's intrusion. Though it was a fairly successful teaching exercise, afterward one student seemed relieved when it was over, and when queried as to this response she said that it was all so "intense." In truth this was probably an unusual experience for a beginning psychiatrist who was just learning to *stay with* another person's inner feelings for prolonged periods. The tendency we all share is to break away from such mutuality of experience as soon as practicable once having decided our own reaction.

Another clinical illustration had to do with a patient who had recently returned from her sister's funeral and was describing the events to her therapist who listened carefully and followed the material fairly well. At one point the patient told of someone acting in an especially kind and thoughtful manner which resulted both at the time and in the recounting in a very profound sadness and tearfulness. The therapist found himself struggling against a full participation in the feeling state of his mourning patient which seemed to signal to him an equally intense episode of tears. He then realized that he was essentially listening "from the outside" or, in other words, using theory either without the data or with a minimum of data. Had he allowed himself to sustain his empathy he would have awakened similar painful feelings in himself, a posture that he naturally resisted. Rather, he had allowed only momentary incursions into the other person's mind: just enough to maintain contact but not so much as to upset. These are the points in treatment where we usually turn to an examination of the analyst's countertransference and/or his inability to be empathic. In all likelihood there is a natural resistance to sustaining one's empathy and a natural inclination to employ the theory as a shortcut.

To restrict empathy to the perfect union is to flirt with the mystical. Better theories will enable the most sensitive person to see even more. Better training will aid the uninitiated to focus on the inner life. Efforts to lift transference and countertransference distortions will assist both the sensitive and the naïve. The misuse of theory will lead to premature closure without enough data, and the supposed accumulation of data without theory leads to the lack of a selective capacity. The latter is always the prevailing state of affairs until someone like Freud shows us just what we have been seeing and hearing but still ignoring. People were exquisitely empathic long before psychoanalysis came on the scene, but they were not psychoanalysts until they knew how to order their data.

One never limits psychoanalysis as such to empathy—in spite of the fact that Kohut (1971) and others have said that it defines the field. The method needs a guiding theory if one is to pick out the significant parts from the massive amount of material offered by a patient. Though sustained empathy may or may not be peculiar to psychoanalysis, our inquiry must also be directed to salient features: that is, we must know what to look and listen for in order to complete the marriage of method and theory. Together they define the field for that period of scientific history during which the theory holds sway. Since theories suffer the fate of replacement by better ones we may say that the method defines the field but never encompasses it. The facts of our field of study grow out of the mutuality of method and theory.

AN ANALYTIC EXERCISE

Psychoanalysts are said to listen for intentions, goals, and purposes. They look for unarticulated, disavowed, ambiguous, or hidden meanings. They do so with a variety of implicit assumptions and formulas. One illustration of the kinds of listening they do is presented here to demonstrate the observation-theory interaction. The reader is cautioned not to assume that this is an illustration of technique; that is not the relevant issue here.

A patient enters the analytic hour and notices the Kleenex tissue on the pillow and announces laughingly that he thinks it is the same one he used for yesterday's hour.

At this point, a psychoanalyst, unlike almost every other form of investigator, asks himself what that means. As we shall see later the simple clarification as to whether or not it is indeed the same tissue or a simple pursuit of the truth or reality of the situation is *not* a psychoanalytic activity.

As the patient talks about his feelings of using a supposedly soiled tissue he presents himself as struggling with a feeling of being taken advantage of by the analyst.

It is this total state of mind that engages the analyst in his determination of the meaning behind the used tissue. He identifies with and recognizes the most general form of configuration of the patient's presentation.

The patient has many associations to others being used and abused, but soon this narrows to a concentration on people who are relatively unmoved by adversity. A special connection is made to his mother who remained stoical under a barrage of angry vituperation from both himself and his father when he was a child. She suffered abuse silently.

The analyst listens to determine if the patient is identifying with the aggressor or the victim. He listens and is guided by a theory that hopes to extend and thereby to elaborate what this means to the patient. Of course this need not be explicit.

The patient talks of his own need *not* to be thrown or upset by others' abuse of him. The analyst has himself associated now to a planned missed session. He asks the patient about this. Patient is somewhat responsive but soon reveals it is more than just that one session.

The analyst shifts his scrutiny to the particulars of the transference and the nuances of the relationship that exists with the patient.

The patient next associates to feeling sad and upset at what the analyst had said a few days ago about the patient's wondering about an extra or fifth analytic hour. The analyst said this would not necessarily speed up the analysis. The patient subsequently felt hurt and devastated. He suspected the analyst of earlier encouraging an interest in another hour and now discouraging it. He [the analyst] probably had the free time when he encouraged it and now had filled his hour with someone else. This selfish sort of an attitude was so typical of him and so typical as well of his father. The important thing was not to reveal how much this feeling of wanting the extra hour meant to him.

The analyst's empathy shifts from that of seeing the patient as abused victim to personal recollections having to do with the entire passive, submissive position that this patient evokes. He recalls Freud's warning that the bedrock of some analyses is the inability of a man to assume a passive stance in relation to another man. He recalls Kohut's modification of this in relation to a developing idealizing transference. He chooses to respond empathically to all the data gathered, processed, and formulated by focusing on what it all means. Though the sequence is, of course, a personal one, the over-all process is a general one.

By "responding empathically" we define empathy in its natural oscillating state between patient and analyst rather than dividing it into an afferent or receptive and an efferent or motor branch. The empathic response maintains and sustains one's connection with the patient and allows us the liberty of joining listening and responding in the single word. Poland (1975) suggests that we listen empathically and respond tactfully, but this may be an artificial division of a reciprocal feedback process.

The exercise is intended to outline the thesis that psychoanalysis employs empathy and a guiding theory in order to determine personal meanings. It is this pursuit of the individual significance of what may seem to be a solitary event, such as a soiled napkin, that launches the analyst on his journey to these quite elaborate psychological configurations that make up a meaning. Unfortunately, meaning does not spring full-grown from individuals, and thus psychoanalysis first must study its development. It has a long, involved growth which necessarily includes cognitive and affective components and which needs multiple perspectives if one is to grasp its totality.

It is impossible as well to situate accurately just where and how we will examine meanings inasmuch as our penetration into the mind of another person carries so much baggage with it in the form of our theories and our inferences. The question of whether the meaning is ours or the patient's or is a mutual construction of the two of us remains to be considered as well. No matter what the resolution of that question may be, it is one that demands the attention of every scientist who cares to consider whether there are really objects (i.e., people and things) in the world to be examined or whether all such objects exist primarily in relation to the perceive rather than autonomously. The coming together of a theory, a method of observation, and the clinical inferences that we choose to make results in the knowledge or the meaning that we attribute to another person.

EMPATHY AND ITS FORMS

Another aspect of the literature on empathy suggests a classification of the phenomenon, and a brief note is in order here. Efforts to categorize and classify empathy from primitive to mature or from "self-referential to imaginative to resonant" Buie, (1981) are based on a sort of telephonic model of communication. They are concerned with the delivery of facts or feelings from one source to another. They involve codes, systems of delivery, and translations and are necessarily and understandably limited by a closed body system of thinking. In contrast, efforts to categorize empathy in terms of open systems of exchange involve issues such as shared meanings, intersubjectivity, and free exchange. It is important for psychoanalysts to realize that these are different approaches to the scientific study of empathic communication, that one is not necessarily better than the other, but that the yield from each of them will be dissimilar. All this is part and parcel of the scientific study of empathy and an effort to reach conclusions about its scientific status. It is essential that one approach these tasks with a clear understanding of the problems inherent in evaluating something as complex as a method of gathering the data of depth psychology.

If, for example, the classification of introspection is contrasted with a classification of direct perception or extraspection we find that an ordering of data in terms of the observer's feelings, preconceptions, or resonance is usually of minimal significance. One classifies apples not on the basis of personal hunger or memories of this fruit but rather on issues derived from botanical science. This is not to say that observer error is not always to be checked and considered, but rather that there are more overriding issues in perceptual categorization. We learn more about objects of perception by a careful attention to sensory data aided by our guiding theories. What is needed for psychoanalysis, as is the case with any imaginative science, are bold and innovative theories used by empathic observers. Only these will allow us to see more, and only these will enable a valid classification of our means of data gathering.

Therefore a future and desired classification of empathy might follow the sort of fundamental distinctions that psychoanalysis often employs, e.g., a developmental model based upon the sharing of experiences ranging from mother-infant to student-teacher communications. One cannot study empathy in isolation. We are always empathic "to" or "with," and the object of our study determines our stance as much as does our own competence and posture.

A second, but by no means secondary, reason for a clearer and more definitive classification of empathy is the need to explain the beneficial effects of one person being understood by another. As we move from thinking of individuals as isolated systems to viewing their participation in open and contiguous systems we recognize that becoming part of a larger system changes our very makeup. So, too, does a position of empathic understanding have marked therapeutic effects on its object. This is best seen in a developmental scheme wherein the mother-infant unit is held together by a communicative feedback that is essential to the infant's wellbeing. The most promising field for a future classification of empathy would seem to be its consideration along developmental lines which would most cogently account for the therapeutic benefit of its employment.

In conclusion one can say that the scientific status of empathy is both reasonable and justified as long as we as scientists treat it as we do any means of data gathering—that is to say as long as we are objective, able to use a variety of theories to guide us, and remain alert to the effects of our own observations. The many colloquial uses of the term seem to have joined with equally vulgar employments of words such as inference to bring about the temporary abandonment of our scientific stance. To recapture the role of empathy in psychoanalysis is but to define it as our method of observation.

Summary

This paper is an attempt to clarify the scientific status of empathy in psychoanalysis. It defines empathy as a method of observation which gathers data that are dictated by a guiding theory. It also clarifies the role of inference as the set of logical deductions that follow from the theory. Inasmuch as empathy seems to have a therapeutic effect when it is sustained, a future classification of empathy that considers relations in an open system and that follows the maturation of empathy in terms of a shared experience is suggested.

References

Brenner, C. (1968). Psychoanalysis and science. *Journal of the American Psychoanalytic Association* 16:675–696.

Brenner, C. (1980). Metapsychology and psychoanalytic theory. *Psychoanalytic Quarterly* 49:207–214.

Brown, H.T. (1977), Perception, Theory, and Commitment. Chicago & London: University of Chicago Press.

Buie, D. H. (1981). Empathy: Its nature and limitations. *Journal of the American Psychoanalytic Association* 29:281–307.

Hartmann, H. (1927), Understanding and explanations. In: *Essays on Ego Psychology*. New York: International Universities Press, pp. 364–403.

Kohut, H. (1971), *The Analysis of the Self*. New York: International

Universities Press.

Poland, W. S. (1975). Tact as a psychoanalytic function. *International Journal of Psycho-Analysis* 56:155–162.

Popper, K. (1963), *Conjectures and Refutations.* New York: Harper and Row.

Ricoeur, P. (1977). The question of proof in Freud's psychoanalytic writings *Journal of the American Psychoanalytic Association* 25:833–871.

Sellars, W. (1963). *Science, Perception and Reality.* London: Routledge and Kegan Paul.

Wittgenstein, L. (1950–1951), *On Certainty,* ed. G. E. M. Anscomb & G. H. Von Wright. Oxford: Basil Blackwell, 1969.

CHAPTER FOUR

Philosophy

In his paper *The Tension between Realism and Relativism in Psychoa-nalysis* (1984), Goldberg's joining of philosophy and psychoanalysis takes firm root and this connection will become familiar in much of his subsequent writings. Here Goldberg couples philosophy with psychoanalysis, by considering realism, relativism and subjectivism as joined by hermeneutics. Hermeneutic understanding concerns itself with what things mean to us. What things mean to us, is of course, open to a number of interpretations.

The philosophical concept of realism aims to determine the makeup of the world with exactness, and relativism considers "the world as variable having no inherent composition save as we choose to categorize it." Subjectivism is a worldview that "posits the subject as primary."

How might these philosophical orderings of the world apply to psychoanalysis? When considering a patient's narrative, for instance, the significance of "what really happened" includes the patient's experience—his psychic reality—of the real event. As we explore what the experience means, we take into account the patient's experience using our theory as well as how we hear and assess what we hear. Here we are "embarked on the investigation of the exchange or dialogue, that is the focus of hermeneutics." In other words, a psychoanalytic understanding of a patient's narrative involves the continual modification of the narrative, as new meanings emerge.

Goldberg notes that particular schools of psychoanalysis have real differences and relative differences. While Goldberg speaks to the science of psychoanalysis, he might also be explaining the process of psychoanalysis itself. As he states, as our knowledge evolves, this "compels us to participate in ongoing negotiations with others of differing viewpoints. Each and every such negotiation can cause us to remake ourselves, and in this manner we thrive on the tension of reality—knowing things for sure—and relativism—knowing things must change." This last statement is worth reading more than once. It underpins much of Goldberg's approach to the way he practices and teaches psychoanalysis.

—GM

The Tension between Realism and Relativism in Psychoanalysis (1984)

Realism is a point of view that considers the world as composed of a variety of things that we sooner or later come accurately to know as matters of fact. That is to say, we learn of the existence of a real world by way of our sense organs and scientific instruments. In its naive form realism is the host of commonsense impressions of the constituents of the world—its apples, tables, and people being exactly what we perceive. Scientifically, however, we agree that a table is "really" a mass of electrons or other basic and more fundamental elements, features, and forms by which we specify our ordinary impressions of it. Scientific realism is thus the effort to determine with exactness the make-up of the world in both its past and present forms (Putnam, 1981).

Relativism is a point of view that considers the world as variable having no inherent composition save as we choose to categorize it. Our sense organs and scientific instruments guide and direct all our observations and, in so doing, determine just what the world is capable of being to us. Kant (1781) was eloquent in insisting that our brains allow us to categorize the world in particular, circumscribed ways, and thus direct a formulation of reality according to that inherent program or design.

Scientific relativism studies how concepts of reality change from time to time in history.

Another world view that needs definition in this context is subjectivism, which may be confused or interchanged with relativism. This position is often attacked as being a matter of purely personal opinion, in that subjectivism is a view of the world that posits the subject as primary. In its exaggerated form, subjectivism can be seen to operate without constraints and so allow one to consider a table as anything one chooses. Many hold that subjectivism may be permitted in nonscientific or artistic endeavors but is suspect in scientific pursuits.

These three concepts—realism, relativism, and subjectivism—do not enjoy agreed-upon definitions in philosophy nor have philosophers arrived at a consensus as to a "correct" point of view. According to Flew (1979), realism is derived from Plato and his theory of universals "For Plato the observed world is only a reflection of the real world, consisting for Plato of the forms which are something like universals." (1979, p. 331). It is perhaps best articulated in modern philosophy by Karl Popper(1972) in his view of objective knowledge. Relativism is derived more from Kant and in some sense is here allied with subjectivism. "To be a relativist is to maintain that there is no such thing as objective knowledge of realities independent of the known" (Flew, 1979, p. 261). Kant moved us away from objective knowledge. Neo-antians have noted that the categories may not be fixed. Modern statements of relativism are associated with the approach of historians such as Thomas Kuhn (1970) and sociologists such as Barry Barnes (Barnes and Bloor 1982). The newly discovered association of psychoanalysis with hermeneutics, or interpretive science, and spokesmen such as Gadamer (1975) and Habermas (1971) calls for a further study of realism, relativism, and subjectivism from psychoanalysis. Hermeneutics seems for some to embrace relativism readily and thus has brought alarm to the proponents of realism.

PSYCHOANALYSIS AND REALITY

Students of psychoanalysis have all traveled the road of the historical moments that led Freud from studying the parental seductions of his patients (Freud, 1925–26) to focusing on the fantasy of these events. As Grünbaum (1983) has so clearly stated, this movement from objective reality to psychic reality remains within the realm of the real. "What really happened" has the same significance for the psychoanalytic investigator as that of any historian, save that the analyst is interested more in the subjective experience of the participant than in a particular "event" as it might be registered by, say, a video camera. Although Freud's patients were not actually seduced, the "reality" of seductions in their psychic lives remains to be reckoned with, and with an equal measure of significance: the personal effect of any given event upon an individual constitutes the psychic reality with which psychoanalysis is concerned.

In this view of reality, we recognize that the subjective begins to assume primacy, and usually we characterize such subjectivism as the different and varied interpretations of an event. At this juncture we also consider the hermeneutic approach to our data. Part and parcel of all psychoanalytic effort is that of interpreting whatever may seem to be merely recorded or registered by other sciences. However, every science is hermeneutic in the sense that it ultimately subjects the registered data to some sort of further theoretical scrutiny, that is, it interprets what is perceived.

The fact of multiple interpretations of any given event seems to unite reality, subjectivism, and hermeneutics. Psychoanalysis aims to interpret and thus to understand a real experience of a patient. Here is a clinical illustration that highlights these points:

During his first analysis, a patient recalled an event that occurred when he was about five years old. He had left school and was waiting on the steps for his father, who was to bring him home. Time passed, everyone else was gone, and father was not to be seen. The boy realized that his father had probably stopped off at a saloon before the planned meeting and had perhaps gotten drunk and/or had forgotten about him. Determined not to be left alone, and frightened that he did not know how to proceed home, the boy set out for the saloon with some dim memory of having been there before and therefore knowing where it might be. He recalled unhesitatingly making his way there, finding his drunken father, and angrily confronting him.

As an adult, he had drawn from this episode the conviction that his father had no particular love or concern for him, and thus that he had to make his own way through life. In a creative writing class, he had submitted an account of this episode, and the teacher had commented on the writer's remarkable success in portraying the emotional state of a lonely, frightened, and neglected child. After his analysis, the patient used this childhood story as a capsulized dramatic presentation of his early life.

The patient underwent a second course of treatment, but the transference on this occasion allowed him to concentrate more upon the ending of the episode. He soon added a finishing touch to the tale by including the father's turning to and addressing the other drinkers and proclaiming, "That kid has a lot of moxie." The emphasis thus shifted from the forlorn child to the aggressive and proud one. Further elaboration of the story also included the fact that the school was run by nuns who lived in an adjacent convent. The boy could have knocked on the door and asked for assistance, but he was either reluctant to be perceived as needing help or else was eager for the adventure. All this material, seemingly available to the patient in the first analysis, was either ignored or minimized in the construction of the interpretations. The same point could, of course, be made of the second treatment and its emphasis on playing down the conclusions of the first.

To recapitulate: a real event occurred that could have been recorded by a video camera showing the boy and his behavior—material that is of limited significance for a psychoanalyst. Rather, from the event, we explore (using our theoretical formulations) the experience of the child and interpret what it means to him. If a cerebroscope were available to view pictures of the boy's internal psychological state, we would be able to interpret those scenes. In a similar way, we interpret the telling or speaking of the event in adulthood or the reemergence of some analogous event in the transference. Thus far we have joined together the issues of reality and subjectivity (psychic reality)—although "subjective" need of course not be equal to conscious awareness—and to this we add the indispensable feature of interpretation. We then might join Grünbaum (1983) in dispensing with the need for an additional term— "hermeneutics,"—which seems to add little to the stated combination of reality, subjectivity, and interpretation.

PSYCHOANALYSIS AND RELATIVISM

The mere observation of events is usually a given, inasmuch as anyone would probably describe what had happened in the childhood scene in a fairly similar manner. A cautionary note is needed at this point, however, since the idea of a *pure* observation has been fairly well eliminated by the dissolution of the assumed dichotomy between theory and observation. This dichotomy had been used to divide the data of pure observation from the workings of theoretical ideas and assumed that everyone would agree on what, for example, was recorded by a video screen. The prevailing view, however, is quite at odds with this (Grandy, 1973), stating that theory determines observation: until one knows what to see, one cannot make any observations. This seems fairly clear in the need for theory to comprehend or "see" the trackings of a Wilson cloud chamber or to "see" the parts of a cell under a microscope. We often balk at the need of theories for the commonplace, but it soon seems obvious that one must somehow know about (that is, have a theory of) apples before one can recognize an apple. Theories are but patterns of putting things together.

With this in mind, we can revisit the episode of the sad and/or proud little boy and notice that some viewers or listeners will observe certain things while others will concentrate on others. All will not be of one mind as to what is seen, much as different camera angles or focuses yield different impressions.

The problem soon grows, and is best illustrated by an example of what is added by the observer to what is observed and the framework or perspective of observation. In Freud's famous case of the Wolfman (1914), a study of the psychic reality of that remarkable patient led Freud to infer that the Wolfman at one or one-and-a-half years of age had seen his parents engaged in intercourse, with the father approaching the mother from the rear. At no time was an actual memory of the event at the time of occurrence recovered, but Freud felt fairly certain that this was a reasonable conclusion (fn. 6, p. 37). While Freud at first suggests only a provisional belief in the reality of the scene (p. 39), he later (p. 97) states that whether or not the experience was real or fantasied is of no great importance. It is important to recognize, however, that even as a fantasy, the event was not recognized as such by the Wolfman but, rather, was introduced by Freud. This is justified by Freud's statement—his theory— that such scenes are inherited endowments that may or may not be actually realized, which allowed him to "see" what no one else had heretofore seen. There is no doubt that his explanation is weakest concerning the contribution of the observer. The validity of the primal scene is established not only by the sense of conviction achieved by patient and analyst but also by its necessity for coherence, or what is commonly called the best fit (Goodman, 1978), offered by this particular explanation. At another point,

Freud drops the idea of the father's annoyance because the analytic material "did not react to it." He demonstrates his own rules of validity in this way (p. 80).

Throughout Freud's case histories we see opportunities for multiple interpretations, as well as the manner in which theory guides, directs, dictates—and even inserts additions to what an untutored observer would note. This has been troublesome to some, such as Niederland (1951) in his pursuit of the history of Senat president Schreber. Here an effort was made to find out "what really happened" between Schreber and his father, and we again must recognize that this conflation of objective and psychic reality is often considered of little or no necessary value in psychoanalysis. For example, an event such as the early death of Schreber's father might have meant salvation to Schreberwhile to another individual it would have been experienced as traumatic. In that respect, one must distinguish between theories that base significance on events themselves and those that consider events in relation to the inner experience of the subjects.

That different theories lend themselves to different observations and interpretations is the hallmark of relativism. One enters the consulting room or any arena of data-gathering with the baggage of preconceptions—one's training in a community of like-minded investigators. We thus pick and choose what we see and how we organize those selections. One's adoption of a particular set of beliefs depends upon the circumstances of the user (Barnes and Bloor, 1982) rather than some fixed set of objective and external standards. This is also congenial to a further elaboration of the hermeneutic circle wherein an interpretation is formed by a continual feedback process in either a reading of a text or a dialogue between persons. And this is also a cause for much alarm amongst psychoanalysts who fear that this approach robs us of a foundation of true beliefs and leads to a medley of "anything goes" narratives, which satisfy only the select circle of the participants (that usually numbers but two). As Barnes and Bloor (p. 13) state, "There is no valid distinction between what is true, reasonable and explanatory and what counts as knowledge, on the one hand, and what is locally accepted as such, on the other. For the relativist there is no sense attached to the idea that some standards or beliefs are really rational as distinct from merely locally accepted as such." Such a stance, which is read as one of unrelieved license, is often associated with hermeneutics and warrants an investigation of that trend which, as we have seen in one version, is highly compatible with the process ofpsychoanalysis or of any manner of scientific pursuit.

REALISM, RELATIVISM AND HERMENEUTICS

The recent popularity of the hermeneutic approach to psychoanalysis was probably initiated by Paul Ricouer in his book *Freud and Philosophy* (1970). Its basic thesis stresses an internal standard of objectivity based upon inner relationships that are lawlike and that themselves constitute the facts. This approach is often traced to the work of Dilthey and Schleirmacher (Ricouer, 1981) and nowadays is currently associated with Gadamer and Habermas. It began in theology and soon grew to be described as the art of interpreting language. For some time, as a result of Dilthey's contributions, the hermeneutic approach was felt to emphasize understanding (*Verstehen*) and was therefore associated with the human sciences, whereas explanation (*Erklaren*) was isolated as the epistemological goal of the natural sciences (Ricouer,1981). Understanding was held to involve grasping of a totality from within; explanation involved features seen from outside. Such a distinction is not now maintained by many who see all science as interpretive and as involving both understanding and explaining (Hesse, 1978).

An incredible misunderstanding of hermeneutics has developed inasmuch as it seems to leave truth and reality behind and to settle for whatever is felt to be agreed upon by the participants in the interpretive act. As in the famous biblical phrase, "Thou art Peter and upon this rock I shall build my church," one may interpret Peter as the Greek *petros*, or rock, and thus conclude that this is the place for the church to stand; or one may feel that Peter is the rocklike person who became the father of the church: it seems to be a matter of personal preference.

So too does one person's understanding of another by introspection or empathy lend itself to an unlimited range of opinion, in contrast to an appraisal determined by an unchallenged set of objective facts. The problem stems from the dilemma of language: a given sentence spoken by different persons or by the same person at different times usually does not mean the same thing. One cannot objectively determine what a sentence stands for without an effort to first understand the speaker. If we add another ingredient to this equation—that of the listener's own personal assessment of what he or she hears—then we are embarked on the investigation of the exchange, or dialogue, that is the focus of hermeneutics. Interpretation of the written word or of the spoken sentence involves the meaning that emerges from the completed circle of the listener (reader) grasping the total content of the speaker (text), which is modified by whatever particular preconceptions the listener brings to the encounter. Whether or not this is qualitatively different from the encounter with the usual objects of science will not be addressed here. Rather, another clinical example will be offered to illustrate this hermeneutic exercise.

This case was presented in an analytic seminar and was offered as evidence of the folly of a hermeneutic approach to psychoanalysis. The patient, a young unmarried woman in her twenties was having sexual problems ranging from physical dissatisfaction with the sexual act to difficulty maintaining a close relationship with a man. The analyst noted that she was seductive and flirtatious in the initial interviews, and his evaluation was consonant with what a listener would call "hysterical personality." The analysis was unusual in that the conviction arose between patient and analyst that the patient had been involved in incestuous relations with her uncle. That fact itself was not as striking as the conclusion that this event (or events) had occurred when she was around 13 years old; yet she could not at all remember this possible happening. Efforts outside the analysis proper were initiated by the patient in concert with the analyst to determine the possible validity of their shared hypothesis. A letter was sent directly to the mother asking if anything had occurred between the patient and her uncle during this period. The mother's ambiguous answer permitted the patient and the analyst to conclude that their suspicions were not contradicted and therefore strengthened. The patient remained unable to recall the event clearly.

When inability to recall occurred in the case of the Wolfman, Freud attributed it to the failure of an 18-month-old child to comprehend adequately what was happening rather than to a failure to lift the repression (Freud, 1914, fn 6, p. 37.). In an hysteric, the latter is felt to be the relevant cause, and this analysis proceeded with this in mind. Despite this supposed defect in the progress of treatment, the analysis proceeded to a successful conclusion, with the relief of major symptoms and an acceptable termination. The analyst was courageous in presenting such a completed case to a group seminar inasmuch as forgotten incest in a 13-year-old seemed a questionable possibility. Yet his claim was that he had not fallen victim to a shared mythical story created by himself and the patient since they had gone outside of the treatment to verify the circumstances. Rather than the conduct of the case *per se*, this, in one sense, was the main thesis of the presentation—that is, one cannot make valid and true conclusions entirely from within the analytic setting since a shared fiction is just as likely to find its place in the light of interpretations as is a true account. Thus the frailty of hermeneutics: it has no checks and balances and seems no more than a conspiracy of agreement.

Donald Spence (1982) has written extensively on this problem and one cannot do justice to his ideas in a brief space. He feels that a number of different narratives may be spun from an analysis since we are not always aware of the background data brought into an analysis. He pleads for a "naturalization" of our data to make it completely accessible to others in order to more closely obtain or approximate the real or historical truth. He thus appears to join the argument between realism and relativism by the process of naturalization. A means of immediate scrutiny of analytic sessions by a number of competent peers would appear to be the antidote to the potential conspiracy of construction of narrative accomplished in the confines of analysis.

Although somewhat belatedly, the analytic case of the young woman was "naturalized" and presented in somewhat detailed form to a group of analysts. This is not meant to be any gauge of Spence's suggestion since undoubtedly he would want detailed presentations with open-ended discussion and this did not take place. However it is of some interest to note the general reactions of the audience. One group felt that this was a perfectly sound analysis with an admittedly unusual case. Another group felt that the analyst and patient had acted out in a manner that did not allow a proper analysis to unfold, and thus the entire story of incest and its possible or probable verification was spurious. Yet another group echoed this last point but did not feel that this mattered in terms of the value of the analysis, since the issue of whether or not a story is true is not of primary importance in an analysis. Perhaps one could also isolate a smaller group of evaluators within the last; they would claim that the reconstruction was more in the nature of a metaphor that captured a general theme of the patient's life and just happened to be cast in that particular mold without it necessarily being a matter of fact. A somewhat ill-defined response perhaps would correspond to a group that said that they would not have gotten the results or conducted the analysis in the manner presented.

To review the case and the responses, we see that the latter, on the whole, seem to support the relativistic view of psychoanalysis, as well as that of multiple interpretations, observer contribution, and variations of a narrative. The realist would opt for some grounding of the facts of the case in a truth-seeking enterprise. Although the analyst claimed a position contrary to that of hermeneutics, he behaved in a manner quite consistent with the approach that maintains that one brings a set of presumptions to an investigation and attempts to comprehend meanings through an ever-expanding set of interpretations gained by coming to understand another person. The problem that remains concerns the tension between the realist position, based on determining facts, and that of the relativist, which assumes that facts are either unnecessary or unattainable—the second state corresponding more to the view that truth shifts with changing perspectives and thus genuine truth lies beyond our grasp.

It is certainly the case that different theoretical persuasions in analysis seemed to yield reasonably good results based on widely differing narratives. Any analyst is familiar with the phenomenon of reading a case that seems totally foreign to his own mode of treatment and yet seems to result in a "cure." Of course we give all sorts of reasons to explain away such cures, but there is no litmus test for a proper cure. In a rather sharp rejoinder to Spence's position of multiple narrative, Malcolm (1983) pointed out that such varied stories are beside the point since the psychoanalytic transference is the only true condition that we confront in analysis. This is unfortunately an arguable point, inasmuch as Freudian and Kleinian and Kohutian transferences do not seem of one piece; yet they remain the one true condition of all of these quite different analyses. The above case was conducted in a seemingly proper manner and the analyst was quite cognizant of the central role of the transference and indeed felt this supported his fundamental stance and his unusual conclusions.

A RESOLUTION OF THE DILEMMA

It seems likely that one can resolve the questions of the reasonableness of the clinical examples and the group responses by examining what is involved in these particular disagreements. This may then answer some other questions that have been raised.

1. DOES REALITY COUNT?

Freud's statement that it matters not if incest was real or fantasied today seems in error. Accumulated evidence in child guidance clinics and in analytic practice has clearly demonstrated that the patient who has experienced incest is a different patient than the one who has not (Gelinas, 1983). Given Freud's conviction of the universal presence of incestuous and castration fantasies, one could be forced into the untenable position that all persons would turn out the same if it were not for the fact that we *do* consider the effects of the environment in neurosogenesis. It is true, however, that we have failed to correlate the features of psychic reality with those of objective reality. Because we are unable to say just what an individual's subjective experience of an event will be, that experience is relative. In the case example, we would likewise have to compare the accumulated empirical evidence of incest in adolescent girls with the clinical picture of that particular patient. We would also consider the accumulated evidence that might warrant irreversible amnesia in such a case. Probably both would be found unable to support the analyst's conviction. These are examples of the gathering evidence from real events to warrant some general conclusion. They contribute to and comprise our general theories of development and psychopathology that are widely embraced by the community of analysts. But more than this carries us on to the next point to consider.

2. WHAT PRECONDITIONS DOES THE INVESTIGATOR BRING TO THE STUDY?

Inasmuch as no one approaches a case with a completely open or closed mind we should determine just what guiding theory this analyst utilized. If he believed that incest in adolescence led to hysterical reactions with complete amnesia, then he was not quite in harmony with the community of scientists, or the way of "normal science," or the disciplinary matrix (Kuhn, 1977) in which he was operating. Although this is reasonable if one is making a discovery or offering a new idea, such moments occur at the outer boundaries of most scientific activity where challenge is expectable.

Theories of all sorts put necessary constraints on one's freedom to devise explanations for cases, and it is necessary that one indicate which one theory or several theories are under consideration. Choice of theory will be considered below, but at this point we can say that the relativism emerging with the practice of different clinicians is often a result of using theories in different ways.

3. HOW CAN THE PATIENT HAVE BEEN CURED IF THE FACTS WERE POSSIBLY MISTAKEN AND/OR THE THEORY ERRONEOUS?

That Jungian, Freudian, and Kleinian analysts spin their own narratives in reporting the analyses of their patients is not a direct challenge to a theory of cure. The curative factor in analyses based on different theories may be the making of the story or a set of as yet unknown and unexamined points. Although several such suggestions have already been offered (Kohut, 1983), we are probably not yet at the point of determining the right theory and are thus living with a good deal of relativism about the nature of cure (Goldberg, 1981).

4. What is the Difference between Theories?

Hesse (1980) and Spence (1982) have noted that theories are underdetermined and thus may examine different areas of inquiry. Also, not all theories seem to work equally well. Further empirical study is therefore needed to determine just what is being explained and how effective it may be. It is not the case that "anything goes" in an analysis inasmuch as one's commitment to any given theory is the ongoing constraint to what data are gathered and what conclusions are reached. Hermeneutics requires us to be aware of our own theoretical convictions as they contribute to our inquiry. What we bring to the field influences the dialogue with the patient and what the patient offers us, in turn, influences us. We understand on the basis of our theories and we interpret on the same set of theoretical patterns. The added feature of self-reflection suggested by many (Habermas, 1971) is a part of a particular theory of inquiry that seems firmly established in the tradition of psychoanalysis.

Since different analysts have somewhat different theories, quite different personalities, and even more varied degrees of self-reflection, the result of their efforts will be quite relative as well. Our conclusions from this case are that the analyst made an idiosyncratic, or at least an unusual, evaluation of the clinical evidence. His theory did not allow for the conclusions that he drew. The benefit that the patient enjoyed belongs to the wide range of unexplained or incompletely explained improvement in many such cases. The role of hermeneutics is by no means challenged from this exercise since facts are not the basis of the problem that emerges from the case; rather, the case falls outside of the constraints of the present-day theories that are utilized.

DISCUSSION

The tension between realism and relativism in psychoanalysis is a direct descendant of the philosophical struggle over the same problem. It leads to our special concerns of whether true histories can be unveiled, correct interpretations made, and rational theories formulated and followed. It raises vexing questions as to whether we manufacture fictional stories of patients' lives, and whether it matters what we say to patients or what school or discipline we seem to represent. This tension further reflects whether we are involved in a scientific enterprise regulated by a logic or sets of principles, or whether, as some insist, ours is an artistic pursuit with *ad hoc* rules and maximum appeal to creativity. Such a tension cannot be resolved by merely taking a firm stand. Perhaps we can subscribe to what Michael Williams (1977) concluded after studying the problem and deciding that no belief seemed unalterably grounded:

> [It is] a picture of human knowledge as an evolving social phenomenon. At any time, we will have a solid core of unquestioned perceptual reports, and the like, against which more marginal and less certain beliefs can be checked. But even this solid core may come in for drastic revision in the interests of deeper insight or theoretical advance. Any belief can be questioned, but not all at once. In this way, the pursuit of empirical knowledge can be seen as a rational pursuit not because empirical knowledge rests on a foundation but because … it is a self-correcting enterprise.

To answer our questions in this spirit, we would say:

1. The real events of a patient's life are significant mainly as they are experienced by the person. The later telling of these events is subject to constant and continual revision according to the context of the retelling. There is no absolute truth to anyone's childhood since individuals often do not "know" what happened to them: each increment of knowledge changes the story and each audience or

listener contributes to the tale—much in the manner Piaget details in describing the child's achievement of concrete operations (Piaget and Inhelder 1959). Fact or fiction are relative matters constrained by coherence, continuity, and good fit, as well as by reigning theories of development that are thus true—for the time being.

2. The interpretations we make to patients are correct not in terms of matching an external historical event to an inner experience but in terms of the "best fit" thesis. They correspond to the requirements Freud made about furthering the analytic process, which, in turn, is constrained by the theory or theories of transference that are likewise felt to be true at a particular time in the history of our science.

3. Our membership in a particular scientific enterprise limits and guides what we see and what we say. Whereas at one point in our science we were able to construct only one narrative with a patient, say an Oedipal one, we now may enjoy a range of narratives offered by, say, Melanie Klein, Kohut, and others. These are options within the field but are not license for any and all productions since their theories are not currently among our acceptable notions. Acceptance occurs by way of and in the context of the logic of discovery and is tested both within and outside the analytic field. For instance, if a self-object transference is discovered in analysis and is posited as a part of normal development, it adds an option to our way of looking at material and is tested for endurance both within analyses and as part of developmental theories considered outside of the analytic setting. Contrast this with the counterexample that the claims of Melanie Klein do not stand up with what we know about the infant's capacity to image and reflect (i.e. fantasize) before the age of 18 months.

4. The particular school or discipline to which we belong is important. This is not a matter of allegiance but, rather, one of articulating just what our theory enables us to do or to say. Thus we have real differences and relative differences. But our awareness of

the fact that knowledge is an evolving social phenomenon compels us to participate in ongoing negotiations with others of differing viewpoints. Each and every such negotiation can cause us to re-make ourselves (Gadamer, 1975), and in this manner we thrive in the tension of reality—knowing things for sure—and relativism—knowing things must change.

5. Whether psychoanalysis is a science of laws or an artistic effort of *ad hoc* rules forces a reconsideration of the puzzle of whether laws are unchangeable facts of life, such as the law of gravity, or whether they are rules created by people to meet situations, much as the rules for playing tennis. At first blush, a difference seems obvious, but looking once again at the puzzle may well open up the reality-relativism problem once again. It does seem to be the case that one gains credibility as a scientist if one discovers and follows the laws of nature rather than if one devises rules to explain problems. Psychoanalysis is caught peculiarly in this dilemma and is often forced to declare itself as art or science by some definition visited upon us by those who know what science is or should be (Von Eckard, 1982). The answer requires too much detail to be worked out here, but one should at least begin by determining whether the definition for scientific activity is a law of nature or a rule constructed by a society of individuals and thus rather easily modifiable.

CONCLUSION

Many people feel that the accumulation of scientific knowledge is progressive, providing proof enough that we are embarked upon a steady advance toward knowing the truths of the real world (Popper, 1972). Others contest this view and declare that we often see an oscillation in the claims of those ultimate truths that, for instance, now see the world in one way and now another, with no clear path of progress, save that of a personal conviction (Hesse, 1980). We do all, however, subscribe to a set of truths that, for the present time, reign and dominate our lives. Occasionally, we are surprised at the findings of anthropologists who report on people who subscribe to a set of truths or world vision entirely different from ours (and we often therefore label these people "primitive"). A similar sort of meeting of different worlds is a fact and condition of psychoanalysis: usually the analyst is felt to be the bearer of reality and the patient more often fills the role of the innocent native or perhaps the misguided and uninformed traveler.

Rather than impose our truths upon patients, initially we view the world from their perspectives. This is but a first step, however, in a process designed ultimately to disabuse the patient of his or her mistaken notions, revealed to both of us in the transference—a situation in which we assume privileged access and knowledge. Locked in as we are by our own set of convictions our capacity to reorder the world is limited, as is that of the patient, who is similarly bound to his or her beliefs.

Thus, we aim to negotiate a reasonable compromise, and such negotiation takes place by way of our interpreting what we understand to be the patient's world. This is the hermeneutic effort, and it embodies and resolves the tension between reality and relativism. Each of our realities is modified by successful participation in negotiation. Sometimes it takes years before we recognize how much these dialogues change us, just as it takes what seems an incredibly long time to confront a new scientific reality. We consider these modifications as progress and only future generations can deliver a final and more sober judgment of the matter.

REFERENCES

Barnes, B. & Bloor, D. (1982). Relativism, rationalism, and the sociology of knowledge. In: *Rationality and Relativism*, eds. M. Hollis & S. Lukes. Cambridge: The M.I.T. Press.

Flew, A. (1979). *A Dictionary of Philosophy*. New York: St. Martin's Press.

Freud, S. (1925–26). An autobiographical study. *Standard Edition* 20: 33–35.

——— (1918 (1914). From the History of an Infantile Neurosis. *Standard Edition* 17.

Gadamer, H. G. (1975). *Truth and Method*. New York: Seabury Press.

Gelinas, D.J. (1983). The Persisting negative effect of incest. *Psychiatry* 46: 312–332.

Goldberg, A. (1981). One theory or more. *Comprehensive Psychoanalysis* 17: 626–638.

Goodman, N. (1978). *Ways of Worldmaking*. Indianapolis: Hackett Publishing.

Grandy, R. E., Ed. (1973). *Theories and Observations in Science*. Englewood Cliffs, N.J.: Prentice-Hall, Inc.

Grünbaum, A. (1983). *The Foundations of Psychoanalysis: A Philosophical Critique*. Berkeley: University of California Press.

Habermas, J. (1971). *Knowledge and Human Interest*. Boston: Beacon Press.

Hesse, M. (1978). Theory and Value in the Social Sciences. In: *Action and Interpretation*, ed. C. Hookering & P. Petit. Cambridge, England: Cambridge University Press.

——— (1980). *Revolutions and Reconstruction in the Philosophy of Science*. Bloomington & London: Indiana University Press.

Kant, I. (1781). *Critique of Pure Reason*. London: Macmillan, 1929.

Kohut, H. (1983). *How Does Analysis Cure?* Chicago and London: University of Chicago Press.

Kuhn, T. (1970). *The Structure of Scientific Revolutions*. 2nd ed. Chicago, London: University of Chicago Press.

——— (1977). *The Essential Tension*. Chicago, London: University of Chicago Press.

Malcolm, J. (1983). *Book Review of Narrative Truth & Historical Truth by Spence*. New York: The New Yorker.

Niederland, W. (1951). New York: Three Notes on the Schreber Case. *Psychoanalytic Quarterly* 20: 579–91.

Piaget, J. & Inhelder, B. (1969). *The Psychology of the Child*. New York: Basic Books.

Popper, K. R. (1972). *Objective Knowledge: An Evolutionary Approach*. Oxford, England: Clarendon Press.

Putnam, Hilary (1981). *Reason, Truth and History*. Cambridge, England: Cambridge University Press.

Ricouer, P. (1970). *Freud and Philosophy: An Essay on Interpretation*. New Haven & London: Yale University Press.

——— (1981). *Hermeneutics and the Human Sciences*. Cambridge, England: Cambridge University Press.

Spence, D. (1982). *Narrative Truth and Historical Truth*. New York & London: Norton.

Von Eckard, B. (1982). The Scientific status of psychoanalysis. In: *Introducing Psychoanalytic Theory*, ed. L. Gilman. New York: Brunner/Mazel, pp. 139–180.

Williams, M. (1977). *Groundless Belief*. New Haven: Yale University Press.

Negotiation, Communication, Interaction and the Process of Understanding

Psychoanalysis and Negotiation (1987) takes up the study of form over content, the "how" something is said from the "what" that is said, the music over the words or the way it is said rather than what is said. Thus every analysis might be considered to operate on at least two levels: what we talk about and the manner in which we do it. This brings us to the topic of the process of negotiation—the "how" of the matter.

According to Goldberg, the issue of rules and the negotiation of rules might offer a source of knowledge concerning the patient's development and psychic structure. Here Goldberg includes the basic rules of the frame: free association, the fee, and the set hours. There is nothing inherently good or bad about these rules, the rule setting or the rule changing, Goldberg simply draws our attention to the negotiation of these processes and their meaning. By negotiation both patient and analyst come to a shared meaning, achieving some sort of shared reality.

How do the analyst and patient reach this shared reality? As Goldberg states, "It is in the crucible of the transference ... Psychoanalysis claims a unique window on the world by assuming that patients will inevitably bring their childhood experiences into the treatment and the disparity between that set of experiences and the reality of the analytic situation will allow for ameliorative interpretations."

The negotiating process is based on a modification of beliefs and in analysis, the negotiation consists of the interpretation of the unconscious content plus the process of working through that content. Here Goldberg offers his understanding of therapeutic change, utilizing the model of mourning to explain the acquisition of structure. It is a two-phase process of understanding and explanation, allowing for a partial merger followed by a disruption. It is this disruption that ushers in the sense of loss or mourning. The sequence leads to minute internalizations of functions. Change is considered to be a result from structural growth. Thus psychoanalysis as negotiation stands in contrast to the traditional concept of it as an unearthing

—GM

Psychoanalysis and Negotiation (1987)

ABSTRACT

Somewhere between the image of psychoanalysis as suggestion and psychoanalysis as unearthing is that of analysis as negotiation. This is a picture of a mutual construction of reality by analyst and patient. Such an interaction allows for reciprocal input of the participants and a possible change in both. This paper sketches the role of negotiation throughout the entire process of treatment—from the initial rules, to the theory of the analyst, to the emergence of the transference, to the goal of the cure. The technique of psychoanalysis is said to lie in the process of negotiation.

INTRODUCTION

The technique of psychoanalysis has not followed a clear advance from a simple set of principles to a deepening and elaboration of those tenets. At times there seems to be a pluralistic approach to technique that borders on an "anything goes" or at least an "everyone does things differently" axiom (Lipton, 1983). A study of technique should focus more on the method or form than on the particulars of the content; this implies that we should divide the "what" that is said from the "how" it is said. Two analysts may share a set of theoretical ideas but differ in their conduct of an analysis primarily in terms of their personal style, which thereby determines much of the conduct of the treatment. This point of form over content, the music over the words, the way it is said rather than what is said, is often felt to be a distinguishing mark of, but not a crucial difference between, various types of analysis. The style of one analyst differs from that of another in ways that are often assumed to be idiosyncratic or personal, which makes them seem more facilitating or enhancing to the conduct of an analysis than central and primary. However, we soon become forced to look at the form of analytic intervention as an integral part of the transaction since periodically it does appear to take precedence.

This paper will attempt to bring the issue of the "how" into a more central position by considering it as inextricable from content in its effect if not in our study of it. This claim can be supported by seeing it as operative at every level of an analysis, although often relegated to secondary status. It thus demands its own theoretical underpinning and its own principles of activity. The latter may be subsumed under the process of negotiation.

WHAT IS NEGOTIATION

The word "negotiate" is so linked to adversarial situations, such as labor versus management, defense lawyers versus prosecution, and foreign powers in disagreement, that one might balk at considering it at all as a part of psychoanalysis. A less disagreeable definition is that it is a communication made to arrive at some settlement of a matter; this definition may relieve it of the negative note in the image of opponents trying to hammer out an agreement. I shall define it in the positive sense of a sharing of meanings.

Upon reading the case of the Rat Man, one sees that Freud (1909) fed his patient without feeling that this hampered or distracted from the analysis in any way. Yet no present-day psychoanalyst can help but wonder about the effects of that or of any other intrusion of the analyst into the process of analysis. The whole question of the analyst's input into the analytic work has undergone a series of scrutinies, arguments, and resolutions in the history of the technical management of analysis. Positions range from the extreme of espousing as total a non-involvement as possible, with any inadvertent intrusion to be carefully examined under the rubric of countertransference (Silverman, 1985), to another extreme of viewing the analyst's input as constituting the main form and content of the analysis (Tower, 1956). Some, like Laing (1967), might hold that the patient is correct in his or her perception of a crazy world that is recreated in treatment. Some, like Melanie Klein (1952), would point to the child's impulses as primarily responsible for the pathology, which is then recreated in the analytic setting. But whether or not one includes the issue of responsibility in considering the reappearance of the life of the child in the transference, there remains the question of whether the analyst can indeed be both a transference figure and an observer of the situation, or whether he or she must inevitably be a participant, witting or otherwise.

Freud's feeding the Rat Man could be seen as involving him in a real interaction to such an extent that the posture of detachment and its associated word, objectivity, was temporarily abandoned. This would correspond to the sort of intrusion that might interfere with a transference based primarily upon the patient's psychology; it might interfere even more with one that is a compound of a two-person relationship. The issue to be addressed is whether one can conduct an analysis with the desired objectivity of a detached yet interested participant, or whether every analysis is a mixture of the analysand's productions and the unpredictable input of the analyst. The first position at least allows for the hope of replicable and predictable data; the second portends a variable product that arises from a mixture of potentially idiosyncratic responses. Regardless of one's position on this matter, the method of exchange or interchange seems to warrant a study of the process of negotiation that goes on between patient and analyst. Only that term seems to capture the issue of two persons with distinct and separate interests working toward an agreement of sorts, and the nature of that agreement seems to depend on the process of its achievements. Thus considering psychoanalysis as negotiation would stand in contrast to the concept of it as an unearthing and so would modify the archaeological metaphor.

There is no doubt that most psychoanalysts would agree to the fact that some minimal negotiation does take place in the treatment process but that it need not, perhaps should not, be much of a factor in the conduct of the analysis. We negotiate issues such as appointment times, fees, and vacation schedules at the start of treatment and often assume (or hope) that they will cease to be problems the remainder of the time. As Freud (1913p. 134) said, "The conditions of treatment having been regulated in this manner, the question arises at what point ... is the treatment to begin?" The conditions, however, do not remain static. On occasion these points become the source of major conflicts in the conduct of an analysis, and we then view them as caught up in the unconscious conflicts of the moment. They are subsequently handled less by negotiation than by interpretation and so belong more properly (and comfortably) within the activities allowed to psychoanalysis.

In truth, negotiation is such a symbolic carrier of action that it is felt to defeat the analyst's proper stance of abstinence. When Eissler (1953) discussed the introduction of parameters into analytic technique, he made it clear that, as necessary as they may sometimes be, they were always something of a nuisance, and one should as speedily as possible return to the single allowed activity: interpretation. The question to be posed is not only whether we have the obvious sorts of negotiations that are familiar to the conduct of analysis, but also whether the word properly belongs to the realm of interpretation as well.

NEGOTIATION AND RULES

Although there is but one basic rule in psychoanalysis, that of saying everything that comes to mind, in fact our patients must subscribe to a variety of rules in order to participate in the process. We set the fee, fix the time, determine the place, and talk when we desire. It is a rare patient who submits to all of our demands and constraints without some sort of reaction; a too willing compliance is even seen as a sign of the concealment of a more profound meaning. It is probably also a rare analyst who has not either lost a patient because he or she could not fit into the analyst's constraints (regardless of their legitimacy) or bent the rules in order to allow an analysis to begin or to continue. Indeed, we often learn a great deal about a patient over this very issue of rules. Here is a clinical illustration:

A patient had had a sequence of negotiations about missing sessions. The analysis had begun with a fairly clear contract that the patient was responsible for all of her sessions and therefore would pay for any that she missed, whatever the reasons. She had no question about this point, although admittedly she was a patient who rarely took issue with any-thing. During one long vacation her husband had protested about paying for missed hours, and the patient had asked if we might renego-tiate the agreement so that it would be like one that a friend had with her analyst. In the contract the analyst tried to fill the hours that were vacated in order to relieve the patient of full responsibility for them. I had deviated from my own rule with other patients. Now I felt that our efforts to analyze the meaning of this issue to this particular patient had been for the most part exhausted, and so I agreed. During the patient's next absence she was beside herself with anxiety over the hours that were taken away from her while she was away. There was no evidence of her feeling a victory over the analyst; instead, she seemed to have to feel that her hours remained hers. We tried to connect this to her childhood feelings concerning the birth of a brother when she was four. He turned out to be a very sickly child who required the concentrated attention of her parents until he died when he was eight years old. The patient felt that this explanation was unsatisfactory inasmuch as she was already in school when her brother became ill, and she could recall no memories of her place having been usurped. Rather, her fearfulness about losing her hours seemed to stem from a general fantasy of hers about dropping from sight in terms of me and my memory. She once noted that I turned away from her as soon as her hour ended to tend to some papers on the desk. She elaborated this into a fantasy that I wanted to be rid of her, or perhaps that I forgot her as soon as she was gone. She wanted to keep her hours even while she was away, in order to stay alive in my mind. Here the issue of rule-making and rule-changing seemed to be of help in understanding the patient.

Examples of rule-setting and rule-changing can do no more than lend support to the idea that there is nothing inherently good or bad about any rule, save how we learn what it means to us and to the patient. We may feel that a good rule is one that follows Freud's (1913) recommendation that it be effective. I take that to mean that a good rule will not impede the development and resolution of the transference while a bad rule will work against that goal. This seems in keeping with the theme of Freud's recommendations, as opposed to the concept of the good or bad having some moral or ethical connotation. Even the fixed rule of free association was explained by Freud (1913) to a patient as being something quite beyond his control, and so he was relieved of insisting on conformity for his own sake. We often wish to extend a host of similar issues in psychoanalysis as belonging to the same category of "it's not up to me but is part of the rules," until re-examining these points betrays our personal investment.

Rules such as length of hours, frequency of visits, and personal contacts between patient and analyst are handled in a separate category having to do with facilitating the treatment. The story that is told of Jacques Lacan's ending some sessions after only a few minutes (Schneiderman, 1983) is reacted to as a breach of ethical standards much akin to those of the analyst who becomes overly familiar with his patient. Indeed, it is usually true of a rule that, because of its institutionalization in our profession, it becomes a part of the right or correct way to do things. Without pursuing the matter of such moral imperatives, it seems clear enough that our rules are or soon become our way of the world. They determine what should be done, how it should be done, and why it should be done. In short, they make up much of the analyst's reality. This particular view of the world then meets that of the patient; in this manner, a situation evolves that calls for some form of meeting of the minds and re-evokes our concern with the matter of negotiation.

NEGOTIATION AND PSYCHIC REALITY

Once the matter of the rules of performance is put aside, we usually feel that we can step outside of participating with the patient in anything like an educative manner. Imagine a patient who tells you that he feels that the world is an awful place, filled with dirt and disease, peopled with evil individuals who wish only to hurt and exploit you, and destined to end in some sort of justified apocalypse. If we choose to treat such a patient, it is assumed that somehow we must be empathic with him and thus must enter his world and experience his reality. We cannot, however, be just another in a line of those who wish to set him straight or cheer him up or talk him out of it. Neither can we indulge in a total immersion in his dilemma and share his view of misery and sadness. It is folly to say that we must, or even can, completely shed our own preconceptions of the world in order to really understand another person. Our very preconceptions that insist that the world is not such a place allow us to begin an effort at what is certainly the goal of disabusing the patient of his forlorn picture of existence. Thus, we neither totally agree nor totally disagree but seek a workable stance for our later interpretive efforts.

If that patient or another patient tells us of a world of brightness and sunshine, happiness and joy, peopled with those who have only your best interests at heart, we should be equally skeptical and equally caught between reality and empathy. It seems that we always weigh the disparity between a sympathetic identification with the patient and some other background concept of how people should and/or do experience the world. Though we may choose to allow the optimistic viewpoint to reign unchallenged, we can never fail to match our own world-view with the presentation of the patient. In short, we can listen to patients only against a background of our own traditions and beliefs, and we pick and choose our interventions on the basis of what we consider proper versus what we feel is deviant. That is how we decide a theory of psychopathology as well as normality. Somehow we know just how people should feel about things, and we act accordingly.

But, of course, no analysis is a process of argument anymore than it is one of suggestion. It is in the crucible of the transference that we determine whatever we choose to see as deviations from a norm. Psychoanalysis claims a unique window on the world by assuming that patients will inevitably bring their childhood experiences into the treatment and the disparity between that set of experiences and the reality of the analytic situation will allow for ameliorative interpretations. Ideally, we should see a transference that follows a somewhat set program responding to a process of interpretation that allows only a minimum of latitude.

TRANSFERENCE AND NEGOTIATION

It soon becomes evident that the ideal equation of transference and interpretation is not easily achieved. One analyst told a story of seeing a patient who had had two previous analyses. She described to her new analyst a series of awful mistreatments bordering on malpractice in these analytic encounters. All the while, she professed her great relief that she had at last found a trustworthy person to help her. The about-to-be christened third analyst informed his patient that although he could not defend the analysts who had abused her, he had no doubt that he too would join the ranks of the oppressors. Being a profound believer in the repetition compulsion, he knew that a fixed program was operating in this patient's unconscious, and that he must allow this to unfold in a nonprejudicial way. And indeed he tells the story in the manner of this patient's psyche seemed to require. Thus the replicable and predictable feature of the transference.

But not all transferences are alike. The very fact that the analyst "knows" what to expect makes him or her a different person from a naïve or untutored partner in some other transaction. Another analyst (perhaps even one of this patient's former analysts) might be more willing to literally mistreat the patient, given her proclivity to call forth this behavior in others, while still another might even have kept these feelings to a minimum. Only in the most ideal of transference enactments are we able to claim a pure form of emergence of childhood experience, and even if that is the case, we do not all attend alike to what does emerge. Sooner, rather than later, every analyst seems to direct or focus the patient's productions by way of his or her own history and traditions, transference and countertansference, and theory and convictions.

Here is an illustration of an analytic intervention taken from Kohut's (1979) "The Two Analyses of Mr. Z." and concerning a dream interpreted differently over a period of years:

> In this dream—his associations pointed clearly to the time when the father rejoined the family—*he was in a house, at the inner side of a door which was a crack open. Outside was the father, loaded with gift wrapped packages, wanting to enter. The patient was intensely frightened and attempted to close the door in order to keep the father out...* Our conclusion was that it referred to his ambivalent attitude towards the father... I stressed ... his hostility toward the returning father, the castration fear, vis-à-vis the strong, adult man; and, in addition, I pointed out his tendency to retreat from competitiveness and male

assertiveness either to the old pre-oedipal attachment to his mother or to a defensively taken submissive and passive homosexual attitude toward the father (pp. 8–19).

In the discussion of the second analysis, Kohut wrote:

> The new meaning of the dream as elucidated by the patient via his associations ... was not a portrayal of a child's aggressive impulse against the adult male accompanied by castration fear, but of the mental state of a boy who had been all-too-long without a father; of a boy deprived of the psychological substances from which, via innumerable observations of the father's assets and defects, he would build up, little by little, the core of an independent masculine self ... the dream constitutes only a tame replica [of a traumatic state] (p. 23).

This is not the place to discuss the many reactions to this set of dream interpretations, which range from outright agreement to serious disagreement. Those who disagree state that the two interpretations are really one, or that the second should have preceded the first, or that either the one or the other was unnecessary, etc. It seems to be of little moment to the critics that for the analyst the dream had a "new meaning" which was in opposition to the previous one. Thus, at a minimum, this dream or any dream means nothing except as seen in the context of the timing, the transference position, and, most important, the theoretical stance of the analyst. Kohut would probably modify this by insisting that the patient's association led to his revised interpretation, but, contrary to Kris (1983), there are simply no observations possible without a theory to direct, guide, and elicit them. One never sees a pattern or follows a theme without a pre-existing schema, and it is simply impossible for any so-called theory-free data to emerge. It is therefore the case that one influences what is seen by the very act of seeing. Alas, we are not and never can be neutral observers. The associations of the patient seem more in the nature of a dialogue than a monologue.

Although the analyst may never openly direct the flow of associations, he participates in two ways. The first has to do with his choice of one meaning over another, since any given dream or bit of analytic material has multiple meanings. This, of course, is the nature of overdetermination. The second is due to the fact that every intervention resets the communication, just as every conversation is made unpredictable by virtue of each participant's need to respond to the input of the other. If we choose to keep our interventions to an absolute minimum by silence, we soon learn that such silences represent an equally significant form of input. We may then choose to move the arena of our scrutiny to studying the effects of intervention or nonintervention upon the associations. In one sense, this concern with form rather than content, a concentration on how things are said rather than what is said, is a natural element in every analyst's armamentarium and is really a theory about a theory, or what may be called a metatheory.

Thus we see that psychoanalysis exists on two levels. The patient talks and we listen, and the patient makes something of our listening. We study what the patient says and how the patient reacts to our silences or our interventions according to our theoretical inclinations. If a patient mentions a common-sense term, such as "apple," we assume we know what it stands for until we may learn of the very special personal meaning it has for that patient. Much of our own sense of the term "apple" is shared by the patient while some part is always special and individual for each of us. In Rangell's (1985) words, "The analyst, by a more informed theory than the patient, produces in the latter further insight and understanding" (p. 83). The how of this process, the manner in which our theory, whatever it may be, is able to change that old apple to a new one is the process of negotiation. But now the question arises of just where the change takes place.

NEGOTIATION AND CHANGE

The theory of negotiation is a metatheory, one that concerns itself with the communicative process that goes on between persons so that they may achieve some sort of shared reality. It stands in marked opposition to a theory of indoctrination, which has associations to submission, compliance, and lack of participation. Results of negotiations are quite different from fixed beliefs which allow for no form of alteration. Rather the negotiating process is based on a modification of beliefs, and, in analysis, consists of the interpretation of the unconscious content plus the process of working through. Merely naming the unconscious content before the patient is ready is of no import, just as doing it only once has a minimal effect. Psychoanalysis has a variety of ways to determine the effectiveness of interpretations: through further associations, increased or decreased resistance, etc. As Rangell (1985) indicated, the achievement of insight is essentially the capacity of the patient to gain a conviction of the truth of the "more informed theory" of the analyst.

There have been many attempts to explain the nature of the therapeutic change in psychoanalysis. It is important at the outset to differentiate such efforts at explanation from those that are descriptive in nature. Statements such as "Where id was, there ego shall be" (Freud, 1933p. 80) or "corrective emotional experiences that occur are crucial … and may well be the single most important aspect of psychoanalytic effectiveness" (Peterfreund, 1983p. 251) are not so much an explanation of a causal relationship as they are a rephrasing of an event. This may be sufficient for many, but usually we look for causal explanations.

Heinz Hartman (1951) offered such an explanation by positing the lifting of countercathexis from repressed material and the subsequent neutralization of the released energy which then became available to the ego. The satisfactoriness of this idea may be limited today, in view of the general lack of acceptance of the entire energy concept.

Heinz Kohut (1984), following Freud, utilized the model of mourning to explain the acquisition of structure that occurred in treatment. He stated that the two-phase process of understanding and explanation allows a partial merger followed by a disruption. This sequence leads to minute internalizations of functions and this is, in turn, explained as a furtherance of the process. Thus change results from structural growth.

Michael Basch (1981), following Piaget and theories of cognitive development, considers the cause of change in treatment to be due to the progressive movement from one state of cognitive development (say, sensorimotor) to another (e.g., concrete operations). He relies on the Piagetian theory of a rather fixed program that will unfold in an appropriate environment. This formulation is similar to those suggested by analytic developmental theorists who liken analysis to a developmental experience.

Barratt (1985) argues against the concept that the curative factor in psychoanalysis resides merely in the new knowledge acquired. For him, the knowing of psychoanalysis is a change in one's being. He insists that one cannot approach or comprehend these changes within the framework of logical positivism. Rather, the method sets in motion what he terms knowing as being, and being as knowing. A change in knowing changes who you are, and a change in who you are alters what you may come to know.

Those who see analysis in developmental terms, including Kohut, feel that the analytic situation encourages and/or allows the maturational processes to unfold. These theorists range along a continuum depending upon what they feel are the proper conditions for development. Thus the analyst must create the climate, lend the language, or correct the deviations in order for the inherent program to be realized. But even the most austere of analytic approaches recognizes that the analyst affects the patient by his presence, his interpretations, and the state of the transference.

The rules of the process, the theory of the analyst, the communicative exchange or metatheory employed, all contribute to any psychoanalysis, and all may be quite different from analyst to analyst and from time to time with the same analyst. It would be folly to say that anything said by the analyst can be considered therapeutic; this would make the words meaningless. But it would also be naïve to say that there is but one true way to proceed. Different analysts do say quite different things at different times, and the fact that these diverse ways of analyzing seem to work demands some explanation that goes beyond the options of nihilism (anything goes) and fruitless comparisons (mine is better than yours). Donald Spence (1982) asks for some naturalization of our data in an effort to pin down some empirical facts. Roy Schafer speaks for alternative narratives which may share equal claims for true historical records (Spence, 1982). What is being suggested here is that every interpretation and/or intervention is an *approximation* of some true state of belief and feeling of the patient. It is couched in the therapist's language, guided by the therapist's theory, colored by the prevailing transference, and open to correction by the therapist's capacity to negotiate. Patients and analysts learn a shared social reality, learn to communicate in a shared language, and learn what one another's expectations are. Inasmuch as we have a sometimes startling and bewildering array of therapeutic interventions, we should attend less to the truth of these propositions and more to the way some sort of agreement is reached between patient and analyst. This is negotiation, and this is what merits study.

THE PROCESS OF NEGOTIATION

A cursory study of Freud's notes on the Rat Man case demonstrates the nature of the negotiating process that went on between Freud and his patient. Freud asked him to bring a photo of his woman friend with him in order to give up his reticence about her. No matter that a modern-day analyst would be reticent about such a request: the words reveal the motive and goal of the analyst. Every page demonstrates some action of Freud's, ranging from "I could not restrain myself" to "I explained to him." Freud persuaded him to reveal things, he suffered through giving explanations that meant nothing to the patient, and he even delivered a lecture on perversion (1909 p. 283). These notes as presented are not to be considered as exemplars of good technique, but it would appear to some that today's analyst would do away with all but the interpretations. I suspect that is both a foolish and an impossible goal, since we, too, persuade, suffer, and lecture, but are perhaps a bit more alert to the consequences.

Many analysts have attempted to divide the components of the treatment into what may be termed the therapeutic or working or real relationship and the transference while others say that all belongs to the transference (Brenner, 1982) and perhaps still others claim the relationship encompasses everything. Some also wish to have this therapeutic relationship assume a background presence so that the real work of analysis may proceed. Putting this feature of analysis into such a framework and seeing it as a positive feature or an impediment seems to minimize the complexity of the process which goes on in every analysis and which underscores how patient and analyst agree or disagree about anything at all.

Brenner (1982), in his recent book, presents a vignette of a woman who argued with him over anything and everything in her analysis. As an analyst, he appropriately considers the question of whether *what* he says infuriates her and then studies the peculiar state that makes *whatever* he says or does not say serve as a stimulus for her irritation. The second consideration which is essentially about the first is of a different logical type, i.e., it is on a different level of inquiry than the first, just as the word fruit is of a higher order than the words apple, pear, and orange. The study of the content is the first level while the study of the exchange irrespective of the content is on a different level. We also say that the second is a meta-study which means no more than a study about something studied.

Brenner does not tell just how this impasse was resolved, but he does mention that the patient tried mightily not to so disagree. She ultimately realized the motives for her persistent arguing, and so we would assume it dissipated. We might also assume that interpretation alone was effective, but one can only wonder about the intermediary steps involved in getting the patient to listen, in convincing her of the truth of one's interventions, in achieving a state of agreement that was so antithetical to her nature. Just how was this negotiated other than by sheer repetition of an interpretation? At one point the patient is said to have resolved to keep quiet until her analyst had spoken. In truth this is an attempt at a negotiated peace; but one which was unsuccessful. It seems that over time the patient was able to see what she was doing.

Heinz Kohut tells of a similar case (Kohut, 1984) of a patient who could not accept any interpretation from him even if it was a correct one (as the patient would later agree). He says that this pattern of refusal in the patient had to do with his own failure to see that the patient felt incompletely understood. When *that* was interpreted, then the analysis could proceed. This is a commentary on the transaction between analyst and analysand, and it coincides with Kohut's conviction that an understanding phase must precede the explanatory phase. But is it always the case that recognizing that something is wrong and interpreting why it is so leads to such prompt amelioration of the impasse? The burden seems to have shifted to the question of how one achieves empathy, i.e., how one manages to have the explanation be an effective one. For Kohut there seems to be a more immediate attention to this level of disagreement, and the analyst seems to be more active in its lifting. But this likewise seems to assume an ease which leaves something out.

To tease apart the factors involved in having the arguing (negative, resistant) patient accept an interpretation, we must recall that negotiation is a two-way process regardless of whether the analyst is silent or verbose. The patient responds to silence or to words by accepting either one as some sort of a negotiating position of the other and carries on from there. The silent analyst may be felt to allow less room for maneuver, but in the exchange between patient and analyst some acceptable compromise is achieved. Over time, the angry patient may agree to the repeated interpretations of the analyst or to the supposedly new and more empathic ones; but ultimately we hope to achieve agreement. What seems to transpire is that the patient, perhaps sooner rather than later, must learn to understand, i.e., be empathic with the analyst. Empathy is operant on both sides, and surely patients learn to comprehend their analyst in a like manner to what we usually say is required of analysts. The intermediate steps may consist of the patient's rephrasing the analyst's interpretation or modifying it or accepting a part and rejecting another part or some other variant. The analyst, in turn, may learn to present only certain parts or to put it in different words or to change the meaning in response to later associations. Together they aim to arrive at a shared meaning. It is a rare analyst who forms and delivers interpretations that need little reshaping, and it is never the case that a patient ends a successful analysis with the same view of his life and the world with which he began.

NEGOTIATION AND THE CHANGE IN THE ANALYST

If the analyst is a participant in the negotiations of an analysis which aim at a change in the patient's view of and theory about himself, can the analyst emerge unscathed? Participants in any negotiating process usually give and take except for those rare states involving fixed beliefs and indoctrinations. Analytic patients change, as noted above, in diverse ways, but we usually assume that the analyst gains only in experience, wisdom, and skill. Yet most of the elements of the analytic change do require some, at least temporary, capacity to see and believe something differently. It probably is difficult if not impossible to grade the potential changes in the analyst in a positive or negative direction, but one can offer the suggestion that each and every patient offers a worldview that demands some sort of accommodation on the part of the analyst. Sometimes this is in the direction of changes in rules (Goldberg and Marcus, 1985), or in theory (Kohut, 1984), or in technique (Freud, 1909). It takes no imaginative leap to realize that these components are also aspects of a total personality, and so we might say that every analysis does indeed cause us to remake ourselves (Gadamer, 1975). The levels of change in the analyst may be primarily cognitive, as when we simply learn more about something from a patient, or they may be affective. The latter may be severe enough to warrant some personal analytic work. But another level would combine these to bring about a change in our science that corresponds to Freud's change of mind and heart about the seduction theory. Perhaps it is not too revolutionary a stand to insist that effective analyses are such meaningful negotiations that they demand that a new analyst emerge. We may or we may not be wiser, but we are (or should always be) different.

Of special moment here is the change in the patient's empathy for and understanding of the analyst. It would be naïve to withhold credit to our patients who teach us how to understand them, who are patient with our mistakes, and who tolerate some of our outlandish interpretations and theories; who sometimes are even quite therapeutic to us! Given the two-way street of empathy it probably means that we, too, are undergoing new experiences, in being understood if not always having things explained to us. Unless we grant this form of the potential for change in analysts, then we fall back on a mechanical version of offering interpretations that are universally and eternally valid; and that position may not be acceptable to many analysts.

SUMMARY

We negotiate the rules of the analytic procedure, our shared version of the world, the meaningfulness of the analytic transference, and the goals and method of cure. When Freud wrote up the case of the Rat Man, he decided, as does every analyst, to present certain facts and to omit others. Among the latter were the host of personal contacts that were felt not to be a part of the analysis. His friendly feeling toward his patient was noted but mainly discounted or subsumed under present-day concepts of the therapeutic relationship. But every analysis operates on at least two levels: what we talk about and the manner in which we do it. When the latter becomes the focus of interest, as often occurs in the analysis of resistance, we still assume yet another level for that discourse. We can never escape the process of trying to reach common ground with our patients. We should agree that no part of the transaction between patient and analyst is ever immune from the effects of the one person upon the other, and no part of the analyst per se does not matter for one or another patient. The history of psychoanalytic techniques makes much of the particulars of allowing a patient to see things and to understand things and to master things that were previously unknown to him. Since we must choose never to suggest or to indoctrinate, we appeal to reason and good judgment in order to move from transference to reality. Each step of the process is suffused with our rules, our theories, and our world views, and each step must entail a negotiation to achieve a shared meaning. Thus the process of negotiations is another way of looking at the technique of psychoanalysis. There is no inherent essence to release that can reveal what a patient is "really like"; rather it is a mutual construction.

At its simplest, psychoanalysis is an effort to change someone else's mind. It is, of course, not confined to the level of conscious decisions but rather aims to reach to the depths to effect such a change. The mere seeing of the truths of the world never seems to be sufficient to convince someone of the folly of his or her position, but psychoanalysis lays claim to a powerful tool that expands one's vision: the transference. It would be a great relief if that were the sturdy platform on which we could all stand to enable insight to emerge, but it seems that our convictions about the transference are as contaminated as all of our other truths and convictions are. Thus we should move on to a study of just how mind changing takes place (while all the time knowing that this as well will be a prejudiced pursuit). The process of persuasion or understanding or gaining insight is a fruitful study in its own right. It consists of all the factors that we study about negotiating a meeting of the minds, i.e., examining the steps that allow for one person to reach agreement with another. This process essentially comprises the technique of treatment, and it in turn includes the whole of our ideas about reality, psycho-pathology, and analytic theory. No step of the process of negotiation is free from this baggage of prejudices, cultural background, and training with which we enter the room, and it is probably equally simplistic to think that we are able to leave the room unchanged. Rather, the job of getting another person to change involves an empathic exchange where-in each participant becomes aware of the other's position. In this manner the technique of psychoanalysis demands that we not only understand our patients but that they understand us as well.

REFERENCES

Barratt, B. B. (1985). Further notes on the epistemic and the ontic in psychoanalytic transformations. Unpublished.

Basch, M. F. (1981). Psychoanalytic interpretation and cognitive trans-formation. *International Journal Psycho-Analysis* 62:151–175.

Brenner, C. (1982). *The Mind in Conflict.* New York: Int. Univ. Press.

Eissler, K. R. (1953). The effect of the structure of the ego on psychoana-lytic technique. *Journal of the American Psychoanalytic Association* 1:104–143.

Freud, S. (1909). Notes upon a case of obsessional neurosis. *Standard Edition* 10.

—— (1913). On beginning the treatment. (Further recommendations on the technique of psycho-analysis I.). *Standard Edition* 12.

—— (1918). From the history of an infantile neurosis. *Standard Edition* 17.

—— (1933). New introductory lectures on psycho-analysis. *Standard Edition* 22.

Gadamer, H. G. (1975). *Truth and Method.* New York: Seabury Press.

Golderg, A. & Marcus, D. (1985). "Natural termination": some comments on ending analysis without setting a date. *Psychoanalytic Quarterly* 54:46–65.

Hartmann, H. (1927). Understanding and explanation. In *Essays on Ego Psychology. Selected Problems in Psychoanalytic Theory* New York: International Universities Press, 1964 pp. 369–403.

—— (1951). Technical implications of ego psychology In *Essays on Ego Psychology. Selected Problems in Psychoanalytic Theory.* New York: International Universities Press, 1964 pp. 142–154.

Klein, M. (1952). Some theoretical conclusions regarding the emotional life of the infant ,In *Developments in Psycho-Analysis* ed. J. Riviere. London: Hogarth, pp. 198–236.

Kohut, H. (1979). The two analyses of Mr. Z. *International Journal Psycho-Analysis* 60:3–27.

—— (1984). How Does Analysis Cure? Chicago/London: University of Chicago Press.

Kris, A. O. (1983). Determinants of free association in narcissistic phenomena. *Psychoanalytic Study of the Child* 38:439–458.

Laing, R. D. (1967). *The Politics of Experience.* New York: Pantheon.

Lipton, S. 1983 Further observations on the advantages of Freud's technique. *Presented to the Chicago Psychoanalytic Society*, October 25.

Peterfreund, E. (1983). The Process of Psychoanalytic Therapy. *Models and Strategies* Hillsdale, NJ: Analytic Press.

Rangell, L. (1985). On the theory of theory in psychoanalysis and the relation of theory to psychoanalytic therapy. *Journal of the American Psychoanalytic Association* 33:59–92.

Schneiderman, S. (1983). Jacques Lacan. *The Death of an Intellectual Hero* Cambridge, MA: Harvard University Press.

Silverman, M. A. (1985). Countertransference and the myth of the perfectly analyzed analyst. *Psychoanalytic Quarterly* 54:175–199.

Spence, D. P. (1982). *Narrative Truth and Historical Truth. Meaning and Interpretation in Psychoanalysis.* New York: Norton.

Tower, L. E. (1956). Countertransference. *Journal of the American Psychoanalytic Association.* 4:224–255.

A Shared View of the World (1989)

In his 1989 paper, *A Shared View of the World*, Goldberg parallels the concept of patient and analyst arriving at a shared meaning to the search for commonality in the larger world of analysis. Goldberg emphasizes the ways in which our theories are our eyes, and as such, the world that we see is defined by our theories. We are warned of the security of having a theory as guidance, as well as the perils of a fixed system. "There is no bedrock of truths in psychoanalysis that allows us to know things for sure, since the essence of the negotiating process is a willingness on the part of both participants to move from their initial positions." With this, Goldberg refers to not only the patient and analyst negotiations that lead both parties to move from a fixed position, but psychoanalysis as well. Whether the subject in question is the patient with fixed perceptions and symptoms, or the analyst with fixed ideas and theories that prevent further inquiry, or the whole of psychoanalysis as insisting on one particular school of thought, if our view is from a fixed position, we are then entering a closed system which is not science. The analyst and patient might begin with fixed positions and ideas, but via negotiations and the introduction of new ideas, they move from understanding to misunderstanding to a more complete understanding.

—GM

*   *   *

The search for a common ground for analysts who work with differing viewpoints has its parallel in the search between analyst and patient for a similar unity of vision: a shared view of the world. No two people live in exactly identical worlds; we mainly manage to communicate with one another by varying degrees of sharing, negotiating and ignoring. Every patient who comes to analysis struggles with a combination of wishes to be understood by the analyst along with hopes that certain aspects of his psyche remain opaque. And every analyst, in like fashion, wants to understand his patient yet also needs and hopes to move the segregated or split-off material into the open.

My thesis here is that the analytic process is one that reverses this sequence of sharing, negotiating and ignoring. It says that this is the essence of commonality both in the analytic relationship *per se* as well as in the larger world of analysis. Let us begin with the first of the trilogy.

SHARING

To some degree we all share a similar perspective with our patients in a wide number of ways. This similarity is what allows us to make a beginning with patients, and it extends from a common language to a familiarity of customs, to an overlapping of like experiences. This need to overlap in a significant segment of life is what is essential for any sort of treatment, and it is why it makes the truly alien person untreatable. Phrases such as 'therapeutic' and 'working' alliance may possibly point to this shared vision that unites people with a minimum of effort. Indeed, the achievement of sharing becomes the major work of analysis as we initially aim to see the world as the patient does and then subsequently to enable the patient to see the world as we do. The world that we see is one defined and delineated by our theories, just as Freud could see things in his patients that he felt that they should ultimately likewise be able to see. Freud asked his patients to look at things in a new and different way: his way. The method of doing this may vary depending upon technique, but the goal remains that of the achievement of a mutually agreed upon view of the patient's life and history.

Some aspects of this effort of sharing are almost automatic, and some require the kinds of communication that all patients and analysts engage in. It is in the exercise of empathy that all people learn about others' inner lives; and this is true of each and every analyst no matter what particular theories he may employ. We aim to see the world as the patient does by a sustained effort of empathic linkage. Though analysts (like everyone else) pick and choose what to see and what to ignore, they must still employ this basic human device of empathy. In a reciprocal manner all patients struggle to understand their analyst and so to achieve this desired-for shared vision. The exercise of empathy does not differentiate analysts one from the other, but the utilized theories certainly do. Although we succeed in understanding one another, a shared state of understanding is short-lived.

NEGOTIATIONS

All analyses begin with enough shared understanding enjoyed by both participants, enough common ground to move on to the inevitable next phase: that of misunderstanding. From understanding, i.e. a basic set of like-mindedness between persons, we move to misunderstanding, i.e. a breach of the unity. The ensuing work of achieving a new understanding from the mis-understood state is that of negotiation. The beginnings of all analytic treatment involve a minimum of negotiation in terms of fees, hours, rules and vacations, the process of free association and a host of idiosyncratic, i.e. personal standards of conduct that every analyst presumes and assumes. But negotiation takes the dominant role in the entire analytic adventure, since analyst and patient are not of one mind, and each attempts to win over the other to his way of thinking: the one by interpretations that lead to insight, and the other usually by some form of special pleading. The patient in one way or another beseeches the analyst to join him in his view of reality, and the analyst exerts his effort to disabuse the patient of that set of supposed facts. It would seem that this is the arena where the patient is most disparate from the analyst, and thus the place where the technical interventions of the analyst become most meaningful. The patient who sees you as the parent feels it as real and does not yet see that this is an arguable perception. Interpretation or learning should allow him to so see that as an error.

The fundamental stance of the analyst in his participation in the negotiating process is governed by his analytic theory. Here is where analyst differs from patient, i.e. a given phenomenon such as a dream or an association is necessarily seen in a different way, because all of our facts are soaked in our theory. We never see any part of the psyche without a theory of the psyche, and thus analytic theories, whether articulated or not, distinguish analysts from non-analysts. They also differentiate one analyst from the next, and here again is where the commonality of analysts falters; and therefore, here is where the practice of negotiation between analysts becomes paramount.

I believe we agree that the major tool of our analytic interventions is the awareness and interpretation of transference. It would also seem to be the case that different analytic theories should and do primarily concern themselves with different comprehensions of transference. Psychoanalytic self-psychology, for example, has added to the list of the observable transferences those of selfobject transferences, i.e. the mirror, the twinship and the idealizing. This is subject to the same sort of negotiating process between analysts as that between patient and analyst, albeit in a more cognitive sense. To not participate in this form of negotiation is not a scientific position but rather reflects a similar sort of insistence on seeing the world in a fixed fashion: an insistence that our analytic patients enjoy to their detriment.

The reciprocal part of negotiation between patient and analyst asks of us to change as well. Inasmuch as we allow every aspect of analytic practice to be subjected to scrutiny, no part of it can ever be immune from reappraisal and alteration. There are no absolute rules for the analytic process save that of freedom of inquiry. The patient's insistence on keeping the world as is, is attributed to transference and is altered by interpretation. The analyst's own insistence on having it his way is considered to be attributable to countertransference along with limitations in his theoretical knowledge: the latter due to ignorance and/or the limitations of the state of the theory. Thus there is no bedrock of truths in psychoanalysis that allow us to know things for sure, since the essence of the negotiating process is a willingness on the part of both participants to move from their initial positions. Since psychoanalysis is not suggestion or indoctrination, it is either revelation or negotiation. It is tempting to believe that it is revelation, but each new finding in our science undoes that neat knot. Only in a closed system which is not science can one ever be allowed to practise the unearthing of revealed truths, but psychoanalysis can never be a finished product. New and unpredictable ideas come into the relationship between patient and analyst in a way different from other sorts of negotiations that begin with fixed ideas and positions.

The give and take of negotiating in psychoanalysis is made unique by the existence of the unknown that resides primarily but not exclusively in the patient. It is this awareness by the analyst that tilts the process in his favour, and it is the introduction of the unknown into that analytic process that makes for the issues that demand negotiation.

THE UNKNOWN

Repressed or disavowed mental contents become a part of the continual misunderstandings between patient and analyst. Because of the nature of the transference, there occur inevitable empathic disruptions or breaks in understanding. These are brought about because the achievement of a stable transference is never a static phenomenon, but rather one that continually makes demands, or has desires, or proceeds to develop. Since transference unfolds, it has changeable demands, and, since transference is repetitious, it has inevitable frustrations. The intrusion of unconscious contents, the existence of disavowed material, and the lack of the necessary structure to process this new set of relationships, all lead to misunderstandings. The re-establishing of understanding from misunderstanding by way of the negotiating process allows for the inclusion of the repressed and disavowed and the establishment of a suitable structure for its tolerance and expression. Thus the sequence of movement is from unknown or ignored material to inevitable misunderstanding; on to negotiation; and then to a shared set of perceptions which represent understanding, i.e. the desired state of sharing. This is the reversed sequence of the trilogy.

Since the analyst knows about the existence of and the forms of repressed and disavowed material, his theory allows him a vision denied to the patient. And it goes without saying that the more one knows the better; and thus no one can ever dismiss Kleinian or Kohutian or Lacanian ideas out of hand, any more than one can do without any therapeutic tool. The potential variants of transference are additional tools to one's analytic and therapeutic armamentarium. The restriction of analytic knowledge to one or another form of theory reveals the same sort of opaqueness that we see in our patients. Analysts who have limited or closed concepts of transferences, who do not learn Kohut or Lacan, who insist that their vision of the world is correct, live analogous patterns to those patients who likewise keep their ignorance at bay.

Even more to the point of the expansion of analytic knowledge being reciprocal to that of the patient is that of the analyst's active participation in the creation of misunderstandings. No matter how inevitable an empathic break may be, it always asks of us that we examine what we did or did not do to cause it and what we learn from it as we negotiate our way to new understanding. This is the part of the equation that consists of the analyst's countertransference or ignorance that in a hoped-for smaller amount adds its input to misunderstanding. Thus the understanding that should follow from this temporary disruption should always include the possibility to the analyst of a level of comprehension that was not previously available to him. In the words of Gadamer, we strive to remake ourselves by way of these cycles of achieving a shared vision of the world. The goal of this process would then be an achievement of a mutually new reality for both patient and analyst. This is not to say that analysis cures the analyst as it does the patient, but rather that no one can emerge from an intense and prolonged analytic relationship in the same way that one enters it.

PSYCHOANALYTIC SELF-PSYCHOLOGY AND THE COMMON GROUND

Since psychoanalytic self-psychology sees itself in the mainstream of psychoanalysis in terms of the formation and resolution of transference, it can make a further contribution in its elucidation of this effort in all analysis. The three phases of sequential action: the activation and intrusion of repressed and/or disavowed material, the misunderstandings, and the ensuing understanding are all conceptualized by way of the self-concept. The formation of selfobject transferences parallels the state of understanding which results from empathic union. The breaks in empathy come from disavowed and/or repressed material that expresses and allows for the emergence of regressive forms of selfobjects. The repairs in empathy lead to a state of understanding that moves toward a firmer self-structure. No matter what theoretical stand an analyst may take it would seem that this sequence has a universal applicability. The major point to be made is that content issues such as castration anxiety or oedipal dynamics play a subsidiary role to those of form and structure.

Such an overview of the work of all analysis is an umbrella. It covers a variety of seemingly different and sometimes contradictory ways of analysing in the sense of explaining why they all may seem at times to be effective. It does not, however, say that all psychoanalytic theories are basically alike or of equal value. Our theories are different, and they cannot and should not be translated one into the other. They compete in the market-place of science, and it behoves every analyst to be skilful enough and knowledgeable enough to make a decision for himself as to which theory explains more and better.

CONCLUSIONS

Psychoanalysis has moved from revelation to negotiation, from the image of a detached analyst enabling unconscious material to emerge, to one of mutuality that demands a new theory to explain how two people affect one another. Such a theory cannot and should not be one that neglects our capacity to see beyond explanations that keep the negotiation on a conscious level, i.e. those of linguistics or sociology or game theory or whatever. Rather we can utilize our analytic theories to explore the nature of change in terms of infantile demands, transference distortions, structure building or similar forms of explanatory concepts. The same should apply to how we change in our scientific exchanges; and one could hardly hope for a better testing ground for our ideas than in our willingness to see how well we can listen to and learn from one another. It is the exercise of a willingness to move from certainty to scepticism and to a resultant posture of openness to new insights that is the mark of the analyst who joins hands with his colleagues in the search for common ground. Such willingness is what we ask of our patients. Can we ask less of ourselves?

Changing Psychic Structure Through Treatment:
From Empathy to Self Reflection (1989)

Changing Psychic Structure Through Treatment: From Empathy to Self Reflection (1989), *Between Empathy and Judgment* (1999), *It Is All Interaction* (1996) and *Enactment as Understanding and as Misunderstanding* (2002), find Goldberg widening his position on psychoanalysis as an open system, where everything counts, there are no time outs, silence counts as much as talking, and all action and inaction resets the communication. There is an assumption, too, that the patient always has an effect on the analyst and that the same holds true for the analyst on the patient. Goldberg takes the position that every analysis causes us to remake ourselves and that the effort to remake ourselves is undertaken by both patient and analyst. "Perhaps it is not too revolutionary a stand to insist that effective analyses are such meaningful negotiations that they demand that a new analyst emerge. We may or we may not be wiser, but we are (or should be) different" (1987).

—GM

*   *   *

The central thesis of this paper is that psychic structure may be considered as a complex system of varying configuration. This configuration can be a microstructure or a macrostructure such as the ego or the self. The issue of changing structure through treatment involves the patient's expanded understanding. The steps involved in this process are sequentially delineated and illustrated with a clinical example. The crucial step of self-reflection is utilized as a sine qua non *of such change.*

There is an old puzzle in philosophy popularized by John Searle (1984) and often called the parable of the Chinese room. It asks that you imagine a man locked in a room with many baskets full of Chinese symbols. The man does not understand a word of Chinese, but he has a rule-book in English which tells him how to manipulate these symbols: something like "take a card from basket one and put it next to one from basket

169

three," etc. The man is then given some Chinese symbols through a window, along with more rules for passing some symbols back out. Unknown to the man is that the symbols passed in are called "questions," and the ones passed back out are called "answers." The rules are so accurate and well designed that the symbols passed out as answers are as good a set of reply as those of a native Chinese speaker. Thus, the man is in a locked room shuffling and passing out Chinese symbols, but clearly not understanding a word of Chinese—indeed, probably not learning any Chinese. The philosophical conundrum is one of observing someone who can behave *as if* he knew and understood Chinese but, all the same, not knowing it at all. The room, of course, can be a computer or simply the inside of a person's skull. The point is that "understanding" seems to demand more than just the manipulating of symbols to yield correct responses. The philosophers wonder just where the understanding may be. Is it in the rules or in the man? Can the whole room be said to understand Chinese? If the room were within a robot, would it then understand Chinese? How does one decide when something is understood? What makes for what we call understanding?

I mention this puzzle because, in a way, it dominates our own psychoanalytic wonder and worry about that moment in treatment when we feel that someone understands something: a moment when we likewise feel that structure (in a definition to be developed) seems to emerge. My own solution to the Chinese room puzzle is not particularly ingenious, but has to do with the fact that no mere adding up of steps or rules or procedures or even knowledge ever leads to the complexity of understanding. That particular state is at a different conceptual level, just as any comprehension of a totality composed of parts demands what Bateson (1972) has called a different logical type. A word is made up of letters, but no study of single letters can ever yield the meaning of a word. The same is true of sentences, faces, and any other totality that is always more than the sum of its components. Structure formation is not a summing up of small insights, but rather a move to a new level or type that makes for a comprehension of wholes which we call understanding. Structure implies organization, and this reflects levels of hierarchies in a complex whole.

The man who is considered the founder of French semantics and a forerunner of the philosophy of structuralism, Ferdinand de Saussure (1916), offers an illustration of the concept of "structure" in his telling of the planned stop of the 8:05 train from Paris to Geneva. This particular train arrives regularly at an approximate time that is fairly close to 8:05 and is thus distinguished from the 7:05 and the 10:05. It likewise is composed of an engine and a number of cars, but these need not remain the same from one day to the next: one day the new cars, and the next the old. Neither the composition nor the elements nor the particulars of the train need be constant in order for it to be the 8:05. Rather, its position in the general pattern of train arrivals and departures and its relations to other trains' comings and goings become the principal issues in considering it the 8:05. The "structuralism" directs our attention to the forms and patterns by which the composite elements connect and relate to one another, while it also diminishes our attention to the particular composition of those elements. To be sure, we often identify the unique element as essentially embodying the structure, since a favorite seat on a favorite train might lead one to feel he is riding the "old 8:05" as it winds its way to a different destination at a different time. It may also appear to some that it is folly to try to distinguish and separate form from content or pattern from composition, since they remain an inextricable unit. However, a great deal of work in fields allied to psychoanalysis, such as linguistics, especially that of Noam Chomsky, has prospered under just such division. For language, it may simply be separating syntax, or formal structure, from semantics or meaning. For psychoanalysis, a similar such project may offer a fruitful road of inquiry. The task for a psychoanalytic division of labor between pattern and elements would be to decide on a proper object of stud, e.g., the ego, for the pattern or organization, and to then determine if it and its stability override issues of composition which would then become secondary—much like the 8:05 might use the cars with seats upholstered in red as well as in yellow leather. The implications of this may or may not be far-ranging, but certainly might, over time, modify our concepts of health and illness. Thereupon, we may be able to classify disorders in a primary and secondary manner: those that have to do with a basic organization would be the primary determinant of psychopathology, while secondary elements would lend only color and substance to fill out the basic program.

There exists a host of mental phenomena that exhibit structure whether we define it as innate constraints, or capacity to act, or as enduring function. Perception, for example, is a mental process that is limited in terms of the quality of the light rays that can stimulate it or arouse a response. It is evoked in a learned manner that can, for example, be investigated by raising kittens in the dark and/or by ablating certain neuronal pathways; and it is adapted in a special manner in certain cultures which, as do the Eskimos with snow, see certain things in a manner that is learned in a very focused area. Any and all mental processes naturally become involved in a psychoanalytic investigation, but only some will show a relevance to the analytic situation and a readiness for change with analytic intervention. Thus, the task becomes narrowed.

If we choose, following Kohut, to select the self rather than the ego as the basic form or organization to study, then a number of principles as well as questions will present themselves. This particular form will be a stable configuration at certain periods of life, and will undergo modifications during growth and development that will follow sets of rules and regulations. Any other organization we choose to study, inside or outside of the realm of human psychology or biology, likewise preserves some fixed aspects that allow it to be considered the same over periods of time, even though it may undergo extensive modifications and even dramatic recastings. The fixed form of the self is a phenomenon of varied manifestations throughout life. Any particular method of studying this form, such as that of psychoanalysis, will reveal crucial or dominant types of this configuration and will allow us to consider the form in its plural sense; i.e., we seem to show different selves at different times. A transformation of such a fixed and relatively stable form means not only that the configuration operates in a manner different from the usual, but that it is governed by different rules. When we see a particular person or self-system engaged in a creative pursuit, we can say that the self is in a transformed state and is functioning according to a different program or set of plans. To be sure, this sort of conclusion is only valid according to the method of inquiry employed and the kind of data one is able to gather. It follows that psychoanalytic observation of creative individuals may or may not reveal whatever is crucial to the unique operations of a creative self.

When we say that a form is operating under certain rules or regulations, we should remember that these range from the constraints imposed by the physical limits of the system (e.g., the retina is not responsive to certain wavelengths of light) and the limits imposed by the particular environment one lives in (e.g., certain sorts of behavior are more acceptable than others, and certain kinds are strictly disallowed). Unfortunately, psychoanalysis does not always have a neat set of rules by which we can observe the proper or healthy operations of the phenomena we study, and we likewise have some uncertainty about the rules we follow in our therapeutic encounters. But we need to know that, either explicitly or implicitly, we do seem to apply a sort of normative program to developmental lines as well as to the process of analytic treatment. Such rules are noted as evidence of proper functioning of the observed system. In somewhat circular fashion, we say that our evaluation of structure is based on unchanging or else slowly changing function. Our rules of governance of a system or organization are a complex amalgam of cultural values, personal prejudices, and empirically tested and validated prescriptions of behavior. Examples of rules, which will need much further elaboration, range from the capacity to free-associate, to Freud's goals of maturity being the ability to love and to work. Examples of not following the rules take the form of acting-out behavior or inability to form and/or sustain a workable transference. Rules become a measure of intact or healthy structure.

The elements or components of a structure call for an important point of differentiation. If a given organization is operating smoothly under certain agreed-upon rules and procedures, then the particular aspects of one or another part of the pattern are of secondary importance or become part of the background. Just as the 8:05 is considered to be doing its job if it arrives, departs and delivers its passengers according to schedule, so, too, is a self considered to be functioning well if it adheres to its own set of plans. Likewise, the makeup of the train, although of interest, is not of primary relevance. This applies equally to the ego and to the self-organization. To follow Kohut's suggestion in this regard, we would say that mirroring, for example, is a function that is able to be carried out by a variety of selfobjects, without attention to their individual makeup. If we grant this assumption, then we might go so far as to say that the particular meanings attributed to any given for of ideation or behavior by an individual are *delivered* by the self-system, but may be essentially of secondary significance. Now meaning *per se* is a hotly debated point in and outside of psychology. What something or someone means is often felt to be the hallmark of a depth psychology. In case conferences, it is frequently delivered in a somber tone, loaded with profound significance. Without in any way taking away from the profundity of that moment, we would offer the idea that meaning(s) is subsumed under the smooth functioning of the self. The structure delivers the meaning. It is the framework within which meaning and its associated term, understanding, are able to operate and to be articulated. Just as rules and regulations demand a more elaborate description, so too does this complex notion of meaning. For now we would note that it may be the case that our attention to particular moments of meaning detract from our comprehension of the underlying framework or matrix within which it lies and can be expressed.

A true structural psychology can be outlined which places structural considerations at the bottom or as the basis of all of our study of individuals. A given bit of behavior may mean something that can be decoded, much as Freud and his successors in psychoanalysis have done with symptoms, parapraxes, and jokes. In a word, there is a story of sorts told within each such unpacking of this or that mental complex. But it is also the case that the delivery of the symptom or joke reflects an underlying structure that is basic and is revealed along with, and as well as, the phenomenon being scrutinized. Some stories are decipherable only if this structure is intact; and whether or not the story is demonstrated in one or another manner becomes of secondary importance. There is no doubt that much of modern psychoanalysis has assumed some sort of structural integrity as a given, and thereupon has devoted itself wholly to the intriguing task of investigating the varied forms of meaning that an intactstructure would deliver. Here we see the myriad ways the oedipal conflict is lived out. But perhaps a case can be made that this is a misplaced emphasis, since it is the system that merits our attention. To pursue our analogy, the train tracks must be intact, and what emerges from the system is understanding.

With this fundamental positing of understanding as the *sine qua non* of structural formation, I can outline what I believe is the manner of its achievement. The sequence is a simple one:

1. The analyst must first understand the patient; he does so by way of empathy. Here we employ any and all theories the analyst uses, and these, in turn, guide and direct our empathy. Such an effort usually demands a lengthy investment in the emotional life of the patient and will, of necessity, be as partial and limited or as broad as our theories and our empathy will allow. Without this requisite understanding, there is little or no relationship, but probably there is always some minimal empathic linkage in any sort of human communication. Thus the spectrum: from minimal to wholehearted comprehension of another person. This is, of course, not to be confused with agreeing with the other or accepting things at face value. Empathy requires understanding in depth.

2. The analyst must explain what he understands to the patient. Here we see the wide range and variability in language and style analysts employ. Patients, over time, learn the particulars of the language of the analyst and soon (themselves) communicate in terms of breasts or penises or conflict or selfobjects. We have no good empirical data as to whether the specialness of the vocabulary matters that much, but it seems to be of relatively little consequence. The capacity of patient and analyst to negotiate a set of reasonable explanations about the patient is one of devising a common language (Goldberg, 1987). The movement from understanding to explaining on the part of the analyst leads to the next step.

3. The patient begins to understand himself or herself. At this point we may employ a variety of theoretical models to make sense of the phenomenon: such terms as the observing ego are commonly utilized here. Essentially, what I propose is that the patient develops a capacity to be empathic with himself. This achievement of self-empathy is patterned after the same kind of empathy that has been experienced by the patient in his relationship with the analyst. This capacity to understand oneself is the essential of structure formation and consists of taking up a position at a different level from that of the mere experience of being understood. This position or level is attained and maintained by the following and last point of structure formation.

4. The patient, once empathic with himself, develops a capacity for self-reflection. This is achieved in the same manner as that in which the analyst manages to reach common ground with the patient, i.e., explaining what is understood. Every patient has to devise some system of explaining himself to himself, i.e., moving from self-empathy to self-reflection. Perhaps this is equally comprehensible as the movement from analogue or totalities to digital sequencing, or from right-brain to left-brain processing. The point of this is that understanding is made communicable by way of some sort of story, just as empathy becomes transformed by way of some logical explanation. We, all of us, become structured in terms of the way we understand ourselves and thereby explain ourselves to us. Only with self-reflection can we say that true structure, in a psychoanalytic sense, has been achieved. This is not to say that this is the way of all structure, say in normal development, but rather to insist that the change in psychoanalysis evolves the specialness of self-empathy and self-reflection. We just do not simply "grow up" in psychoanalysis, but rather accomplish an integrative task that does what normal development might be said to have done. This last point is to contrast the understanding a child requires for normal growth with what an analyst offers to a patient. Every child requires an atmosphere of understanding others to prosper, and all

parents utilize a variety of explanations to deal with the mysteries of such growth.

This sequence then corresponds to the set of responses that differentiate the person who does something correctly from one who is able to consider the how and why of what he does: the man who merely responds correctly in Chinese from the man who understands it.

It is, of course, impossible to compress any clinical example into a demonstration of this sequence of structure formation. I can only give the barest outline of such an occurrence while assuming that a host of material must be taken for granted.

CLINICAL EXAMPLE

My patient is a male homosexual who came into psychoanalysis not so much to change his sexual preference, but to gain some control over it. He seemed unable to limit his sexual contacts both in terms of frequency and perversity, and he feared doing something that would damage his physical well-being as well as his social status. I shall briefly recapitulate the above-listed steps.

1. Prolonged empathic immersion is the phrase employed to designate the process by which the analyst gains access to a patient's inner states. My own guiding theory contained the thesis that the patient's sexual behavior was designed to handle other more painful affect states. I naturally had other preconceptions and prejudices, which made up my theory, which, in turn, would allow me to understand the patient. Such an understanding takes a long time to accomplish, because it is both a matter of trial and error and of introspective scrutiny. The necessary ingredients of regression, alliance, etc., allow for continual empathic contact with the patient, which becomes focused on the transference, or my particular version of transference. The transference enables empathy to function in depth and allows empathic access to repressed or disavowed psychic contents.

As the patient feels understood—and this is not a matter of some mystical resonance, but rather a continual recognition of someone else who is attuned in the manner that all of us ascertain when we are understood or misunderstood-his sexual behavior seems to diminish and vanish. Since this is a composite case, I can attest to this phenomenon being almost commonplace.

2.   My explanations of what I understand are not so clearly delineated from the how and why of my understandings as I might wish. They do, however, fit primarily into the category of transference interpretations. So much has been written on this subject that I can do no more than point up that, for me, these have to do with the ongoing relationship with the analyst, and they in turn are buttressed by reconstructive narratives. One only turns to the past to confirm what is noted and narrated in the present-day transference. Of course, my explanations are couched in the language and sense of my theoretical bias, but more often than not the patient and I develop a very personal language that best characterizes him. This particular man is an academician, and so I find myself speaking in a more erudite manner than with others.

The nature of my explanations had to do with the emergence of the aforementioned sexual behavior following analytic separations or disruptions whether physical, as over weekends, or emotional, as in misunderstandings. The patient's parents had divorced when he was five, and the father had visited erratically until he was thirteen. He was always caught between the parents, especially over money issues and most severely when his mother was forced to go to work when he began school. During the analysis he recalled returning home to an empty house after school when he was around eight. He took off his clothes, dressed himself in a sheet, stood naked in front of a mirror, and employed various other erotic maneuvers to soothe himself. So, too, was the loneliness of analytic absences handled by some form of sexual diversion. His sexual behavior allowed for a feeling of mastery and control over the disorganizing state that ensued with the loss of the father.

3. This particular patient's capacity to experience the painful affects he had otherwise handled by sexualization, characterized this next stage of self-empathy. Just as Freud (1917) noted in "Mourning and Melancholia," the move from investment in another to investment in oneself is the primary mechanism wherein one takes over a function or a characteristic or a symptom. Patients who experience empathic immersion in their lives soon become able to perform in this manner to themselves. This man observed the emergence of profound loneliness preceding a vacation that had been noteworthy for a period of intense sexual fantasies that seemed to have no corresponding impetus to action. He was intrigued and even amused by the variety and frequency of his sexual thoughts, yet showed no interest in visiting the old bars and haunts of his previous life of excitement. With the cessation of his perverse activity, and the persistent manifestation of his sadness, he began to see himself in a different light and to consider the whys and wherefores of the same sadness of his childhood. This then leads to the next point of self-reflection.

4. Language is the main medium of analytic traffic, and is the dominating theme in our discourse. It enables one to "nail down" the global or physiologic, or even mysterious feeling states that are a part of every analytic treatment. Everyone, whether an analytic patient or not, proceeds through life by using a variety of explanatory constructs to handle the uncertainties of the world. All parents, likewise, employ a range of devices to explain and predict the behavior and development of their children. Some of these theories are quite simple, some bizarre, some animistic, and some quite sophisticated. The degree of effectiveness of a theory, i.e., the pragmatic criterion, usually determines its survival.

    As we go through life with this capacity to self-reflect, we may achieve some mastery over ourselves and our world. The self-reflection of the analyzed patient is most congenial to this mastery, based as it is on self-empathy and guided by the "most-informed" theory (Rangell, 1985) we have offered the patient. My own patient now is captured by an intense effort to make sense of his life in terms of explaining to himself why he feels the way he does and (using an analytic theory) how it came about. He relates more and more to the absent father and to his yearning to recapture that missing experience.

One must assume that this particular patient's story about his life has validity or is "true" in the sense that it accurately pictures or represents the past. This is the point of contention that leads to a preoccupation with the tally argument (Grünbaum, 1985) and that allows psychoanalysis to claim a place as a historical discipline. Freud offered a variety of ways to determine the validity of an interpretation in terms of the ensuing associations, but there seems to be no solid way that one can establish whether the past does tally or whether a fiction is being constructed. Many stories and many meanings are created and told during treatment. If psychoanalysis aims at the establishment and maintenance of an intact structure, then it may be important to recognize that these narratives are more in the nature of epiphenomena than they are related to the formation and dissolution of psychopathology. It is our capacity to understand, to feel understood, and then to reflect on this totality that is primary: the narrative is what the train delivers, but the intact system is what underlies the capacity. Self-reflection is the exercise of the system.

Such reflection is not to be equated with the popularized self-analytic function. That term refers, for the most part, to a mechanism available for conflicts and problems that require, conscious or otherwise, an active re-enactment of an analytic experience, albeit in miniature. Self-reflection, like structure, is an ever-available and continually used attribute by which we make our way in the world. So now my patient considers, scrutinizes, and explains his feelings to himself in a different, more controlled, and more effective manner than was previously available to him.

As in our Chinese parable, the work of self-reflection is at a higher level or of a different logical type than that of whatever behavior one may manifest or consider. It is an act of examination that frames the other act and by so doing allows for the (quality of) regulation we attribute to structure. But structure can no longer be considered to be the dams or channels or levees that a theory of energy flow might suggest. Rather, structure is pattern, and patterns lead to words such as organization and system which, in turn, suggest the hierarchic levels we have outlined.

The broad reconstructions that my patient employs as part of his new story about himself are based on his missing father who disappeared at a crucial time in the patient's development. This loss did not allow certain psychological consolidations to take place. They do not so much take place in analysis as they might in childhood (with the now available analyst); rather, the patient accomplishes an analogous process *vis à vis* the analyst. The process of such accomplishment has to do with the nontraumatic and phase-specific losses of the analyst and his function (i.e., empathy and explanation) substituting for the traumatic experience of childhood. The filling in of one's life or one's self or one's personal narrative constitutes the content that is used in self-reflection. My patient had to retrace in the transference the variety of feelings of rage and discontent at the absent father, longing and its concealment for the possibly visiting father, and unbearable excitement at being with the father. These are the elements that, once recaptured, can be thought about, considered, and lifted to a new level of self-comprehension.

Conclusion

Structural changes in psychoanalytic treatment come about by way of the transference, and form on the basis of the explanations given to this relationship. The transference develops from the empathic links established between patient and analyst. Although transference is ubiquitous and universal, only a continual level of empathic attunement allows for a workable transference. The understanding achieved by the stable transference must be subjected to the varieties of explanation employed by analysts. They are all but approximations of whatever is the true state of affairs. Some work better than others, and it would be folly not to be as informed as possible about alternative explanations. But since they are all but partial answers, they all have varying degrees of success. Thus every patient can expect improvement in varying degrees, and it is rare treatment that has no yield whatsoever. In this sense, some structural change can be seen in every treatment, and we hope that the most propitious one is the one we have to offer. Like the man in the Chinese room, we must do more than make the right moves; we must be able to understand and explain what we are doing to others.

REFERENCES

Bateson, G. (1972). *Steps to an Ecology of Mind.* New York: Ballantine Books.

Freud, S. (1917). Mourning and melancholia. *Standard Edition* 14.

Goldberg, A. (1987). Psychoanalysis and negotiation. *Psychoanalytic Quarterly* 56:109– 129.

Grünbaum, A. (1985). *The Foundations of Psychoanalysis.* Berkeley: University of California Press.

Rangell, L. (1985). One the theory of theory in psychoanalysis and the relation of theory to psychoanalytic therapy. *Journal of the American Psychoanalytic Association* 33:59-92.

Saussure, F. de (1916). *A Cause in General Linguistics* New York: Philosophical Library.

Searle, J. (1984). *Minds, Brains and Science* Cambridge: Harvard University Press.

Between Empathy and Judgment (1999)

A patient of mine, whom I shall call Karl, said that he wanted very much to write a letter to Ann Landers or Dear Abby. He had come to me after seeing several therapists preparatory to his "coming out" as homosexual, and in each case these therapists were on hand to help him implement this decision of his. Because of my own admitted uncertainty about what he "really" was, and for other reasons based on my inquiring and expressing concern about his life apart from his avowed sexuality, he decided to go into analysis with me. In the analysis, he discovered that his homosexual fantasies were serving what essentially were nonsexual purposes, and he soon became for the first time rather actively heterosexual.

A friend of mine who is a gay therapist—that is, someone who is himself gay and primarily treats gays—tells me that my patient is really heterosexual, and this is now what my patient claims, and what he wants to tell Dear Ann and Dear Abby. He wants them to know that one should never urge anyone to declare himself gay or be directed to a gay therapist or to take any such definitive steps until and unless one knows for sure. And so here is the crux of the matter. Karl says that his analysis allowed him to discover what he really was—i.e., he was able to know for sure, and without this, he may well have decided to become gay. That possibility now offends him. He feels that he was very close to a terrible mistake. Interestingly, he feels there are lots of other aspects of himself that are likewise what he really may be or seems to be or would like to be, and that he wishes he could be made different. He would have liked his analysis to change these for him as well. He wishes he were more sociable—why hasn't his analysis helped him there? He feels he is somewhat lazy and now insists that analysis should make him more industrious. When I suggest that he seems to be willing to discover and modify certain things about himself—like his sexuality, say—and to regard these as a mark of authenticity, while at the same time he comes upon other qualities—say, a certain aloofness in relationships—and considers them questionably authentic but eminently alterable, he agrees. But he cannot settle for analysis being confined to the mere unlocking of potentials. Is it not meant to do more? Should it not only allow or enable us to be different, but to make us so?

Karl says that he thinks analysts feel that a patient is like an unlit Roman candle on the Fourth of July. The analyst lights it and steps to the side to watch, hoping to admire the display. Some Roman candles are splendid, and some are duds. Blame the factory. But surely one needs to take more responsibility for the display, since no one really seems to step to the side. Karl agrees that his own analysis could not be said to have been clearly weighted on the side of heterosexuality, but he has always suspected that I had a bias in its favor. The neutral stance that I claimed was, in truth, more related to a personal confusion of mine than to a principled conviction. He and I shared a goal, and to say otherwise would be to hide behind a cloak of neutrality that seemed more transparent than real. Or so he says.

This variation on the nature-nurture argument has in the past had a rather clear solution in psychoanalysis. Part of the solution is the existence of real physical constraints. We cannot make people taller or shorter, but perhaps when it comes to weight we are a bit less certain. However, as each new evidence of the physical or biological makes its appearance, we tend to retreat. When we learn of the neurological basis for obsessive-compulsive disorder, we come to read the case of the Rat Man with a different eye. When we become convinced of the genetic basis of bipolar disease, we begin to think less of the dynamic formulations once ascribed to it; but when these same genes are called into question, we quickly rethink our psychological position. Thus we become prisoners of the latest and best physical basis for the psyche. And surely sexuality is bedrock—or is it?

The other part of the solution for what can and should be done for patients, and thus what is in their best interest, is our own set of standards and norms. These tell us how people ought to be, and we work to get our patients as close to them as possible. We have all devised some set of developmental steps that we consider normal and therefore desirable. To travel along the correct path of development and achieve a goal that we consider optimal is the blueprint, secret or open, against which we measure our patients. Thus, in our supposed willingness for patients to follow a path of self-fulfillment, we also posit a map that tells us just about where they should end up.

Sexuality and gender seem to be, or should be, easy. For a while there, everyone had to be heterosexual. Of late, psychiatry and (reluctantly) psychoanalysis have moved to a clear espousal of normal homosexuality. For each of these poles there seems to be a pathology as well; i.e., there exists a pathological heterosexuality that serves to cover over or defend against a variety of painful situations, up to and including homosexuality. The situation is ever more complex. We regularly see heterosexually promiscuous or deviant men or women who struggle against homosexual intimacy, just as we see gay promiscuity defend against heterosexual closeness. At one point in his treatment Karl said that he might have gone either way, and so one surely has to consider bisexuality as yet another aspect of normal sexual performance. Is it really the case that psychoanalysis allows people to determine what they really are, without the analyst also making some determination? Is it not possible that there is no such thing as what a person really is?

In an excellent review based primarily on Ogden's variation of Kleinian thinking, Sweetnam (1996) argues that gender, being dialectical, may feel fixed at certain times and fluid at others. She claims that different psychological positions—the paranoid and the depressive—provide a context for the anxieties, defenses, object relationship, subjectivity, and symbolization that alter the quality of gender experience within a context that goes beyond a linear developmental timetable or the comprehension of singular identifications. Sweetnam's intention is to balance the biological determinism ascribed to Freud with the newly popular cultural determinism of other investigators, by proposing a framework that embraces both fluidity and firmness. The essential point of her effort is to reveal our psychology as constrained, perhaps trapped, between biology and culture, the body and the world.

At any given moment in analysis we seem to making some judgment of the way things ought to be, and we tend to direct the process according to that judgment. It is a judgment based on what we claim to be correct and real and true. But just as biology seems to help at certain times, so at others cultural factors seem to weigh in. There can be little doubt that people can go more than one way in more than one domain. It seems a bit naive to say either that we let the patient decide, or that we allow normal development to unfold. We are not merely watching. However, once we relinquish our neutral stance as untenable, we are committed to standing somewhere. Lest we too quickly claim allegiance to a newly popular embrace of "authenticity," we should probably recognize that one can be an authentic scoundrel as well as a saint. Where once we felt that we need only be empathic with our patients, we now find that we cannot help but judge them as well. Sometimes the two stances seem to be at odds, in need of some principle of unity. And so now to the reconciliation of empathy and judgment.

Two Perspectives

At the outset I would like to clarify some of the basic positions that I see as fundamental to psychoanalysis. It is first and foremost a psychology devoted to what some philosophers and many scientists have called a first-person perspective—that is, one that centers on a subjective view of the world that says that *I* know, *I* see, *I* experience. The contrasting viewpoint is that of the third person: objective, external, making statements about him, her, or it that sees, knows, experiences. First-person perspectives are available to introspection, conscious personal scrutiny, and assessment, and are regarded by some as incorrigible, since one is, or should be, the sole determinant of a personal experience. By contrast, a third-person perspective is available to objective, public examination and testing, and is the clear winner in a scientific tug-of-war. To complete the picture, we consider a second-person perspective, the experience that *you* are having, to be graspable by another by way of an inner comparison or vicarious introspection. It has been the sad fate of psychoanalysis to have been ever tempted by a third-person perspective as an ultimate goal to be reached. Most neurophysiologists lay claim to a third-person perspective as allowing a complete description and explanation of any and all brain phenomena and so as the goal of all studies of behavior. But most, if certainly not all, scientists also agree that first-and third-person psychologies are irreducible, one to another. There can be no elimination of the "I" experience. Biology and social psychology can never replace depth psychology. These remain complementary but distinct perspectives.

It is worth a moment to explain and justify this thesis of the irreducibility of first-and third-person perspectives, since the tendency to treat depth psychology as a way station to some sought-for biosocial final explanation seems solidly entrenched. Psychoanalysis thus becomes wedged in between biology and social psychology in a scientistic effort to explain from an objective point of view all there is to know about people. But just as no study limited to the make-up of DNA can reveal the final phenotype, so too the study of neuronal pathways demands an experience if we are to identify precisely the fate of this or that brain activity. When we know just how and why the brain produces the color brown, we still need to determine exactly what color is experienced. Nor should we be fooled into thinking that knowing enough about the brain will close the gap. There exists such a gap for both empirical and conceptual reasons. No matter how much we subscribe to the premise that all phenomena are ultimately neural, as surely they are, we need to recognize with equal certainty that psychological phenomena are not thereby eliminated. Indeed, a famed perceptual physiologist has stated recently that "perceptual findings must be considered primary, and if the neurophysiological data do not agree, the neurophysiological data must be wrong" (Uttal 1997, p. 300). The first-person perspective is essential.

On the social side of the ledger is the evidence recently accumulating that calls into question the biological innateness of sexuality, especially as regards women, some of whom seem capable of choosing their sexual identity (Golden 1997). Research seems to suggest that some women who identify themselves as bisexual find they are able to entertain the possibility of choosing to be lesbian or heterosexual. In the presence of powerful social and cultural factors, biology seems to take a back seat. The fluidity of sexuality is, however, perhaps called into question by reports of that ridiculous experiment by Money (*Chicago Tribune*, March 14, 1997), who advised parents to raise as a girl a boy whose penis had been accidentally amputated. After countless surgeries and hormone treatments, the child finally insisted on becoming the boy he knew he was. One may theorize that biology or early imprinting was a factor here, but I suspect that an analytically informed observer could see that simply everyone around the child knew he was a boy masquerading as a girl and that the communication of that fact, however unconscious, was omnipresent. Thus, it seems sometimes that biology rules the day and at other times that social factors predominate. Nonetheless, a first-person psychology remains valid, despite whatever third-person issues are raised, because only such a perspective allows us entry into the personal experiences of the subject. It must be admitted, however, that sole reliance on a first-person perspective has caused problems that continue to plague our field.

The effort to establish psychoanalysis on what was felt to be a firmer, more scientific ground certainly began with Freud's 1895 Project. That effort was taken up later by Heinz Hartmann, who insisted that psychoanalysis was an explaining, rather than an understanding, psychology. Hartmann said that the study of forces in opposition, of energy and its expression, was the scientific ground of psychoanalysis. For him, an understanding of psychology is necessarily unreliable and so fails to be a science. Only an explanation of causal relations in the mind, he believed, could bring psychoanalysis to its rightful place in science, and these causal connections are made not from reports of subjective experience but from (in his words) the actual mental connections. Empathy not only is rife with potential errors, but neglects that part of our personality— the unconscious—that is fundamental to psychoanalysis. Hartmann wanted an objective psychoanalysis that was reliable and capable of validation. His was essentially a plea for a third-person psychology in which our judgments or truths must rule.

The love affair of analysis and objectivity was certainly cooled, if not shattered, by the central role assigned to empathy by Heinz Kohut and his colleagues. Although the two Heinzes were friends socially, ideologically they were quite far apart. Kohut's concentration on empathy as vicarious introspection indeed moved psychoanalysis back into a first-person perspective. This focus has been taken up in countless variations on the theme—from an insistence on seeing things primarily from the patient's point of view to the embracing of a postmodern or relativist position that calls into question the very existence of truth or fact or objectivity. Things are what they are felt to be and not what others say they are. What happened to the patient as a child is a question not of history but of meaning. Rashomon becomes the new cultural symbol of psychoanalysis, as at our conferences "it all depends" becomes an introductory mantra. To see the world from the perspective of the patient as to suspend judgment and to enjoy, perhaps momentarily, a trial identification with the other.

A problem that presents itself in any singular focus on empathy is that it is either a sustained or a momentary inquiry into a conscious experience. When one steps into the shoes of another to vicariously introspect, the material available is by definition that which is conscious.

A first-person perspective entails experiences that have qualities and are realized. We own our experiences, and they are a conscious part of us. Imagine the difference between a name you cannot remember and one you cannot possibly have known. The first is felt as something that must be brought back into awareness, while the second allows no ownership claims and remains outside the psyche. For those who would limit our data to the empathically accessible, therefore, the role and even the existence of the psychoanalytic unconscious becomes problematic.

To be sure, the complex role of empathy in psychotherapy and psychoanalysis is not diminished by a recognition of its inherent limitations. But we need to add a crucial component to the data obtained by empathy. A component that belongs to the observer, it may be thought of as consisting of preconceptions or perspectives or theories, but it is essentially derived from the eye of the other. It is a judgment. The balance to the purely subjective experience of the patient is offered by the judgments brought by the observer. These are the observer's theories, preconceptions, morality. If the observer believes in the unconscious, it is added to the mix. To gain access to another, we carry ourselves and our beliefs along, and so every first-person perspective, every study of individual meaning, is seen and then changed by the onlooker. (And it needs perhaps to be said that every third-person perspective also carries with it the subjective coloration of the observer.) The psychoanalytic observer, the empathic student of a patient, carries convictions and judgments not only about the patient's reported experiences but also about what is known at first only to the analyst: the content of the patient's unconscious. Initially this is felt by the patient as foreign and separate. The unconscious is experienced not as first-person phenomena but as something alien and apart. To bring it into subjective experience, to realize Freud's "Where id was, there ego shall be" (once considered the work of psychoanalysis), is to move from the third-person perspective on the contents of the unconscious—however conceptualized—to the first-person perspective of subjective ownership and individual meanings. The two Heinzes—Kohut and Hartmann—must be joined in this reconciliation of empathy and judgment.

The autobiography of the analysand is "since Rousseau a construction, not a representation" (Bernstein 1995, p. 70), and into it is introduced what the analyst knows/presumes to be present, primarily if not exclusively, in the patient's unconscious. These additions are the shifts or switches between facts and meanings, objective and subjective, judgment and empathy, that we all live with as we understand our patients while simultaneously judging them. It should perhaps be emphasized that empathy or understanding or first-person psychology is certainly not opposed to judgment or explanation or third-person psychology; rather, the two interpenetrate. A similarly false dichotomy is often drawn between creativity (ascribed, erroneously, exclusively to artistic endeavors) and discovery (falsely attributed exclusively to the scientific). The argument over whether psychoanalysis is an art or a science is played out on the same erroneous basis, as these are ends on a continuum rather than separate domains. To fault the empathic approach by noting its contamination with inferences is as wrong as condemning objectivity by seeing the subjective component in it. These are conceptual errors. Empathy and judgment must penetrate one another, as do discovery and creation. However, since an analysis is an exercise in first-person psychology, we need to see it as what one writer has called "a theory-mediated autobiography" (Bernstein 1995, p. 70). Thus we see that all sorts of theory, from Freudian to Kleinian to

Kohutian to Lacanian, can be used for an acceptable redescription of childhood and indeed all personal experience. All these redescriptions may be true, since the autobiography is shaped by those who create it. What emerges from a psychoanalysis is a first-person account of a life, written by two people, an empathic account interpenetrated by the judgments of the other.

CLINICAL IMPLICATIONS

A return to Karl will afford us a better view of psychoanalysis as a first-person psychology. Karl manifested a type of clinical state that some of us have been studying for some time: the narcissistic behavior disorders. Some of my friends, however, both in psychiatry and psychoanalysis, seem genuinely puzzled by this diagnostic category. They either consider it the result of too much empathic immersion or politely ask me just what those words are supposed to mean. My answer to that question is that these are pathological conditions characterized by behavior considered distasteful, abhorrent, or antisocial, and felt by the actor to be performed as if by another person. Thus, a perfectly respectable citizen will periodically find himself stealing something, a perfectly moral woman will find herself picking up strange men in bars, an otherwise honest person will find himself lying. My patient Karl was a voyeur who would fairly regularly find himself looking at men's penises in locker rooms and masturbating with the immediate image or the memory of it. Karl hated himself for this behavior and spoke of its occurrence as if it were done by someone else, as if he could not, and would not, own it. The cases that a group of us have studied show this phenomenon of disavowal rather routinely; a split in the self seems to allow the coexistence of parallel personalities with different sets of goals and ambitions, different values and needs, indeed seemingly different psychic organizations. Typically, one personality is acknowledged and the other despised; i.e., one is understood and the other is harshly judged. That both are conscious gives no clear answer to the problem posed by the split: one is me and the other is him.

In writing of repression, which Kohut called a "horizontal" split, Freud emphasized the patient's ignorance: "It is a long superseded idea, and one derived from superficial appearances, that the patient suffers from a sort of ignorance, and that if one removes the ignorance by giving him information (about the causal connection of his illness with his life, about his experiences in childhood, and so on) he is bound to recover. The pathological factor is not his ignorance in itself, but the root of his ignorance in his inner resistances; it was they that first called this ignorance into being, and they still maintain it now" (Freud 1910, p. 225). By contrast, the split of disavowal, first noted by Freud in the fetishist (1927), is vertical rather than horizontal; here the patient knows and yet does not acknowledge, as would happen if the contents of the unconscious were made known to the patient and were therefore conscious but not really owned or experienced as part of the self. It is thus a matter not of ignorance but of abhorrence regarding what is known. These patients judge themselves, but not like those who suffer guilt from a harsh superego; rather, they treat themselves as others whom they would shun; they see themselves from a third-person perspective and so disown a part of themselves.

We often note that the anxious or depressed patient is *unable* to step aside from a symptom in order to disavow it. By contrast, a patient of mine with an eating disorder spoke of her binges as if in retrospect she very much disliked that person who stuffed herself with Oreos. In treatment, more often than not, the therapist or analyst joins with the patient in this harsh judgment. The college professor who steals books in an unpredictable and uncontrollable manner very much expects the analyst to be as critical of his behavior as he is. Save for those patients whose behavior disorders dominate their psyches, these patients with vertical splits live a life between understanding and judging and ask the same of their analyst. This now becomes a virtual laboratory for a study of the tension between empathy and judgment. The analyst, struggling to understand and not condemn, shares the split of the patient, while almost simultaneously being asked to condemn until understanding is achieved. When one treats a scoundrel, be it a thief, a liar, a voyeur, or an addict, it is foolhardy to claim neutrality for ourselves. We always take a stand. And some of us even, in turn, judge ourselves harshly or benignly for the stand that we take.

Perhaps one of the more interesting phenomena to have emerged from our study is the wide range of tolerance or intolerance claimed by the analysts in our group. While one of us may be quite content to have a stalker as a patient, another may be totally unable to sustain a therapeutic stance toward such behavior. The analyst who comfortably treats a thief is considered to be himself mildly unusual, but only by some members of the group—until that moment in our discussions when he betrays his own quite corrupt self. And when that moment occurs, he is as astonished as anyone to see himself as a kindred soul to his dishonest patient. The movement from tolerant understanding to critical judgment becomes a rather routine feature of our group discussions, with some members resting more easily in one phase than in another. The dishonesty of one of us is sharply attacked and condemned by the others until, in time, we begin to sense the lack of purity, the inherent contradiction, in all of us. What once were sharp lines of demarcation between right and wrong, truth and falsehood, become shaded into vague areas of personal opinion. We seem unable to find our footing as we shift between the parallel selves of our patients, as we discover shades of the same split within ourselves.

The transition from one perspective to the other is graphically demonstrated by a Lacanian, Slavaj Žižek (1992), who describes the story of a serial killer in the movie *When a Stranger Calls*. He presents the killer first as an unfathomable object, with whom no identification is possible, and then makes a sudden transposition into the perspective of the killer himself. Žižek discusses the two points of view, that of victim and that of murderer, and the sudden twist of the movie: "The entire subversive effect hangs upon the rupture, the passage from one perspective to the other, the change which confers upon the hitherto impossible/unattainable object or body, which gives the untouchable thing a voice and makes it speak, in short, which subjectivizes it" (p. 57). Once captured by the identification with a murderer, we find it difficult to depart from that position to once again objectify and despise him. We are denied the comfort we had previously enjoyed of knowing for sure, a comfort best thought of as a warning, since the interpenetration of empathy and judgment makes for the unstable state more proper to the life of a psychoanalyst. We do, however, manage to carve out positions of resolution, and those positions share both the judgmental condemnation suggested to us by Freud in his consideration of the endpoint of analysis, along with the self-empathy needed to restore balance to an ever-present uncertainty and lack of closure. This resolution maintains, however, the interpenetration of judgment and empathy.

EMPATHY, JUDGMENT, AND TREATMENT

Let us consider empathy as discovery, more or less, and judgment as creation. Moving back and forth between empathy, which aims to discover what is there but at times is inaccessible, and judgment, which creates something by bringing in new materials, is both a paradox and a sought-for state. The autobiographies we create are necessarily shaped by the theories we employ—our judgment—to mediate what we hope to discover in our patients by way of empathy. We discover, by using our theories, what is in the unconscious, but we do so by knowing beforehand what is there to be found. Similarly, our patients come to recognize the split-off areas as really belonging to them, as the foreign territory of the repressed and the disavowed, the psyche split off horizontally or vertically, is joined with the rest of the psyche. In treating patients with behavior disorders, we become able to be empathic first with one side, then with the other, and ultimately with both. We must, however, realize that seeing things exactly as the patient does makes blind men of us both. We need to remain objective about our subjectivity; we always judge or evaluate our meanings as we step aside and see ourselves as we would see another.

This oscillation between empathy and judgment has a counterpart in our consideration of what we find in a patient versus what we bring to our investigations. With Karl, I knew I wanted to rid him of his voyeurism, but I could also rather easily identify with that activity; I was more puzzled than anything about his both wanting and hating his homosexual longings. Over time, as I became convinced that they represented a sexualization related to the transference, I brought my judgment into his analysis and created a new configuration.

The history of psychoanalytic technique has itself made this journey from discovery to creation. The earliest pioneers in the field were intent on discovering the contents and makeup of the unconscious; the latest contributors, advocates of the various interactive theories, address the jointly created products of analytic and therapeutic work. Most contemporary investigators seem to seek a resolution to the dilemma through some sort of fifty-fifty compromise. No one seems any longer to deny the importance of the analyst's person. Nor is anyone likely to say that the patient's past and unconscious are not to be reckoned with. Unfortunately, the resolution seems often to be reached by means of a popularity poll, and more often than not is generalized to apply to all of our patients. But what I have learned from Karl and so many others is the simple truth that sometimes I matter and sometimes I do not. I may matter when I wish I did not, and when I really wish I did, I often don't. It is different with every patient, just as I am different myself with each of them. One might even say that Karl found what he wanted in me: that peculiar combination of being able both to understand him and to judge him, a combination that differed enough to allow for a change but was close enough to allow a connection. With perfect empathy he would have had no chance; with unrelenting judgment he would have had no space.

Because of the moral issues that are so salient in them, behavior disorders are striking in their appeal to our individual judgments. However, moral concern exists to some extent in every treatment we conduct. It is regularly concealed within our theories and in our particular views of what we consider right and proper, normal and expectable. Every form of psychopathology calls forth a variety of beliefs or opinions, which essentially are our prejudices (Warnke 1987). There is no way we can see a patient without our preconceptions and prejudices, but they do not have the same effect on all patients. Sometimes, with some patients, empathy dominates the treatment, while others seem most attuned to our individual inputs: to both our personalities and our theories. Today's psychoanalysts run the risk of attributing either too much or too little to their presence and, thereby, of losing sight of the individual patient's varying needs. We must always focus on the first-person perspective, which requires that we consider the impact of our input on the patient, but the great need of future psychoanalytic research is to better access which patient has that as a central concern and which as peripheral. We cannot discount the possibility that the idea of our significance may be just another prejudice of ours. Being empathic surely must entail being able to judge what we mean and what we have brought to our patients. This can be neither disregarded nor made too much of.

Biological and physical constraints, in ourselves and in our patients, become interwoven with subjective experience and the culture in which we find ourselves. The necessary interpenetration of first-and third-person perspectives makes for the continual reassessment of any particular bit of analytic data. There are no pure forms, and probably no fixed percentages of types of input. Sometimes biology matters a lot, sometimes a little. The same can be said for sociocultural factors and for our own contributions as analysts. Co-construction does not mean equal partners. Transference does not mean that we are just doing our jobs with no ulterior motive. Perhaps this is the feature that makes psychoanalysis so interesting, inasmuch as it has a built-in level of uncertainty.

One last antinomy that seems to bedevil our field is one that most analysts find especially obnoxious: the contradiction that supposedly exists between history and fiction. Since Freud we have been urged to liken ourselves to archaeologists, unearthing the hidden and doing so carefully, cautiously, in order to avoid disturbing the past or contaminating the relics. But these relics are but traces of the past, and they demand an imaginative interpretation to allow us to see, in one scholar's terms, "what I would have witnessed, if I had been there" (White 1978). When we form these imaginary mediations (Ricoeur 1988), we interweave fiction and history, fashioning our reconstructions according to one type of preferred story rather than another. This fictionalization of history allows us to construct at times a tragedy, at other times a comic novel. We begin to write our own imaginative interpretations of what is remembered as history but is recast as a present moment.

A very common psychoanalytic event is the retelling of significant episodes from a patient's childhood. Each recall carries with it a new possibility for reinterpretation and perhaps a new and better understanding. For Karl there was the momentous time, after his parents' divorce, when his father came to take his sister and him out for the weekly parental visit. This historical event, characterized by Karl's feigning sleep so as not to join his sister, became the nucleus for a whole set of scenarios. Sometimes Karl hoped his father would return for him alone. Sometimes he fantasied having time alone with his mother. Sometimes he would give up his act and race to join his father and sister. As analyst, I would imaginatively revisit the scene and silently write the script I hoped was history as represented, but realized was being newly written as a sort of fictionalization of history.

Once again we see an interpenetration, here of history and fiction, just as we did with the first- and third-person perspectives, with discovery and creation, and with empathy and judgment. The mix in each instance, however, is to be considered not as contamination but as enrichment.

POSTSCRIPT

The answer to Karl's lament was offered by himself when he came to see me shortly before his marriage and some months after his official termination. It is apparent to any analyst who listens to this tale that my patient's complaint was composed around that remaining bit of transference directed to the parent who had failed to be perfect and to make his son perfect. Karl told me that he still occasionally wanted to look at men, but that that was something he could manage and live with. His gratitude to me was properly tempered with the disappointment that must accompany any treatment. I was pleased and a little hurt, but was comforted by recognizing that analysis as a profession, and as an individual encounter, is a very mixed bag.

REFERENCES

Bernstein, J.M. (1995). *Recovering Ethical Life*. London: Routledge.
Freud, S. (1910). "Wild" psycho-analysis. *Standard Edition* 11:221–227.
—— (1927). Fetishism. *Standard Edition* 21:152–157.

Golden, C. (1997). Do women choose their sexual identity? *Harvard Gay and Lesbian Review*, Winter 1997, pp. 18–20.

Ricoeur, P. (1988). *Time and Narrative*. Vol. 3. Chicago: University of Chicago Press.

Sweetnam, A. (1996). The Changing Contexts of Gender: Between Fixed and Fluid Experience *Psychoanalytic Dialogues* 6:437–459.

Uttal, W. R. (1997). Do theoretical bridges exist between experience and neurophysiology? *Perspectives in Biology and Medicine* 40:280–302.

Warnke, G. (1987). *Gadamer: Hermeneutics. Tradition and Reason*. Stanford: Stanford University Press.

White, H. (1978). *The Tropics of Discourse*. Baltimore: Johns Hopkins Press.

Žižek, S. (1992) *Enjoy Your Symptom: Jacques Lacan in Hollywood and Out*. New York: Routledge.

It Is All Interaction (1996)

Somewhere between viewing the analyst as detached observer and in-formed interpreter of the analysand's associations and viewing the analyst as active participant in the patient's psychic life, there lies a truth about the nature and degree of analyst-patient interaction. In another sense, however, there is a very certain participation of the analyst in every patient's psychol-ogy. Perhaps this lies at a different level from whatever the analyst may or may not do; that is, it is beyond overt interaction. It comes from the fact that inaction may count as much as action, silence as much as talking, and understanding as much as misunderstanding. There is no certain path to neutrality and/or nonparticipation, since the proper stance of an analyst is always to be able to be surprised at the results of his or her presence as well as behavior. Everything seems to matter, and so interaction needs to be considered along a spectrum of accidental to intentional, as well as inci-dental to meaningful.

If we assume that the patient always has an effect on the analyst and that the same holds true for that of the analyst upon the patient, then we need to clarify both the nature of the proper constraints of an analysis and how to manage and explain this inevitable mutuality of interaction. As to the first, it is clear that we evoke moral and ethical limits to ana-lyst-patient interaction. We likewise insist upon actions or restraints that facilitate treatment. We abstain from physical contact, both because we feel it improper and because it impedes the treatment. But not every-thing is so easy since what belongs to the second category of helping or hindering the analysis is only determinable by our theory of analytic process. And this is where the trouble starts. We fall back on theory as guide, and we are not all on the same road.

One device employed to handle the supposed problem of interaction has been to posit analysis as either a one-person or body, or two-body event. The first lays claim to everything happening within the patient or within the mind of the patient and so might support a stance of noninteraction, save for those (Boeskey, 1988) who claim that we can and do interact while still holding to the intrapsychic posture. The second, or two-body, model is always a variant of interpersonal activities. This assumes persons to be clearly defined entities that pass messages between one another and so effect one another. The analyst influences the patient but is equally liable to be touched and even changed. Interaction here, that is, between persons, becomes the whole ballgame, while interaction in the one-body system is more of an interference of the process or an alerting mechanism to the analyst. We need to study how we talk about this mutual influence.

WHEN DOES A PERSON BECOME AN OBJECT? WHEN DOES AN OBJECT BECOME A REPRESENTATION?

Psychoanalysis adds a gloss to this minor debate about one or two persons by making persons into objects. I think it a fair question to ask: "Just when does a person become an object?" since the latter term enjoys a place in analytic theory that more often than not becomes a shorthand for the former and so leads to an uncertainty of definition. Persons have relations with other persons, persons usually have names, and persons are social beings. Objects are derived from Freud's claim that they are the aim of drive gratification. The words are not interchangeable. Objects are stimulators of instincts, gratifying of instincts when serving for discharge, or binding, or damning of instincts when frustrating of discharge. Without a psychoanalytic explanation or theory, there is no sense to the concept object. Thus, what happens between persons (as opposed to objects) is interpersonal or better: social psychology. It is the interaction between two persons viewed from the outside by an observer, and, fortunately or not, it is not a psychoanalytic perspective. For that, we must turn to the object concept, since that term only comes about by way of analytic theory, and so the field of object relations must somehow link up with a theory that depends either upon the drives or else upon another place of the term in the theory, that is, in the formation of the ego or of any psychic structure. To speak of object relations in terms such as closeness or intimacy or meaningfulness is to confuse the social world of relationships with the rather strict and confining place of objects in psychoanalytic theory. This, I believe, has led to one major confusion about interaction in psychoanalysis, since there is a tendency to conflate social, that is, visible, behavior, between the analyst and the patient with that of intrapsychic phenomena. But we know that what is seen or intended may be a far cry from what is felt and experienced. The first is interpersonal, the second intrapsychic, but both are interactions.

The second great major confusion comes from the long struggle of psychoanalysis to adequately position the mind. Perhaps no one of our great analytic theoreticians was more guilty of sowing this particular conceptual disorder than was Edith Jacobson. In her monumentally significant paper, "The Self and the Object World" (1954), which she later expanded to a book (1964), she led our theory down the two-world path: an inner world of images and an outer one of the real world. As she says (1964p. 19), "From the ever-increasing memory traces of pleasurable and unpleasurable ... experiences and of perceptions with which they become associated, images of the body as well as images of the love objects emerge, which, at first vague and variable, gradually expand and develop into consistent and more or less realistic endopsychic representations of the object world and of our own self." There is is: two sets of entities or worlds, the external one of objects and the internal one of somewhat accurate images. The tremendous appeal of this model has led psychoanalysis into the present era of two worlds: the real world of action that is visible to all and a miniaturized one of unseen replicas or representations that are inevitably tainted or contaminated by fantasies or drives or whatever. The resulting disparity between these two worlds in this model has led us to all sorts of trouble. It is a neat model for explaining the supposed failures to accept reality. It is a model of treatment designed to reconcile the disparity between fantasy and reality. It is basically a computer model of input, registration, and output. It is marvelously convenient and clear. And it is probably wrong.

That is not to say that the world may not be represented in some way or other but, rather, that this model treats the mind as a sequence of operations: first, we perceive the world, we then search for a comparison or match in the mind, and then we respond. This is a model made popular by Artificial Intelligence researchers: one that insists that a mental state is a relation to a representation. When we see an apple, we compare it with an inner representation of an apple to see if it matches. When we want to tie our shoe, we search for the shoe-tying program, activate it, and proceed. The program or the representation is interposed between the world and the subject. The world is real, the representations are facsimiles, and a proper match is our aim. Indeed, our treatment is posited on this disparity of worlds.

In contrast to this model is one that says that a mental state can be a direct relation to an object. The difference is that this alternative second model removes the dichotomy of subject versus object, as well as that of the subject standing outside of and perceiving the world. A new model literally opens the self to the world. Thus, there is but one world. But it is not the same world for all of us. Our perceptions are not those of the supposed "real world," but are themselves determined by whatever unconscious elements our theory proposes, that is, drives, fantasies, or deficits. Representations of the mind participate in the construction of this world. They do not, as some theorists suggest, operate in a separate theater of activity. To do this requires creating a miniaturized inner world populated with images and endowing these so-called images with all sorts of qualities and abilities and attributes. Following is a description of projective identification from a recent psychiatric article (Goldstein, 1991):

> [I]n step 1 the patient projects onto the analyst an object representation of a powerful parent, while identifying with a self representation of a helpless victimized child. Then, in step 2, the patient projects onto the analyst a self-representation of a victimized child, while identifying with an object representation of a powerful parent. Step 2, in this example, includes a second and different projection and a second and different identification. [If instead] in step 1 a self-representation of a little, victimized self is projected, then step 2 simply adds intensity to the original projective process [p. 158].

The article professes to explain a mental condition by this fantastic and scientifically unlikely series of phantom entities jumping back and forth across a boundary between two people. There is also a step 3 of reinternalization, which only compounds the improbability of the whole scheme. The problem of this two-world scheme of external world versus internal world is that of assuming a difference between the two, which must be rectified. Any interaction between persons is translated into something like "What does that really mean?" where the *really* becomes the carrier of truth. What seems to be happening in the world is assumed to be but a shadow of its inner significance.

What is the alternative to this two-world scheme? Well, it's basically seeing the mind as part of an open system that connects to and with others. This maneuver allows us to cease the fundamentally flawed argument about interpersonal versus intrapsychic, as well as to examine with some credibility just what the nature of analyst-patient interaction consists of. In a word: it is all interaction. Psychoanalysis, however, is primarily concerned with certain intrapsychic phenomena, and for this the analyst becomes a part of the system of the patient. There is no separation or dichotomy, nor need there be. Interaction versus noninteraction is a nonargument. It is in the psychoanalytic examination of the action that one distinguishes analysts from nonanalysts. It is not to be found in the imaginary realm of internal objects.

Interaction is not what you overtly do, and abstinence is certainly not noninteraction. Just being there is action enough. There is a direct relation between patient and analyst: they are or should be coupled. Once this model is considered, then everything that goes on is an interaction, and only then can the particulars of the theory start to explain the nature of, the reactions to, and the proper consideration of this coupled system.

WHAT DO OBJECTS DO?

It may come as a surprise to learn that most extant analytic theories limit the field of object and object relations to the two above-mentioned points: the involvement with drives and their function in the formation of psychic structure. The many and varied descriptions of relationships that derive from interpersonal and/or interactive psychiatry must either be translated back to these two issues or must be recognized as belonging to the social field, until and unless a new theory or a new dimension to the theory is offered. The analyst who refuses a Kleenex to the patient does so in order to frustrate a drive. The analyst who mirrors a patient does so in order to participate in the psychic structure of the patient, that is, to strengthen a structural tie. And all of the transference and countertransference phenomena that develop and are interpreted should flow from these rather limited roles of objects, that is, parts of psychic structure or the aim of drive gratification. It is probably desirable that all sorts of other issues present themselves in an analysis—issues such as kindness, promptness, generosity, and consideration—but one must take care not to treat them as overriding this more fundamental point. All of these admirable traits are but facilitators for the basic position. Now the whole business is made easier (for some) by recognizing that psychoanalytic drive theory with its dual instincts is pretty much out of date and more wrong than right (Basch, 1988). But to put that to the side for the moment allows us to concentrate on one of the acceptable roles of psychoanalytic objects, which is as a structural component of the psyche or, in one lexicon of terms, as a selfobject.

SELFOBJECTS AND CONNECTIONS

When other persons are seen in a psychoanalytic perspective as participating in the composition of the psyche, much as the analyst participates in the open system of the patient, then we are able to study the nature of the connections. These persons are then translatable into a sort of psychoanalytically legitimate object—a selfobject—and the form of, as well as the degree of, coupling or connection becomes a proper object of study and therefore a clue to the conduct of the analysis. Connections become the basic issue of interaction, and breaks in connections, as well as the establishment of lasting connections, become the focus of proper psychoanalytic technique. But more important than this somewhat abstract consideration is the fact that connecting leads to understanding. Whatever word you may choose—coupling, connecting, or linking—may be seen as equivalent to that of understanding. That empathy is the tool to such a state of connecting is a felicitous happening and one shared by all analysts who employ this tool. Empathic breaks, discontinuities, uncoupling, all become equivalent to misunderstanding, and this, too, is a state common to us all. Therefore, the problem of correct or incorrect interaction falls back upon the capacity to understand. Within proper moral and ethical constraints, anything is allowable that help us to understand, to connect. We thereby establish a baseline for our treatment and now can join this with our previous insistence on recognizing the singular world of each and every individual.

The vision of a self as connected to others as selfobjects is a one-person model and, thus, is also an intrapsychic one. There is no self demarcated by a boundary, separated from an object, and so interacting with the object by projection or introjection. Rather, there is a self composed of and/or constituted by selfobjects, and it is the nature of the strength and function of the connections that call for study and examination. This is a different model, one that insists upon the self or subject as a participant in the world and so quite different from one that sees the self or subject as looking out at the world. A very cogent illustration of this participation in the world comes from biology, which has taught us that the enzyme that breaks down the sugar lactose to provide energy for bacterial growth is manufactured by bacterial cells only when lactose is present in the environment. The so-called environment is really a part of the system. From the cell to the self, we remain open systems and networks of interconnectedness. The vision of the solitary subject or the isolated patient is untenable, and thus, our self-formed boundaries may be a source more of conceptual difficulty than of theoretical aid.

Since we all live in one world, we tend to feel that ours is the right one, until we come to recognize that the same conviction exists in everyone else. Worlds differ just as people do, but we must caution ourselves not to be convinced of the certainty of ours and ours alone. When analyst and patient come together, there inevitably results the matching, as well as the clashing, of the different worlds. To the degree that the analyst connects or understands he or she is able to see and comprehend the world of the patient. This is the place where we must heed those (Schwaber, 1983; Stolorow, 1988) who ask us to limit our own preconceptions and see the world from the patient's point of view.

But the rationale of such a stance is not a lasting one, unless we feel that patients need only to be affirmed in their perceptions, feelings, and experiences. That is true of everyone for a while. To that degree we may affirm, but soon we dissent.

The next stance (of this disagreement) is one that Jacobson would probably agree to, and that is one that assumes and follows from the conviction that the analyst does indeed have some sort of privileged access to the "real world." I can both agree and disagree. The analyst has access only to his or her world, and parts of it must necessarily be duly delivered to the patient since we assume that his or hers is the better world. The prejudices and preconvictions of the analyst must thus carry a greater weight than those of a patient, and treatment is always tilted in favor of that patient needing something from the analyst. Analysis is, thus, not to be seen as intersubjective, a stance that suggests a mutuality of contributions from the participant. Nor is it an exchange of the patient's psychic and neurotic reality for external reality. That, of course, is a colossal conceit. Rather, it is a negotiated compromise carried out in the transference. We must insist, however, that it is the patient's transference that tilts this process and so demands that it remains within the psyche of the patient. The process of change is negotiated over and around the connections and disruptions in the transference, and it follows the sequence of understanding, misunderstanding, and, once again, understanding. The understanding comes from your connecting to the patient. The misunderstanding comes from your seeing the world differently, for whatever reason, such as countertransference, and so breaking the connection. The reconnection comes *not* from further agreeing with the patient but, rather, from a negotiated compromise, and the latter carries the seeds for the analyst's changing his world as well.

DIFFERENT ANALYSTS AND DIFFERENT WORLDS

One can only posit an analysis assuming a certain fixed course by considering the patient as having a sort of stable pathology and the analyst equally having a sort of stable theory. If we all share this theory, then only our personalities will alter the course of an analysis. This is the so-called common-ground position (Wallerstein, 1988), which says we are all pretty much the same and all act pretty much alike. It does allow for variations but claims some essential sameness. It says as well that our differences, even in theory, may level out in action and so result in a commonality of technique regardless of the vocabulary we may employ to describe just what we do. The subtle, but compelling, temptation of this conviction is that of allowing us to dismiss other ideas as merely "old wine in new bottles" and so never to have to do more than glance at supposed opposing ideas. It leads to a sort of topsy-turvy world of multiple explanations for a single phenomenon in stark contrast to a scientific stance that aims for a single explanation for supposedly multiple phenomena. It does this by dissolving the differences. If we all do the same thing, we need not care for theory. However, if we all do different things with similar results, then theory is paramount, since only theory will field the single explanations. Periodically, we see a wave of protest against theory, a kind of debunking of jargon with a plea to divest ourselves of our theories or our "explanatory metaphors" and to just "listen to the patient" or "tune in to the affects." One recent article espousing this supposedly "atheoretical as possible" approach (Lindon, 1991) illustrates this as follows: "[in] the process of patient's maternal transference to me; I know I am a man yet I push that 'theory' aside and try to attune to the patient's experience of me" (p. 33). Now, although that may seem neutral and clear, relatively jargon free, it is certainly a very powerful theory. It tells you what to know, what to see, and what to do. I have no complaints about its value, but it is downright foolish to claim anything anywhere is atheoretical. Our theories are our eyes.

Once free of this naive approach to "the stark facts," we must recognize that we have more than one set of eyes and that we do things quite differently. Our common ground is that we can talk to one another; it is not that we say or do the same things. And if, indeed, our theories literally see for us, then there is no separation of theory from method. To separate a "theory of the mind" from the method of free association (Kris, 1990) is to practice a sleight of hand. The very idea of associations presumes that we see the mind as functioning in that manner, that is, of going from one signifier to another. But the mind of the frog (as well as we can know it) does not associate. The frog does not, as he flicks out his tongue for a fly, think about the last fly he caught or the prospective taste of this one (Lettvin et al., 1959). And the Lacanian analyst (as well as one can know that as well) also works with a different theory of association and so does not interpret at the same point as does the Freudian. No part of our analytic stance is free of theory, and to even insist that the analyst's obligation is to make no intervention except those that foster freedom of association is, once again, to assume that the analyst can be the single judge of such a state. Theory does not belong only to special, complex models of metapsychology, but as some have said: "Everything is theory." And the theory of connective individuals who share a world is simply not that of bounded individuals with internal, somewhat comparable worlds. It is necessary to distinguish these points of view and to realize that they lead to separate sorts of results.

IMPLICATIONS

One result of this altered theory has to do with interaction and the concept of countertransference, a term that usually has to do with the analyst's input that is less than neutral or realistic or even, at times, helpful. Ideally, the analyst manages or handles these reactions and ultimately works them out to the benefit of the analysis and the patient. At the termination of the analysis, we often assume that the analyst emerges unchanged, save for being a bit older and wiser. But a true picture of interaction is one of mutuality, and so it is quite likely that the analyst should, indeed must, change as well. Analyst and patient are coupled, which makes it unlikely that only one party is affected. Sadly, most considerations of the analytic process do not look to the necessary alterations in the analyst but rather consider them as adventitious or even problematic. We do not study the lasting changes in the analyst, both specific and general when we insist upon a theory of minimal participation, with the latter word closely related to notions of contamination and/or interference. My suspicion is that a proper study of changes in the analyst, those that are inevitable results of the process, would do much to aid in our understanding of many of the problems of analysis from the declining enthusiasm for the practice in some to the dogged insistence on standards in others. Interaction goes both ways.

CONCLUSION

Each of us lives in a world of similarities and differences, and some worlds rarely work better than do others. Patients and analysts join in a program of mutual connection. They share in a system of negotiation directed to a reasonable and partially shared reality based upon a structural and organizational developmental process. They both change, and although we usually concentrate more upon one, the patient, than the other, the analyst, we have much to gain from a more careful study of the latter.

REFERENCES

Basch, M. (1988). *Understanding Psychotherapy.* New York: Basic Books.

Boesky, D. (1988). Comments on the structural theory of technique. *International Journal of Psycho-Analysis* 69:303–316.

Goldstein, W. N. (1991). Clarification of projective identification. *American Journal of Psychiatry* 148:153–161.

Jacobson, E. (1954). The self and the object world. *Psychoanalytic Study of the Child* 9:75–127..

Jacobson, E. (1964). The Self and the Object World. New York: International Universities Press.

Kris, A. (1990). The analyst's stance and the method of free association. *Psychoanalytic Study of the Child* 45: 25–42.

Lettvin, J. Y., Maturana, H. R., McCulloch, W. S. & Pitts, W. H. (1959). What the frog's eye tells the frog's brain, *Procedures of the Institute of Radio Engineering* 47:1940–1951.

Lindon, J. A. (1991). Treatment techniques in evolution. *Bulletin Menninger Clinic* 55(1): 30–37.

Schwaber, E. (1983). Psychoanalytic listening and psychic reality. *International Journal of Psycho-Analysis* 10:379–392.

Stolorow, R. (1988). Integrating self psychology and classical psychoanalysis: An experience-near approach. In: *Learning From Kohut,
Progress in Self Psychology, Vol. 4*. Hillsdale, NJ: The Analytic Press,
pp. 63–70.

Wallerstein, R. (1988). One psychoanalysis or many *International Journal of Psycho-Analysis* 69:5–22.

Enactment as Understanding
and as Misunderstanding (2002)

The author considers the concept of enactment as a ubiquitous event that is best seen as part of a sequence in the process of understanding a patient. As such, enactments are not unusual or special save as they are often subject to disavowal or to being singled out by the analyst as especially subject to scrutiny. Once recognized, enactments need to be interpreted: not so much in terms of their unconscious origins, but more with regard to the need to include them in the analytic dialogue.

*   *   *

Most of us, most of the time, aim to understand others, and we acknowledge our understanding by some form of affirming communication, verbal or otherwise. Normal conversation proceeds by a series of exchanges that try to clarify any misunderstanding, and change it into an agreed-upon understanding. The gestures and words that compose our everyday discourse are, however, necessarily decreased and minimized by the structured form of psychoanalysis, which is regularly conducted without face-to-face contact and in an atmosphere of much reduced verbal exchange. Over the years, our attention as analysts has been alerted to the inevitable impact of the out-of-sight and often mute analyst upon the analytic process, and we have profited from this. We also owe a considerable debt to those who have tried to isolate and demarcate the so-called enactments of analysis as they serve to illustrate special times of interaction (Chused 1991; McLaughlin 1991).

Enactments are circumscribed moments of behavior that have been defined variously (and among other things) as "symbolic interactions between patient and analyst which have unconscious meaning to both" (Chused 1991, p. 615), or as "regressive interactions experienced by either as a consequence of the behavior of the other" (McLaughlin 1991, p. 595). These definitions are further circumscribed by Anderson's assertion that they "enact rather than [maintain] the separate thinking and inquiry necessary to the analytic stance"(Anderson 1999).

If we turn a bright light on these definitions, we see that only the terms *regressive, unconscious*, and *symbolic* serve to differentiate enactment behavior from ordinary run-of-the-mill action. And if we turn an even brighter light on those particular words, it is difficult to claim that any single bit of action is free from the qualities ascribed to enactment. Indeed, the very notion of action or behavior seems to fail the test by definition, inasmuch as silent inactivity can readily be seen as regressive, symbolic, and laden with unconscious intent. The theoretical claim that psychoanalysis can be divided into a time of thoughtful inquiry and a time of regressive, defensive action may well be more of a hope than a reality. The ordinary activities of arranging schedules, setting fees, and managing the day-to-day conduct of a practice, coupled with such extraordinary actions as extra appointments, phone conversations, disclosures of personal information, and so on, are never easily compartmentalized as to whether they are "enactments" or "interactions." If a patient offers a hand to shake, our response is surely an enactment; and it has, just as surely, an unconscious reverberation. If we agree to modify a schedule or reduce a fee, we act as a consequence of a request, and so can hardly claim that our responses are not regularly a mixture of regressive as well as thoughtful behavior.

Yet it seems that over the course of an analysis, only one person—the privileged analyst—is allowed to highlight some forms of behavior as enactments, while simultaneously dismissing or disregarding others. The crucial issue seems to be why we choose to select certain forms of behavior as enactments, and what *this* choice and *this* behavior may mean. It would seem folly to consider enactments as bad or infantile or defensive, since they may be initiated by either party (Jacobs 1986). They might more properly be seen as efforts at understanding: from the one to the other and in both directions. For a start, we must agree upon just what constitutes understanding.

UNDERSTANDING

Psychoanalysis regularly makes a place for understanding in the realm of cognition; that is, one knows something that has heretofore been hidden or repressed, as when the ego is made aware of the contents of the id. Understanding is more than knowing per se; it is part of a larger process. Understanding or *Verstehen* is at least one-half of the under-standing-explaining complex and, for some patients, is said to be the more crucial part of treatment. Lots of effort has been directed toward a better grasp of the position of understanding, especially in psychoanaly-sis, and especially as it relates to interpretation (Hartmann, 1950). One perspective has it that interpretation is the link between understanding and explaining; that is, one interprets something, say a transference resistance, which allows understanding to emerge and in turn be ex-plained, say by a genetic reconstruction. Another perspective says that we understand one another by way of empathy, and that this connects us to one another. This resulting connection is then the area of explanation, both in its origins and its vicissitudes. Both of these perspectives allow understanding to be seen as moving us from one place to another—not so much, or only, in the form of increased knowledge, but in opening us up to more possibilities, or, perhaps more accurately, in freeing us to be and do more. It may not be too far afield to say that understanding makes one a different person. No matter how one chooses to conceptu-alize the status of understanding, it clearly serves a central role in analytic therapy.

The achievement of understanding is a product of verbal discourse in most analyses, and the failure of this achievement is sometimes attribut-ed to action: behavior that is not, for whatever reason, reformulated in discourse. Indeed, it is often the case that action by itself, instead of words, is felt to be inconsequential, even deleterious, either because it cannot contribute to understanding or because it is misunderstood. Yet it may also be true that certain actions or behaviors are themselves efforts at understanding, and these bits of behavior may be successful even when they are not made a part of the "talking cure." If all enact-ments are seen as efforts at understanding, then some are successful (albeit perhaps of little or no consequence), others are successful and remain quite outside of the analytic discourse, and some few are unsuc-cessful and become loci of misunderstanding. These last are the usual places of concern for many analysts. Behavior that is misunderstood seems to be characterized as enactment more often than behavior that is understood, but this may be an error. Much behavior falls into this category—that is, acts of misunderstanding that are open to understanding, and are either of no import or become objects of investigation which are resolved, i.e., understood. Some behavior, however, remains misunderstood and unresolved, and therefore an object of concern. Action that lies outside this circle of concern may or may not be attended to, but rarely does it enter the discourse of the treatment. It is misunderstanding that stands out and calls for recognition, and is therefore sometimes properly reckoned with. Understanding is regularly left as is.

MISUNDERSTANDING

Gadamer discusses misunderstanding as a state that must itself somehow depend upon understanding, since we are only able to claim that we misunderstand or are misunderstood if we have some baseline of reference (Gadamer 1962). Most psychoanalysts and psychotherapists can distinguish a case that is "not at all understood" from one that is "misunderstood." We may claim that we simply did not "get it" about one patient, and equally insist that we misunderstood another. And clearly these casual descriptions do aim to differentiate two quite separate sets of conditions. The first is not based so much upon error as upon a lack, an absence, of connection. The second is more in the nature of a faulty connection. To be sure, there is no black-and-white distinction between "not getting it" and "getting it wrong," but the latter speaks to the finer points of interpretive work; the former addresses a more complete cognitive or empathic failure. When we are out of touch or completely lost, we try to make a connection. When we are a bit off, we try to clarify. Without in any way dismissing or not recognizing the many areas of gray that exist between these extremes, it may still be possible to understand better why some enactments stand out as significant and worthy of examination, while others are readily classified as trivial and of no import.

To be sure, we all differ a great deal in our ways of "getting it," and our patients all provide different challenges. One analyst might struggle more than another to comprehend certain patients. The psychology of analysts varies, both in terms of their wishes to understand, and in terms of their propensities to ignore what is not understood. The same is true of patients, who feel understood and who in turn understand the analyst. Seeing the analyst-patient dyad as an effort to enhance mutual understanding and diminish misunderstanding may allow for a changed perspective on the problem of enactments. These can then be recast as moments of misunderstanding that break the connection between analyst and patient or as efforts to reconnect without the use of interpretation. That is, they are acts centered upon the mutuality of understanding. Those that remain outside of our discourse and are never attended to are areas open to future investigation by ourselves or others.

One way to maintain a connection that is in danger of being broken, or to reestablish one that has been lost, is to disregard whatever threatens it. This disregard can be classified as a minor issue of turning a blind eye to something, or to a more classical condition of disavowal. Thus two persons who seem to understand one another may approach an area of potential disagreement, one temporarily not amenable to negotiation or resolution by interpretation, and reckon with it by implicitly agreeing to exclude it from notice. A silent conspiracy develops, by which each participant is drawn into splitting off or disowning the troublesome area. We shall call this *pseudounderstanding*. It is achieved by an act of disavowal. It seems necessary to invoke this idea of a silent—that is, an unspoken—agreement if we are to comprehend the broad range of definitions and recommendations about enactments.

CLINICAL EXAMPLES OF MISUNDERSTANDING

In an extensive review of the many contributions to the general problem of enactment, Frank (1999) notes that the entirety of patient-therapist interactions can be seen as enactment, and so one runs the twin dangers of too broad and too limited conceptualizations (pp. 45–65). Over and over, decisions as to "what counts" as an enactment seem to be either arbitrary or somehow connected to self-deception. Setting a schedule is a good example of enacting that can sometimes be dismissed as trivial and yet may be at other times the site of a significant unconscious conflict. Here is an example taken from the psychoanalytic literature.

CASE I

This case is taken from an article on enactment written from a Kleinian point of view (Anderson 1999). The author reviews much of the relevant literature on enactment and proposes the idea that enactment derives from a pressure upon the analyst to avoid sensory bombardment issuing from the patient. Without pursuing the theoretical issues discussed in the paper I will focus upon the clinical material, which involves an initial compliance by the analyst to the patient's requests for what are called "minor deviations from the analytic frame." These are usually changes made in response to schedule alterations. Following these "enactments," the patient dreams of a debilitated analyst; this leads the analyst to decide not to comply further with the patient's requests. Her refusal leads to new material about the analyst's "cruelty" and other important "hidden elements." Thus the analyst's changed position, which is characterized as a move from enactment to neutrality, is said to have redressed the analyst's mistaken initial compliance.

One need neither ascribe to nor dismiss the Kleinian considerations in this study to pursue briefly some critical points. To begin with, the author seems not to make much of the fact that her refusal to comply is just as much of an enactment as was her previous agreement. The evidence of supposed primitive hate and the attributions of cruelty to the analyst that ensue from the refusal would seem to be fairly expectable. Would an enactment of generosity or indulgence on the analyst's part have resulted in material that would also support the offered theory? Many enactments of this sort that occur between patient and analyst— the kind in which "painful reality" is no longer avoided—seem peculiarly to center on the analyst as one who does less or gives less. Need this always be the case? Is all compliance an avoidance of reality? The enactment is *not* only the refusal of the request; it is also the very act of the analyst in either accepting or refusing—that is, it is the delineation of a frame and the change in the frame. This delineation and subsequent change must take precedence as the focus in the analysis, since the analyst says that "her best analytic judgment" caused her to change her mind, and the patient agreed with this judgment. Although one need not take issue with this judgment, it would seem obvious that such an agreement between analyst and analysand is the stuff of transference that could well be the central point of the enactment—that is, unless the transference is disavowed. Yet this clinical vignette is offered as if this central point of agreement were but a preamble to the real one—the cessation of the analyst's compliance with the patient's requests, and the patient's resultant rage. In truth, one is no more real than the other. To insist that the analyst enacts as a defense against the patient's terrorizing threat may open the door to questions about whether the refusals of analysts *as well as* their earlier compliances enact another defense, disavowal; and this may be the more significant arena of inquiry. Thus a seemingly minor act of schedule arrangement illustrates a sequence: supposed understanding or agreement (in the analyst's solving of the schedule change), followed by misunderstanding and the patient's compliance with the analyst. This compliance may then be a sign of objectionable material that is split off and disavowed.

The analyst and patient begin the treatment with a set of understand-ings about the "frame" of analysis, although surely much of this remains in the background. The analyst may feel a struggle within herself over some of the niceties of the arrangements, but nothing need be an issue until the emergence of a moment of misunderstanding. In the above case, this misunderstanding took the form of a set of dreams, which led the analyst to conclude that the patient saw her as weak, and that there was thus rage hidden behind the patient's requests for a schedule change. In addition, the analyst tells us, there were further requests for change from the patient. One might here say that these changes and requests had unconscious meaning to both patient and analyst (Chused 1991), and that each at this juncture in some sense misunderstood the other. This mutual misunderstanding is the ideal occasion for an inter-pretation that can lead to or restore understanding. Too often, of course, such misunderstandings are not seen as mutual, and so they become arenas for what may be misguided analytic work aimed at a compliance that masquerades as understanding. In this case, the misguidedness takes the form of the analyst introducing a new rule: one of refusing requests.

I would say that this enactment moved from mutual understanding to misunderstanding and on to further enactment without mutual understanding, although the analyst herself believes that she well understood her patient. I would consider this claim valid only if such understanding could be confirmed by the patient, and clarified by interpretative work. Here is another example, with an illustration of how understanding can be achieved by interpretive work.

CASE II

This young professional man came to see me upon referral from an analyst whom he had been seeing in another city. The prospective patient had moved because his wife had been offered an important and promising position in this new location, and he felt that up until now she had sacrificed her career for him. Their finances had not at all improved with this move, and finances became of immediate concern in my taking on and treating this potential new patient. He told me that his previous analyst had begun seeing him on a once-a-week basis at a somewhat reduced fee, and had proceeded to reduce the fee further as the frequency of hours increased to four times weekly. He said that this was a common practice in the community from which he had come, and he wondered if the same were true here, and if I could accommodate him in an equally negotiable manner.

Reducing a fee for a patient was not a new experience for me, and I did not consider the amount of money at question significant. Therefore, it seemed reasonable to put aside any question of this action having much of an impact on me. The patient seemed interesting, my self-esteem was enhanced by the referral, and so I agreed to start at a lower fee. In the event of an increase in the frequency of sessions, I would decrease the fee, just as the other analyst had done. In retrospect, I felt uncomfortable from the very start at having to make an accommodation that matched that of another analyst, rather than one fashioned by myself. I tried to put this nagging discomfort to the side and attributed it to some competitive feelings with the other analyst, trying to convince myself that no matter who made the decision, it was all for the patient's good. Here we are on the cusp of disavowal.

I was wrong. As the once-a-week meetings began, the patient spoke more and more of the burdens that he had assumed with this move, which had been made primarily in his wife's interest. As his anger toward his wife became more open and focused, I found that my initial mild discomfort with the financial setup was growing more uncomfortable. At what seemed an appropriate moment in the treatment, we began to discuss money: first in a general way, then more specifically in the here and now as it related to his wife and family, and then even more specifically in his lifelong relationships with his father and mother. It was interesting and revealing to learn that his parents gave him and his wife a yearly gift allowed by the IRS, but with the stipulation that it was really a loan that would one day have to be repaid. These parents were well-off financially, but seemed unable to give any gifts without attached strings. When they came into the arena of treatment, we were able to discuss the feelings of guilt at receiving along with the rage at "not getting." We could next see how I was feeling a similar set of feelings at being placed in a position akin to my patient's, and we saw how others were likewise putting my patient in a situation that resembled one familiar throughout his life: that is, of making a sacrifice, feeling angry at having to do it, and feeling guilty both because he was angry and because he felt ungrateful. However, a basic and essential aspect in all of these interactions—in his family, with his wife, with his first analyst, and initially with me—was that much if not all of this remained unspoken. For a while it was segregated, but finally it entered into the conversation. I should mention here that this discussion did not entail changing the agreed-upon fee in any way.

This single event—lifting behavior into the therapeutic dialogue— sometimes routine but often surprisingly a source of great discomfort, becomes a crucial turning point. Thus this particular enactment was able to be different from other enactments, because it was not allowed to rest unexamined among the "usual and ordinary" behaviors of the analyst. We see how it moves from the status of the disavowed to a place of importance and recognition. The crucial question—the reticence of the analyst to bring it into that place of discussion—is basic to the problem of enactments. This next case illustrates enacting that is never addressed, either by action or by interpretation.

CASE III

This case is an example of a mutual enactment; its initiation was unclear, but probably belonged to the therapist. It appears to present no particular moral issues, and so could readily be classified as innocent on that basis. It does, however, qualify as an enactment that passed unnoticed and remained so.

This case of a middle-aged, well-known female theatrical celebrity was presented for consultation because the therapist felt the treatment was at a stalemate. The hours with the patient were said to drone on and on; the patient reported events, leaving little time for any sort of interventions, and had no tolerance whatsoever for transference interpretations. In the recounting of one hour, the therapist began by focusing on his patient's infidelity to her husband, primarily with a much younger man whom she would meet in out-of-the-way and/or secluded hotels in order to avoid discovery.

These secret liaisons were of vital importance to the patient, and her therapist often attempted to contrast their significance with his own insignificance, as his patient expressed it. This woman felt that it was vitally important not to be seen with her young lover, since not only her marriage but her public persona as well would suffer.

In a more detailed examination of a representative hour, the therapist began with a description of how he let his patient in by a private door, so that she would spend no time in the waiting room and so that her entrances and exits could not be observed by other patients. The therapist recounted this in a matter-of-fact manner, and could not recall if it had begun with the patient's request for secrecy or the therapist's suggestion for the same. When the supervisor called attention to the fact that this bit of behavior seemed to parallel exactly some of the activity associated with the patient's secret rendezvous, the therapist seemed quite literally stunned. He had never noticed, and he certainly would have never chosen to discuss this with his patient. Yet he had no difficulty in seeing that this bit of behavior that was going on in a regular fashion between his patient and himself might well be connected to his own feeling of frustration over the lack of meaningful discussion of important issues with the same patient.

Without going into the case discussion in any greater detail, we can now pursue a more careful inquiry into the therapist's conduct. He could readily see that he was engaging in an action that he then proceeded to deny or disavow. Indeed, he said openly that he felt somewhat alienated from that action and decision of his, almost as if they had been made by someone other than himself. He felt embarrassed at this disclosure but, perhaps peculiarly, did not at that moment feel able to confront his patient with his new observation. As much as he could consider the entrance and exit of his patient as behavior that might conceal a host of other complex meanings—that is, it was symbolic and carried unconscious content—and as clearly as he was convinced of the need for this enactment to be brought into the therapeutic discourse, he felt a clear resistance about contemplating the former, and a clear reluctance about pursuing the latter. This seems to qualify as significant nonverbal behavior that remained outside of the arena of interpretive activity; that is, it was disavowed and kept away.

It is important to recognize and underscore that this particular enactment might mean little or nothing for one patient, and could well be discussed with another patient. There is nothing inherently deleterious about the behavior, save as it exists within the context of the treatment.

ONE EXPLANATION

It would be foolhardy to attempt to offer a single explanation for all enactments, especially if one subscribes to the view that they are ubiquitous. However, it may be possible to focus upon enactments that occur in one analyst and are experienced as unusual by that particular analyst. Such personal experiences may involve external scrutiny, as happens in supervision, or may be recognized in a private sense of uneasiness or guilt or embarrassment. For every person there is a sense of disruption in the movement from personal comfort to unrest, from innocence to blame, and from pseudounderstanding to misunderstanding. The corresponding view from the outside may of course be one of a more or less moral or ethical evaluation. Within this area of judgment lie the rules and regulations of whatever system of psychoanalysis or psychotherapy is embraced. Therefore, if one assumes that anything—from a handshake to a hug—belongs to the ordinary routine of practice, then this imaginary line of meaningful enactment has not been crossed. Although one person's enactment may be another's routine behavior, short of clear-cut ethical misbehavior, a proper explanation can belong only to that one person. This particular approach to understanding, therefore, is devoted to the psychology of the analyst and to what it means when he somehow steps outside of his "ordinary and usual" behavior. Each of these cases allow for different responses, and these enable us to categorize enactments as ignorable, or able to be handled by counteractions, or resolved by interpretation.

DISCUSSION

Enactments may be distinguished among the larger category of interactions between analyst and patient, but only by virtue of their having a special psychological significance; and this aspect of significance is one that is assigned by the analyst. If both enactments and interactions are ubiquitous, then we must segregate out the special group of interactions that is therapeutically meaningful. The arbitrariness of this decision has led to a vast literature that struggles to characterize enactments either as unusual, or as possessing some special status. The problem with this is that some enactments certainly do escape the notice of analysts or are disavowed, because of the analyst's theoretical stance or personal psychology, while others seem to defy such ignoring. Thus, rather than remaining bound to these poles of recognition or nonrecognition, we have to carve out a better way to conceptualize enactments. When Chused says, "To want anything from patients, … even to be understood accurately, is to be vulnerable to the experience of one's own transference and thus be susceptible to an enactment" (1991, pp. 616–618), she suggests that "not wanting" is some pure, albeit unattainable, state of neutrality rather than a very powerful form of interaction of its own. Alas, not wanting is no protection from enacting.

In reformulating the concept of enactment in terms of understanding and misunderstanding, my effort is to place interpretation in the center of the solution to the conundrum. The core concern of the analyst need not be to restrain action or "not want," but rather to understanding what he or she did or did not do.

ENACTMENT AS PSEUDOUNDERSTANDING FOLLOWED BY MISUNDERSTANDING

Much of the interaction in psychoanalysis is felt to be trivial, and so ceases to be a part of the analytic discourse. When patient and analyst are "in sync" they usually are involved in information gathering or in the consolidation of new information. They feel connected and, ideally, understanding goes (or should go) both ways. We are loathe to speak of "enactments" in the context of these periods. But one problem that may occur during them is disavowal—that is, disturbing material that has the capacity to disrupt the connection is allowed to remain outside of the treatment. The case of the celebrity let in by a side door illustrates this form of disavowal. My case of the reduced fee illustrates an apparent understanding—a *pseudounderstanding*—that clearly negatively affected one member of the analytic pair but was never allowed to be completely split off from the analysis. In these two cases an effort was made to maintain a comfortable connection with the patient and so not to rock the boat. The analyst's reaction was one aimed at better understanding the patient, but this necessitated having disruptive material split off from discussion, at least temporarily. If and when it is brought into the discourse, it leads to misunderstanding: a misunderstanding that is vital and necessary.

Analysis must necessarily move away from pseudounderstanding to misunderstanding if change is to be accomplished. This misunderstanding derives from or follows pseudounderstanding, and is often an occasion for enactment in the more common usage of the term. *Something happens.* These occasions of disruption may or may not be behavioral, and enactment in its common sense is often noted at these times, especially if the misunderstanding is seen as lying somehow outside of the ordinary conduct of analysis. This is best illustrated best in the case involving the changes in schedule. The analyst acceded to other requests of the patient, became troubled, and herself moved to action. One problem that occurs in these instances is that of action being met with reaction which then leads to resolution by compliance rather than to a return to mutual understanding. The inevitable misunderstanding that follows pseudounderstanding is the engine that moves the treatment.

INTERPRETATION AS RESOLVING MISUNDERSTANDING

There is no doubt that interpretation as a general concept can be either behavioral or verbal, and that interpretation per se can run the gamut from a casual nod of agreement to a meaningful recognition of an unconscious configuration. Psychoanalytic interpretation, however, is different, and so is quite restrictive and focused. Moving from a state of misunderstanding to one of understanding in psychoanalysis, as opposed to the host of other forms of resolving differences, demands a concern with transference and countertransference and a recognition of the unconscious derivatives of the misunderstanding. We know that we need not have a dream presented to us to engage us in interpretation, but we are often reluctant to recognize that many of the supposed minutiae of psychoanalysis have equal value as portals to the unconscious. When something goes wrong in our procedures, we tend to right them in order to attain our usual level of comfort. This pull on us to react should of course be a pull to understand and to interpret. To move from allowing schedule changes to no longer allowing them—that is, from one kind of enactment to another—is an example of handling misunderstanding without psychoanalytic interpretation. So, too, are all forms of abstinence and/or gratification that alter or resolve a problem without an increase in mutual understanding. Too often, all that is achieved is comfort. There is little doubt that most analysts do interpret with a personal conviction of understanding their patients, but there exists an added requirement in psychoanalytic discourse, and that is that the patient as well must feel understood. Ultimately this understanding is raised to a cognitive level by way of explanation. But that is another story.

INTERPRETATION IN DEPTH AND BREADTH

The usual view of psychoanalytic interpretation is one of unearthing something that is hidden: that is, allowing the repressed unconscious to be raised to consciousness. In contrast to this image, of movement from depth to surface, is the image of integration, of gathering separate or split-off segments into a congruent whole. This latter conceptualization is the one that corresponds to the inclusion of disavowed contents in a process of ongoing scrutiny. Just as we need to bring unconscious issues into the ongoing transference relationship and subject them to interpretation, so too must we recognize that disavowed content must join in the conversation. Enactments are regularly left out of the ongoing verbal exchange either by choice or out of psychological resistance. Our faith in the "talking cure" is rewarded when we recognize that everything "counts," and so everything deserves a place in the dialogue.

SUMMARY

Enactment, like so many overused words in psychoanalysis, has an undeserved popularity. From its original status as an indicator of something gone wrong, it has, over time, been used simply as a description of the normal range of interpersonal occurrences (Frank 1999, p. 55), and sometimes is even encouraged as therapeutic (Bacal 1985). Inasmuch as we may have a legitimate right to say that it is all interaction (Goldberg 1996), we can perhaps better circumscribe enactment as those interactions participating in the analytic dialogue that may be conceptualized either as transference and countertransference issues or as contributors to the pseudounderstanding/misunderstanding sequence. In the latter conception we come a bit closer to the mutual experiences of the two participants, and therefore may have an easier time grasping that something is amiss.

When something is wrong we can usually agree that one of us— patient or analyst—does not understand that "something," which may have been brought about by an enactment. The state of something being wrong may be resolved by an interpretation, or by yet another enactment. Enactments can thus be positioned as part of the sequence of creating and resolving misunderstandings. The critical point for psychoanalysis is that we recognize that interpretive work is called for to resolve whatever is amiss. Enactments are never right or wrong or good or bad. They are properly seen as spurs to psychoanalytic understanding, our primary task. As such, they lose their special status even while they serve to remind us when we occasionally forget what our first effort must be. There is little new in this way of thinking about enactment; I offer it as a way to understand better a word that is often misunderstood.

REFERENCES

Anderson, M.K. (1999). The pressure toward enactment. *Journal of the American Psychoanalytic Association* 47:503–518.

Bacal, H. (1985). Optimal responsiveness and the therapeutic process. In *Progress in Self Psychology*, vol. 1, ed. A. Goldberg. Hillsdale, NJ: Analytic Press, pp. 202–227.

Chused, J. (1991). The evocative power of enactments. *Journal of the American Psychoanalytic Association* 39:615–640.

Frank, K. (1999). *Psychoanalytic Participation Action, Interaction, and Integration*. Hillsdale, NJ: Analytic Press.

Gadamer, H-G. (1962). *On the Problem of Self-Understanding in Philosophical Hermeneutics*, ed. D.E. Linzi. Berkeley: University of California Press, pp. 44–58.

Goldberg, A. (1996). It is all interaction. *Psychoanalytic Inquiry* 16:96–106.

Hartmann, H. (1950). Comments on the psychoanalytic theory of the ego. *Psychoanalytic Study of the Child* 5:74–96.

Jacobs, T. (1986). On countertransference enactments. *Journal of the American Psychoanalytic Association* 34:289–308.

Mclaughlin, J. (1991). Clinical and theoretical aspects of enactment *Journal of the American Psychoanalytic Association* 39:595–614.

CHAPTER SIX

The Correct Place of Pragmatism, Pluralism and Psychoanalysis

In a series of papers, beginning in 1981, Goldberg turns his attention to the place of self-psychology within psychoanalytic theory. In this first paper, *One Theory or More*, Goldberg locates the place of self-psychology in the traditional and established theories. In a later paper, *Self-Psychology Since Kohut* (1998), he distinguishes self-psychology from intersubjectivity theory and relational theory, both tributaries of self-psychology.

Given that psychoanalysis, according to Goldberg, tends to sprout diversity with abandon, how can we order this diversity among the various schools of psychoanalysis? Goldberg makes a case for pragmatism in determining usefulness and effectiveness, among the many schools of psychoanalysis, in his paper *American Pragmatism and American Psychoanalysis* (2002). Goldberg then calls for tolerance of diversity in his paper, *Pity the Poor Pluralist (2007)*. Why and when an approach works best needs to be given a hearing, especially as we are "living in the time of evolution of psychoanalytic thought."

One Theory or More, (1981) asks the question, "Do we have one theory or do we have two or more?" The efforts to locate the new findings of self-psychology within the established and "correct" practice of psychoanalysis fell into three camps: 1) deficit versus conflict in assessing clinical data, 2) a resistance to self-psychology, which was assumed to be an encroachment into the area of classical psychoanalysis, and 3) the radical view, which situated Oedipal pathology not as inevitable or as bedrock, but as one form of aberrant self-development.

Self-psychology further distinguished itself from prevailing theories in areas of developmental considerations in several different ways: in the different domains of inquiry (for instance, the nature of the self-object tie), methods of data gathering (vicarious introspection) and insight serving as the expression of a developing self.

—GM

One Theory or More (1981)

INTRODUCTION

Pioneers in psychoanalysis, as in any field of scientific inquiry, are few and far between. In fact our science may still be too young for us to determine who the significant leaders are since it is often only in retrospect that one can assess the meaningful contributions in the history of a science. So many of the seemingly great chemists and physicists of their time have faded into obscurity that it will be little surprise to our future historians to note that the many, to us, meaningful figures of today will have contributed little of lasting significance to our science of psychoanalysis. Erich Fromm was undoubtedly a pioneer and only the future will reveal if his contributions will continue to take hold on our minds as the edges of psychoanalysis are further explored. This essay will be directed toward examining some facets of the reception of new ideas before history can make a more reasonable assessment.

One of the very great difficulties in the establishment of new ideas in the field of psychoanalysis, perhaps more so than in other scientific pursuits such as physics and mathematics is the heritage of our ideas from one man, Sigmund Freud, and a form of trusteeship of his ideas that seems to carry on from generation to generation. Trustees are usually assigned the role of guardianship and at times they feel a necessity to decide issues of truth or falsehood in terms of the reigning ideas. I have been particularly interested recently in the impact of the new ideas of self psychology on the overall field of psychoanalysis, and I have often been struck by the wave of responses which these new ideas have evoked. Although some of these responses are quite challenging and provocative, a number of them seem to fail to meet the minimum demands for scientific theory and inquiry. The most recent one that struck me was a statement in a book review in a psychoanalytic journal (Gediman 1980) which said that Heinz Kohut's ideas were incorrect. I should like to expand upon that seemingly innocuous matter of opinion in order to pursue what I think is an erroneous form of criticism of scientific ideas, one that stems from a conviction that there is a "correct" theory and/or that one must protect and guard and judge new ideas in comparison to such correctness.

The criticisms of self psychology at times seem confined to a mere protest that all of these ideas are not very new or different; they are no more than every good analyst has done all of the time and thus need no particular attention to be paid to them. I suspect this is more a problem in sociology than in psychology since there seems to be no consensus among analysts as to the originality or popularity of the ideas. Some seem to feel them as revolutionary or deviant or dangerous; and this hardly squares with the old wine in new bottles thesis. Of course the best example of such a criticism was the one that followed the publication of "The Two Analyses of Mr. Z." (Kohut 1979); one that dismissed that report by saying these two inadequate analyses should have really been one adequate one. The fact that these analyses were at times contradictory and that the central dream was interpreted quite differently in the separate treatments seems to have escaped these readers (Rangell 1980). But more importantly the question arises as to what guiding theory would allow one to see these two analyses as one or would compel one to face the conclusion that the theories, though perhaps compatible, are really quite different.

Do we have one theory or do we have two or more? If we have one theory which is essentially the correct one should we work toward translating supposedly new ideas back into the old language and should we make minor changes or adjustments in our accepted theory in order to accommodate new finding? This, of course, is what Thomas Kuhn (1962) felt was the job of normal science. On the other hand we might have to face a problem of different theories which, by certain standards, are necessarily what some philosophers of science have called "incommensurable" or seemingly lacking in any basis of comparison. Karl Popper (1963) feels that any theory worth its salt would necessarily overthrow the old one because it must be, by definition, revolutionary and, thus, a really new finding cannot long exist in the confines of an old theory. Yet another school of philosophy (Feyerabend 1975) believes in a multiplicity or plurality of theories which co-exist for times until the best survives. It is important for any proper evaluation of the pioneers of our field to try to determine whether these are political movements characterized by schools and personalities, whether they are significant additions within the realm of normal science or whether they have presented us with a vision that challenges the basic "facts" of our old theory. But, especially in these evaluations, we should pursue as objective and scientific a course as is possible. I think we are now witness to such an inquiry into the theoretical status of self psychology, and I believe we can profit from relinquishing a preoccupation with correctness in favor of one of usefulness, i.e., that of the breadth, depth and elegance of the explanatory yield of the theory.

THE CONTROVERSY

At a conference on self psychology several years ago, Heinz Kohut started a discussion of the "one theory or two problem" by likening it to that of the dim appearance of a figure of a man who approached the viewer from far away down a road. At first one could not make out whether it was the one or the other of two men. As the figure came closer there was more of a tendency to commit oneself to a decision; and, finally, as he came clearly into focus there would be no doubt as to who the person really was. So too, it was felt, most of the questions that confronted the either-or problems of psychoanalytic psychology could be likened to that stage in our scientific investigations at which a certain level of uncertainty necessarily dominated our perceptions. A resolution and an absolute conviction as to the one truth remained a bit beyond our ken. It is important to note that, at least at that point in our scientific study, most of the controversy seemed to be posited around seemingly rivalrous positions i.e., either it was a problem of narcissistic pathology or it was one of a structured neurosis, either it was an oedipal or a pre-oedipal problem, either the analyst was a real object or a selfobject, etc., etc.

I should like to take this opportunity to pursue this matter since I think there remains a good deal of ambiguity in these controversies. There are at least three different opinions which can be considered: In brief, they are:

1. The view of one school of thought, best articulated by Robert Wallerstein (1980) states that it is not a question of either/or but of both/and. Essentially this orientation pays close attention to the deficits of developmental arrests but claims that analytic material is too fluid to make a sharp dichotomy between deficits and regression. It especially espouses what is felt to be a variant of Waelder's multiple functions principle by stressing multiple vantage points in assessing clinical data. Although this approach seems most flexible and liberal it tends to evolve into its own either/or question, i.e., a question of the crux of pathology as being either due to deficit *or* due to conflict and the latter does seem to win the day. Therefore, there remains a tendency to subsume the new findings of self psychology under the rubric of classical findings and to stretch the umbrella a bit to make the definition of conflict as "any opposition of any kind involving any aspect of psychic functioning in any form." I think that is worth pondering.

2. The second approach to the either-or problem takes a much firmer stand and seemingly divides the world of psychoanalysis into narcissistic pathology and structured pathology, and only occasionally allows oedipal pathology to have narcissistic features. There is a marvelous convenience to this kind of strict dichotomy in that one can even separate analytic practitioners into those who are treating narcissistic disorders and those who do not. But, in all seriousness, these somewhat political considerations stem from the early writings of self psychology and they resist the encroachment of self psychology onto the area of classical psychoanalysis. They admit of a category of narcissistic disorders but they are strict segregationists. While the first position is all inclusive, this one treats self psychology as an aberration of sorts.

3. The third position is the most radical one. It posits self psychology as subsuming classical oedipal pathology as but one form of aberrant self development. It states that the natural culmination of normal self-development is oedipal resolution, but that failures in

such resolution always reflect underlying problems in the self-selfobject matrix. And although it allows for a focused concentration on the oedipal conflict in a neurotic, it always looks beyond this to a developmental defect. In a rather obvious way this is also the most radical point of view in terms of development since it states that oedipal problems are developmental ones that are not inevitable but are determined by the vicissitudes of normal development.

There are other positions to be sure. They range from an utter dismissal of the existence of any of the findings of self psychology to an equally absurd embracing of the primarily clinical material in every possible encounter whether psychoanalytic or therapeutic or social. Such severe stances which liken self psychology to a cult, or claim it to be some sort of gratification exercise, are probably best classified as non-scientific efforts which are, fortunately or otherwise, themselves only capable of being understood by a self-psychological approach. But leaving these exaggerated poles aside I would offer these three positions as being at the heart of the controversy.

Now initially I want to sidestep these different stances to say a few more words about theories in general since the three positions of both/and, either/or or entirely one, are essentially three different clinical theories.

To begin with we must accept the fact that all scientific theories are underdetermined. That is to say that there is never a one to one correspondence between theories and fact; but rather we know that any given theory allows us to see some things and to miss others and to make of many things what we wish them to be. Our theories do pretty much direct our perceptions and, unfortunately, they probably belong in the category of "preconceived ideas". This is not so unfortunate as long as we retain a certain flexible capacity: that of recognizing a misfit when it occurs and of realizing that a theory is valuable only in terms of its usefulness, i.e., its utility as a kind of a map or visual aid. The remarkable beauty of Freud's discovery of the oedipus complex, a clinical theory in itself, was its enabling us to see, understand and explain a host of disparate phenomena which had previously made no sense. The phobia of Little Hans is now revealed in a way that was not previously possible. And, of course, once one can and does see phenomena in a new light then they will never be the same as before. In a similar sort of manner the theory of selfobjects makes for a perception of relationships and transferences that is also similar to a new map over foreign terrain, and this allows for a kind of explanation of patient-analyst relationships that was heretofore lacking.

The other point about theories that I want to emphasize is that they are always wrong and are waiting for a better one to come along. Any good and new theory should be revolutionary and should overthrow the old one. This certainly does not mean that rival theories do not co-exist for long periods of time, but ultimately one of them manages to dominate because of the aforementioned points of simplicity, elegance and explanatory yield. But theories that continue to live side by side are either explaining different phenomena or are waiting for a single theory to replace both of them. In the history of any scientific enterprise one sees periods or relative agreement about the value of a theory followed by the introduction of a new set of ideas. This is often accompanied by a form of social and/or political dispute until the practitioners of the science reach some sort of consensus on how they do their work. Naturally this sequence need not be clearly demonstrated or easily observed, but a few salient periods do seem to stand out. One of these is the task of tampering with the old theory to incorporate the findings of the new one. I think we see this in the first position outlined wherein the usual and customary tenets of classical psychology are modified to accommodate self psychology. These efforts are praiseworthy since old theories should never be abandoned without extremely good reasons. However, ultimately there occurs an eroding of the old theories. Certainly Waelder's Principle of Multiple Function (1930) had nothing whatsoever to do with multiple vantage points of observation except in the most generous of interpretations. And if conflict theory is allowed to equal any sort of opposition that one experiences including that of a conflict over developing further because of the lack of sufficient structure, then it probably can embrace just about everything and thus runs the risk of trivializing its original meaning.

Let us focus on the conflict issue. We all know that it enjoys a narrow definition, such as offered by Brenner (1979) who confines it to the instinctual wishes of childhood, or to that of Anna Freud's (1965) more broad and inclusive one that includes conflicts between the child and his environment, the ego and the superego and between drives and affects of opposite quality. The direction of the extension of a definition of conflict is certainly outward, since for Sandler (1976) it even includes an adult's use of a childhood defense in a particular circumstance.

My own thought is of an analytic case, a homosexual, who for the first time was entering into heterosexual activity. I suppose one could say that he was filled with conflicts of all sorts. Perhaps one could say he had a conflict between being homosexual or heterosexual. One major problem of his was that of a need to have his masculine striving responded to. He had had a childhood of ridicule in this regard, having been dressed in girl's clothing. His penis was an object of scorn for his sister and mother, and he had been ashamed of his body for all of his life. Much of the period in his analysis had to do with the emergence of exhibitionistic fantasies of his masculine self and the concomitant need for a reflecting selfobject. My own way of conceptualizing the new developmental achievement is simply not able to consider this as much of a psychoanalytic conflict situation. It is a matter of ongoing new experiences being confronted. I have no doubt that some heroic stretching of classical theory could make it a conflict, but it seems at some point to have lost its moorings in the original sense of Freud's. This, I think, is a fine example of theory tampering and is probably cause enough to say that the theory really cannot do the task assigned it. To say that conflict should embrace what are essentially conscious decision problems i.e., a movement into a new state of affairs versus maintaining the old, should I do this or should I do that?, is, to my mind, no longer a psycho-analytic effort. Even the material of child and infant observation can remain on a descriptive and superficial level if one reports that the child departs and returns for refueling because of a conflict over separation. Psychoanalysts must ask exactly what the child communicates to the mother and vice versa. Of course going back and forth is a conflict of sorts but it is not quite what Freud had in mind about the clashing of forces. If everything is "conflict" then conflict is nothing.

Another step in the historical sequence of theory ascendency is the attempt to isolate the new one by admitting its value but assigning it to a different domain of inquiry. Sometimes we see the development of new methods of investigation in this manner. At other times, however, these efforts are doomed to failure because new theories are, as emphasized, essentially incompatible and revolutionary. I think we see this dilemma in the field of self psychology in terms of the very concept of the selfobject. Either one grows out of such a relationship, leaves it behind and advances to clear and permanent self and object differentiation, or else a whole new way of conceptualizing normal growth and development must be entertained in order to comprehend the existence of lasting and mature selfobjects.

Let us compare the clinical situation in terms of the data gathered and conclusions drawn as an analyst listens to a patient who is upset or concerned about a pending separation. If one listens with a theoretical assumption that normal development involves a movement toward individuation and gradual independence, then one would probably concern oneself with the struggle over such freedom and the conflict over leaving the libidinal object with whom one is attached. The typical sequence of behavior seen in separation-individuation conflicts and translated back into fantasies about the relationship with and the ties to the analyst or parent may or may not lead to different analytic results than that derived from an alternate theory. But a typical statement such as: "The analyst continued to sense the patient's need to evoke the hated and wanted intrusiveness in the transference, followed by resistive withdrawal" certainly sounds like the theory is dictating the kind of information one obtains from a patient (Selma Kramer 1979). Other elaborations of the need for the patient to experience rage (Rothstein 1979) insist that one will do a disservice to a patient by neglecting a consideration of the patient's sadism and aggressiveness. This seems to support the position of most philosophers of science that one cannot separate observation statements from theoretical statements (Grundy 1973) and to confirm that we see what we look for.

If one contrasts this guiding theory with one that states that the individual wants and needs continuing relationships with his selfobjects and that individuation is not separation but rather a change in the nature (controlling vs. being controlled) of the relationship, then a new and different form of data emerges. Rage is not a necessary condition of separation but rather is a reaction to selfobject failures. Termination is not a working through of a particular individuation conflict but rather one of the attainment of empathic connections. (Kohut 1979) Much, if not all of the material elicited sounds and looks different and even the technical interventions become changed. But this soon is seen as *not* a matter of translating one theory back into the other but rather that the very facts that they gather are so theory laden as to defy comparison.

The important and really only significant point about the lack of compatibility of the two ways of looking at separation is not that one is right and the other wrong. This is simply not the case with theories and for any critic to show incorrectness by stressing incompatibility is to merely underscore the obvious. The question is a much more difficult one and has to do with a lengthy examination of the value of one theory against the other. Therefore if one examines a new set of ideas and finds them in conflict with old established ones, this is not an occasion to write a critique. It is a call for proper surprise and curiosity in order to ascertain if certain old unanswered problems may now lend themselves to better understanding. Of course all new theories are incorrect. That is as they should be; or else one only relearns what one already knows.

This, of course, brings us to the final position of the three, the one that posits a psychoanalytic theory of self psychology that includes and replaces that of the primacy of the oedipal conflict. Again, without making a claim for its correctness I can suggest what we must expect of it: it must encompass everything we already know, and more. If it fails to do this then it indeed is but a minor variation on a theme which will ultimately be absorbed into our existing views of psychoanalysis without any fundamental radical upheavals. This is where we are today and that is the problem that confronts us.

To return to some clinical material I would like to reconsider a point that we are all familiar with that demonstrates the seeming paradox of good analytic work followed by depression and despondency. A patient, for example, gains insight into a phobic avoidance and instead of this resulting in feeling better, feels worse. There are many ways to talk of this: certainly as one variant of a negative therapeutic reaction. Either the patient felt guilty about getting better, or was afraid to get better, or the correct interpretation undid repressions which released aggression which was turned inward. And yet another way of seeing what happened is quite different. It is that the very act of interpretation takes place within a self-selfobject matrix and that one must subsequently respond to the patient to confirm him or her, to positively mirror an achievement, much like one must respond to the oedipal achievements of the developing child. Inasmuch as some analysts might agree with this technical advice it still is necessary to recognize that there is a significant theoretical difference between the insight alone making the change and the insight also serving as the expression of a developing self. There should be no question that one needs to interpret the need for confirmation in turn; but there is a distinct difference between the two clinical theories in terms of levels and breadth of the interpretive work. The introduction of so-called structure building features in psychoanalysis is certainly not new or confined to self psychology. There are two points to be made which might illustrate how the psychology of the self may go beyond what we know in this regard. The first is that the selfobject transferences enable one to conceptualize, literally to see the unfolding development of how the self as structure accomplishes such an increased capacity to be self-regulating. This is a more congenial and more clinically relevant picture than an abstract concept such as one of "ego repair." The second feature that needs our careful consideration is the one that suggests that interpretations per se are structural alterations which proceed by transmuting internalization; and the interpretation of the meaning of an interpretation might therefore be a necessary activity of every analysis. Every interpretation is capable of a new feeling about one's self.

Since theories are undetermined as to facts and since alternative theories seem to handle the data equally well at a certain level of investigation, how are we to decide which one to follow? It is certainly not a case for an indiscriminate choice of theories but the answer (and there is one) may be hard for some to take. In order to decide which theoretical approach is of maximum utility one must commit oneself to it and use it in a non-prejudicial way for a period of time. Only a test of usefulness is worthwhile and only a complete understanding of the theory will allow such a test. Unfortunately and incredibly so much of the criticisms of self psychology are based on those basically irrelevant comments which range from a claim to the nonexistence of selfobject transferences to the insistence that the conduct of these analyses is no different from what everyone has been doing all along.

The final acceptance of one theory over another is not arbitrary. No matter how long parallel theories may co-exist there do exist criteria for choosing one over another. Philosophers of science (Harre 1972) sometimes suggest two poles of the epistemology of science: phenomenalism and realism. Some sciences like anatomy are more suited to realism, and some like physics more suited to phenomenalism. So too are some theoretical statements directed to real things and some to "fictions" which have a degree of plausability. But regardless of how we position psychoanalysis in our consideration these same philosophers list criteria for choosing one theory over another (Popper 1963). Until we come to grips with the essentials of our analytic observations, with the true facts of psychoanalytic evidence we must content ourselves with criteria of comprehensibility and coherence in our selection of theories. But the first and essential step is to utilize the theory to see just what we can learn.

The person who claims never to have seen an idealizing transference must first learn what to look for. The person who claims he has known this all along and/or has been doing this all along, as in the typical critiques of Mr. Z., betrays both a suspect honesty and a glaring misconception of the basis of scientific theory. One can only wonder what would be the psychoanalytic explanation behind a statement of the need to confirm the patient's accomplishments in dealing with a phobia; one that would be capable of being communicated to others and is part and parcel of a classical approach. Niceness, kindness, support; those are not answers since even these social amenities are capable of being explained. The claims of doing what every good analyst does are both foolish because we simply do not all do the same things, and insubstantial because the next generation of analysts needs a framework for operations. I, for one, do not see a place in classical psychoanalytic theory for this particular kind of intervention except, perhaps in the usual effort of expanding the theory.

It might be quite worthwhile to examine just what so many of the so-called pioneers in psychoanalysis do offer us. I think it is an opportunity: one that allows us a choice to see if our old map is as good as ever or if we can go further with a new one. Theories are never right or wrong. No theory can be conclusively refuted. No theory is absolutely acceptable (Hesse 1978). The criterion of pragmatism is the single best guide to adopt; and this certainly calls for a maximum of tolerance and a minimal conviction of certain truths.

CONCLUDING REMARKS

Self psychology has presented psychoanalysis with a challenge by way of allowing certain observations to be made. This includes a theory of self-development that uses the concept of maturing relationships with selfobjects. It is a holistic theory which posits an overall open system of the self and that suggests continual viable relationships with ones' selfobjects. It likewise places the center of the treatment of many individuals on the development and resolution of the selfobject transferences.

Psychoanalysts must come to grips with these ideas of self psychology by testing their utility in the service of explanation. Such an inquiry involves an acquaintance and understanding of the working through of these selfobject transferences. Unfortunately most critics of self psychology seem to restrict their activities to citing deviation and difference. This is not the proper avenue for the critique of new ideas. On the other hand, to neglect a careful study of the contributions of pioneers is to rob ourselves and our patients of a chance at an advance of our science. This is hardly tolerable in any effort that aims to help and is equally unfair to our wish to know.

New ideas are not new paradigms. That unfortunate word has been so abused that its greatest popularizer (Kuhn 1977) has now disowned it. His intent seems to have been to describe an event in the sociology of knowledge. But pioneers who present new ideas essentially offer us epistemological tools and the reactions to these changes in perception are not necessarily an accurate gauge of their value. To change a set of convictions is always an effort, but psychoanalysts should be *more* rather than less capable of this task. Sigmund Freud was as "incorrect" as Erich Fromm was and as Heinz Kohut (1979b) now is. We owe our gratitude to that pioneer who has the courage to be wrong.

REFERENCES

Brenner, C. (1979). The components of psychic conflict and its consequences in mental life. *Psychoanalytic Quarterly* 48:547–567.

Feyerabend, P. K. (1975). *Against Method.* London: New Left Books.

Freud, A. (1965). *Normality and Pathology in Childhood: Assessments of Development.* New York: International Universities Press.

Gediman, H. K. (1980). The search for the self Selected writings of Heinz Kohut. Special Book Review *in The Psychoanalytic Review* 17 4 1980–81.

Grundy, R. E. (1973). *Theories and Observations in Science Introductory Essay.* Englewood Cliffs, New Jersey: Prentice-Hall, Inc.

Harre, R. (1972). *The Philosophies of Science* Oxford: Oxford University Press.

Hesse, M. (1980). *Revolutions and Reconstructions in the Philosophy of Science* Bloomington and London: Indiana University Press.

Kohut, H. (1979a). The two analyses of Mr. Z. *International Journal of . Psychoanalysis* 60:3–227.

—— (1979b). Concluding remarks on the Conference on Self Psychology Los Angeles, California, October 1979.

Kramer, S. (1979). The technical significance and application of Mahler's separation-individuation theory. *Journal of the American Psychoanalytic Association* 27 (Suppl): 251.

Kuhn, T. S. (1962). *The structure of scientific resolutions.* Chicago: University of Chicago Press.

Kuhn, T. (1977). *The Essential Tension.* Chicago and London: University of Chicago Press.

Popper, K. (1963). *Conjectures and Refutations.* New York and Evanston: Harper Torchbooks, Harper and Row.

Rangell, L. (1981). From insight to change. *Journal of the American Psychoanalytic Association* 29:119–141.

Rothstein, A. (1979). Toward a critique of the psychology of the self (manuscript).

Sandler, J. (1976). Actualization and object relationships. *Journal of the Philadelphia Association for Psychoanalysis* 3:59–70.

Waelder, R. (1930). The principle of multiple function: Observations on overdetermination *Psychoanalytic Quarterly* 5:45–62.

Wallerstein, R. (1980). Self-psychology and 'classical' psychoanalytic psychology: The nature of their relationship. A review and an overview Presented at the Boston Psychoanalytic Society and InstituteSymposium on Psychology of the 'Self' Boston, Massachusetts, November 1, 1980.

Self-Psychology Since Kohut (1998)

The place of self-psychology within psychoanalysis is taken up by Goldberg in his paper, *Self-Psychology Since Kohut* (1998), not as an effort to locate the place of self-psychology in established tradition, but to distinguish self-psychology from its developing branches, or "separate tributaries," of the intersubjective, interpersonal and relational. Self-psychology seems to have passed from the radical new to the established tradition.

The major conceptual contributions of self-psychology include the description of the self-object transferences, their clinical elaboration, the concept of the self-object as well as the area of the narcissistic behavior disorders (addictions, delinquencies and perversions) that are considered a particular form of self-disorder and characterized by a vertical split. The position of empathy as the basis of all depth psychology and the altered consideration of aggression as reactive rather than primary are other notable features of self-psychology.

According to Goldberg, intersubjective theory has a different definition of empathy, as it holds a different view of the curative process and the focus is on the shared construction of the patient and the analyst.

Relational self-psychology claims a distinction from traditional self-psychology in its insistence on optimal gratification to promote change. In this view, according to Goldberg, the object is considered separate from the self, and there seems to be an absence of an interpretive approach in bringing about therapeutic change.

Neither intersubjective nor relational theory has a serious consideration of the role of unconscious fantasy. In this way, both differ from self-psychology. Goldberg states, "Kohut's development of the foundation for the notion of self-objects went hand-in-hand with the modification and transformation of unconscious fantasy." In response to a patient who wonders if her analyst is preoccupied, an intersubjective response might include the analyst scrutinizing her participation in this view. A self-psychologist might wonder if this perception stems from a grandiose fantasy struggling for recognition and modification. The line we draw determines the approach we take.

—GM

The changes in psychoanalytic self psychology since its origination by Heinz Kohut are described as differences in three branches: the traditional, the intersubjective, and the relational. Each claims both a distinctiveness and a major influence within self psychology. These are described and contrasted. It is suggested that an effort to integrate all three is premature, and that they will continue to grow separately.

INTRODUCTION

This is in the nature of a historical progress note. For many students of psychoanalytic psychology, the advent of self psychology was an interesting moment in the growth and development of depth psychology, one which began with the publications of Heinz Kohut and which continues on with the adoption of several of his ideas and concepts. Most psychoanalysts do not keep up with the literature of self psychology, and most have only a casual acquaintance with its vocabulary and even less familiarity with its internal struggles. Kohut's original aim for self psychology to have an established place within organized psychoanalysis has given way to its rather surprising emergence embodied in a solid group of clinicians and investigators outside of the psychoanalysis that Kohut knew. This has been accompanied by conflicts, disagreements, and, perhaps predictably, different branches. That a significant partisanship has arisen within the domain of self psychology is one of those inevitable events that plague much of psychoanalysis, but it should not conceal the fact that self psychology, itself, has seemed to travel along distinctly different ideological lines.

It is always difficult to lift out the pure theoretical concepts from the political surround, but there does seem to be a rather clear clustering of concepts that differ from one another while still claiming an allegiance to self psychology, an origin from self psychology, as well as an advance of and beyond self psychology. Only one of these branches has a definite name, i.e., intersubjectivity, and so one is immediately at a disadvantage in pursuing an effort to single out and describe these other chosen branches without falling into the political pitfalls of organizational controversy. My attempt therefore will be to sketch the separate tributaries of self psychology without, in any way, laying claim to either completeness or correctness. This will necessarily result in certain omissions, such as the role of social constructivism, the concept of motivational systems (of Lichtenberg, 1989), and narrative theory. These are significant and important issues in contemporary psychoanalysis, but they seem to me to be less representative of a movement in self psychology than of general themes in psychoanalysis. Each, however, does play a significant role in the growth of self psychology but has not, as yet, become more of a member of one branch than another, i.e., they are ecumenical.

One often hears of a fantasy involving the return of an originator, like Freud, to consider what has happened to his or her brainchild. One example of this would be to recall the time when the rules for admission to candidacy were so strict that it was claimed that Freud would never have passed muster. Just as that period in time has also passed, so has the question of whether or not Freud would have embraced one or another advance in psychoanalysis, such as ego psychology. The field is too fluid. The same is true of self psychology, since fidelity is often more to persons than to ideas. Beyond the cry of whether or not Kohut might have agreed or disagreed with any idea lies the more powerful plea of whether or not the idea is a worthwhile one. The answer to that remains more with the perspective of history than anything else. Much of the original work of Kohut has found a significant place in psychoanalysis. The significance of the narcissistic transferences, the perception of the maturation of narcissism, the focus upon the phenomenology of narcissistic disorders have all entered into the ordinary discourse of most analysts (Gill, 1994).

The continuing evolution of self psychology has articulated with the emergence of a number of other psychoanalytic excursions such as seen in interpersonal and social constructivist concepts (Hoffman, 1991). Thus the path of self psychology can be seen as a clue to the entire postmodern era for psychoanalysis (Barratt, 1993). Viewing psychoanalysis as an evolving system allows us to see the emergence of a host of ideas that may or may not survive the rigors of clinical experience.

Inasmuch as the varied branches that have emerged in self psychology, perhaps because of their shared origin, have survived in a competitive atmosphere, it is almost impossible to describe them in anything approaching pure form. Each claims a status that seems to depend upon being different from the others, and so any listing or description carries a weight of a value judgment. With the impossible goal of even-handedness, the bibliography will therefore be directed primarily to a few representative works and will aim to avoid as much as possible the spirit of competition that presently exists in and about the students of self psychology. It is selective rather than inclusive.

Following from the excellent book review by Morton and Estelle Shane (1993) which emphasized the differences of opinion about the basic tenets of self psychology, all of which derived from different authors, my essay will be directed toward the trends or movements in self psychology which are crystallizing out without a particular allegiance to a particular person. Just as self psychology is working itself free from an absolute allegiance to Kohut, so, too, will we see these branches survive less on the basis of their fidelity to their founders and more on the basis of what we hope will be essentially pragmatic factors. Although a theory may be inextricably tied to its originator, its destiny depends upon its use over time. And for many it is much too early to judge their staying power.

One unhappy result of any selection of current forces in self psychology, as in any dynamic field, is an arbitrary delineation of exclusion and inclusion. Some people insist that they are not self psychologists although they seem to be. Some insist that they are but appear otherwise. Probably it does not matter except in an overview such as this which aims to identify trends within the field. Therefore, it seems best to minimize the personal references and to highlight the ideas, and so some omissions are therefore inevitable.

I will exclude some issues that seem closely tied to self psychology but have over time become integrated into all of psychoanalysis. Prominent among these is the position of empathy which Kohut felt was the basis of all depth psychology but which he insisted had no particular tie or special affinity to self psychology. There is no doubt that there are a number of different emphases on the nature and role of empathy, but, at present, there seem not enough crucial differences in its definition and employment. Its popularity may be ascribed to self psychology but not its utilization. Everyone now seems to include empathy as an essential component within psychoanalysis.

Another notable feature of self psychology has been its altered consideration of aggression as reactive rather than primary. Putting aside the enormous misunderstandings that have grown up outside of self psychology about aggression, there does not seem to be much serious debate within self psychology itself about Kohut's original position (Ornstein, 1993). That position certainly had room for normal assertiveness alongside that of narcissistic rage. The parallel issue that has had only a minority of psychoanalysts preoccupied, i.e., the place of inborn destruction and the death instinct is probably one that self psychology has effectively bypassed. Indeed, the entire consideration of psychoanalysis as posited on drive psychology is not one entertained by self psychology, and is now embraced beyond self psychology (Lichtenberg, 1989).

With these provisos in mind, I will now turn to a brief examination of three main trends in self psychology since Kohut.

TRADITIONAL SELF PSYCHOLOGY

The major theoretical contribution offered by Kohut in his delineation of psychoanalytic self psychology was that of the selfobject, and the major clinical contribution was the description of the selfobject transferences: their formation, working through, and resolution. The work that followed upon and flowed from these central theses was primarily one of elaboration and variation on these themes. All kinds of forms and types of selfobjects were considered and described. These ranged from non-animate things, such as musical themes, and animals to a further categorization of selfobjects from archaic to mature. As might be expected, the concept became overloaded, with almost anything that seemed to play a role in growth and development quickly and readily being assigned the role of a selfobject. In the evolution of any idea a popular term becomes over popular and then—usually after a plea to dispense with it entirely—it starts to get a more focused definition. This happened within and outside of self psychology with the overuse of empathy, which still awaits a rescue from its overzealous proponents.

Selfobject was originally intended by Kohut to mean another person who served to perform a function which one could not perform for oneself. He meant this to be thought of as a forerunner for psychic structure, since he described the phase-specific taking over of these functions as resulting in further structuralization. That some selfobjects remain with us throughout life seemed to allow a modification of this theoretical contribution, since it opened the door to a new definition of maturity which seemed to have room for lifelong structural deficiency, i.e., the selfobject was even needed to maintain the self.

Along with the ongoing work on a better definition of selfobject, there has been a continuing debate about whether the selfobject needs to be considered as an inner experience or an actual entity. This struggle over the correct positioning of the psyche in the world is equally waged throughout all of psychoanalysis which has yet to clarify the true nature of objects. Noteworthy, however, is that the selfobject is a theoretical bridge to the controversy that goes on between one-person and two-person psychologies; and self psychology is no stranger to this debate. For some the selfobject is a part of the self and thus is best considered as a one-person psychology. For others it is a connection to another and is therefore a clear example of a two-person psychology. The concept of the selfobject and its reliance on a theory of self development, however, does serve to differentiate it from most of the other two-person psychologies.

Without too much of an excursion into some knotty philosophic issues, the distinction between one- and two-person psychologies must begin with some agreed upon and accepted definition of a person. From William James on, we have learned not to limit the notion of person to that which is contained within one's skin but to extend it to a larger area involving ownership. Since self psychology regards selfobjects as part of the self, it extends the concept of the person to include those others who function as part of the self. The self is composed of or constituted by its selfobjects. Therefore, the concept of a person seen socially or from the position of an external observer becomes transformed into that of the person seen in a psychological sense, i.e., from within a mind. Two persons in conversation seen by an observer is the social or interpersonal perspective. However, from the vantage point of the inner psychology of one or the other social person there may be only one self with his or her selfobjects; therefore self psychology is now conceptualized as a one-person psychology (Goldberg, 1990p. 126).

The clinical elaboration of the selfobject transference is also a definite demarcation for self psychology. The literature of self psychology has followed a trend seen in much of psychiatry outside of psychoanalysis in a pursuit of shorter modes of treatment. There seem to be more reports of psychotherapy than psychoanalysis and thus more inferences about the nature of the transference rather than a fully explored and resolved description of its course. Concurrent with the abbreviation of the therapeutic efforts has been the use of what are called principles of self psychology in child therapy, couples therapy, family therapy, and even organizational psychiatry (Goldberg, 1985, 1986-1996). Since this trend too has usually been felt to be a dilution of psychoanalysis, it needs to be carefully studied as to its ultimate value.

One area of inquiry concerns the narcissistic behavior disorders, a diagnostic category of the addictions, delinquencies, and perversions that Kohut felt were a particular form of self-disorder. These pathological states have been examined in terms of their self structure, which is characterized by a vertical split, a form of self pathology described by Kohut, There is as well a particular kind of interpretive intervention that seems applicable in the analytic treatment of the disorders. An offshoot of this inquiry has been a significant amount of clinical material that highlights the analyst's enactments during treatment. The change of the position of the analyst from dispassionate observer and interpreter to active participant and performer is being discussed throughout psychoanalysis and psychotherapy, and so it is natural to see its significant emergence in self psychology (Bacal and Thomson, 1996). Perhaps it is most fitting to launch our description of the other trends in self psychology by considering the change in their conceptualization of the place and role of the analyst.

INTERSUBJECTIVITY

Intersubjective theory is presented as a field or system theory. In one sense all of psychoanalytic theory can be considered an open system, but the original ideas of Kohut were certainly confined and limited to a narrow consideration of the self and its selfobjects. Therefore, one must alter his or her perspective in thinking of "reciprocal interacting worlds of experience" versus intrapsychic structural relations. There certainly must be a gain and loss in each perspective, and one result of a new or different outlook is a new vocabulary. Some critics claim that a retranslation of some of the new words and phrases back into familiar words such as that of "unconscious organizing principles" back into "transference" will show no essential difference between the two lexicons, but that, of course, may rob the new theory of much of its originality and scope (Ornstein, 1995). Therefore, the ideas of intersubjectivity theory ask for a shift from drives to affectivity and a consideration of the psychoanalytic situation as a system with a fluid boundary between patient and analyst. The interplay between patient and analyst is viewed as a situation of conjunction and disjunction. The first characterizes assimilation of experiences into familiar configurations, the second into configurations that alter meanings for the patient. Both patient and analyst make contributions to the therapeutic action.

Intersubjectivists claim few concrete recommendations to style or technique in therapy, since they wish it to be a perspective broad enough to accommodate a range of practice. Indeed, intersubjective ideas are said to be but a call to an increased sensibility (Orange, 1996) or a theory, perhaps like information theory, that can accommodate a number of clinical theories. In order to achieve this position, however, it may be a contradiction to make certain clinical claims, such as those made about transference (Stolorow and Atwood, 1996). These views are not simply another statement about the analyst as growth-promoting versus the analyst as an objector old. The crucial difference between traditional self psychology and the theory of intersubjectivity is that for the latter the transference is felt to have two basic dimensions: the selfobject dimension and the repetitive dimension. The first is said to encompass development enhancing experiences, and the second to illustrate experiences of developmental failure. The essence of transference analysis lies in investigating the dimensions of transference as they take form in the ongoing intersubjective system. This system is formed by the interplay between the transference of the patient and that of the analyst. The focus is ever upon this shared construction and not upon the singular contribution of the patient projected onto the analyst.

At first blush one can hardly take exception to many of the views of intersubjectivity; it must await a test of usefulness to see if it adds much to the traditional approach. However, further difficulties have to do with the recent claim that intersubjectivity is more broad based than the singular concept of the selfobject, has a different definition of empathy, a different view of the curative process, and originated independent of Kohut's contributions (Trop, 1995). Unfortunately, problems of territoriality seem to contaminate many scientific arguments. It may well be the case that some ideas need to stake out a claim of independence in order to prosper. This does seem to be the present direction of intersubjectivity theory.

From the stance of the selfobject as a component function of the self to that of the analyst as a reciprocal interacting world of experience, we move on to the next category in which the selfobject is a variant of an object relation and in which the analyst necessarily has an impact upon the patient.

RELATIONAL SELF PSYCHOLOGY

This category is less of an organized movement than is that of intersubjectivity theory, but there is no doubt that a significant number of self psychologists see themselves as concerned with a better delineation of the object as separate and as gratifying. We can loosely call this group relational self psychology (Bacal and Newman, 1990).

Heinz Kohut originally conceived of narcissism as a separate line of development: separate from the known and accepted line attributed to objects of love and hate. Over time he seemed to modify this duality as he moved the study of the self to center stage, and as the self and its selfobjects became the fundamental features of all psychopathology.

With his emphasis on oedipal self-objects, he made these the pivotal issues for this developmental phase, and so relegated the objects of love and hate to a secondary role in the transference neuroses. Thus, the self became central, and the independent objects moved to the periphery. To bring the object as an "independent center of initiative" back to the fore does ask one to develop some scheme of relations between the self and the object. To do so involves either a commitment to the drives, which self psychology has abjured, or a looser use of the term "relations," which is not uncommon in much present-day analytic writing. The insistence on relations between the self and objects has led some to focus on the need for the person to be aware of the presence, needs, and impact on others and to include these factors in assessing growth and development. It is said that traditional self psychology has simply by-passed this area and that no treatment can make a claim to comprehensiveness without recognizing the status of the other as a separate entity. The affinity to schools of interpersonal analysis is apparent (Mitchell, 1988).

The other area where self psychology differs from the standard view of growth and development of the self has to do with the insistence by Kohut that optimal frustration is the sine qua non for the structuralization of the psyche. His viewing this as a result of interpretation has been challenged by those who claim that optimal gratification is a more felicitous description of what serves to promote change (Shane and Shane, 1996). From this there is but a short step toward concluding that interpretation per se need no longer carry the sole burden in the therapeutic effort for change. The comparison of the child's learning a language is offered as the best example of a major step in growth occurring in a properly gratifying and supportive environment with no need for frustration to serve as impetus or indeed as at all a factor. With a perspective on analytic treatment as a new growth experience, an entry becomes available to parallel the features of analysis with those of optimal development. The knotty problem of "critical periods," those that allow for language acquisition and reading comprehension and others, is yet to be solved, since in this crucial area analysis is clearly not the same as the child's experience of growing up. How can analysis recreate a period of development that has been closed? Language acquisition seems to occupy a very special place in development and so perhaps is not a valid example of how a gratifying environment can aid in structure formation. For the most part the claims made for an optimal environment suggest that growth takes place both in the life cycle and in the treatment situation without frustration (Shane and Shane, 1996). This, of course, differs from Kohut's original position.

THE PLACE OF UNCONSCIOUS FANTASY

It seems likely that any evolving branch of self psychology will strain against tradition and at some point move on into an independent course. If one considers the role of unconscious fantasy, as an example, it is not difficult to see that both the branches of intersubjectivity and relational self psychology either make little use of it or dispense with it altogether. Rather than concern ourselves with the faithfulness to tradition of the new enterprise, we perhaps can think about the point at which—just as in biological evolution—we decide that a new species has emerged. If we do embark on a new course, much like what may have happened with self psychology and classical analysis, we are justified in reexamining all of the taken-for-granted concepts that constituted the old one. Surely the concept of unconscious fantasy is a legitimate member of that group of tacit assumptions. To the degree that any core concept is eliminated, one can expect a certain ripple effect as others will necessarily be altered or themselves eliminated. No doubt this sort of straightening out of the disorganization that follows from a radical restudy is often left to be done by others at a later time. One needs to be aware, however, that even minor modifications can have significant repercussions and lasting effects.

There is little doubt that Kohut, who was well schooled in psychoanalytic theory and practice, wanted to retain what he felt were the foundations of his own training and beliefs, and that he developed self psychology as a step in the evolution of that theory. Quite aside from the social and political pressures that come from fidelity to a group dogma, he initially believed that self psychology was a natural outgrowth of the tenets of psychoanalysis. He felt that, just as Heinz Hartmann had seen it necessary to expand ego psychology with the elaboration of the concept of neutralized energy, he had to expand the theory of narcissism with the description and elaboration of the fate of unconscious fantasies by way of the deployment of selfobjects. Kohut's development of the foundation for the notion of selfobjects went hand-in-hand with the modification and transformation of these unconscious fantasies. The fantasy of greatness, which can have a pathological printout in megalomaniac visions, can also fuel the mirroring needs and have an adult resolution in the internal feeling of pride. Such fantasies are the underpinning of ambition. The fantasy of connecting with a powerful and benevolent other, which can have pathological deviance in the influencing machine, can fuel the idealizing needs and result in an adult resolution characterized by an internal feeling of enthusiasm. The initial poles of self psychology were posited on the existence of a transformation of a set of unconscious fantasies without which there seemed no psychological sense to their continued existence. The unconscious fantasy appeared to be the motor for ongoing growth, and its fate the measuring rod for the success or failure of this growth. Change could be measured with this yardstick, and pathology could be viewed with this as a background barometer. If it becomes viable to consider new and different selfobjects, such as adversarial selfobjects or twinship transferences, then it seems proper to see if there was a corresponding set of fantasies that can accompany the path for their developmental course.

These minimal considerations about unconscious fantasy must be played out in the future against the further development of the different branches of self psychology. If a patient enters your office and remarks after a bit that she feels you are somewhat preoccupied, the range of options that present themselves for appraisal and scrutiny is quite clearly derived from your own position and stance vis-à-vis these options. You may wonder about your own participation in her view of you and thus see the intersecting subjectivities as forming this present state. However, a stance that reduces your contribution, albeit without eliminating it, might focus upon the patient's struggle with some grandiose fantasy that she fears will not be properly mirrored. A response on your part about her perception of you and your needs, along with the question of whether or not you should aim to correct that perception, would direct the treatment along an entirely different path than a mere interpretation of a grandiose fantasy struggling for recognition and modification. No one would argue for one position as necessarily exclusive; and most would agree with the absolute necessity for considering and ideally integrating all of the possible perspectives. But any one of them has a certain magnetic pull of its own, as it tends to encourage one approach rather than another. From the concentration upon a possible unconscious fantasy, one is inevitably led toward thinking about the next point in the sequence that asks whether it is from her or from me or from both of us?

The unconscious need not be thought of as a thing or a place. Instead, it is a way of looking at things: we assume that manifest issues have concealed meaning behind them. It is what Kohut called a part of our introspective intentions. One approaches reality only by way of a background of experience, and a part of a psychoanalyst's background is the concept of the unconscious. Every encounter with a patient can be studied within a frame that allows for a major contribution from an unconscious fantasy or for a major contribution from the immediate actions of the participants. The line that we choose to draw determines our varied approach to the patient (Goldberg, 1990p. 127). Much of present-day self psychology seems to divide along this line.

INTRAPSYCHIC VERSUS INTERPERSONAL

Kohut's study of the self was the study of a psychic structure, and he considered the selfobject a component of that structure. He often contrasted his stance with that of interpersonal psychology and usually managed to denigrate the latter in spite of his protest of innocence. His main criticism of the interpersonal was that it was from a third person perspective, but the implicit criticism was that it was superficial. He felt that psychoanalysis studied the makeup of the psyche and that empathy was the tool for such a study, while social interactions were exteroceptive inspections by more distant observers. Gill was one person able to be clear in his view that analysis was interpersonal, and so that we did study the goings on between persons. He never could quite understand why self psychologists could not see that. It takes no great feat of intellect to see that looking at what you think goes on inside is different from what you think goes on between, and that thinking about what A does to B is different from what B does to A. Putting aside all arguments about methods and models, it seems unlikely that a concentration on an unconscious fantasy will not take precedence over a supportive comment from a therapist if one chooses up sides with Kohut versus if one goes along with Gill. The patient's perception of the analyst's feelings counts more for Gill than does the patient's projection of her own discontent. That is how it should be in our world of heterogeneity; it underlines the differences that exist between the branches without in any way valuing one over the other, save in their ultimate usefulness to both patient and analyst. These three branches do seem to separate out once again when we choose to look for emphasis. The failed parent of Kohut comes necessarily from the patient, is co-constructed with the analyst by Gill, and asks for a new and potentially curative response from our third group. Although such oversimplification does a disservice to all three groups, it does do the service of recognizing that they are not all of a piece. From whatever common core they derive, they are spreading apart, and it seems highly likely that they will continue to do so.

DISCUSSION

Organizations make for easy distinctions, while the distinctions made of a heterogeneous field may seem quite arbitrary. However, a greater problem seems to occur if the non-members of a scientific field assume that it is a static one, and that one need only refer to whatever original works have endured in order to be informed. This is surely the case with psychoanalytic self psychology no less than with any other sector of the psychoanalytic world. One may wonder how Freud would consider the present-day content of a literature in the field about his own brainchild; this is an equally imaginative exercise for Heinz Kohut, Melanie Klein, Jacques Lacan, and many others.

It may or may not be true that the changes within self psychology are a microcosm of the changes within all of analysis, but there is no doubt that they give hints of general trends. These trends have to do with the recognition of the dialectic exchange that takes place in all of treatment, the more careful study of the different forms that treatment can take, the application of the data and knowledge of the treatment outside of the one-to-one setting, and the incorporation of information from other disciplines into the overall comprehension of therapy. This, of course, is not to mention the enormous changes brought about by the changing place of analytic treatment in our society that ranges from altering training and credentials to modifications in practice. The accompanying social changes that characterize self psychology are, of course, a topic for another discussion.

In conclusion, if we confine ourselves to the clinical and theoretical aspects of self psychology, we see that the central concepts have given birth to a set of separate tributaries, each of which lays some claim to serve as the major voice in the field. The traditional, the intersubjective, and the relational may go on to have distinctive lives of their own or may become reabsorbed in one another or evolved in a totally new form. It may be most important to recognize that efforts to diminish differences or to integrate disparate ideas into some sort of uniformity could turn out not to be in the best interests of the field. That remains to be seen, and it is to be hoped that we shall all continue to look.

REFERENCES

Bacal, H. & Newman, K. (1990). *Theories of Object Relations: A Bridge to Self Psychology.* New York: Columbia University Press.

——— & Thomson, P. (1996). The psychoanalyst's selfobject needs and the effect of their frustration on the treatment: a new view of countertransference. In *Basic Ideas Reconsidered: Progress in Self Psychology, Vol. 12*, ed. A. Goldberg. Hillsdale, NJ/London: Analytic Press, pp. 17–35.

Barratt, B. B. (1993). *Psychoanalysis and the Postmodern Impulse: Knowing and Being since Freud's Psychology.* Baltimore/London: Johns Hopkins University Press.

Gill, M. M. (1994). Heinz Kohut's self psychology. In *A Decade of Progress: Progress in Self Psychology, Vol. 10*, ed. A. Goldberg. Hillsdale, NJ/London: Analytic Press, pp. 197–211.

Goldberg, A., Ed. (1985). *Progress in Self Psychology, Vol. 1.* New York/London: Guilford.

——— (1986–1996). *Progress in Self Psychology, Vols. 2–12.* Hillsdale, NJ/London: Analytic Press.

——— (1990). *The Prisonhouse of Psychoanalysis.* Hillsdale, NJ/London: Analytic Press.

Hoffman, I. Z. (1991). Discussion: toward a social-constructivist view of the psychoanalytic situation. (Discussion of papers by L. Aron, A. Modell, and J. Greenberg.) *Psychoanalytic Dialogues* 1:74–105.

Leider, R. J. (1996). The psychology of the self (self psychology). In *Textbook of Psychoanalysis*, ed. E. Nersessian & R. G. Kopff, Jr. Washington DC/London: Amer. Psychiatry. Press, pp. 127–164.

Lichtenberg, J. D. (1989). Psychoanalysis and Motivation. Hillsdale, NJ/London: Analytic Press.

Mitchell, S. A. (1988). Relational Concepts in Psychoanalysis: An Integration. Cambridge, MA/London: Harvard University Press.

Orange, D. (1996). Remarks at the 1996 Self Psychology Conference. Washington, DC.

Ornstein, P. (1993). Chronic rage from underground. In *The Widening Scope of Self Psychology: Progress in Self Psychology, Vol. 9*, ed. A. Goldberg. Hillsdale, NJ/London: Analytic Press, pp. 143–158.

——— (1995). Critical reflections on a comparative analysis of "self psychology and intersubjectivity theory." In *The Impact of New Ideas: Progress in Self Psychology, Vol. 11*, ed. A. Goldberg. Hillsdale, NJ/London: Analytic Press, pp. 47–78.

Shane, M. & Shane, E. (1993). Self psychology after Kohut: one theory or many? *APA*, 41: 777–797.

——— (1996). Self psychology in search of the optimal: a consideration of optimal responsiveness, optimal provision, optimal gratification, and optimal restraint in the clinical situation. In *Basic Ideas Reconsidered: Progress in Self Psychology, Vol. 12*, ed. A. Goldberg. Hillsdale, NJ/London: Analytic Press, pp. 37–54.

Stolorow, R. D. & Atwood, G. E. (1996). The intersubjective perspective. *Psychoanalytic Review* 83:181–194.

Trop, J. L. (1995). Self psychology and intersubjectivity theory. In *The Impact of New Ideas: Progress in Self Psychology, Vol. 11*, ed. A. Goldberg. Hillsdale, NJ/London: Analytic Press, pp. 31–46.

American Pragmatism and American Psychoanalysis (2002)

Goldberg explores the appeal for relinquishing correctness in favor of usefulness in his 2002 paper, *American Pragmatism and American Psychoanalysis*.

Where is the place for pragmatism in the field of psychoanalysis? Pragmatism concerns itself with what is most useful in terms of increasing our capacity to better make our way in the world and the most useful tools of the trade being the most justified. In other words, only the test of effectiveness should cause us to choose one set of ideas over another. The yearning that we may find one vocabulary, one set of techniques and procedures that puts it all together in a neat package must give way towards acceptance that pluralism dominates psychoanalysis. Further, that "we would do best not to try to translate the workings and language of one into another. One integrating concept is the effort to understand another person in depth." It is this claim for understanding that unifies the "diverse bundle of claims and techniques."

—GM

* * *

The author compares American pragmatism with American psychoanalysis in an effort to place the existence of the many diverse schools and theories of psychoanalysis in a historical context. Pragmatism is seen as a theory of instrumentation or a collection of tools for accomplishing goals; it claims that many of our efforts to know and seek truth are based upon myths. Psychoanalysis, too, can be seen to pursue certain theoretical claims based on myths. The present climate of pluralism in psychoanalysis is not a phase, but an indication of our diverse ways of achieving in-depth understanding of another person.

INTRODUCTION

Psychoanalysis, as it is understood and practiced today in the United States, is a much different phenomenon than it was fifty or even twenty years ago. It is also equally distinct from what is identified by the same name outside of the States—say, in Europe or South America. Although many of its adherents study, teach, and claim psychoanalysis to be a monolithic set of ideas and procedures, in truth, it is a diverse and heterogeneous bundle of claims and techniques held together by a somewhat vague allegiance to the seminal ideas of Sigmund Freud.

Indeed, periodically, even that line of tradition to its founder is given little more than a nod to an association more historical than ideological. The sometimes futile efforts to draw borders around the field by giving it a definition and a set of established technical procedures more often than not ends in acrimony and discord, with a resultant further separation and estrangement of one set of beliefs from another. Every thought-provoking issue, ranging from niceties of the setting—such as frequency, use of the couch, and duration of analyst-patient contact—to the more hallowed principles of technique—such as free association, sharing of personal information about the analyst, and even the way to interpret dream material—has, at one time or another, come under scrutiny, attack, and either alteration or dismissal. The field is seen either as a mess or as a victim of bad science in need of straightening out.

I think it is important for thoughtful students of analysis to take a step back from their personal islands of propriety and affiliation in order to see if we are part of a particular historical process, one that is not unusual or necessarily one to be condemned or despised. Such a step might pave the way for consideration of a particular movement in philosophy that at one time had, and has again recently seen, a popularity and vigor that may well be peculiarly American. That movement is American pragmatism. In proposing such an inquiry, I am not by any means suggesting that this is the only or best way to study changes in psychoanalysis. I do hope, however, to dispel fears about dilution of the scientific tenets of the field, and even to reawaken some of the enthusiasm that once attended the discipline we practice.

Discussions of philosophical points are usually not readily embraced by psychoanalytic readers, because such discussions are essentially nonclinical and often seem to bear little relevance to analytic practice. However, a philosophical viewpoint is called for in order to explain certain socio-historical features that are overtaking the practice of psychoanalysis. Furthermore, it seems fair to assume that most practicing analysts are interested in issues related to technique, and pragmatism is considered a philosophy of instrumentalism or one devoted to the tools of a trade. It also seems fair to conclude that most students of analysis are interested in the field's intellectual history, and the history of pragmatism seems to parallel that of analysis. For these reasons, a marriage of the two holds promise.

What is Pragmatism?

The intellectual history of pragmatism began in the early 1900s, with William James, Charles Pierce, and John Dewey. Each of these men warrants a lengthy historical exposition of his life and ideas, but that effort must be put aside in order for us to pursue the essential idea of pragmatism: "Thought is an integral and constitutive part of historical experience. Truth is something that happens to an idea within the exigencies of a particular time and place" (Pettegrew 2000, p. 3).

Pragmatism's most popular and vocal spokesperson today is Richard Rorty (1979, 1982), who is considered by some to be a menace, while others see him as the most original and important philosopher writing today (Brandon 2000). The menace label derives from Rorty's status as a debunker of the tried and true, while the perception of originality reflects his insistence on a total reframing of philosophy. He has been the one most responsible for a revival of interest in pragmatism, but he gives due credit to Dewey for the origin of the bulk of his ideas. The grounding of these ideas in Dewey allows for a distinction from the many other ideas associated with pragmatism, ideas subsumed under the rubric of relativism and postmodernism, and ones also regularly trounced or misunderstood by both casual readers and large numbers of scholars and critical readers. Thus, the revival of pragmatism in America is sometimes termed *neo-pragmatism*, in order to keep faith with the principles laid down by Dewey and reignited by Rorty.

These principles are best encapsulated in Rorty's (1982) claim that:

There is nothing deep down inside us except what we have put there ourselves … We produce new and better ways of talking and acting— not by a reference to a standard but just better in the sense that they come to seem clearly better than their predecessors. [p. xxxvii]

Rorty (1979) claimed that we should give up our hope of being able to accurately represent the world as it really is, and should instead come to realize that all efforts to find foundations for objective knowledge are based on misconceptions. Essentially, his position has been that we are mistaken in thinking that we can look out at the world and objectively perceive, record, and study it. Rather, he said, our personal and historical makeup causes us to regularly, and often radically, construct and reconstruct the world.

Although Rorty was and is the major American voice for pragmatism, he has been joined by several European contributors who propose basic principles regarding the undoing of dualisms of subject and object, fact and value, and knower and known. The best known of these non-American philosophers is Jurgen Habermas (2000), who wrote that we unknowingly live under three myths: (1) the myth of the given; (2) the myth of thought as representation; and (3) the myth of certainty. These myths derive from our assumptions that: (1) we know our mental states better than anything else; (2) knowing takes place essentially in the mode of representing objects; and (3) the truth of judgment rests on evidence that vouches for this certainty.

Habermas noted that Rorty replaced the relation between subject and object with another place, *symbolic expression,* which in turn accords validity for and in an interpretive community. For Habermas, the philosophy of language á la Rorty states that

The objective world is no longer something to be reflected, but is simply the common reference point for a process of communication between members of a communication community who come to an understanding with one another with regard to something. The communicated facts can no more be separated from the process of communication than the supposition of an objective world can be separated from the intersubjective shared interpretive horizon within which the participants in communication already operate. Knowledge no longer coincides with the correspondence of sentences and facts. [Habermas described in Brandon 2000, p. 35]

Habermas went beyond Rorty in his own pragmatic perspective, which emphasized successful intersubjective communication to achieve a sought-after understanding within a communicative community. However, Habermas has surely remained within the tradition of American pragmatism.

One can readily see dangers lurking in the proposal that we do not correctly perceive the world, but instead gather about us a group of people who agree with us. We do not collect facts in order to obtain truth and knowledge that will be good for all time, but rather we hold a medley of workable opinions. Our thinking is not a record of representations of the real world, but is a series of more or less successful operations upon the world.

Acceptance of such statements may very well cause us to abandon fundamental or foundational beliefs about the world in order to join with the pragmatic rebels. This movement away from a philosophy of certainty or positivism is, not surprisingly, just what has been happening to a large extent in American psychoanalysis. Unfortunately, this change in analysis has not been seen and studied as part of a historical process, but has instead been criticized as evidence of disloyalty to Freud and to classical analysis, as reflective of mistaken ideas about science, and (most unfortunately) as simply bad philosophy.

To paraphrase the pragmatists and apply their philosophy to psychoanalysis, if there is "no way the world is," is it also true that "there is no way a patient is"? This question has been seen as a consequence of Nietzsche's perspectivism (Allen 2000, p. 141), which seems to say that your view (or guess) is as good as mine. Pragmatists argue that consensus and only consensus is the governing rule for what is right and correct. They refer back to what is most useful as being most justified, and therefore, they insist that it is *what accomplishes such an endpoint* that becomes the bearer of the way the world is.

If there is no way the world is and no way a patient is, then it may readily follow that there is no single way to either act upon the world or to properly treat a patient. If what works becomes the guiding light for therapeutic intervention—as it does for the activity of just about any accomplishment espoused by pragmatists—then one need not evaluate therapeutic behavior against a background of a set of correct or pre-scribed rules and regulations. Rather, one practices with an eye both to the chosen activity being effective *and* to the maintenance of a consen-sus of like-minded persons who constitute a community of support. Only then can we claim validity for what we do.

It is surely at this point that many people part company with pragma-tism (along with the more denigrated relativism and postmodernism), inasmuch as they begin to feel that the ground is going out from under them, along with the set of personal beliefs and principles of personal training by which they have lived (and even prospered).

WHAT, THEN, IS PSYCHOANALYSIS?

The parallel between pragmatism and psychoanalysis requires that we describe the present state of the one along with that of the other. One way to sum up pragmatism is to see it as a form of naturalism, or simply the way human beings cope with the world. To sum up much of today's psychoanalysis, we might describe it, too, as the variety of ways analysts cope with the problems of their patients. Of course, at each and every presentation of one or another method of such coping, a critical eye may determine that this or that is no longer qualified to be considered a proper component of the analytic community. And so at each and every presentation of a particular method, the effectiveness of the treatment may take a back seat to the issue of credentials, i.e., remaining within a tradition. It may be best to initially put to the side that consideration of loyalty and fidelity and to return to the three myths suggested by Habermas (2000):

1. *The myth of the given.* This is the assumption that true facts exist in the world and that, in one way or another, we can gain access to

them. Eagle, Wolitzkey, and Wakefield (2001) insisted on the assumption that there "exist stable mental states, dynamics, defenses, wishes, needs, desires, schema and so forth on which the analyst takes a perspective" (p. 481). These authors quoted Cavell (1988) as stating that the idea of a subjective perspective makes sense only if there is an objective world. The fundamental thesis is that there is certainly a way the world is, as well as a way a patient is.

The pragmatists' answer to that conviction is that to speak of facts at all is to talk of something that has conceptually already been shaped and structured. This shape is something that can be given only by a vocabulary. Conceptual norms (like dynamics and defenses) are creatures of vocabularies: no vocabularies, no conceptual norms. Rorty (1989) wrote: "Since truth is a property of sentences, since sentences are dependent for their existence upon vocabularies, and since vocabularies are made by human beings, so are truths" (p. 21).

Before there were humans, there were no truths, so if there are no true claims, then there are no facts (Brandon 2000, p. 161). We have created the list spelled out by Eagle, Wolitzkey, and Wakefield (2001)—"mental states, dynamics, defenses, wishes, needs, desires" (p. 481)—in our psychoanalytic community; it is there because we put it there. Once again, pragmatism denies that we can escape the conventions and contingencies of language in order to connect with a world of experience outside of texts. Once we buy into using the word objective, we become enslaved by it and are forced into the dualism of subjectivity versus objectivity. We must remember that the words come from us; they are not God-given.

As Davidson (2001) has said, "There is a good chance these dualisms will be abandoned" (p. 43).

2. *The myth of thought as representation.* This is a rather basic assumption in much of psychoanalytic theory, one based upon the representational world and one or another elaboration of this world of internal objects. This schema underscores Cavell's (arguable) assumption of a dualism (1988), and naturally locks one into thinking that one can and should compare the internal world with the external world.

Pragmatists say that norms of relations (i.e., the relation between an inner and an outer) are exclusively intra-vocabulary. The world does all sorts of things to us, but once we use our language to describe that world, we wrap those things into our vocabulary, causing the world to lose its independence. It is no longer a thing represented in our mind. It is no longer privileged, but is a product of ours.

Wedded as we are to a world of internal representations, it is difficult for us to tear ourselves away from this picture. Although Moore and Fine (1990) defined a psychic representation as a "more or less consistent reproduction within the mind of a perception of a meaningful thing or object" (p. 166), both computer science and neurophysiology have moved to the recognition that these replicas do not exist as such. There are no accurate reproductions, but rather useful reactions. We should not mistakenly view the printout from a computer as containing a sentence within it, any more than we view the thinking of the mind as containing the pictures within.

Today's psychoanalysis recognizes that the individual does not sit apart from the world with his or her internal representations, but rather engages in active interaction as an open system. We might now say that "my grandmother is encoded or registered in my mind and brain," but we understand that codes are not replicas or translations, but are rather directions for a process. The DNA for an arm contains no semblance of a limb, but is a series of directed steps or a program that, with the proper surround, will yield an arm. The surround or context is often the crucial ingredient in the determination of just what the programmed code will produce. Thus, one cannot call up an image of old; instead, one makes what works for the occasion.

3. *The myth of certainty.* The authority of the analyst is made available to him or her by the collective knowledge of the analyst's theories, the careful scrutiny of the transference and countertransference, and the validity of the interpretations made. Eagle, Wolitzkey, and Wakefield (2001) claim that we should aim for "humble realism" in order to un-

derstand as accurately as possible the patient's psychic reality (p. 486). Hanly and Hanly (2001) seek "critical realism," by way of which the analyst can know enough of the patient's psychic reality to accomplish the therapeutic and scientific purposes of analysis (p. 515). Others, such as Renik (1993), suggest that all the analyst's activities are so infected by one's individual psychology that one can never know the patient's psychic reality with any certainty.

Of course, the pragmatists would claim that all these authors have bought into both the myth that things can be known for sure, and subject-object dualism. The idea presented by Klein as projective identification suggests that we indeed *can* know "what comes from whom" (Hanly and Hanly 2001, p. 527). This would probably be dismissed by pragmatists with the belief that it really makes no difference. Pragmatists suggest that we need be neither humble nor critical about realism, but rather resigned to giving up the search. Thus, the pragmatists' answer to the anti-positivists is that the battle is best avoided.

In addressing psychoanalysis, pragmatism would ask that we abandon these myths and recognize that we are engaged in conversations aimed at increasing our capacities to better make our way in the world. Each of these conversations employs a favored vocabulary. Only the test of effectiveness should cause us to choose one over another. And effectiveness is always relevant to time, place, and consensus.

TODAY'S PSYCHOANALYSIS

Although there may be a good deal of disagreement, it does seem to be the case that differing schools of psychoanalysis help many people, and they seem to do so in roughly equal numbers. Tb be sure, one particular patient may not profit at all from one approach while doing quite well in another, but no school of treatment is a complete bust or can claim one hundred percent effectiveness. They all work. None can trumpet its superiority over the other based on a track record of cure or improvement or patient appreciation. We presently have no comparable statistics, so we rely on folklore. Therefore, the relevant question is why and how such diverse, and even oppositional, ways of practice can enjoy relatively equal effectiveness.

Unfortunately, that question is usually either dismissed or not even asked. The preferred question we typically hear is how so many thoroughly erroneous or wrong-headed approaches have managed to fool so many people! There is a good deal of attention paid to issues of deviance or difference, rather than to those of consensus. We tend to listen to others while marshaling an argument, rather than being open to what may be beneficial for a particular patient.

American pragmatism would make the claim that today's psychoanalysis is continually asking the wrong questions because it is consumed by the myths of our ability to gain and represent certain knowledge. We argue over who is right and who is wrong, who is loyal and who is unfaithful, and who can wear the banner of certitude. As long as we accept the dualism of subject versus object as a reality, we shall labor mightily over whether the patient's ideas have somehow found a home in our mind and managed to take over our thoughts. As long as we believe in the world of facsimiles of persons populating our minds, we shall worry over whether these representations have become better or worse organized, more split or more whole, and, especially, closer to looking like we would like them to look. And as long as we know what is best for our patients, what is the right way to live and think, we shall be able to make a claim as to whether the patient has finally gotten it right. The pragmatist would ask that we work at doing without these fundamentals and foundations; he or she does not say that these fixed positions are wrong so much as that they limit one's freedom.

I believe the pragmatist would also ask us to change our question about the mistakes of other schools to one that asks what each does that works. Our hope for this commonality of inquiry should be directed toward an appreciation of the effectiveness of diversity. Somehow, somewhere, we must all be doing something right. That rightness cannot be dismissed as suggestion or transference cure or just plain luck, although all of those factors may also be operant. There is more to it than that, and our preoccupation with differences has blinded us to whatever it may be.

In an effort to understand why a Kleinian and an interpersonalist can explain a patient in totally different vocabularies and help a patient in what may seem to be totally different methods, we would do best *not* to try to translate the workings and language of one into the other. That is often a leveling process that aims to reduce the one into the other. That is a search for a common ground, a pursuit that serves to ignore what is distinctive about each theoretical stance. Instead, we must be able to respect differences and recognize that we are embarked on an inquiry of learning about human understanding and communication. A likely commonality of various theories is the investigation of the basis of and pitfalls in humans' understanding of one another. Such a respectful stance that recognizes commonality is more wholesome than one of insisting either that the others have gotten it wrong, or that *you* are the one who knows what is really going on.

WHY TODAY?

To discuss the history of pragmatism in America is to appreciate its rise and fall and recrudescence. Hollinger (1980) wrote: "Pragmatism is a concept most historians can do without" (p. 88). Yet soon after that comment was written, pragmatism returned in full force and revitalized the entire field of intellectual history.

More than once, we have heard and read similar indictments of psychoanalysis as something many psychotherapists can do without. In truth, however, there is a similar revitalization going on in analysis today, though it is clearly one that lives outside of the tried and true tenets of classical analysis. Pluralism is what dominates today's psychoanalysis, and pluralism is the watchword of pragmatism. It is important to see this pluralism in its own right, not as a steppingstone or a temporary phase that will culminate in some final, unifying, overarching theory that puts it all together into a neat package. Today's analysis is composed of a host of different communities employing different vocabularies to help patients in different ways. There is little doubt that some patients do better with one such vocabulary over another, and that some of these communities seem to make no sense whatsoever to some of us. There is a good deal of doubt as to how this all came about and why it continues to dominate the scene of contemporary psychoanalysis.

Take, for example, the ongoing discussions noted above about the analyst's access to an objective reality. The very framing of that issue assumes a dualism between subjective and objective, as well as a conviction that somehow we can know and grasp reality. These assumptions direct one to an unresolvable endpoint that is handled by the suggestion that one should appeal to humility or give up absolutism. In response to this lack of resolve, opposing schools, such as social constructivism or intersubjectivism, have risen to claim a mutual construction of reality. Such a resolution offends some, while causing others to claim that the truth comes in many versions (Schafer 1996, p. 251), to insist that the word *objective* has two meanings (Gabbard 1997), or to declare that one knows one's own mind only in relation to another mind (Cavell 1988, p. 877). All of these solutions may be worthwhile, but may also be futile.

Compare these efforts to Dewey's comment that we should aim to create a culture in which the question of whether *truth* (or objective reality) is within our reach would not arise, because nobody would attempt to define it. "The image of thoughts or words answering to the world would go by the board, and be replaced by images of organisms coping with their environment by using language to develop projects of social cooperation" (Rorty commenting on Dewey in Brandon [2000], p. 263).

It may well be the case that the development of such cooperative projects is exactly what psychoanalysis today is trying to do in the consulting room. Midst the many schools of jargon and babble, there really does exist a host of pragmatic efforts to reach accord, but these efforts are drowned out by the din of arguments. Disagreements about whether there is a reality that can be grasped, if the analyst knows that reality better, if it is made up by the two of them, or any other variation of the typical dilemmas-perhaps, in the long run, the only difference made by these inquiries and their various answers is that they cause us to differ.

All of the solutions offered to the problem of objective reality employ a vocabulary that is designed to shape and support its basic premise. The perfectly sound thesis that one knows one's mind only in relation to another mind (Cavell 1988, p. 877) is underwritten by an assumption that a mind lives within the skin and skull of a subject. An alternative vocabulary (and one that is quite popular these days) proposes that one's mind includes other individuals. That perspective changes the entire position of how minds affect one another.

With an eye toward seeing various perspectives as tools of investigation, there need not be only one correct way toward an answer to a problem. The many approaches to so-called objective reality allow us either to settle on one, or else to dismiss it as a pseudo-problem. Pragmatism advises us to focus on the possibility that we may be captured by one or another of the above-mentioned myths as we struggle to resolve the unresolvable. Knowledge must be seen as a tool for adaptation, rather than as a picture of reality.

DISCUSSION AND CONCLUSIONS

From a rather fixed set of concepts and principles laid down by Freud, psychoanalysis has moved to a hierarchical arrangement of training centers governed by seasoned scholars who certify students according to their capacity to comprehend and utilize Freudian concepts and principles. For a multitude of reasons, ranging from financial factors to the rise in popularity of psychopharmacology, psychoanalysis then began to fragment. Training became more diverse. Practice became more varied. And a multitude of schools and theories emerged, with each championing a claim to universal validity.

One reaction to this multiplicity has been a retreat to Freud, with a profound reverence for his words. This made for authenticity. Another reaction was to plead for dialogues between competing schools, with the hidden agenda of winning over dissidents. The most tolerant reaction was that of live and let live, but that tolerance seemed to depend upon the hope that someday it would all come together into an integrated whole. Maintaining that pluralism is here to stay has not been a very popular stance.

The yearning for convergence of the tower of Babel into one universal language seems both reasonable and understandable. However, it is probably not attainable without a more fundamental comprehension of our mixed vocabularies, coupled with a better fix on the essentials of psychoanalysis. The first of these efforts may rest on our recognizing the dualisms that haunt our field. The second is a work in progress. Such work demands our dispensing with certain prescriptions and concerns, such as frequency of sessions, the use of the couch, and so forth—points that have been shown to be nonessential. However, in that dispensing, we must search for what lies behind these techniques that have been championed by some and not by others.

Analysts agree that most of the trappings of psychoanalysis exist in the service of facilitating the work, but we regularly and unfortunately collapse the facilitating processes into the essence of the work. To get behind these externals, to reach the essence of psychoanalysis, need not mean anything approaching a uniformity of methods or theoretical tools. These differences are probably here to stay. We might be better off to recognize that the myriad contributions to the analytic enterprise that suggest changes in technique and theory should be thought of more as options than alternatives. One integrating concept is the effort to understand another person in depth. To say this is to suggest a foundation—ironically, in a plea that seems to aim to do away with foundations as such.

But my foundation need not be yours, just as my so-called effectiveness may not be yours. We must abandon our yearning for something we can all agree upon as grounding our inquiry. I make a claim for understanding, because for me that is the essence of human discourse and the crucial yield of psychoanalysis. I believe that this is where the debate over pluralism should be centered, with the hope that such a debate will open us up to more possibilities for analysis. Everything that works toward that end should be seen as the yearned-for unity of analysis.

We shall someday recognize that our differences in reaching an understanding are not divisive as such. They reflect a freedom of inquiry, and that freedom brings us together in the spirit of Freud, if not in the mimicry of his behavior. American psychoanalysis is today's representative of pragmatism's effort in that direction. As Stanley Fish (1999) wrote:

Pragmatism is the philosophy not of grand ambitions but of little steps; and while it cannot help us to take those steps or tell us what they are, it can offer the reassurance that they are possible and more than occasionally efficacious, even if we cannot justify them down to the ground. [p. 308]

REFERENCES

Allen, B. (2000). Is it pragmatism? In *A Pragmatist's Progress*, ed. J. Pettegrew. Lanham, MD: Rowman & Littlefleld.

Brandon, R., ed. (2000). *Rorty and His Critics*. Malden, MA: Blackwell.

Cavell, M. (1988). Interpretation, psychoanalysis and the philosophy of mind. *Journal of the American Psychoanalytic Association* 36:859–879.

Davidson, D. (2001). The myth of the subjective. In *Subjective, Intersubjective, Objective*. Oxford, England: Clarendon Press.

Eagle, M. N., Wolitzkey, D. L. & Wakefield, J. C. (2001). The analyst's knowledge and authority: a critique of the "new view." *Journal of the American Psychoanalytic Association.*, 49(2):457–489.

Fish, S. (1999). *The Trouble with Principle*. Cambridge, MA: Harvard Univ. Press.

Gabbard, G. (1997). A recommendation of objectivity in the analyst. *International Journal of Psycho-Analysis* 78:15–26.

Habermas, J. (2000). Richard Rorty's pragmatic twin. In *Rorty and His Critics*, ed. R. Brandon. Maiden, MA: Blackwell.

Hanly, C. & Hanly, M. A. (2001). Critical realism: distinguishing the psychological subjectivity of the analyst from epistemological subjectiveness. *Journal of the American Psychoanalytic Association* 49(2):515–533.

Hollinger, D. A. (1980). The problem of pragmatism in American history. *Journal of American History*, 67, June.

Moore, B. E. & Fine, B. D. (1990). *Psychoanalytic Terms and Concepts*. New Haven, CT: Yale Univ. Press.

Pettegrew, J., ed. (2000). *A Pragmatist's Progress*. Lanham, MD: Rowman & Littlefield.

Renik, O. (1993). Analytic interaction: conceptualizing technique in light of the analyst's irreducible subjectivity. *Psychoanalytic Quarterly* 62:553–561.

Rorty, R. (1979). *Philosophy and the Mirror of Nature*. Princeton, NJ: Princeton Univ. Press.

—— (1982). *Consequences of Pragmatism*. Minneapolis. MN: Univ. of Minnesota Press.

—— (1989). *Contingency, Irony, and Solidarity*. Cambridge. England: Cambridge Univ. Press.

Schafer, R. (1996). Authority, evidence and knowing in the psychoanalytic relationship. *Psychoanalytic. Quarterly* 65:236–253.

Pity the Poor Pluralist (2007)

In his 2007 paper, *Pity the Poor Pluralist*, Goldberg again undertakes the question of what psychoanalysis should do, especially as "unity and single-mindedness do not appear to be happy members of the psycho-analytic enterprise. We sprout differences with abandon." While there does not exist one principle that underlies all forms of psychoanalytic thought, nor do we have an over-arching theory that covers everything "this diversity may be considered the solution rather than the problem". Pluralism solves the debate of how one best decides what works best for each patient. "Pluralism answers this question by alerting us to the possibilities that psychoanalysis must be seen as an evolving set of concepts with variable applicability." As there is no one-size-fits-all in the practice of psychoanalysis, we might do well to have "enough famili-arity with what others do to allow for reasonable exchanges." Perhaps, also, may be advantageous to recognize our limitations, so that we might admit the dictum "in my house there are many mansions, is mistaken as most of us live in only one. And while we do occasionally gaze at and wave at our neighbors, we feel happiest at home."

Though we are happiest in our own familiar psychoanalytic home, Goldberg calls for a tolerance of diversity. "Every idea deserves a hear-ing, no matter how foolish it may appear. One can never predict the ultimate outcome that best serves adaptation." One enduring element in Goldberg's thinking seems to be that, mistakes and errors, rather than problems, might well be considered solutions.

—GM

INTRODUCTION

Imagine, if you will, that after a certain period of therapy that might range all the way from psychoanalysis to psychotherapy to cognitive-behavioral therapy on to psychopharmacologic treatment, we were able to determine fairly exactly that some particular neuron-al connections in the brain were significantly altered. Based upon these alterations, we could further determine just how effective this or that particular therapy had been. In truth, as of now, there *can* be seen certain brain changes by way of PET scans after both psychotherapy and antidepressant drug therapy in patients treated with these modalities. Alas, it is only after talking to these patients to determine if they themselves claim improvement that we can make much of anything of these brain changes.

As eagerly as we long for some sure way of knowing if what we are doing is working, we have to fall back on merely asking. And even then, we cannot be sure. Some patients say they are better in order to please us. Some say they are not in order to hurt us. Sometimes we insist that patients are better in spite of contrary evidence. And sometimes we ourselves refuse to recognize improvement. So somewhere between those tell-tale brain connections and our own personal sense of certainty come the authors of this volume.

Rather than discussing each contribution individually, I should like to see the collection as representative of a long-standing problem that has existed in psychoanalysis. The problem begins with analysts' expectations about just *what* psychoanalysis should do, along with the decision of *when* psychoanalysis should be considered. The background to this problem of decisions and expectations consists of the attitudes and training of these various contributors. The result of the very distinct differences of training and approaches presents itself as a problem for us all.

THE GOALS OF TREATMENT

One would hope that the authors of these contributions would be of one mind in terms of the very issue, noted above, of our patients getting to feel better. Owen Renik begins his essay with such a declaration: i.e., one aims to afford the patient a feeling of greater well-being. He insists on this as universal. However, Marilia Aisenstein makes the familiar claim, one that most psychoanalysts have heard in extremis, attributed to Freud and later rather enthusiastically embraced by Lacan, that—on the contrary—insists that the analyst should not be interested in therapy per se.

Though it may be of some comfort to claim, along with Aisenstein, that we are primarily interested in the process, with improvement as a mere byproduct, it is difficult to collapse the analyst such as Renik who wants the patient to feel better, to remove symptoms, and so on, with the analyst who, in Romulo Lander's quotation from Bion, wants the patient to "be what he is" (p. 1500). There is surely a certain vagueness in such a goal, and this vagueness is continued in this collection in the positions of Claudio Laks Eizirik and Charles Spezzano, who claim, respectively, that being listened to somehow reduces psychic pain, and that redoing one's life story is equally effective.

In contrast to these unarguable but somewhat evanescent statements, R. D. Hinshelwood tells us that Klein advocated containment as a very specific process of modification of the patient's distress, and Kenneth Newman presents Kohut's position that a particular developmental process takes place in analysis, and this necessarily makes for symptom relief and health. Sander M. Abend is a bit more cautious in championing Brenner's idea that the goal of treatment is but to alter those compromise formations that account for symptoms to those that afford more satisfaction of wishes. That last does seem to come closer to the Renik stance, but it is noteworthy that we start off with a medley of goals ranging from *helping* to *learning*. Our contributors are not of one mind.

In some sense, all our authors want to help their patients, but they vary greatly in terms of the level of their personal therapeutic zeal. It is, of course, unfair to focus on a few selected quotations. And, surely, not all the views presented here are in clear opposition, but they may serve to highlight one crucial distinction in terms of therapeutic action, and that distinction resides in a certain attitude that our authors present about their work. This attitude can be characterized in various ways—as, for example, one stance being a somewhat detached and intellectual exercise devoted to unearthing and exposing infantile conflicts, versus a stance that stresses an emotional involvement directed toward helping the patient better adjust to present life circumstances. Anyone reading these contributions is able to differentiate the author in terms of this attitude toward the work, and this is best seen in the differing discussions of just what each thinks about the *relationship*.

THE RELATIONSHIP WITH THE ANALYST

Abend is clearest in his discussion of the analytic relationship, and he is equally clear in presenting his personal opinion about its usefulness and potential danger. He does not in any way diminish its significance, but feels it is not something he would champion as the major agent of therapeutic action. Renik takes a strongly opposing view in that he sees the analyst as a partner, as participant-observer, and as co-constructer of analytic material. He stands at a 180°-position away from Abend.

This discussion of the analytic relationship requires that one distinguish the usual analytic work of listening and interpreting from a more active participation and revealing of the analyst's own personality. This is not the same as the concern with understanding and handling one's countertransference, which all the authors consider in some detail. Rather, it involves some crucial decisions about analytic neutrality and analytic enactments. In reading Spezzano's contribution, I find little doubt that he allows his own personality to be a part of his traffic with his patients, and one cannot help but feel the same about Aisenstein. Interestingly, Spezzano seems to place his behavior squarely in the center of his theory, while Aisenstein has a certain disconnect in her description of a fascinating clinical vignette and her advocacy of a theory that is neither Lacanian nor classical (and which in no way seems relevant to her vignette).

A similar contrast to that of Abend and Renik can be seen in the pairing of Newman and Eizirik. Newman presents Kohut's position as one that has the analyst functioning as a critical factor in filling in the uncompleted psychic structure of the patient. While this is said to take place within the confines of the self object transference, the various subsidiary contributors to self psychology all seem to concentrate on one or another actions of the analyst in terms of frustration and/or gratification, actions that seem, obviously, to go beyond the neutral stance of the analyst. Analytic neutrality, on the other hand, is underscored by Eizirik, who, while allowing for spontaneity and naturalness, emphasizes the need for a distance from the five points that he feels determine analytic work. One cannot help but see such a concept of "distance" as in opposition to that of frustration and/or gratification; there is no brief for co-construction in this stance.

Lander makes a distinction about the analytic relationship that differs from all the other authors' in that he differentiates neurotic from psychotic patients and recommends a pedagogic activity on the analyst's part. For Lander, the analyst teaches the psychotic analysand to survive. As a matter of fact, most analysts who stress the relationship as being itself therapeutic do tend to do a good deal of teaching and advising.

Hinshelwood considers psychotic patients as well, but in no way differentiates them from neurotic ones. He refers to Bion's treatment of a schizophrenic and links this to Klein's work with socalled disintegrative egos. One striking difference between the authors who declare themselves as more or less following in the footsteps of Freud, and those who show more allegiance to Klein, seems to be in the consideration of treating neurotics and personality disorders, as opposed to psychotics. Kohut seemed to draw the line of analytic work at borderline personality disorders, while others feel analysis is indicated in these patients.

For the most part, the authors in this collection do not concern themselves too much with diagnostic categories or with the concept of analyzability. In reading these contributions, one cannot help but conclude that, no matter how much each lays claim to being a psychoanalyst with an allegiance to Freud, they are also quite different from one another. Identifying just what is the commonality and what is the difference seems to call for an explication.

PLURALISM

At a recent conference of psychoanalysts, a clinical presentation was discussed from five different analytic perspectives. These perspectives were essentially presented as different theories, of both technique and therapeutic efficacy. This particular conference was an offshoot of an earlier one in which different ways and ideas about analysis were felt to be incompatible, and the resulting split in that meeting led to a new hoped-for unity, which lasted but a short while, until it, too, spawned first one, then two, and now five different sets of ideas and ways of thinking. One can fairly safely predict that some, if not all, of these five perspectives will undergo further refinements and generate offspring. Unity and single-mindedness do not appear to be happy members of the psychoanalytic enterprise. We sprout differences with abandon.

Pluralism is a philosophical doctrine that says there is no one principle that underlies all forms of thought. Thus, much alike the overdetermination of behavior that is familiar to all psychoanalysts, there need not be a single explanation to encompass all theories or techniques of therapeutic action. Therefore, an improvement in a patient's well-being as a result of psychoanalysis can be explained as a byproduct, a reaction to the warmth of the analyst's personality, a developmental achievement, an example of the efficacy of insight, a learning of how to handle discouragement, or all other manner of explanatory devices. All are capable of carrying die weight of explanation, but all are obviously not of one piece.

It is vital to clarify that pluralism demands more than a name change. Some essential differences must carry the weight of the separation of one idea about theory and technique from another. Sadly, many splits and changes are often more political than scientific, as time frequently makes clear.

Before further pursuing the answer to the riddle of such a disparity of explanations, we may find it worthwhile to examine its origin. One striking conclusion in reading these varied contributions is that no single author seems to be aware of, or at least to pay much attention to, any of the others. There exists a dogged insularity in each of these papers that, aside from a mere mention of what someone else may have written, follows a single line of conviction and conclusion. Indeed, some of the papers mention writers who are hardly household names, but who are brought forth as representative of something akin to a school of thought. Although Strachey is given more than his due, he mainly serves as a historical launching point to pursue what is likely to be a very regional set of ideas. A famous American politician, Tip O'Neill of Boston, once said that "all politics is local," and that quote might well serve to explain the psychoanalytic pluralism of today. It all seems to depend on where you live, who your teachers were, and who your personal analyst was. In other words, the pluralism that so reigns in psychoanalysis may well be more political than we would like to believe.

Lacan is a good case in point. His work is enormously popular in Europe, yet rarely taught in psychoanalytic institutes in the United States. His ideas about therapeutic action are almost incomprehensible to someone who follows Kohut. But Kohut is also a sterling example, inasmuch as his followers, for the most part, have little or no familiarity at all with the teachings of Bion about therapeutic change. More important, this insularity in psychoanalysis is not only promoted, but is everywhere routinely perpetuated by an atmosphere of disdain toward the dissidents. It is extremely unusual to find an analyst who is familiar enough with the work of Bion, Lacan, and Kohut to be able to carry on a discourse about all of their thinking. Rather, we find analysts who are wedded to one or another, let us say, school of thought, and familiar enough with, let us say, the dissidents to brand them as such. Although this is a sad state of affairs, it merits something more than either disappointment or outrage; it calls for a study, and this valuable collection of essays is an excellent place to begin.

There are five clinical vignettes and a dream described in this group of papers. Although each is presented in order to illustrate or demonstrate a clinical application of the particular writer to his or her particular theory, it is not especially difficult to read them as illustrative of another of the writer's points of view. Aisenstein offers a vivid portrayal of an interaction with her patient Vanya. On one occasion, Vanya speaks of feeling forgotten and of thinking his analyst has disappeared. His analyst tells us of her worry about him and of his own disappearance. As an exercise, I read this vignette with Spezzano's point of view in mind—that of the analyst finding a home in the patient's mind and vice versa. I did this with no attempt to discredit Aisenstein's clinical work, of course, but rather to suggest that her efforts to connect what she does to the work of Green seemed no more telling than to a host of other writers.

Later in the same case, Aisenstein beautifully describes some postanalytic work (which, although it is given a French name, is hardly a particularly French activity), and so proceeds to make a statement about co-generated conclusions. Once again, I read this with Renik's very powerful insistence on the intersubjective nature of analysis, and wondered if the "theoretical" discrepancy might actually be one of language and vocabulary.

If we contrast the cases presented by Eizirik and Renik, we immediately note the active interventions of each of these analysts. One can read these interventions in a number of ways—as instances of countertransference, of self-revelation, or of introducing psychotherapeutic activity into a psychoanalysis. Likewise, one may choose to rationalize what may otherwise be considered nonanalytic enactments by reference to learned scholars. Once again, we find that something that seems close to personal opinion or theoretical predilection inevitably comes to rule the day. It is not clear to the reader what guiding principle would allow Eizirik and Renik to come so alive with this patient and not with another.

It is apparent that many of these contributors do pretty much the same thing in conducting an analysis, but with different names and attributions. What is less apparent is how to determine when and why they do what they do, and if it always works. Again, this comment is not meant to argue with success as much as it is to wonder about failure.

And so to make a case for failure. My good friend Marian Tolpin, a distinguished analyst in her own right, once said that what we really need is a collection of and discussion about our failed cases. I believe that most of the initial presentations of innovative techniques and theories developed out of a lack of success with the tried and the true. Klein had to develop a different technique to deal with children, and I suspect this sort of impasse leading to creative expansion has been true of almost all the major contributors in psychoanalysis. I know this was the case with Kohut, who developed his ideas about narcissistic personality disorders because, for him, classical analysis seemed to fall short in providing a theoretical base for treating these cases.

Now, it is certainly fairly obvious that if all your cases do well and none is unsatisfactory, then you have no cause whatsoever to learn much about what others are doing. But if not, you surely have a debt to pay for your ignorance. And it seems more likely that the approaches of the contributors of this collection are best seen as working well with some patients and not so well with others. My reading of Lyotard (1984) and postmodernism is that there are no overarching theories that cover everything, but one needs to see what works best under what situations

The position of Renik that rather dramatically describes how he helped his patient following his irritation at her whining is a wonderful example of local applicability. However, there may well exist a cohort of patients for whom such a theoretical and technical approach is contra-indicated. But the conviction of Abend that belies the value of the analytic relationship seems to fly in the face of Renik's. Is it not possible that Abend is also correct, but again, only with selected patients? There is little doubt that both are sometimes right and sometimes wrong. Newman seems best in explaining this supposed dilemma in his presentation of the shortcomings of self psychology. In fact, shortcomings exist only in the usual overextension of all these theories and techniques. I cannot, for example, believe that Hinshelwood thinks Kleinian interpretations apply to everyone; but perhaps he does.

It should be clear that psychoanalysis has thus far been unsuccessful in answering the question of what works best for which patient. I cannot imagine how it will ever be successful in such a pursuit as long as we are prisoners of our parochialism. In Aisenstein's description of the case of Vanya, there is a sentence that describes their meetings as occurring three times per week, face to face. Aside from the unconscionable but true fact that this way of working would not be considered psychoanalysis in present-day accredited institutes in the United States, the intriguing question should really be just *why* and *when* this approach works best. Seeing someone three times per week face to face ought to be a decision based on more than convenience and cost, as important as these factors may be. There is now some developing research on the issue of frequency, and this needs as much investigative scrutiny as does the Lacanian technique of varying the length of the analytic session.

Once again, I believe much of this comes down to political rather than scientific opinion. I am not here calling for empirical research into various techniques, as desirable as that may be. I just doubt very much that there are any analysts who are familiar enough—say, with self psychology, for example—who are willing and able to practice that on certain patients, switch to Kleinian technique when that is appropriate for other patients, and then on to Lacan or Bion for still others. My own admittedly limited contacts with analysts who are committed to, say, classical analysis indicates that they learn just enough self psychology to trash it, and just enough Lacan to dismiss him. That is the present sad state of affairs.

AND EVOLUTION

I am emboldened to add a personal note to offer my own idea as to the explanation for the present state of seeming disarray in psychoanalysis. Knowledge, much like plants and animals in biology, undergoes an evolution of its own (Munz 1999). Knowledge generates a variety of ideas and concepts that enter the intellectual marketplace and aim to find niches for survival. Some concepts endure and some fail. A few, analogous to the Galapagos finches and turtles described by Darwin, manage to survive intact for fairly long periods because of their isolation from other sources of influx and influence. I suspect this may be true of our own islands of certainty where, for example, there is an insistence that one analytic theory and its interpretations apply to everyone, everywhere. Some theories have moments of extreme popularity, only to dissipate and disappear rather quickly, and so to be labeled as fads. All must ultimately face the crucible of public scrutiny and testing, and, ultimately, only the fittest survive.

It is important to recognize that we are living in the time of the evolution of psychoanalytic thought, and thus in a time that calls for maximal tolerance of diversity. Every idea deserves a hearing, no matter how foolish it may appear, inasmuch as evolution always proceeds by stages, and one can never predict the ultimate outcome that best serves adaptation. We should also remind ourselves that evolution takes a long time, and so we must suffer fools gladly and with patience.

Summary and Conclusions

This collection of essays on the theory of therapeutic action from various theoretical and conceptual vantage points presents the reader with a set of expert, varied, and well-thought-out guidelines. Each writer delivers what is an overview of how he or she works with patients, and much of this is offered in the spirit of ecumenism or universality. Just as we might appreciate from a collegial gathering of various religious faiths that emphasizes tolerance and respect for differing opinions, there seems little doubt that, in our hearts, we all know we are right. Thus, the stage is set for a struggle between opposing sets of truths, and the reader is given the freedom of choice versus rejection of each set.

My personal opinion is that the dictum of "In My House, There Are Many Mansions" is a mistake for our field, because, like it or not, most of us live in only one. We do occasionally gaze at and wave at our neighbors, but feel happiest at home. The comfort and security of sticking to one expert or one domicile is immensely increased by diminishing the attraction of any other. I recently attended a meeting devoted entirely to demonstrating that Kohut's ideas could be eliminated or seen as unnecessary by an exercise in extending some of Freud's ideas. I could not help but feel that this was such a wasted exercise that it should be left to theological debaters. The question remains: how do we best decide what works for which patient?

Pluralism answers this question by alerting us to the possibility that psychoanalysis must be seen as an evolving set of concepts with variable applicability. What psychoanalysis needs is genuine scientific pluralism. Given the unlikelihood of any one analyst's having familiarity with and competence in all the approaches presented in this collection—not to mention the approaches that have not been included—it seems that, in certain cases, the best we can do is to recognize our limitations and to refer the patient to one who has such competence. That, of course, demands enough familiarity with what others do to allow for reasonable exchanges. The publication of this volume is a step in that direction. Each contribution should be read as part of such a step and not as a "one-size-fits-all" program.

REFERENCES

Lyotard, J.-R. (1984). The postmodern condition: a report on knowledge. *Theory and History of Literature, Vol. 10.* Minneapolis, MN: Univ. of Minnesota Press.

Munz, P. (1999). *Critique of Impure Reason.* New York: Praeger.

CHAPTER SEVEN

Rules, Boundaries, Correctness
and Ownership

Goldberg discusses the issue of rules, correctness, questions of certainty and absoluteness; the distinctions between the moral and the ethical and the place of boundaries in these considerations in a series of clear and cogent articles written between 1999 and 2008. Reading these papers, it seems that there is no position that is not worth our re-consideration. One might consider, after reading these papers, the delight that accompanies this view of the world from a position not so fixed.

Goldberg turns our attention to the distinction between the moral and the ethical in his paper *Boundaries as Pre-Conditions* (1999). According to Goldberg, the moral concerns itself with what is correct and the ethical is concerned with aims or the goal being pursued. In psychological treatment the ethical belongs to that area which furthers the treatment. Boundaries, then, belong to our ethical behavior, or in other words, as the conditions that allow for a plan to proceed. As Goldberg states, "A reconsideration of boundaries as pre-conditions for effective therapeutic action moves them from the area of morality to that of pursuing an optimal treatment process: an ethical aim."

The boundary, then, is that area of operation that allows us to accomplish our aims of treatment. Taking a patient for a cup of coffee or the analyst's offer of condolence or a hug to a patient, are activities that are in bounds if they enter into the analytic discourse. "Nothing can escape the need for meta-communication, i.e. talking about what just happened ... It matters not so much what you do but rather that it must be examined." Do not let your eyes move too quickly from this last sentence. It is at the heart of Goldberg's analytic stance, where what just happened must not escape examination.

—GM

Boundaries as Pre-Conditions (1999)

Boundaries in psychoanalysis and psychotherapy can be considered either as indicators of moral transgressions or as guidelines for therapeutic intervention. This paper suggests that these categories be better delineated in the hope that less attention be paid to that of moral mistakes and more to that of treatment effectiveness.

The intent of this paper is to distinguish between the view of boundaries as loci of transgression or moral issues from the concept of boundaries as practical points of treatment or ethical considerations.

It is not always clear just how we distinguish between the definitions of the moral and the ethical. If we borrow from Ricoeur (1992), we may highlight the difference as being between that of norms and that of aims. The moral is to be considered as what is felt to be good and normal, and so it lays claim to a universal status. It consists of the rules of correct behavior. The ethical has to do with the aim or goal being pursued, and so it directs us to the proper way to live. Ricoeur feels that ethics therefore encompasses morality.

To transpose this distinction to psychological treatment, we might say that we have a variety of moral standards or norms in dealing with patients, while having a goal in mind as to what we consider best for an individual patient. We behave in a certain way that we consider moral, but beyond that, we impose other standards in order to promote our goal of treatment. It may not be wrong in and of itself to tell our patients personal matters about ourselves or to have a cup of coffee with them, but it may not promote the treatment to do so. In this case, it is clear that ethics includes and determines morality. On the other hand, some may say that certain (for some) morally offensive or repugnant behavior is truly in the patient's best interests. These, of course, become arenas for argument and disagreement, as first occurred between Freud and Ferenczi.

Putting those possibilities momentarily to the side, it seems prudent to consider our concern with boundaries as more properly belonging to our ethical behavior. As such, boundaries are the allowable constraints for achieving our goals and are not so much our moral norms. This is quite familiar to some analysts who recognize that certain perfectly normal forms of behavior, such as sharing a cup of coffee are considered breaches of proper technique. It is less familiar to some therapists who feel that sharing a cup of coffee is so natural as to make us seem foolish to decline. The difference is a product of a plan: a plan of doing good. Therefore, it may be more profitable to see boundaries as the conditions that allow for the plan to proceed, and so they may be termed pre-conditions. With this in mind, one can begin to examine and clarify just what are the proper pre-conditions that are necessary for just what therapeutic action. Mistakes in the recognition of boundaries are not necessarily moral failings, although they well may be, but rather are more often technical errors. A reconsideration of boundaries as pre-conditions for effective therapeutic action moves them from the area of morality to that of pursuing an optimal treatment process: an ethical aim.

What may at first seem a fairly easy delineation of boundaries, i.e., the analytic claim of neutrality, has had a recent re-examination (Renik, 1996) and is held by some to be untenable, even unusable. However, it seems more to the point that supposed neutrality is, for some, but a synonym for the respect of boundaries. Little is gained by the substitution of phrases until we spell out just what is ethically demanded of us.

The usual image of neutrality (or what has been an acceptable substitute definition: staying equidistant from id, ego, and superego) is an image of immobility, of the analyst's refraining from making a difference. The usual image of boundaries is one of allowing action or sometimes even encouraging action up to a point. Therapeutic action makes a difference. The difference between neutrality and operating within a boundary represents a shift in our thinking about the requisite action of analysts and therapists, i.e., what needs to be done in order to accomplish one's goals. Therapeutic alliance, rapport, empathy, a host of recommended stances all speak to our doing or being something that is needed, rather than to our being nothing that gets in the way. It is in the areas of doing too much or too little, or making mistakes, that the issue of boundaries arises. Perhaps one should therefore focus upon the allowable and necessary actions of analysts and therapists rather than on the usual concern devoted to errors of commission. To return to ethics, we can say that we need to operate within an arena that allows us to accomplish our aims of treatment. This arena of operation assumes a recognition of norms and standards, but these do not determine the boundaries of the arena. Rather it is bounded by what is needed to achieve the best interests of the patient.

It seems fair to say that most discussions about boundaries in psychotherapy and psychoanalysis have to do with violations and transgressions. As such, they focus upon both of the moral considerations of the concept: the standards of propriety and the breaches of good conduct. Within these discussions (Gabbard, 1994, 1995), there lies a clear message about the impact of such violations upon the treatment process, but there is no clear-cut delineation of the nature of the boundary. To be sure, the discussions of boundary problems are inevitably linked to investigations of transference-countertransference problems that lie with the therapist or analyst, but there remains a lack of clarity about just what is the status of this entity. For example, a recent list of recommendations (Day, 1994) for practicing psychiatry in rural communities was directed toward points of caution in maintaining what could only be described as an aloof and diplomatic stance in order to (once again) avoid boundary violations. Yet it would seem to be obvious that one needs more than such a series of constraints to properly position oneself vis-à-vis a patient. What one *should* do is therefore more a matter of describing the conduct that becomes a caring and interested professional. None of these guidelines seem to define a boundary as part of a treatment process rather than as a signpost of a moral failing. My effort here is to consider the simple and perhaps obvious view of boundaries as pre-conditions.

What Is a Pre-Condition?

A pre-condition is the sum of factors that allow one to effect a therapeutic intervention. It can be thought of as the stance of a therapist or analyst that should exist in order to proceed with whatever action is being considered. The ensuing action may then breach the boundary.

There is no absolute point of effective intervention, and naturally the kind of intervention planned will determine the particular pre-conditions. There is surely an ideal pre-condition for certain forms of interpretation as well as for particular moments of optimal frustration or gratification, etc. We need to study and define these ideal conditions in order to better define just what a boundary does and how it functions. Before one can possibly detail the violations, it seems a wise course to describe the proper dimensions of a boundary, and these would seem to vary with the nature of the intervention being entertained. A therapist who, for example, believes in optimal gratification of a patient might well assume a different position than one who supports optimal frustration. A therapist who is planning to teach something to a patient will surely have a different set of pre-conditions than one who eschews that position. Without in any way supporting or discouraging these particular stances, we must examine them more carefully before we can consider any particular action as a violation of a boundary. In this sense, one distinguishes between boundary crossings and boundary violations (Gabbard and Lester, 1996), in that one necessarily crosses boundaries in treatment but need not thereby commit a violation.

Do Pre-Conditions Differ?

A perhaps apocryphal and unreferenced story told about Freud describes his ending an analytic hour with Helene Deutsch and having her sit up. Freud is then said to have explained to her just what had transpired during the previous analytic hour. This rapid transition from analyst to teacher illustrates the altered conditions required for his being the one rather than the other. His function as an analyst demanded of Freud a commitment to his own definition of neutrality (which may have been a liberal one) while his performance as an instructor could be said to take advantage of a certain transference element that would lend strength to his educative efforts. Each of these positions lived within a set of boundary conditions that, while having some similarities, clearly differ from each other. As we consider the varieties of actions attributed to analysts, it is difficult to insist upon a single set of pre-conditions for what is now felt to be a range of activities that go beyond the single and most familiar one of interpretation. We call them pre-conditions because they are the necessary pre-existing conditions that allow for the ensuing activity, which, for some, may have interpretation as a final common pathway, but, for others, a whole series of activities ranging from trial identification to instruction to more active involvement.

ONE EXAMPLE

Arlow (1979) lists the nature of an analyst's experience as going from passive listening to a change involving introspection of some material that intrudes into the analyst's consciousness. That change speaks of an identification with the patient and the taking on of the role of observer-interpreter. This is followed by intuition which consists of a silent and effortless organization of data. A third process, according to Arlow, is that of empathy, which is said to make intuition possible. These three components form the first part of the interpretive work. The second part is based upon cognition and the exercise of reason. Side by side, these two parts allow for interpretation to take place.

There seems to be no set position for an analyst or therapist to allow all of the above to proceed. The boundary for passive listening, if such a thing exists, seems not to coincide with that of trial identification or active interpretation. We are surely in different places at these different times. As Rangell (1979) says, "the analyst roams." He or she moves between transference and non-transference and avoids fixation points. Rangell refers to his and Fenichel's "necessary activity" and even goes on to note the emotional experiences that are corrective or therapeutic in all analytic procedures.

At the point of this "necessary activity," one sees the step beyond the concept of a boundary as a pre-condition and enters the arena of actions that are held to be therapeutic in themselves. It is often the case that boundary violations are rationalized being in the patient's best interests, and so it may follow that a particular act can, in that way, be rescued from the category of misbehavior. However, this should better be thought of not so much as a boundary that demarcates a place of therapeutic action as a proposal for the supposed violation taking its place as a part of the therapy. One does or does not do something to a patient for the patient's benefit. There are a host of such maneuvers that have been offered over time — from yelling at patients to hugging them, from scolding them to applauding them, from the giving of gifts to accepting them. All of these actions become anointed as part of the treatment rather than as violations of a boundary. And, as such, they are not moral mistakes but rather are incorporated into one's ethical aim. Such actions lay claim to a status equal to that of analytic interpretation and so are defended as necessary. This, of course, is the major refuge for therapeutic misbehavior. It is therefore the crucial area for distinguishing the ethical from the moral viewpoint.

For the most part, analysts take refuge in the principle of abstinence. This stems from the theoretical assumption that one must frustrate the instinctual drives in order to develop an interpretable transference. Brenner (1979), in espousing this principle, agrees that some gratification is inescapable, but he takes issue with Stone's statement that there are occasions when an analyst should give advice to a patient or offer condolences when a patient suffers a catastrophe. Brenner feels these are not in accord with good analytic practice. But surely the failure to take these actions could be just as "gratifying of an unconscious infantile wish" as would the acts themselves. Neither position is a guarantor of an ensuing successful interpretation. Brenner rightly says, for example, that to express sympathy for a patient's loss of a loved one may make it more difficult for the patient to express pleasure over the loss. But to withhold it seems equally to run a risk of a different sort. Indeed, there is no sure way of knowing what your action or inaction will lead to, especially since much of what is communicated remains unconscious. Is it possible for one to feel sympathetic, withhold sympathy, and still remain within the bounds of effective interpretive work? Is it equally possible to feel unsympathetic, yet offer sympathy and then proceed to analyze the patient's reaction to the loss? It seems more likely that each position runs the risk of going outside of the boundary required for effective interpretation.

Abstinence is no longer the insulated position for the conveying of insight, since the word may have lost its original meaning. Silence, all forms of withholding, all standards of anonymity, carry a powerful message, one that may convey more information than does talking, advising, and exposing. One must be very cautious in attributing a virtue to what is essentially a kind of negative behavior. Not answering a question can be creating a condition that inhibits interpretation just as much as does a prompt response. Abstinence as a form of the frustration of gratification can readily be seen, on occasion, as gratifying, just as action of many sorts is liable to be frustrating. Offering a tissue to a crying patient or refusing to do so speaks primarily to the therapist rather than to the theory of technique. There is no easy way to predict the effects of our involvement, and yet we are always involved.

What seems true of most analysts and therapists is the construction of one's own particular boundary within which one lives and operates. This may be termed one's style, but here it refers to one's conditions for therapeutic action. Given the usual moral norms, we all try to develop the optimal pre-conditions that allow us to be effective and efficient. Just as the taking of notes seems to work for some and to impede others, so too an entire system develops that becomes the most agreeable setting for the individual to function. Indeed, the interesting work on matching of analyst and patient (Kantrowitz, 1996) seems to support the notion that a host of factors come together that allow for a workable dialogue. This leads to the conclusion that not every patient will realize every transference with every analyst. It also suggests another conclusion that all sorts of behavior are allowable without any danger of indulging or conspiring with the patient or complying with the patient's distortions (Rangell, 1979, p. 93). To consider that question, I turn to another example.

NON-INTERPRETIVE INTERVENTIONS

It is important at the outset to try to separate the customary behavior of a therapist — what some would call his or her basic style — from those actions of the therapist which are felt to be particularly directed toward an individual patient. To be sure, some actions are felt to impinge of necessity on any patient, and so there remain a large fuzzy area that defies easy categorization. One would suppose that if one hugs every single patient, it could become a matter of style, just as never uttering a word could be seen as the same. But let us proceed to examine interventions that can be seen as involving moving out of the established set of conditions or boundaries to effect a change just as an interpretation might optimally do.

Interventions that are felt to be therapeutic yet do not rely upon insight usually fall under the broad category of the "relationship" or perhaps the "therapeutic relationship." That term is an umbrella for the various kinds of connections of persons. There are different theoretical explanations for the ways that people connect or relate to one another. Object relations theory may posit the relationship as gratifying a drive while other theories may see a relationship as offering a psychic structure. The benefits derived from these relationships encompass a range of psychological terms, from holding to nurturing to growth enhancing. Most, if not all, of the benefits attributed to these relationships are posited on some scheme of development. Thus, a growth relationship may substitute for a failed development or may enhance a defective development or may allow for an arrested development to proceed. Inasmuch as there are variations in these concepts of development, there seems to be no agreed-upon set of explanations as to just why relationships are ameliorative. However, in the broadest sense, relationships are seen as functioning as supports or substitutes that are needed as a result of pathological development. A problem arises when one attempts to explain how a therapeutic relationship can lead to a long-lasting improvement once the relationship has ended and has done so without the benefit of interpretive work. That problem has bearing upon the issue of boundaries as pre-conditions, since we assume that the relationship is some sort of vehicle for therapeutic change and so is or should be both clearly delineated and necessarily limited. Otherwise, it runs the risk of being an unending relationship, a form of addiction. Or else it must have a mystical component that defies explanation. On the other hand, the cessation of the relationship accompanied or followed by interpretive work is very much like the analytic situation of a bounded posture which allows for interpretation: it is just a different set of limits.

Relationships can thus be seen as extended boundaries that can be effective and are capable of being terminated. The ending of these relationships can then be interpreted with hope for insight, or terminated in such a way that development proceeds, as is posited in the formation of psychic structure. The crucial variable would seem to be that the cessation of the relationship leads to a positive change: something felt to be offered by the relationship can have a long-lasting effect. With this in mind, one can re-examine the issue of boundaries as preconditions, i.e., what sort of a relationship allows for a reasonable termination that results either in insight or in increased psychic structure? This serves to distinguish this category from transference cures and never-ending relationships. These last two, though not necessarily to be condemned, are variants of psychotherapy that call into question the very point of an ethical determination of what one considers best for a patient. However, the clearer category of a limited relationship returns us to the notion of an individual boundary for an analyst or therapist from which he or she can operate *and* which can be terminated to the patient's benefit. Relationships must therefore be seen as temporary way stations which, when interrupted, can be utilized by the patient. Unless a relationship can be dissipated by discussion, it tends to bind the patient to the therapist and the therapist to the patient. Therefore, for example, not offering condolences requires a discussion about what fantasies this evoked in the patient, just as does having a cup of coffee with the patient. Nothing can escape the need for metacomments, i.e., talking about what we just did. This scenario, which says that it matters not so much what you do but rather that it must be examined, both redefines neutrality and gives us a powerful tool to better delineate our concept of boundaries.

TRANSFERENCE AND BOUNDARIES

If boundaries are to be seen as the pre-condition for analysis and/ or psychotherapy, then the entrance into the area of therapeutic work, either interpretive or non-interpretive, is an entrance into transference issues. Perhaps best emphasized by Gill (1979), the most reliable guide to the transference is what is actually going on in the analytic situation. Resolution of the transference can be seen as parallel to the resolution of the therapeutic relationship: the first by interpretation, the second by whatever developmental considerations may be entertained by the therapist. Persistence of the transference, though recognized as ubiquitous by all analysts, is reluctantly accepted with the hope for its ultimate diminution. Persistence of a therapeutic relationship falls under the category of the kind of maneuver encouraged by Basch (1995) in certain forms of psychotherapy, or else is to be otherwise explained. More often than not, this becomes the site of a host of boundary violations that are not in the best interests of the patient, primarily because they reflect a wide variety of unacknowledged, unspoken, and unresolved transference issues.

Relationships that are not interpreted can surely be vehicles for patient improvement, but it would seem to be critical to the improvement that they be the focus of the treatment. For example, if a patient improves in treatment partially because of the imposition of the regular event of treatment times in the patient's life, then the therapist must consider whether such regularity is now an added part of the patient's psychology and can be readily transposed to his or her life outside of treatment. I believe this to be a common occurrence in some noninterpretive treatments, although it may at times be a minor factor in itself. However, that example is one that primarily flows from the needs of the patient. When we examine aspects of therapeutic relationships that are products of mixed therapist/patient needs, we begin to see how difficult these may be to resolve, if indeed they demand resolution.

Once a commitment is made to an examination of all aspects of the analytic or therapeutic relationship, then no one part can be ignored. If a patient and a therapist have a cup of coffee together, it must be made the center of inquiry. There may be little difference in an analyst's asking a patient how she felt about his failure to offer condolences and a therapist's asking what the patient's fantasies were during the coffee period. In each of these cases, one attends to the actual reality of the analytic or therapeutic encounter and studies it for its transference implications. An inquiry such as suggested by Brenner — to allow a patient to express his or her feelings about a recent loss — is essentially one that removes the analyst from the equation. The transference is therefore not the focus of this exchange; instead, the focus is on an outside commentary about the patient. The same may occur with a variety of interactions in many therapeutic relations. A shared cup of coffee is not a moment outside of the treatment, and so it can be neither condemned nor promoted, but rather must be made a part of the treatment.

Unfortunately, many aspects of these relationships that are not interpreted or otherwise resolved fall into the category of being unresolvable or, better, are never discussed. Every such discussion of an event or encounter places a bracket around the event and so segregates it from the ongoing relationship. It essentially says, "Let us step to the side to see just what transpired," and so in its own way, it destroys the moment. It also re-creates a boundary, one of inquiry and investigation, and in this manner, it undoes the relationship. It thus seems obvious that this is often the reason these issues remain undiscussed. Times of physical contact, of self-revelation, of gift-giving and gift-receiving, of emotional outbursts, all tend to evolve into conspiracies of silence, of awkward efforts to erase or rationalize the possible misstep. Analysts who yell at their patients insist that this is for the patient's benefit. Therapists who accept gifts from their patients claim it to be a natural part of the relationship. In either case, the event does not actively participate in the treatment either by its being understood or supported by a reason outside of the therapist's own needs. Once again it must be noted that each of these supposed missteps has a right to be brought in as a natural part of an ongoing treatment as long as one can demonstrate it as both needed and temporary. And no one can easily distinguish between a defense of any such behavior as either well planned or rationalized after the fact. The struggles of Ferenczi are an interesting study of that very uncertainty (Jones, 1957, p. 164).

Two Examples

Kohut (1984) tells of allowing a patient not to pay his analytic fee for several months in order to make a later purchase (p. 73). He states that the reason for the request and the meaning of the response only became clear much later in the treatment. He took a chance and perhaps was correct, but it was done in the process of the examination of the act.

At one time I saw a female patient who told of being in analysis with her husband's analyst during the same period of time. She insisted that this analyst never revealed to her anything that her husband said, but she said that she could not help but feel and even see that he knew a great deal more than she told him. It is difficult to see just how this could be claimed to be in the patient's best interest, but I have no doubt that such a claim would be made. It is only by keeping in mind the dual point of "temporary" and "necessary" that we can properly claim such probable boundary crossing as justifiable.

The Problem of Relationships

A review of a rather provocative book entitled *When Boundaries Betray Us: Beyond Illusions of What Is Ethical in Therapy and Life,* by Carter Heyward, an Episcopal priest, is a fascinating examination of what seems to be a confusion about boundaries, morals, and ethics. In the book, Heyward tells her own story about her encounter with a psychiatrist who, while agreeing to treat her, refused her request that they be friends. She goes on to say that this refusal was unethical and also a betrayal. The book reviewer disagrees and claims that the psychiatrist's error lay in her not setting boundaries clearly and early. This reviewer, Marie Fortune (1994), herself a minister and therapist, writes of the patient's mistaking a "healing" relationship for a peer relationship and assumes that the psychiatrist did not feel that a mutually intimate friendship was in Heyward's best interest.

The published review article is followed by a response from Heyward, who claims that she had indeed found just what she was looking for in her therapist who, at one point, agreed that only her professionalism was an obstacle to this mutually intimate relationship desired by the patient. Heyward goes on to say that this allows pre-set rules and codes to dictate what may not be in the best interests of these participants. Inasmuch as this particular psychiatrist said that she would have liked to have been her patient's friend, one may feel that the issue is clouded by countertransference, but in its own way, it is clarified by this frank admission of the therapist. Before discussing this, mention should be made of Fortune's reply to Heyward. This last is a review of what is felt to be the respect of boundaries and a clear call to distinguish between professional relationships and those of intimacy. The plea is supported by an unarguable claim against exploitation of patients.

At first blush, one might quickly side with the reviewer who feels that this psychiatrist and her patient simply did not stick to the rules. However, an analyst might well wonder just why and how the need for this particular kind of relationship was understood and interpreted. As long as the wish to be a friend is taken as a potential violation rather than as a symptom, it remains a part of the struggle between patient and therapist. And sadly, with no mention of the unconscious determinants of this particular wish, our reviewer seems to join in by mistakenly considering this as a possible or potential boundary violation. However, one soon begins to side with the forsaken patient, who is never shown that relationships need not be either indulged or frustrated but rather must be understood.

The reason for the psychiatrist's refusal to be Heyward's future friend should not be seen in terms of potential transgressions, but rather as an impediment to her understanding what it means to the patient. The failure to adequately explain how one relationship differs from another, i.e., "healing" from "mutually intimate," stems from a barely concealed failure to understand what relationships are all about. This can only be solved by some sort of theoretical stance that squarely sees the relationship as a temporary place for a specific task. Regrettably, the word has itself gained a mystical aura that allows some therapists to claim an inherent "healing power" that relationships offer. With this claim, boundary problems seem inevitable, since some relationships seem morally correct while others are felt to be beyond moral norms. However, this misplaced judgment fails to say if the relationship is part of the treatment, i.e., is ethically correct. Being a friend is not immoral, but seeing it as a boundary violation blinds the reviewer as well as the psychiatrist from seeing it primarily as demanding an explanation rather than as a warning sign.

DISCUSSION

To revisit the intent of this paper is to see that boundaries can be viewed either as practical roads to an end or as moral injunctions. We need to take a long-term view as to whether or not what is done will facilitate or impede the treatment, all the while knowing that some effects may not be predictable.

Boundaries may be seen as launching pads for treatment. Their supposed violations are both inevitable and invaluable. When we step across a boundary, an enactment takes place, and we thereby change our relationship with our patient. If the enactment is one of interpretation, then it may either lead to insight or to a different position for both patient and therapist. We are unable to move from a neutral bounded place to interpret and then jump back to a safe neutrality, since the conditions have now been reset: sometimes a little, sometimes a lot. These new conditions become the boundary for the ensuing work. And just as every interpretation calls for re-examining our position, so does every other sort of action or inaction. It is only the failure to recognize these resettings that allows for the prolonged realization of unresolved transference configurations and persistent untherapeutic relationships. Just as Sigmund Freud moved from analyst to teacher with Helene Deutsch, so too do we all inevitably modify our boundaries, and therefore we need to be aware of these ever-changing positions. It might even have been suggested to Freud that his mini-lecture to Deutsch be the focus of the next analytic hour. Nothing goes away, and everything counts. With this in mind, we may see that the attention that one must pay to boundaries is better seen as an ethical consideration — what is the best way to accomplish what this patient needs? — rather than a moral one — what have I done wrong?

The monitoring of one's boundaries can be burdensome as well as painful. That would make clear, from an ethical point of view, why such things as physical contact, financial arrangements, and social interactions are the ruination of analysis and therapy: they are much too complex for any one person to scrutinize and interpret. Only one's personal unresolved megalomania would allow one to have dinner with an analysand: this is not a moral issue, but rather one that requires understanding that the general difficulty of this complicated state of affairs makes it nearly impossible to be handled in a treatment. Certainly, one cannot stay alert to all of the unconscious enactments (Hoffman, 1991) and the shifting boundaries of an analysis or psychotherapy, but the clues to those relationships that remain unexamined and unexplained become available for study as one's own grandiosity is subjected to personal scrutiny and questioning. Therefore, the effort to rationalize a boundary transgression is usually designed to avoid the proper inquiry as to what it meant to the treatment process. Thus, we should not so much limit our actions on the basis of the violation of moral norms as on the very practical point of our own very limited capacity to understand all that goes on between ourselves and our patients: events that should mainly accrue to the benefit of the patient.

I began this paper with the hope that a reconsideration of boundaries as the pre-condition for effective therapeutic action will move them from the arena of morality to that of ethics, i.e., pursuing an optimal treatment process. In this light, interpretations as well as various forms of relationships that aim to help patients can be seen as actions that cross and modify boundaries. New boundary configurations depend upon the recognition and, often, the discussion of what has transpired between the analyst or therapist and the patient. Without the examination of just what happens following an interpretation and/or an enactment, the newly formed boundary can unfortunately cease to be a pre-condition for further therapeutic activity and can thus become an uninterpreted or a not understood lasting situation. The continual scrutiny of the existing boundary configuration is a powerful antidote to the grandiose fantasy of being able to be more than just an analyst or a therapist. That should once again place us on a proper ethical path.

References

Arlow, J. A. (1979). The genesis of interpretation. *Journal of the American Psychoanalytic Association* 27:193–206.

Basch, M.F. (1995). *Doing Brief Psychotherapy*. New York: Basic Books.

Brenner, C. (1979). Working alliance, therapeutic alliance, and transference. *Journal of the American Psychoanalytic Association* 27:137–157.

Day, J. (1994). APA's Corresponding Task Force on Rural Psychiatry.

Fortune, M. (1994). Therapy and intimacy: confused about boundaries. *The Christian Century*, June 1–8.

Gabbard, G.O. (1994). Psychotherapists who transgress sexual boundaries. *Bulletin of the Menninger Clinic* 59:124–135.

Gabbard, G. O. (1995). The early history of boundary violations in psychoanalysis. *Journal of the American Psychoanalytic Association* 43:1115–1136.

Gabbard, G.O. & Lester, E.P. (1995). *Boundaries and Boundary Violations in Psychoanalysis*. New York: Basic Books.

Gill, M. M. (1979). The analysis of the transference. *Journal of the American Psychoanalytic Association* 27:263–288

Hoffman, I.Z. (1991). Discussion: toward a social-constructivist view of the psychoanalytic situation. *Psychoanalytic Dialogues* 1:74–105.

Jones, E. (1957). *The Life and Work of Sigmund Freud*, Vol. 3. The Last Phase, 1919–1939. New York: Basic Books.

Kantrowitz, J. (1996). *The Impact of the Patient on the Analyst*. Hillsdale, NJ: Analytic Press.

Kohut, H. (1984). *How Does Analysis Cure?* Chicago/London: Univ. of Chicago Press.

Rangell, L. (1979). Contemporary issues in the theory of therapy. *Journal of the American Psychoanalytic Association* Supplementn81–112.

Renik, O. (1996). The perils of neutrality. *Psychoanalytic Quarterly* 65:495–517

Ricoeur, P. (1992). *Oneself as Another*. Transl. K. Blainey. Chicago/London: University of Chicago Press.

Postmodern Psychoanalysis (2001)

While following the rules might unquestionably be considered correct and right, Goldberg alerts us to the risks in assuming that there exists a singular proper and correct method for conducting an analysis. This theme is explored in Goldberg's paper *Postmodern Psychoanalysis* (2001). By post-modern, Goldberg recognizes that we have a multitude of approaches that do not happily link together in an overarching theory. In this Tower of Babel, with conflicting languages, vocabularies and sets of rules, we need to adopt an attitude not of "anything goes," but rather, "everything matters." This includes the application of rules. If an analyst, for instance, declines the offer of a gift from a patient under the guise of rules, this application of a rule is imposed by theory. Goldberg warns of the possible risks applying rules, advising that they may remove the analyst from the dynamics of the situation and shut down the analytic process of inquiry. While Goldberg does not offer his own set of rules on rules, he does offer this advice: "One is doing the right thing as long as one understands what one is doing ... *nothing* is free from being the object of such sought-for understanding." Packed into this last statement might be the condensation of much of Goldberg's approach to psychoanalysis.

—GM

*   *   *

In keeping with the spirit of the postmodern, the author suggests that psychoana-lysts should be wary of subscribing to a set of rules and/or a proper method for the conduct of psychoanalysis. He puts forward instead the suggestion that some patients do well with certain rules and not with others, and offers a brief report concerning a group of patients who were unable to live by the rules to support such a viewpoint. He suggests that a corollary of this perspective is one that links the analyst's own capacity to live within or outside of rules to his or her effective-ness with these particular patients. From this unique illustrative group, the general conclusion is offered that only the singular goal of understanding in depth is the proper guiding rule of psychoanalysis.

INTRODUCTION

Correctness permeates and envelops psychoanalysis. From our worry over boundary transgressions to our hope for the correct interpretation, we struggle to be both honourable and helpful, to do the right thing. This rightness and propriety are nowhere more prominent than in the efforts to practise according to a prescribed and proscribed method. All analysts thereby claim to honour and respect the psychoanalytic method, a collection of rules which, if properly followed, should lead, by a sort of internal logic, to a correct endpoint. Much to our initial surprise and eventually to our disappointment, those of us who adhere to this plan have learned that sometimes we cannot seem to be able to follow the rules, at other times a seemingly faithful following may result in unhappy results, and on some occasions a complete disregard of the rules turns out to be the most felicitous route to an agreeable resolution. One can only then wonder if he or she did indeed follow the method correctly or if, perhaps, our rules are misguided or even if, peculiarly, psychoanalysis and correctness do not easily line up together in a comfortable union.

The practice of psychoanalysis or the application of the method entails, as does every procedure that lays claim to a method, a commitment to following the rules. Everyone who wishes to learn analysis has a group of books that explain how one is to act, a supervisory experience that allows for the study and adjustment of errors, and a professional life with patients, all of which are designed to sharpen one's skills and, like it or not, to gather together one's own set of rules, which regularly are seen to conform to books, supervisors and patient success or failure.

At the outset we need to distinguish, as Wittgenstein (1967) emphasised, following a rule from understanding a rule. This distinction may not be as easy as it may appear.

There can be little doubt that psychoanalysis has of late witnessed a variety of changes in method, which some say results from a relaxation of the rules. Others insist that any such change is a modification of the rules. Still others dismiss all change as a disregard of the rules, at times leading to a conceptual banishment from membership in the psychoanalytic community. Not only do these changes affect frequency of appointments as witnessed in an erosion from five to four to three times to even once weekly analysis, but they extend to rules that one would once have once felt were sacrosanct. Some analysts dispense with the couch. Some describe analysis by telephone. Many analysts encourage revealing personal feelings about themselves to their patients, even to the point of asking patients if they are interested in what would otherwise be private information (Aron, 1996). Indeed, at the point that one is encouraged to share positive, loving feelings towards a patient, a sharp outburst is often heard claiming that this is no longer qualified to be called analysis. Other than drumming out the disbelievers to maintain some semblance of conformity, one wonders if and how one can possibly circumscribe all of the changes in the rules and the method. We may begin with a goal that is concerned less with the issue of correctness and more with an enquiry as to the source of all of this present-day 'wild analysis'.

Background

A search for the source of psychoanalytic method and the rules to be followed (or ignored) finds itself not on a road that Freud laid out and with which all analysts are familiar, but rather one that sits unsteadily between two quotes. The first is attributed to the analyst Wilfred Bion, saying: It is difficult to stick to the rules. For one thing, I do not know what the rules of psychoanalysis are (1990, p. 139). The second is derived from the philosopher who has championed postmodernism, Jean-François Lyotard, who tells us both that the postmodern is 'incredulity towards metanarratives' and who claims that all of science legitimates itself with reference to a metanarrative, which is a set of rules of the game (1984, p. xxiv). Thus Bion is ignorant of the rules, while Lyotard is untrusting of them. And although Bion was perhaps practising a certain sort of playful elusiveness, he was also communicating a deeper truth that may join with that of Lyotard. Thus each of these men voices a scepticism and wariness about the adoption of rules that lead to a method that may, by virtue of its insistence on correctness, serve less to direct than to constrain and even to distort.

The postmodern outlook in its most general sense speaks for a multiplicity of approaches that cannot be linked together in a grand narrative or an overarching theory. It allows for many languages, and the resulting Tower of Babel in turn has led many of its critics to condemn it as saying that 'anything goes'. It is thus unsettling and frightening and threatens to undermine the solidity of any rule-governed enterprise. I think this is an unfair and naïve comprehension of postmodernism, which is best illustrated by Lyotard's statement that each self lives in a fabric of relations that is more complex and mobile than ever (1984, p. 15). Seeing the mind in this sense of its complexity allows us to recognise that such complex and open systems are neither predictable nor determined. Indeed, in an extension of Freud's concept of overdetermination, one can list a series of differences by which rule-based systems differ from complex networks or interconnected systems. These range from self-organisation (compared to pre-programmed options that are defined *a priori*) to a multiplicity of final solutions (compared to a specific endpoint) (Cilliers,1998, p. 91). In brief, the postmodern approach moves from the general theory or metanarrative, which aims to explain everything, to particular ones that depend upon the set of local conditions, i.e. the context.

If one grants such a step towards flexibility and the existence of uncertain borders that complex systems call for, then a move can be made towards considering many of our rules and the subsequent method as devices that need have no or little overall validity. Rather, they all must be recast into a particular moment or moments of applicability, i.e. they are local rather than general. The caution that must of course be a constant companion is one that is unfortunately regularly disregarded, i.e. that a rule that may be alterable in one set of circumstances cannot therefore be seen as unnecessary in another set. We are unable to generalise with ease. We are not so much in an arena of 'anything goes' as much as in one of 'everything matters.' This then calls for a persistent activity of framing, of 'meta' examination of all that transpires but, again, only within its particular context. We no longer can take anything for granted.

CLINICAL NOTES

A rather innocent, yet strikingly illustrative anecdote in our literature (Akhtar, 1999) tells of an analyst refusing a patient's gift of fruit while tactfully explaining the rules, i.e. reasons, for this refusal. This seemed to be done primarily in terms of the need to frustrate instinctual drives, and the patient complied with this explanation. This *may* be seen as an example of the method gone astray because of this very point of general-isation, of an overall metanarrative being in place. The application of this or any rule that is imposed on the analysis by a general theory may indeed be necessary or even innocent, but it regularly falls outside of the analytic process of enquiry. This illustrates the following of a rule rather than understanding of it. This particular patient could be one who needs to give a gift quite in contrast to this analyst's precondition, but, again, that can only be determined in the context of the moment. To apply a rule can (or perhaps must) remove the analyst, with his or her own presence, from the dynamics of the situation, since the rule comes from elsewhere. All of our usual and necessary concerns with the question of what this dream or fantasy or enactment means, to both patient and analyst, become sidetracked with the introduction of the issue of cor-rectness or the excuse of proceeding according to the rule. I believe that one can honestly attribute that position of non-generality to Bion who, by saying that he was ignorant of the rules, may have meant that they have no bearing outside of a particular patient at a particular time and, therefore, one is best served by not knowing beforehand.

CLINICAL RELEVANCE

Recently, my colleagues and I have been engaged in a study of a group of patients who could conveniently be classified as not living by the rules (Goldberg, 1999, 2000). These are patients who are usually considered as having behavioural disorders and who run the gamut of misbehav-iour from lying to stealing, from sexual eccentricities to unlawful perversions. They are also people who are ordinarily either not consid-ered for psychoanalysis because of the severity of their pathology or because of their inability to conform to the rules of analysis. The study of these patients has allowed us to turn a searchlight on analytic rules and method, inasmuch as we became forced to develop rules in an *ad hoc* manner in our therapeutic efforts, or, as Lyotard would say, rules with local validity and applicability. Our patients routinely could not fit into our individual methods of analysis, and each of them required some sort of individualised method. Perhaps this becomes true of many if not all of our patients in some more subtle manner.

CASE EXAMPLE

Conrad was a lawyer involved in client litigation who developed sudden acute anxiety when arguing in courtroom trials and so was forced to suspend all such public appearances. He felt himself extremely fortunate to have earlier purchased a disability insurance policy that paid him handsomely as long as he was unable to pursue his normal occupation, which for Conrad was appearing in court. It did not matter for this policy that Conrad could pursue other forms of legal activity, and he quickly chose to be disabled and to collect on his insurance. Not surprisingly, the policy demanded a regular validation of Conrad's condition to be submitted by a psychiatrist, i.e. Conrad needed to be seen by someone who would agree to such a contract. Initially this was no trouble for Conrad, but his first analyst, a psychiatrist, balked after a bit, inasmuch as Conrad's need for such a disability certification seemed to be interfering with the treatment. Conrad went shopping. A few analysts agreed to treat him but all insisted on staying clear of this insurance requirement. Finally Conrad found an analyst who agreed to see him and to regularly certify him as disabled.

No doubt, at this point many analysts would claim that a bona fide analysis was impossible, since the rules of analysis were not being adhered to, and rather than a therapeutic alliance, this arrangement might more properly be termed a financial negotiation. This extreme example of a deviation from the analytic method is offered not as an instance of an ethical deviation that is a separate subject, but rather as an opening to an enquiry as to whether rule changes are feasible and so can themselves be subject to analysis. In brief, this analysis was felt to be workable for some time until, despite the patient's improvement, a termination seemed difficult if not impossible. The analyst presented this case to a group and was roundly criticised for being corrupt and having colluded with this patient. The protest of the analyst began with his insistence that if I did not do it, someone else would. However, the group was unrelenting in its blame and shortly thereafter, a chastised and depressed analyst sought supervision for his conduct. He discovered much about his own greed and dishonesty and subsequently saw it confirmed in the material that had emerged in the analysis. After some time he was able to revisit the analysis with some new insight and soon thereafter, the patient decided independently to discontinue his disability benefits and to terminate his analysis. The case was then again presented to the group that remained critical but also less certain. Was this indeed a case of an analysis that simply could not follow the rules? Without resorting to a familiar 'this is not analysis', is it possible for some analyses to live outside of the usual rules as long as these exceptions ultimately become themselves scrutinized? Perhaps most intriguingly, does one need to share some similar pathology in order to be able to help some patients?

THE ANALYST AND THE RULES

What our group did learn from a study of a number of such rule-breaking patients was that almost all of the analysts had what can best be called a corresponding, albeit often unconscious, inability to stick to their own preformed rules. Indeed we soon came to believe that *only* a rule-breaking analyst could hope to be effective with our misbehaving patients. Conrad's analyst was able to examine his own preoccupation with money, and he thus later claimed that his own movement from financial chicanery to professional honesty was a mark of this movement and its later effectiveness.

If we could allow the truth of that position, we might be able ourselves to make a parallel claim that all of our rules derive from our personal, i.e. individual, needs that become sanctioned by membership in groups that are like-minded. Once again we must remind ourselves that this does not and cannot lead to licence. Rather it raises a more fundamental question as to just what can be said about the analytic method that does not devolve into the niceties of the ritual such as gifts, couch and frequency? Put in another way, what enables an analyst to function as an analyst? How can one understand rather than conform to a rule?

THE PATIENT AND THE RULES

One lesson learned by our group as we discussed each of these cases was that not every one of us could do what was required of us by each patient. Whereas one analyst might help a thief but not a cross-dresser, another could easily reverse his or her predilections. The most outstanding conclusion that we reached was one that involved a rather persistent and significant blindness that accompanied our preferences and convictions. Just as Conrad's analyst seemed to disavow his own obvious (to others) dishonesty, so too could we see similar defensive positions operant in all of our behaviours. Out of these combinations of personal rationalisations and denials, there seemed to emerge a collection of procedures that we tried to apply to all of our patients. If we could free ourselves from these preconceptions, we might better explain the variability of success and failure with patients. In a nutshell, the inevitable conclusion is that some patients require certain rules while having no problem with others. Thus one cannot operate according to a fixed set of rules and an expectant analytic method, any more than one can operate with a totally flexible set of rules and an equally unexpectant method. The question of what enables an analyst to function as such is equally applicable to a patient and his or her comparable ability to be a patient. The task of any analysis is to determine the requirements of a given patient as they differ from that of another and then to see if these requirements articulate with the capabilities of the analyst. It makes no sense to assign qualities such as optimism or openness or even neutrality to analysts, since each of these rather admirable qualities may not serve any particular patient well and may not be natural features of any single analyst. Nor does it make sense to insist that patients should not read analytic books or should not marry or should not bring gifts, since each of these injunctions may or may not be in the best interests of the analysis. We need to take a step back to grasp what is essential about the analytic method and its applications.

DISCUSSION

Psychoanalysis is grounded in understanding; not the casual understanding seen in relationships that prosper according to its achievement, but an in-depth understanding that is conditioned by the complexities of the transference and the unconscious. It is a form of understanding that puts comfort and agreement into a secondary position. There is no doubt that Freud felt that he achieved this form of understanding by the technique and conditions that he employed, or to put it differently, by the method that he felt was most likely to allow the development of the state of transference that was desirable. Many analysts have felt the same, and one cannot possibly discard the knowledge that derives from that tradition.

However, there is also no doubt that other analysts might achieve that understanding under different conditions. If the method of such understanding requires a sustained empathy on the part of the analyst, then one needs to attend to the conditions that enable both patient and analyst to make that possible. If one feels that other forms of data-gathering are required, then that too becomes a mutual undertaking by both patient and analyst. Since people are different both in personality and pathology, it seems foolhardy to insist that Freud's tradition applies to all. It seems equally foolhardy to claim that nothing whatsoever need apply to all. Thus we aim not for some intersubjective state of agreement but for a state allowing an optimum enquiry of one person by another. To oversimplify: one is doing the right thing as long as one understands what one is doing. That requires that everything can be bracketed as a local metanarrative with local rules and thus be scrutinised. And *nothing* is free from being the object of such sought-for understanding.

REFERENCES

Akhtar, S. (1999). Distinguishing needs from wishes. *Journal of the American Psychoanalytic Association* 47: 113–51.

Aron, L. (1996). *A Meeting of Minds*. Hillsdale, NJ: Analytic Press.

Bion, W. R. (1990). *Brazilian Lectures*. London: Karnac.

Cilliers, P. (1998). *Complexity and Postmodernism*. London and New York: Routledge.

Goldberg, A. (1999). *Being of Two Minds*. Hillsdale, NJ: Analytic Press.

Goldberg, A. (2000). *Errant Selves*. Hillsdale, NJ: Analytic Press.

Lyotard, J.-F. (1984). *The Postmodern Condition: A Report on Knowledge, Theory, and History of Literature*, Vol. 10. Minneapolis, MN: Univ. of Minnesota Press.

Wittgenstein, L. (1967). *Philosophical Investigation*. Trans. G. E. M. Anscombe. Oxford: Blackwell.

Who Owns the Countertransference? (2004)

Who Owns the Countertransference (2004) and *A Risk of Confidentiality* (2004) find Goldberg advising against assuming an absolute position. Here, he states that even rules considered absolute and universal—including those that require confidentiality and privacy—need to be open to investigation and further inquiry. The title of his paper, *A Risk of Confidentiality*, is wonderful and witty and worth a double take. Who but Goldberg would lead us to question the sureness of confidentiality?

—GM

*   *   *

A recent series of articles published in the *Journal of Clinical Ethics* (Harvard Ethics Consortium 2003) presents a published case study of a patient in psychotherapy, along with the responses of a number of readers, including a response from the patient himself.[1] The basic point of these essays has to do with the patient's consent for the publication of his case and the repercussions that ensued from his reading about himself from his psychiatrist's point of view. The latter report included a good deal of the psychiatrist's feelings about treating this patient, feelings that he had not previously shared with his patient and that turned out to be quite hurtful to the patient. Although the patient had given his consent to have his case published, this consent had been agreed to long before the case was written up, and indeed, the patient hardly remembered that moment of agreement until presented with the finished product.

The *Journal* includes essays by both the psychiatrist and the patient, with discussions by a number of ethicists who themselves seem quite committed to the dual task of allowing a patient to read what is said about him or her, while ensuring that such a reading will not be harmful or injurious to the patient. Most readers will probably conclude that the delicate effort at a balance to the problem has not resulted in a happy solution.

---

[1] I am grateful to Carlye Perlman for alerting me to this publication.

SOME BACKGROUND

I shall not review here the extensive literature on confidentiality of psychoanalytic publications, which has been adequately reviewed and discussed by Gabbard(2000) and Galatzer-Levy (2003). Rather, I wish to pose our particular dilemma as one between the stance of the International Committee of Medical Journal Editors(1995) and the Committee on Scientific Activities of the American Psychoanalytic Association (1984). The guidelines of the first, as summarized in the second, say that published information must be "essential for scientific purposes" (p. 440), and "the patient or proxy must give written informed consent for publication" (p. 441). This has the form of a law and is decisive.

The second group does not demand consent, but leaves it up to the author to protect the patient. Protection ranges from alteration or omission of material to thick disguise of the patient. The latter usually demands that no one other than the patient can recognize him- or herself as the one being written about. This takes the form of a calculation and a judgment.

Each of these two positions centers its attention on patient protection and gives the vulnerable patient the maximum concern, yet each has a status of its own and is set up in opposition to the other.

OWNERSHIP

The crux of the issue of revealing something about the treatment of a patient often comes down to a question of ownership. Although the property status of human tissue is controversial (National Bioethics Advisory Commission 1999), the *Journal* states that patients clearly have ownership of their stories (Joffe 2003), and so lay claim to privacy.

The narrative that is constructed in the formation and presentation of a case history is felt to belong solely to the patient, who must either give permission for its distribution or must be protected from any harm that could result from its publication. Thus, at one end of an imaginary line that we could construct, we would have the treatment—be it psychoanalysis or psychotherapy—as an activity done solely for the benefit of the patient, with all issues such as property rights belonging to the patient. Midway on our imagined axis we can fashion a co-constructed narrative, which is both a product of two authors and an entity that would allow for a claim of dual or shared ownership. Finally, at the pole opposite to that of patient ownership, there could be a point that seems to belong to the therapist in its entirety.

It is often a poor analogy to place physical medicine alongside psychological treatment, but we surely can agree that (say) a surgical technique that is honed and perfected on one or more patients can be used effectively on future patients. That technique or knowledge is now the property of the surgeon, with all due gratitude to the patients who lent themselves to its development. So, too, in psychotherapy and psychoanalysis, each patient is a potential laboratory in which to develop our own skills until, over time, these become so much a part of a practitioner that she or he is hard pressed to point to its origin. The fuzziness begins in the middle; only at the extremes does clarity ensue.

CASE ILLUSTRATION

An interesting case in analysis presented a bit of clinical material that I felt had not heretofore been represented in the literature. I wrote up the case, with the major pertinent issues revolving around my countertransference reactions to the clinical material. I showed the written-up case to a consultant, who felt that this was a significant contribution and should be published. The wisdom of this conclusion is not the issue here, but the dilemma is. In truth, the value of most contributions is determined over time and cannot be readily apparent.

Although this case could be disguised from being identified by anyone but the patient, it could certainly not be concealed from the patient. If he or she were to read of my countertransference reactions, it seemed to me that it would be potentially harmful to the conduct of the analysis. Nor could I show the written case to the patient for consent to publish, since it might readily recapitulate the sad events written up in the aforementioned *Journal*.

In that case, the hurt and angry patient did return to his therapist to work out the derailment that had resulted from his reading of the case, and the therapist felt that both he and the patient had profited from this unfortunate circumstance. It seems that the harm can come at any time, even after termination. But one can hardly make a case for the supposedly ameliorative effects of a return's being universally true.

Stoller's (1988) advice is to let patients edit and disguise their own cases, but this advice is given in the form of a universal rule, and I have no doubt whatsoever that it would not apply to my patient and my countertransference. Nor was I eager to test my conclusion. Rightly or wrongly, I felt that thick disguise would destroy the point I wished to make, and I saw no way out. No solution seemed to fit.

DISCUSSION

The benefit of the case presented in the *Journal* is that, for the most part, it represents a situation in which everyone would have been better off if the write-ups had never been seen by the patient. Of course, the best but not the only way to achieve this is never to publish anything save fiction or theory. Many potential but unwilling writers, or those who simply cannot write, take refuge behind this solution. Indeed, one often finds the most zealous defenders of patient protection to be filled with the ranks of the nonwriters. The other solutions available to solve the dilemma are nicely listed and discussed by Galatzer-Levy (2003), but he shows them all to have their own failings. In fact, he concludes his article by joining Gabbard (2000) in stating that all supposed solutions face difficulties.

If we move away from the very valuable point on the continuum that is devoted to patient protection and patient ownership, we may arrive at a point closer to one of therapist ownership, as in my countertransference, coupled with a possible benefit to future patients. The risk is clear. The answer is less so, but not beyond us. It begins with our dispensing with a commitment to any set of rules that govern all case presentations and publications. If we embrace pragmatism, then we need to recognize that some patients should indeed be consulted beforehand, some disguised minimally, some disguised thickly, and perhaps some disguised not at all. Stoller (1988) may have carved out a group of patients who can edit their own cases, while others may delineate those who should never have to reckon with such publication. There is a grave danger in treating all patients alike, as well as in our taking for granted that a higher moral code exists to which we must all conform.

When Gabbard states that no approach is without its problems, he argues that a clinical decision must be made in each case regarding whether it is the best strategy to use thick disguise, to ask the patient's consent, to limit the clinical illustration to process data without biographical details, to ask a colleague to serve as author, or to use composites. Once again, the goal is to minimize potential harm to the patient while maximizing the scientific value of the contribution (Gabbard 2000). Those are excellent guidelines, but the above-noted *Journal* case and my own quandary seem to suggest that there is simply no way to know beforehand, no guarantee of achieving the goal anticipated by Gabbard. Not only is no approach without its problems, but the potential problem is not usually readily apparent in making one's clinical decision. Can it be that we cannot write without risk?

There is an interesting discussion by Derrida on ethical decisions, in which he affirms that every such decision requires confrontation of its essential, irreducible undecidability. Caputo (1997) summarizes Derrida's point:

> The opposite of "undecidability" is not decisiveness but is calculability. Decision-making, judgment, on the other hand, positively depends upon undecidability. So, a "just" decision, a "judgment" that is worthy of its name, one that responds to the demands of justice, one that is more than merely legal, goes eyeball to eyeball with undecidability, stares it in the face (literally), looks into that abyss, and then makes the leap, that is, "gives itself up to the impossible decision." [p. 137]

Alas, just as psychoanalysis is one of the impossible professions, it is also burdened with impossible decisions.

CONCLUSION

Most ethicists and moralists aim to form laws of behavior that cover all persons, such as is embodied in the golden rule of doing unto others as you would have them do unto you. However, most persons decide their behavior on a more pragmatic, ad hoc basis, and this may well result in behavior that ranges from the utterly selfish to the most altruistic. What psychoanalysts have learned is that all behavior is complex, much of it is unconscious, and so we are more often befuddled than confident about the meanings of behavior. Ethicists who promulgate universal rules may indeed do us more harm than good. Absolutes in psychoanalysis and psychotherapy are conveniences that can inhibit and blind us. We may profit more from devoting time to better categorizing our patients into those who may not care at all if they are presented as case material, those who care just enough to be disguised, those who would give consent if they could edit the case, and those who would forbid any sort of publication. This is not meant as a solution but could lead to a better clarification of the dilemma. It may simply not be true that from the point of view of others, confidentiality is an absolute privilege that must always be observed, or that privacy is a fundamental right of all patients. Rather, confidentiality and privacy may be proper objects of investiga-tion—investigation that is waylaid by those who would claim certainty about the right way to behave.

The investigations that are necessary to better equip us to make a proper determination about privacy and confidentiality are probably not those that divide therapists and analysts as to their preferred procedures. As interesting as that research might be, it is not of paramount im-portance. What is needed is a clearer idea of how we balance the risk of disclosure with the need for disclosure. Both patient and therapist should enjoy rights to attain this balance. Analyses are co-constructions and lend value to each of the participants. We surely cannot devise a risk-free answer while maintaining our credibility as scientists. Both obligations and ownership go both ways.

REFERENCES

Caputo, J. (1997). *Deconstruction in a Nutshell.* New York: Fordham University Press, p. 137.

Committee On Scientific Activities Of The American Psychoanalytic Association (1984). Ethical conduct of research in psychoanalysis. *Bulletin of the American Psychoanalytic Association* 40:439–445.

Gabbard, G. (2000). Disguise or consent: problems and recommendations concerning the publication and presentation of clinical material. *International Journal of Psycho-Analysis* 81:1071–1083.

Galatzer-Levy, R. (2003). Psychoanalytic research and confidentiality. In *Confidentiality: Ethical Perspectives and Clinical Dilemmas,* ed. C. Levin, A. Furlong & M. K. O'Neill. Hillsdale, NJ: Analytic Press.

Harvard Ethics Consortium (2003). *The Journal of Clinical Ethics* 14:88–133.

International Committee Of Medical Journal Editors (1995). Protection of patients' right to privacy. *British Medical Journal* 311(7015):1072.

Joffe, S. (2003). Public dialogues and the boundaries of moral community. *Journal of Clinical Ethics* 14:101–108.

National Bioethics Advisory Commission (1999). *Research Involving Human Biological Material.* Rockville, MD: U.S. Dept. of Commerce.

Stoller, R. J. (1988). Patients' responses to their own case reports. *Journal of the American Psychoanalytic. Association* 36:371–391.

A Risk of Confidentiality (2004)

The concept of confidentiality is examined from its absolute position espoused by some psychoanalysts to the many exceptions to this position allowed by others. The suggestion made in this paper is offered as a psychoanalytic one which urges us to see confidentiality as posing risks in both positions, that is, the absolute and the necessary exceptions. Confidentiality is representative of many, if not all, of the rules and methods that are implicit in the conduct of an analysis and thus may well be taken for granted. The suggestion offered is for a periodic re-examination of the implicit background of psychoanalysis.

INTRODUCTION

The idea of a 'background' is prominent in certain philosophical circles (Searle, 1992), but it is often a rather elusive idea to define. It has to do with the tacit assumptions or things taken for granted in any situation from a social gathering to a workplace. These assumptions are said to be both basic and not in need of attention being paid to them. Such a background operates, say, when we go to a restaurant and assume that there will be a menu of sorts, that we can purchase food and that a bill will be offered to us: all things that need not be spoken of overtly. We can imagine such a set of assumptions in many other normal situations, and it takes no stretch of our imagination to see how it may apply to psychoanalysis and psychotherapy. These last examples are somewhat notorious in that they claim to want to draw attention to even the most minor of issues, yet they too have a host of unspoken and taken-for-granted ideas. Over time the ordinary and accustomed ways in which we as analysts and therapists operate become so routinized that they fade into the background and no longer become issues of concern and attention. With such comfort and convenience a certain risk may become operative.

In a previous submission I discussed how the development of the rules of psychoanalysis have led to a sort of moral commitment to their adherence (Goldberg, 2001). Such a commitment tends to give these (often implicit) rules a certain air of absoluteness which may, in turn, detract us from analyzing them. Rather than our becoming alert to every nuance of analysis we allow our routine to fade into the background.

There should be little doubt that many if not all of the tried and true principles of psychoanalysis may profit from being subjected to periodic re-examination and scrutiny to see if their status remains as telling and relevant today as it did when first developed and observed. This sort of re-evaluation has been brought to bear on such issues as frequency of visits, the use of the couch, self-disclosure etc., and, more often than not, it leads us regularly to confusion and debate rather than to certainty and closure. This unhappy endpoint would, however, appear to be quite unlikely with an issue such as confidentiality, an issue claimed to be 'a basic patient's right and an essential condition for effective psychoanalytic treatment and research', as so stated in the *Ethics case book of the American Psychoanalytic Association* (Dewald and Clark, 2001). This particular case book is meant to serve as a guideline of general principles. It proceeds to present a series of potential problems for all sorts of ethical dilemmas with those concerning confidentiality offering enough exceptions to this aforementioned basic right to cause consternation to any psychoanalyst or psychotherapist. I should like to develop the idea of the fading of ideas into the background utilizing this assumption of a basic right of confidentiality. My aim is to demonstrate that this basic belief has allowed us to fall back on an absolutist position which in turn carries a risk of its own while its relativistic counterpart is equally problematic.

The exceptions to the maintenance of confidentiality in psychoanalysis range from disguised supervision, to insurance reports, to communication to lawyers and courts, to talks with family members, and on to publications in professional journals and the lay press. These are all defensible and desirable. One immediate response to this plethora of possible breaches in confidentiality is a conviction that there are no easy answers. Yet another response is admirably presented in a book by Bollas and Sundelsen who offer a compelling case to support the claim that: 'a patient who sees a psychoanalyst is guaranteed that absolute confidentiality is assured and maintained, [and] then the door is shut to any and all requests from third parties for clinical notes and testimony by the clinician' (1995, p. 155). The single exception allowed by the authors is for consultation with a supervisor with the patient remaining anonymous. That exception is allowed for the benefit of the patient alone.

In order to handle the inevitable pressures brought upon a therapist for breaks in this absolute position, the authors offer the position of 'social therapist' as one (in sharp contrast to a psychoanalyst) who both treats the patient as well as actively intervenes in the patient's life. The book insists that one cannot practice psychoanalysis with the basic premise of free association if one does indeed step outside of this fundamental rule, and it bemoans the sad state of much of today's analysis which seems to regularly betray such an absolute condition. Such betrayals other than consultations are seen as done for the benefit of third parties.

AN OUTLINE OF THE PROBLEM

If one were to line up and list the rather ordinary requests and demands for breaks in confidentiality, they would fall into two categories. The first would have to do with those which would benefit the treatment, the second with those which would benefit others but may either harm or benefit the treatment. For Bollas and Sundelsen the first category would have but one entry: that of consultation with a colleague or supervisor with an adequate disguise of the patient. For many others, as in the *Ethics case book*, there are a host of situations which do ultimately benefit the patient, such as informing insurance companies, albeit at a price. For the most part the second category is filled with benefits for others with an undetermined harm to the patient. The absolutarian standard of Bollas and Sundelsen is both reassuring and comfortable. But one should wonder. In a very telling quote from a psychoanalyst who struggled with a law prohibiting psychiatrists from testifying without a patient's permission, we read, 'this honorable attempt to protect the patient misses the essential point that he [the patient] may not be aware of unconscious motives impelling him to give permission'. One might also exchange that quote to end with 'to conceal information'. And one may extend that dilemma to include the psychiatrist in the exchange. Without in any way diminishing the passion and point of the absolute stance on confidentiality, one should surely wonder if such a stance also serves to bypass unconscious motives in the therapist in the guise of a noble pursuit.

Our two suggested categories divide along the line of a concentration on the effectiveness of the treatment with particular concentration on transference-countertransference issues in contrast to a separate focus upon ethical issues involving a concern for the greater good. Thus a betrayal of a patient who was about to harm someone, as in the Tarasoff decision (Bollas and Sundelsen, 1995, p. 4), is a clear step away from the patient on to the protection of society. In contrast to this breach, one could readily see how writing up a patient for publication while getting the permission from the patient to do so (Dewald and Clark, 2001, p. 30) is a step aimed at both aiding patients and benefiting the greater good. However, the separation into the two categories may be a clue to one risk of confidentiality: a clue offered by the slight chink in the absolute armor of Bollas and Sundelsen: the consultation.

Case illustration

Phil was a lawyer in analysis who, after a rather productive period in treatment which had resulted in a significant diminution of his presenting complaint of depression, came to somewhat of a standstill in his analytic work. Phil's analyst was troubled over the lack of progress in his otherwise valued patient, and he sought private consultation with a supervisor whom he had often gone to for assistance. Phil's analyst felt that he had much profited from this supervisory visit and returned to his patient with some new insights and vigor. Phil himself could not help but be aware of this change in his analyst's stance, and the analysis seemed now to proceed in a most promising direction. Shortly after this period of improvement, Phil asked his analyst why and how he accounted for this alteration in the treatment and even went so far as to enquire if the analyst had sought outside help. The analyst confessed—if that is the proper word—and Phil became outraged at what he felt was a breach of confidentiality. He had always felt this analysis to be a contract of privilege and privacy, but also he had thought of his analyst as possessed of all the knowledge necessary for his treatment. He was deeply disappointed.

Although this patient had in no way been identified to the supervisor and so clearly fell into the category of permissible breaches of confidentiality, it seems difficult to distinguish the issue from similar such actions, inasmuch as Phil had no concern as to his being identified. In this particular case there was a wonderful opportunity offered to analyze the patient's over-idealization of his analyst and to work through the ensuing de-idealization. In retrospect Phil and his analyst saw this period of analysis as a moment of positive progress. Phil felt he could see the similarity in his rage at his father's shortcomings, and his analyst felt that he could better struggle with his own conflicts about needing help and having to do things on his own. This mutual benefit from the breach seems to suggest more such benefits from some other breaches with minor and major differences. This sort of consultation is the sole exception to confidentiality allowed, and it seems to hinge on helping the patient without revealing his identity. These two parameters seem worthwhile, but it remains to be seen if they can serve as guidelines to the entire problem around confidentiality.

The crucial distinguishing point about this case surely has to do with the analyst's own psychology. Perhaps an analyst less able to struggle with his own inadequacies would not seek supervision, would pursue a different and less rewarding therapeutic action or would even discontinue the analysis. If we focus upon this single but crucial point, we may be able to construct a number of scenarios in which the analyst, constrained by confidentiality, would fail to do something which might benefit the treatment. Some of these scenarios could include identifying the patient as well. The inclusion of the third party does not come without a series of problems and risks and even opportunities.

CASE ILLUSTRATION

Dr G is analyzing a very volatile patient who has been placed on psychotropic medication by a consulting colleague of Dr G's. Much of the time of the hours of the patient had been devoted to the lambasting of the psychopharmacologist by the patient who accused him of being cold, insensitive and downright sadistic. Some of this doctor's interventions seem to be more harmful than helpful and even undermining of the therapeutic work with Dr G. Finally Dr G called his colleague and asked about the interactions with the patient. Much to his surprise, he learned that this other doctor has been a model of propriety and correctness and much of the patient's vituperative attack on this man had been misplaced and distorted. Dr G now compares this hostility toward his colleague with the over-adoring attitude that the patient has toward him and reluctantly becomes aware of the development and maintenance of a split transference involving these two therapists. Indeed, most of the negative feelings that may have been directed to Dr G have been directed to and drained off to the psychopharmacologist. Dr G realizes that he has enjoyed and participated in this arrangement, but he wonders if this problem would not potentially exist in any analysis wherein one set of feelings are successfully diverted to a figure outside of the analysis. However, something about this seemed different. There was a real bona fide connection between these two doctors, since Dr G had felt a need to be in touch with his patient's medication management, and he had made it a rule not to abdicate what he felt was a necessary responsibility. One of Dr G's other colleagues divorced himself entirely from the pharmacological management of his patients, but Dr G felt that position for himself made him more anxious and unable to intervene when necessary. More than that, he felt that his patient wanted him to be connected with the psychopharmacologist, and the conversation that resulted from his phone call was a necessary part of the treatment.

This case of a consultation with an identified patient opens the door a bit further than the single crack offered by Bollas and Sundelsen in the previous case, but the door should not be taken as a window of opportunity to dispense with confidentiality. Rather it might allow us to better understand the analyst's need to connect outside of the consulting room; a need that is especially notable in cases of a split transference.

CASE ILLUSTRATION

Mrs. S had been a child of an early divorce followed by a quick remarriage of her mother to a man who sexually abused Mrs. S. Mrs. S had endured this childhood trauma in complete silence, since she was convinced that reporting her stepfather's behavior to her mother would be overwhelming to this fragile woman who had suffered enough from her first marriage. This vow of silence and secrecy followed all through her adult life and was especially maintained in her weekly visits to her own father. That relationship was a loving and enjoyable one, but one equally captured by secrecy and concealment, inasmuch as Mrs. S's mother could not tolerate the idea that her daughter was happy with her ex-husband, the biological father of Mrs. S. Thus the stage was set for Mrs. S to live a life of compartments and concealments, a life which later manifested itself in addictive and delinquent behavior. By no means could one directly correlate such concealment and secrecy with the later delinquency, but it did seem to live on in much of this behavior.

Mrs. S had treatment before coming to Dr B, but she assumed from the start that he would never report anything about her to anyone; and Dr B happily joined in this assumption. He soon learned of both her repeated delinquency and misbehavior and its parallel concealment from both her husband and her long list of therapists. She recreated the sad configuration of her childhood of her not telling her mother about either father or stepfather, both of whom seemed to enlist her in somewhat pleasurable and forbidden behavior. This, not surprisingly, was also recreated in the transference with the analyst either being unconsciously invited to collude in misbehavior (as described in a previous publication (Goldberg, 1999)), or assigned the role of the knowing but mute parent.

As the patient's delinquency decreased in treatment and soon disappeared entirely, she became more and more depressed, and her legal problems now took center stage. She asked Dr B to write a letter to her lawyer, and he referred her to a legal consultant for this help. It soon became clear to Dr B that only he could offer the necessary material for a legal defense, and he reluctantly did write a letter. Shortly after that, the patient's mother inexplicably asked the patient if her stepfather had ever abused her. The patient was flabbergasted at the truth finally coming out, and both she and Dr B wondered if some change had occurred within her that communicated itself to others: a change of bringing a split-off aspect of herself into an integrated whole. Of course, this seemed only a speculation that could not be verified, but it started the treatment on the road to integration.

No matter how anyone may evaluate this particular act of breaking confidentiality (i.e. the letter to the lawyer), it would be problematic to classify it as derailing or damaging the analysis. Nor is it possible to say that it could have been completely avoided, yet have the treatment continue. However, it may serve to once again blur this distinction between acts focused solely on helping the patient and those that go outside of the treatment in both openly identifying the patient and enlisting others: the latter ostensibly for the greater good of society. The claim that one can rationalize many breaches of confidentiality by insisting that ultimately this is for the good of the patient, a claim disputed by Bollas and Sundelsen, is readily available in this and any case that allow the person to get the necessary treatment or to continue treatment. For Mrs S the involvement of the lawyer allowed her to continue in treatment. One must wonder if the retreat to absolute confidentiality is but a place for the analyst to hide, especially from analyzing the nature of the third party involvement.

DISCUSSION

The exceptions that have developed over the years to the physician-patient privilege are considered by some to be so plentiful that the entire concept is without significance (Slovenko, 1974, p. 650). When one is invited to consider all the exceptions to both the privacy of the patient and the ethical requirements demanded of the clinician, there may be little room left for this 'privilege' which is supposed to allow individuals to withhold information especially from the courts but also to a variety of interested parties. Without this privilege, enjoyed readily by priests, spouses and lawyers, therapists are set adrift in a sea of ethical uncertainty. We quickly lose sight of our fundamental focus and become amateur ethicists and moralists.

To rescue ourselves from the life of bewilderment, we adopt rules of conduct such as in HIPAA which enable us to feel both honest and helpful, and surely one of the best of these rules is that of confidentiality. As the rule becomes confining and difficult to maintain, we begin to modify it. One modification is to obtain a patient's permission to break a confidence. Unfortunately we have learned that patients are often unable to be free enough of transference issues to be in a position to really give informed consent. A patient may agree because of a positive feeling or disagree because of a negative one, while neither would accurately reflect an objective and rational decision. Another modification offered to aid our uncertainty is that of patient disguise, especially in terms of consultation or publication in professional journals. But this last is limited to patients who are not in the field and/or will not 'come by such writing' (Bollas and Sundelsen, 1995, p. 189). That, of course, excludes what might be a valuable literature on the analysis of psychoanalytic candidates. At each and every turn we seem to confront a problem that either seems more inhibiting of our practice or of our freedom to function as members of a free society. If we limit ourselves to issues that deal only with the patient and the analyst, our first category, there probably can be no opening to a third party without a variety of implications: both good and bad. If we open the door to issues that go beyond the patient and the analyst, our second category, there can be no easy guideline to what is and is not allowable. I should like to propose a trial of a psychoanalytic solution to the quandary.

If we return to the fundamental thesis of the two books that compose the bulk of references in this essay, it is that one must try to shut the door to any and all requests for information and intrusion by third parties. Ethical problems present themselves when the door is completely shut, but less so by far than when it is allowed to be ajar. Substituting 'social therapists' as doorkeepers seems one form of solution that effectively bypasses rather than solves the problem. The shut door is an absolute position that devotes itself to the patient's welfare. The open door is a relative position that makes for the introduction of interests that may coincide with or override those of the patient. However, it may also be helpful to make a psychoanalytic assessment of the inclusion of the third party without any preconceived value judgments.

The concept of a split transference, a vertical split as conceptualized in self-psychology, directs our attention to a divided set of feelings: one group directed and focused upon the analyst, another devoted to an area of concern and/or behavior in persons and issues outside of the analysis. One obvious solution to this divide is to bring the split-off material into the analysis and on to the person of the analyst. This is not always an easy accomplishment, and sometimes an analyst may unwittingly keep the material out of the analysis. One interesting aside here is that of a case in analysis for approximately eight years without ever mentioning to his analyst that he regularly stole books from his university bookstore. In a subsequent treatment he realized that this first analyst had communicated non-verbally to him that she could not handle that information. Thus we see that it is up to the analyst to somehow allow the split-off material to participate in the analysis. This rather simple idea goes far beyond the analyst's willingness to listen to warded-off material, inasmuch as some of this sometimes presents itself only in the form of behavior, as witnessed in the above-noted book thief, as opposed to ideation. There are patients who must be seen as unable to talk, rather than as unwilling to do so. They are prone to inviting the analyst to collude with them rather than to interpret what they cannot speak of.

If the analyst betrays the confidence of a patient by opening the door to a third party, he is essentially enacting but probably no more than if the door is effectively barred. Both closing and opening are actions, but one is regularly more prized than the other. We are regularly lulled into thinking that silence, like inactivity, is the proper atmosphere for analytic work, but there is no guarantee that free association prospers in a field of such deprivation. Surely some patients may do well with a more responsive analyst, even though some analysts may feel most patients do best in those original parameters of conduct. Just as surely there may be patients who do better by the action of an analyst who opens the door to consultants, pharmacologists, lawyers and the like. The crucial issue is that of analyzing the action. I suspect this central element is one that is ignored or neglected by the assumption of some absolutarian posture. If we are convinced that confidentiality is an absolute and basic right, we become seduced into believing that it is beyond investigation and interpretation. It runs the risk of fading into the background and only being attended to in its breaches. Unfortunately, too often such attention is composed of worry over ethical issues rather than of a careful examination of the transference implications of the presence of a third party. Of course, a relativist position invites other sorts of dilemmas.

The action of an analyst who breaks the bond of confidentiality is best thought of as one kind of enactment that demands investigation and interpretation rather than as an error of commission worthy of condemnation. This sort of stance treats analysis as an activity that corrects itself by the process of interpretation rather than one of adherence to a set of procedures and rules. Of course we may not always be able to effectively understand and interpret our actions, but we are always better off wondering why we do what we do rather than chastising ourselves for our supposed errors.

The entrance of a lawyer or an insurance company into the sanctity of the analytic dialogue, however welcome or unwelcome, turns the two-person dialogue into a conversation of three parties. Many times the analyst is blind to the transference implications of this entrance, but many other times the analysis will not or cannot proceed without such a connection. There need be no automatic injunction against the analyst examining privately or openly what this third person means to him as well as what that presence means to the patient. The exclusion of the lawyer or the insurance company may offer a feeling of comfort or smugness, but such exclusion could well assist in the analyst's remaining unaware of his unconscious motives in such rigorous rule adherence.

Summary

Absolute positions are snares that routinely betray their dangers by the introduction of selected exceptions. This is seen in the assumed and inviolate absolute basic right to confidentiality which begins with an exception allowed to consultation with a colleague and then proceeds to a list that seems to have no end. We soon seem to leave the arena of our expertise and move to one of the study of ethics. This is no brief against the proper concern with ethics but rather is an alerting call to our having missed the point. Once we do become alert to our standing in the wrong place, we tend to go back, to retreat to our absolutarian stance. Both directions, that of exceptions and that of retreat, make for a neglect of our work as analysts.

Embracing confidentiality as an absolute right runs a risk of allowing unconscious material which could be brought into the analysis to remain outside as split off and unintegrated. In one sense, an analyst may collude with a patient in maintaining confidentiality as well as in breaching it. The former stance is supported by our established procedures and is certainly one best embraced by our profession, but it is not one that should be immune from psychoanalytic enquiry. Opening the door to third parties is a move decried by our established procedures and is certainly a move to be very cautious in considering. However, it too should not be classified as a prohibition without exceptions. Both stances are too risky. Everything in analysis is to be seen as an interesting site for investigation and interpretation.

CONCLUSIONS

Psychoanalysis sits uneasily between an allegiance to a proper way to function and an openness to a variety of paths which can lead to a form of methodological anarchy. My personal solution to this delicate balance is to see analysis as an heir to the field of American pragmatism. What is demanded of us is an ever-ready alertness to whatever we may feel is taken for granted, all the while recognizing that we may need to abandon our yearning for something that we can all agree upon as grounding our enquiry (Goldberg, 2002, p. 249). Just as absolute positions raise problems so too do relative ones. Pragmatism is not relativism, since at times the pragmatic path may espouse an absolute stand.

A re-examination of the promise of confidentiality as an absolute right of patients results in the same opening to uncertainty as happens in the re-examination of many of the seemingly unalterable rules and procedures of psychoanalysis. This sort of house cleaning can be upsetting to many of us who take comfort in the supposed proper conduct of an analysis under proper conditions. However, it is equally likely to cause a reconsideration of what many feel is the more correct and proper pursuit of psychoanalysis, that is, the understanding of a patient in depth. There may be no single road to achieve such a goal.

REFERENCES

Bollas C, Sundelsen D (1995). *The New Informants*. Northvale, NJ, London: Jason Aronson, Inc.

Dewald PA, Clark RW (Editors) (2001). *Ethics Case Book of The American Psychoanalytic Association*. The American Psychoanalytic Association.

Goldberg A (1999). *Being of Two Minds*. Hillsdale, NJ: The Analytic Press.

—— (2001). Postmodern psychoanalysis. *International Journal of Psycho-Analysis* 82: 123–8

—— (2002). American pragmatism and American psychoanalysis. *Psychoanalytic Quarterly* LXXI: 235–50.

Searle I (1992). *The Rediscovery of Mind*. Cambridge, MA: MIT Press, Bradford Books.

Slovenk R (1974). Psychotherapist-patient treatment privilege: A picture of misguided hope. *Catholic University Law Review* 23: 649–73.

Some Limits of the Boundary Concept (2008)

Goldberg further examines the boundary concept in *Some Limits of the Boundary Concept* (2008), making distinctions between violating a boundary, disobeying a rule, breaking a law and the separation of technical issues from any evaluation of moral conduct. Given the present climate of pluralism, Goldberg argues that a universal applicability of boundaries and rules is unlikely.

—GM

*   *   *

A reexamination of the boundary concept and its applicability to different theoretical approaches to psychoanalysis reveals it to be of questionable usefulness in the present climate of psychoanalytic pluralism. In the light of clinical illustrations, it is suggested that an underlying problem with this concept may be a failure to discriminate between technical and moral dimensions. The necessity of separating the legal issues involved is also indicated. Recognizing the existence of separate domains and considering the rules that apply to each are offered as an alternative to focusing on boundary concepts.

INTRODUCTION

In a series of clear and cogent articles, Gabbard and others have outlined and described issues surrounding boundaries in the practice of psychotherapy and psychoanalysis (e.g., Gabbard 1999; Gabbard and Lester 2003). Boundaries are defined as structural characteristics of the therapeutic relationship that allow the therapist to create a climate of safety, and essentially are the components that constitute what is considered to be the therapeutic frame. The crossing of such boundaries may be seen as benign, isolated, attenuated, and discussable, while violations are felt to be damaging, egregious, discouraging of discussion, and tending toward repetition (Gabbard 2005).

One can imagine the concept of a boundary as separating two enclosures. One person is situated inside one enclosure, and messages are sent back and forth to another. Thus does the analyst or therapist remain in one space and the patient in another, and forays take place outside the enclosures or lines of delineation. Such intrusions are deemed either crossings or violations, each of which is an occasion for scrutiny and commentary. Of course, the use of the words *frame, structure,* and *enclosure* should not be taken to diminish the fact that boundaries are but concepts that allow an analyst to organize the to and fro of the dialogue. There are other ways as well to deal with the exchange, but the focus here is on the boundary concept.

In describing a somewhat simplified version of but one classical view of psychoanalysis, we might say that the patient's libidinal and aggressive drives are directed at the analyst who, by frustrating their gratification, enables an interpretation or a message to be delivered to the patient. A boundary crossing or violation can thus be visualized as a breach in the enclosure due to one or another form of drive gratification, which in turn necessarily leads to a situation that cannot allow for a remedial interpretation, and so effective treatment may be stymied. This would seem to be in keeping with Fenichel's (1945, pp. 569–576) explanation, as well as those of others.

Other forms of theory do not rest easily with this form of imagery, since they do not warrant a picture of separate and distinct communicating entities. In a self psychological orientation, for example, the patient and the analyst or therapist do not reside in self-delineated arenas, but rather there is a patient–therapist connection through a self-selfobject relationship. Instead of crossings or violations, the crucial disruption in a therapeutic atmosphere consists of an empathic break. Such breaks may be benign, isolated, attenuated, and discussable, and so would correspond to boundary crossings. So, too, may they be damaging, egregious, discouraging of discussion, and tending to be repetitive, and so correspond to boundary violations. However, a crucial distinction that does not permit a parallel between the first image of separate entities and the second of connected ones is the axiom that *empathic breaks are a necessary part of the analytic or therapeutic process.* No such ameliorative quality can be attributed to boundary crossings as a mechanism to drive the therapeutic process.

One of the conditions for defining boundaries is flexibility. This qualification permits crossings to be tolerated through means such as empathy, projection, introjection, and projective identification (Gabbard and Lester 2003). However, the attribute of flexibility seems consistent with the above-suggested image of enclosures, and so highlights a certain ambiguity in the entire concept of *crossing*. It may be that there is an inherent contradiction in present-day thinking about boundary crossings and boundary violations, a contradiction exposed by the recent popularity of theories such as intersubjectivity and self psychology, which seem to assume an ongoing crossing as a sine qua non for effective treatment.

If one focuses for the moment on the therapeutic process posited in self psychology, the achievement of a sustained empathic connection is seen as the single most basic requirement for an effective treatment. This fits with the flexible nature of a boundary crossing. The inevitable failure of this empathic connection or of this "allowable" boundary crossing sets the stage for an effective interpretation and a hoped-for, resulting understanding that is accompanied by a modicum of psychic structure. One would be hard-pressed to explain how a boundary cross-ing followed by a retreat from said crossing could or would lead to a substantive result.

In a far-ranging discussion of Greenberg's (2001) contribution on the technique of relational theory, both Greenberg and his discussants focused on the analyst as engaging with the patient in a risk-taking manner. This seems to be quite at odds with any sort of frame that consists of a boundary, but rather is said to be centered upon negotiated interventions. There is an emphasis on spontaneity and a portrayal of enactments as valuable because they embody otherwise inaccessible, unconscious currents. Indeed, many relational techniques seem to promote boundary crossings and to flirt with boundary interventions.

The dynamical systems theory advocated by the Boston Change Pro-cess Study Group (2005) states that psychoanalytic interaction is necessarily sloppy, and that it centers upon the moment-to-moment activity of patient and analyst. This theory seems to encourage surprise and unpredictability, and it is difficult to see how a frame of any sort would fit into this group's technique, although they also disclaim any effort to promote one therapeutic efficacy over another (p. 701). This disclaimer does not erase the lack of utility of the boundary concept.

Therefore, it may be both interesting and profitable to consider other ways to speak about and to understand therapeutic fallacies and mishaps. (Of course, changing a word or employing a different vocabulary can hardly be offered as a solution to the above-mentioned limitations of the boundary issue.) It seems apparent that the distinction between crossings and violations is fundamentally a moral one in that the underlying difference between the two is a conviction that a wrong has been committed; and the distinction between a mistake and a wrong is a significant one, as we shall see in what follows when we suggest the use of rules.

For the most part, I feel that there is an underlying moral code in much of our treatment, one that seems to justify assigning the adjective *wrong* to most violations (Goldberg 2007). All sorts of examples can be offered, ranging from breaks in confidentiality to the acceptance of gifts, in order to illustrate how violations—in contrast to crossings—somehow involve a moral code of propriety and ethically correct conduct. We shall here use *moral* as the adjective to cover the imperatives and prohibitions that regulate ethics.

I have asserted that the usual knee-jerk reaction to boundary violations, as opposed to crossings, is that someone has done something wrong. However, we are all equally aware of wrongs that are visited upon patients that seem to have no moral status whatsoever. The analyst or therapist says something that is later regretted, and soon this is clearly seen as the wrong thing to have been said. We have made a mistake. Or the analyst or therapist fails to say or do something, in retrospect coming to believe that this was equally in error. These technical mistakes may make one feel guilty or ashamed, and are often categorized as wrong, but these wrongs should not be considered moral failures. Yet we often do conflate such technical wrongs with moral ones, and we may feel bad about them, almost as if we had sinned; and at times; some supervisory sessions may raise chastisement to the level of what might be expected following a moral transgression.

Not surprisingly, there are all sorts of examples in which the single quality of "damaging" is absent from an instance of boundary violation. If a therapist chooses to conduct an analysis or therapy while taking a walk with a patient, some might perceive no hint of a moral mistake, while others might consider it a gross boundary violation. So, too, if an analyst chooses not to have tissues in the office (an honest-to-goodness position of a member of the profession), we might feel that he or she is possessed of bad taste, but not of mistaken morality. While many so-called boundary violations may indeed be identified as ethical errors, there seem to be enough exceptions to allow for a separation between the two. Here is an example.

CLINICAL ILLUSTRATION

A female patient of Dr. A was not feeling well, and after examination by her internist, was diagnosed as having a particularly ominous form of cancer. She was subsequently admitted to the hospital, where her condition worsened, and a grim prognosis was offered. She telephoned Dr. A and asked him to visit her, which he unhesitatingly did. During the hospital visit, he held her hand in response to a request of hers, and he otherwise behaved as he might to any friend in distress. He later puzzled over whether he had felt at the time that he was her analyst, i.e., a person behaving as an analyst, or someone who was but another person connected to an individual in distress. He could not decide.

Dr. A speculated as to whether or how the analysis could be resumed if the patient recovered, and he rationalized his dilemma by assuming that this was a recognizable boundary crossing that could hardly be said to be damaging. However, after a few such visits with hand-holding accompanied by shared discussions about the fears associated with death and dying, Dr. A felt that he had surely violated an analytic boundary. He speculated that some consulting analysts would inevitably conclude that this analysis could not be resumed if the patient recovered, while other analysts might well commend his behavior and insist that it in no way would preclude resumption of the analysis. (It should be noted here that one is solely concerned with *behavior* in speaking of boundary issues, and not of fantasy or unconscious material.)

This seemed to be representative of a case in which a boundary violation had no moral or ethical implications whatsoever. However, Dr. A wondered if a similar set of circumstances with handholding and shared intimacies could possibly be countenanced by any of the above-imagined consulting analysts if conducted in a coffee shop, or in any setting other than a hospital. The shadow of a moral opprobrium was cast upon such an exchange, which apparently gained social acceptance only within the context of Dr. A's having to put aside his analytic identity.

Dr. A could see that his behavior would not allow for a continuation of the analysis if either he or the patient were being gratified without the opportunity for an interpretation to be made. He also recognized that this boundary crossing could be seen as a violation, albeit it would be a moral problem only in some settings (e.g., a coffee shop) rather than in another (a hospital). Dr. A could also claim an ability to maintain empathic contact with his patient in each of these settings, and so to conclude that his position as analyst remained intact up to and including the capacity to discuss what had transpired; however, he was not so convinced that he could dismiss the moral issue in the imagined background of a coffee shop.

Separating the Moral from the Technical

Without in any way proposing an advantage of one technical approach over another, it seems evident that different theories of technique see boundary crossings and violations differently. Historically, this may be the result of a one-time universal manner of conceptualizing psychoanalytic technique, and consequently of concluding that a deviation from that technique was in error and wrong. This wrong came to be seen as justifying the adverbial addition of *morally* to *wrong*.

In truth, the very use of the word *boundary* assumes and conjures up an image of a technical stance that can be called into question. Boundary violations, by their very definition, manage to tie two concepts together, so that it is fairly automatic to assume that a boundary violation is equivalent to, and means, a moral break. One proposed solution to this mixing of boundary violations with moral transgressions is the separation of technical issues from any evaluation of moral conduct. In order to separate boundary issues that enter into moral arenas from technical ones that do not, we might consider the introduction of another word: *rules*. Both moral concerns and technical standards invoke rules, and remembering this may aid us in clearing up the difference between the two.

THE CONCEPT OF RULES

A rule is a guide for conduct or action, and like any sort of guide to behavior, it is capable of being applied in a way that results in a moral error. However, it is broad enough to encompass all forms of technical activity and does not presuppose a particular structure or therapeutic frame that might be used, for example, to conceptualize psychoanalysis or psychotherapy. More important, rules have a meaning and a philosophical heritage that might add weight to their application, replacing the concept of boundaries in our examination of when and how we adjudicate right from wrong.

Rules regulate practices ranging from driving one's car to conducting psychoanalysis. One is said to conform to rules without necessarily understanding them. One obeys a rule when the rule is more or less internalized. As a person becomes trained in any sort of a practice, he or she is said to be brought into conformity within a community. When the justification of a practice is not required, we see patterns of behavior develop, and a true practitioner is one capable of engaging in full-fledged rule-obeying behavior. Some say the novice conforms and the skilled actor obeys. In our pluralistic world of psychoanalysis and psychotherapy, it seems clear that different communities are involved in a varied collection of patterns of behavior, according to their training and subsequent demonstration of rule-obeying behavior.

A complex and complicated philosophical discussion (Kripke 1982) concluded that rules can never be the result of an individual decision, but rather are social products, i.e., they come about through community practice and sanction. A good example of this is offered by Boesky (2005), who describes a case presentation of a patient's being physically touched. He reflects upon the writings of twenty-five authors who have offered their own commentaries on the technical pros and cons of whether or not to hold a patient's hand. Although Boesky discusses the need for controversies to be contextualized, he nonetheless offers an opportunity to examine how rules of technique vary from one group to another, all the while agreeing that these issues are technical differences that may also have dynamic meanings that are insufficiently understood. At one point, Boesky states that "gross boundary violations are always wrong" (p. 849), leaving it to the reader to decide what exactly is a "gross boundary violation." It seems that sometimes it is a group decision, and at other times it is universal and so termed "gross"

One example of such a gross violation is discussed in a paper presenting the results of a study of sexual boundary violations (Gabbard and Peltz 2001), in which an analyst who was accused of sexual misconduct defended himself by stating that what he did was standard practice at the time of the occurrence. He was rebutted by evidence that it had never been standard practice. After worrying over and arguing about behaviors ranging from touching to sexual intercourse, the participants in this discussion appear to have reached a resolution centering on rules of technique buttressed by community practice. The moral dimension remained in the background, but was clearly the crucial voice. Gabbard and Peltz's article is entitled "Speaking the Unspeakable" (2001) to underline this moral lapse.

In a discussion of sexual misconduct, there is both an agreement that there exists a universal vulnerability to transgressions and a suggestion that such transgressions are mainly quantitatively different from what ordinarily goes on in analysis. Michels (see Foehl 2005, pp. 958–960) lists the various perspectives available to examine sexual misconduct, but they all seem to be dependent on "too much" of one quality or another. Gabbard insists that such moral misbehavior is possible in all of us. Once again, the point at which a crossing becomes a violation, when something mild becomes something gross, remains in a peculiar way something believed to be obvious to everyone, yet equally unexplainable to many of us.

The effort to distinguish acceptable from unacceptable behavior based upon proper use and application of rules of technique might seem promising. One might say, for instance, that sustained empathic immersion would be impossible in moments of boundary violations; if the analyst becomes overly involved in the patient's transference fantasies, it is more difficult to explore and interpret the patient's participation as the originator of the fantasy (Foehl 2005, p. 959). Yet a reading of the relational perspective would seem to champion just such an involvement by the analyst (Greenberg 2001, p. 385). Similarly, a self psychologist must spell out just which empathic breaks are discussable and capable of being utilized to form psychic structure, and which are incapable of such a sequence. Yet a reading of the Boston Change Process Study Group's (2005) findings insists that the participants do not, and indeed cannot, reflect on what has transpired (p. 697); implicit relational knowing is said to occur outside of conscious verbal experience.

All in all, misbehavior may be rationalized in terms of proper or improper technique, but there is no tight fit between analyzing correctly and behaving correctly. Standards of behavior and standards of technique are best thought of as residing in different domains. Rules for practicing psychoanalysis differ from rules for proper moral behavior, yet they are continually collapsed so as to conclude that a good practitioner is a good person as well. Bad practice may or may not involve moral indiscretion. The same may be said of good practice, depending upon which moral barometer one employs. Here is how this is possible.

RULES IN DIFFERENT DOMAINS

We have noted that rules are patterns of behavior that are developed by a community joined by a common language. One may belong to a community of analysts characterized by a particular set of technical rules, and these rules may be quite different than those espoused by another group of practitioners. Most of us are also members of a community that offers standards of proper moral behavior. Confusion results when we assume that our technical standards direct or prescribe our moral ones. The reason not to hold hands may or may not be based on technical standards. The reason not to have sexual intercourse is generally based upon moral standards. Efforts to put both of these on the same continuum mistake quantitative issues for qualitative distinctions.

A similar problem occurs when we assume that good people who are morally beyond reproach will be good practitioners. My colleague who forbade tissues in his office may have been a morally limited individual who was also a competent analyst. Issues such as honesty, confidentiality, gift giving, etc., must be reexamined in terms of their therapeutic efficacy set apart from their moral status.

A further source of potential confusion comes from a lack of clarity concerning the legal issues involved in a discussion of boundaries and rules. Just as boundaries seem best to accord with a set of technical procedures that may have a limited usefulness, and rules have a universal applicability that demands a careful set of assumptions, legal issues in turn present a possible added dimension for discord. There are laws against certain forms of behavior, such as sexual intercourse with a patient, just as there are laws requiring some breaches of confidentiality. For the most part, however, the practice of psychoanalysis and psychotherapy is regulated along the standards of medical practice. Occasionally, there is a collapse in the distinction between violating a boundary, disobeying a rule, and breaking a law. An extended discussion of these distinctions is called for, but for now one must keep in mind the need to maintain these arenas of concern as separate and independent ones.

BACK TO BOUNDARIES

The thesis offered here is that a concentration on boundary crossings and violations confuses technical issues with moral ones. Teasing apart these two domains is an exercise that must be done in order to develop clarity and relieve confusion. Here is one example.

In a paper on boundary issues, Gabbard (2005) illustrates a point with a vignette in which a therapist in training was offered a diamond necklace by a grateful patient at the conclusion of treatment. After meeting with her supervisor, the therapist in training explained to the patient that she had to decline the gift. The case was chosen to illustrate that expensive gifts can herald potential boundary violations. It is assumed that the end of treatment might not allow for discussion of the offer, but it is also implied that such gifts should never be accepted.

In a case conference that I attended some years ago, Franz Alexander told of being offered an expensive watch by a patient, which he had to reluctantly decline because the offer occurred at the beginning of the analysis. However, once the offer had been analyzed, Alexander was able to accept the gift.

Comparison of these two incidents leads one to conclude either that accepting gifts is wrong in and of itself, or that gift giving is an analyzable act that need have no particular moral status. The first position makes the acceptance of expensive gifts a moral mistake that stands outside the treatment, while the second makes it an analyzable condition that need have no particular moral overtones. One can surely complicate the first vignette by introducing the possible return of the patient to treatment at some time in the future, and one can also wonder whether Alexander's countertransference was blinding him to the moral issues. However, the point of the exercise is that of separating the technical and therefore analyzable issues from the moral and therefore unassailable ones. The rules that regulate the one are not at all the same as those that regulate the other. Each requires a separate decision.

If we are to define boundary violations as damaging, egregious, discouraging of discussion, and repetitive, we must also recognize that the first two attributes of this series—i.e., damaging and egregious—are felt to lie in the realm of correct behavior and are not considered relevant to the rules of any particular psychoanalytic school, while the latter two attributes—i.e., discouraging of discussion and repetitive—do not make sense in the light of some analytic theories, such as that of the Boston group, where, as we have noted, reflection about what has transpired is not encouraged. All these attributes become joined into a single series only when analysts are held to a higher or different moral standard than, say, surgeons or internists (who might well accept expensive gifts). This is not the place to question the origins or basis of an ethical code that is selectively applied to analysts and therapists, nor is it at all the place to deny its existence or appropriateness. Such distinctions are evidence, however, that rethinking many of our assumptions about violations would be worthwhile.

Summary

A reexamination of the boundary concept suggests that it is an amalgam of technical and moralistic standards. The technical ones have developed from a particular classical analytic theory based upon a model of two separate individuals who engage in psychic mechanisms, such as projection and introjection. Other psychic models, which utilize concepts of shared psychological substrates, make the concepts of boundary crossing and boundary violations somewhat less useful. Moralistic standards derive from an entirely different sets of rules, but have become impreccated with technical ones, so that judgments such as *good* and *evil* stand in for those of *correct* and *incorrect*. Teasing apart the technical rules—according to whatever psychological models and theory one employs—from the moralistic ones, derived form an entirely different historical time and place, is a task that is much needed.

One example of the intertwining of technique and morality can be seen in the long-established principle of confidentiality. It is held by some to occupy such a hallowed place of esteem that it is said to be "constitutive" of psychoanalysis, i.e., it is felt to be embedded in the very practice of psychoanalysis (Lear 2003). However, an effort has been made to demonstrate that the unexamined acceptance of this principle can carry a certain risk (Goldberg 2004). At times, the patient's best interests may well be served through a violation (if that is the word) of confidentiality. However, it is only when one attempts to apply a vision of confidentiality as a distinct and independent principle that one can grasp the idea that it is not universally applicable.

The use of illustrative ideas such as crossings and violations seems to carry with it the burden of distinguishing right from wrong. In contrast, the use of rules as sometimes applicable and sometimes able to be dispensed with may lend freedom to the use of a variety of techniques. Such an embrace of pluralism also offers the freedom to interpret moral standards as either valid or without meaning.

Although the domains of technique and morality interact, they also have a certain independence from each other. One may rationalize certain seemingly unethical acts by insisting that they are part of technique, just as one may refrain from other behaviors by a supposed submission to the rules of technique. It might well be salutary to examine morality and technique each in its own right.

It may be the case that Nietzsche (1878) was correct when he said:

> Perhaps a future survey of the needs of mankind will reveal it to be thoroughly undesirable that all men act identically; rather, in the interest of ecumenical goals, for whole stretches of human time special tasks, perhaps in some circumstances even evil tasks, would have to be set. [p. 31]

That, of course, makes morality possibly as pluralistic as our present state of psychoanalysis.

Boundaries are best seen as local phenomena that have mistakenly been given universal applicability and status. They are useful if kept within one set of technical rules, but they highlight the need for recognizing how other technical systems call for other kinds of investigation. The benefit of this recognition is that of allowing moral considerations to stand alone, without being defended or dismissed on the basis of the proper technical conduct of psychoanalysis.

REFERENCES

Boesky, D. (2005). Psychoanalytic controversies contextualized. *Journal of the American Psychoanalytic Association* 53:835–864. http://www.pep-web.org/document.php?id=apa.053.0835a

Boston Change Process Study Group (2005). The "something more" than interpretation revisited: sloppiness and co-creativity in the psychoanalytic encounter. *Journal of the American Psychoanalytic Association* 53:694–729. http://www.pep-web.org/document.php?id=apa.053.0693a

Fenichel, O. (1945). *The Psychoanalytic Theory of Neurosis*. New York: Norton.

Foehl, J. C. (2005). "How could this happen to me?": sexual misconduct and us [panel report]. *Journal of the American Psychoanalytic Association* 53:957–970. http://www.pep-web.org/document.php?id=apa.053.0957a

Gabbard, G. O. (1999). Boundary violations. In *Psychiatric Ethics*, ed. S. Block, P. Chodoroff & S. A. Green. New York: Oxford University Press, pp. 141–160. http://www.pep-web.org/document.php?id=apa.043.1115a

—— (2005). Patient–therapist boundary issues. *Psychiatric Times*, 25(October):28–33.

—— & Lester, E. P. (2003). *Boundaries and Boundary Violations in Psychoanalysis*. Washington, DC: American Psychiatric Publishing. http://www.pep-web.org/document.php?id=sgs.003.0379a

—— & Peltz, M. L. (2001). Speaking the unspeakable: institutional reactions to boundary violations by training analysts. *Journal of the American Psychoanalytic Association* 49(2):659–673. http://www.pep-web.org/document.php?id=apa.049.0659a

Goldberg, A. (2004). A risk of confidentiality. *Int. J. Psycho-Anal.*, 85:301–310. http://www.pep-web.org/document.php?id=ijp.085.0301a

—— (2007). *Moral Stealth: How "Correct Behavior" Insinuates Itself into Psychotherapeutic Practice*. Chicago, IL: University of Chicago Press.

Greenberg, J. (2001). The analyst's participation: a new look. *Journal of the American Psychoanalytic Association* 49:359–426. http://www.pep-web.org/document.php?id=apa.049.0359a

Kripke, S. (1982). *Wittgenstein on Rules and Private Language*. Cambridge, MA: Harvard University Press.

Lear, J. (2003). Confidentiality as a virtue. In *Confidentiality: Ethical Perspectives and Clinical Dilemmas*, ed. C. Levin, A. Furlong & M. O'Neil. Hillsdale, NJ: Analytic Press, pp. 3–18.

Nietzsche, F. (1878). *Menschliches, Allzumenschiches (Human, All Too Human)*, trans. M. Faber & S. Lehmann. Lincoln, NB: Univ. of Nebraska Press, 1996.

CHAPTER EIGHT

Differentiation

Early in his psychoanalytic training, Goldberg's mostly admired and always imposing teacher, Max Gitelson, proclaimed that the goal of psychoanalysis was not one of symptom relief, but "to allow patients to better understand themselves." However, teacher and student did not share this view. Charles Kligerman, another teacher of Goldberg's, offered a different opinion on the goal of analysis. According to Goldberg, Kligerman took the position that "analysis did something that was lasting and was more than just freeing someone from psychic pain. The goal of analysis involved some significant alteration in the patient." Goldberg, who thought that feeling better must somehow figure into the aims of analysis, began his query into the goals of psychoanalysis. He writes about this topic in his paper, *Me and Max: A Misalliance of Goals* (2001).

Given these three goals, that of self-understanding, a lasting alteration in the psyche, and the relief of distressing symptoms, Goldberg considers the connection among these essential goals, while noting that one goal is not prized over the others and that there is not a "one size fits all" theory. Goldberg then offers the alternative possibility of joining the three goals.

How might these goals be integrated into one approach? Symptom relief can be accomplished by a variety of means, but for the relief to be lasting, there are two issues that need be joined, that of self-cohesion and self-reflection or self-understanding. The necessary connections that allow for a firm sense of self-cohesion with self-objects, providing symptom relief and lasting value, may be attributed to psychic structure, which is "a way of talking about one's stability over time."

Goldberg differentiates his thinking from his teachers Gitelson and Kligerman, whose absolute certainty did not match with his own uncertainty regarding the goals of analysis. However, it might be this very atmosphere of uncertainty "that makes analysis the rich field that it is." Uncertainty is not a state from which Goldberg feels the need to be free of. And he encourages us to share his comfort with uncertainty and discomfort with absolute authority.

—GM

Me and Max: A Misalliance of Goals (2001)

INTRODUCTION: MAX

One of the burned-in memories of my lengthy life as an analytic candidate is of an event that took place in a case conference chaired by Maxwell Gitelson. Gitelson was a sort of crotchety and imposing man who was fairly humorless and could easily and honestly be characterized as opinionated. This particular moment of meaning of mine occurred when, to the best of my memory, a student said something or other about either his and/or the patient's hope (and goal) that the patient would soon feel better. Gitelson proclaimed (rather than offered) his opinion that psychoanalysis was not meant to make people feel better or to relieve symptoms; rather, the goal of analysis was to allow patients to better understand themselves. Relief of symptoms was a sort of chance byproduct of such understanding, but it was definitely *not* the goal of analysis. Nor should any psychoanalyst pursue that essentially secondary effort.

My silent reaction to Gitelson's "Bah, Humbug" appraisal of symptom relief was my own "Bah, Humbug," since I was convinced that almost everyone I knew in analysis wanted to feel better, and if self-understanding was what had to be swallowed, then that medicine could and would be endured, but it was hardly the goal that I personally would rank as number one. It seemed clear that one person's goal was just not properly or necessarily made for another. Rather than one size fitting all, it seemed that the goals of the patients and the goals of the analysts, and the goals of the field of psychoanalysis, might well lie in separate areas of concern. They need not be in opposition, but they surely are not and cannot be reduced to identical significance and importance.

The combination of my desire to be a good student, plus my near-total intimidation by Gitelson, allowed me over time to adopt his singular goal as mine. I periodically and often surprisingly found myself saying and even believing that the goal of analysis was self-understanding, especially when my patients would point out that I was not helping much with their psychic distress. I could readily recognize the comfort that this adopted stance offered, inasmuch as it allowed me to cast myself as someone in pursuit of this more noble effort of a variation of "truth," rather than settling for the lesser metal of mere comfort and relief. Also, the analyst's view of symptom relief as a happy though accidental companion of analysis enables the analyst to achieve a feeling of personal pleasure without the encumbrance of satisfying someone else's (the patient's) wishes. In this way, I found myself allied with what I imagined were the more lofty aims of the field, rather than joined with those of the individual patient: selfish but safe.

Sooner or later, one must surely realize that concern over the proper goals for what one achieves or what discipline one espouses is basically a moral issue. The pursuit of doing well readily collapses into doing the right thing, and so a conflict occurs, at times, between making the patient feel better versus, say, satisfying Freud's axiom of "where id was, there shall ego be" (1933, p. 80). Unless the satisfaction of the axiom yields an equal degree of contentment for the patient, one cannot reduce the latter to a byproduct of the former. The relief of symptoms and the happiness of the patient become the goals, according to this moral stance, and that of self-understanding sort of trots alongside. One could, of course, eliminate the problem if these two or three goals always emerged and then merged together, but we are regularly haunted by analyzed patients who claim that they feel no better, alongside happy ones who seem quite psychologically opaque. My loyalty to Gitelson was severely tried.

CHARLES

My next memory, a bit less severely etched, comes from another teacher, Charles Kligerman, who was anything but crotchety but probably equally opinionated. He would regularly say that analyzed people are just different from nonanalyzed ones. He would also pronounce this with a certain sense of the former belonging to a very exclusive club, and with the secondary message that one would do well to limit one's acquaintances, friends, and certainly spouses to that membership. Putting aside this seductive elitism, Kligerman's position made it clear that analysis did something that was lasting and was more than just freeing someone from psychic pain, since that latter quality would never by itself lead to this exclusive club admittance. Therefore, the goal of analysis involved some significant alteration in the patient, one that went beyond symptom relief, and perhaps even beyond that ephemeral state of understanding. It made one a different person—and at least to some, a better one as well.

Somehow, the goals were beginning to become better demarcated, although perhaps not in the way Max and I might have wished for. They were not singular in that they had to satisfy a multiplicity of needs. But perhaps the most striking alteration or addition to this original and somewhat encapsulated version of goals offered by my mentor was that the change was not limited to the patient, but seemed to extend to the analyst as well. That is to say that the practitioners of analysis are different, both because of their personal analyses, and because they practice the somewhat noble enterprise of turning out special people. To combine the views of my two mentors might well lead to one being overwhelmed by elitism, as well as by the altitude of this rarified atmosphere.

The challenge that presented itself to me was that of reconciling or somehow unifying what seemed to be a threefold set of goals: that of self-understanding, of relief of discomfort, and of a lasting or relatively permanent change or enhancement of value. Each of these three seemed essential and each seemed connected to the others. Thus, the focus upon one or another should contain some element that would lead to the others. Without in any way denying the multitude of subsidiary benefits of treatment, which could range from a happier marriage to a more fulfilling sex life, these three endpoints should be all-encompassing. So now to examining each in turn.

SELF-UNDERSTANDING

The dominance of the ego and the accumulation of insight into one's unconscious, taken together, are assumed to lead to a body of knowledge that enables one to comprehend one's self differently. This difference may take the form of a narrative of one's history, or on other occasions, might narrow in on a retelling of a more focused event, such as a particular moment of trauma. Patients surely differ in the manner in which they reflect back upon their analyses. No matter how much one insists upon analysis being an activity in which the participants engage in narration (Schafer 1992), or one of the recovery of memory (Fonagy 1999), these are more properly seen as one or another *form* of the procedure, rather than as the fundamental goal. There can be little doubt that some patients prefer telling their life stories, some wish to concentrate on the here and now with little reference to personal history, and some seem peculiarly devoted to elaborate Proustian reminiscence. That such a personal preference is regularly seen to match the preference of the analyst alerts us to the value of looking for this particular form of the goal of analysis as sometimes lying outside the essence of the process.

Consider the following patient: A young professional man entered analysis with the clearly defined and stated aim of getting married. He claimed to have had a host of involvements with marriageable women, but not to have done much more than living with one for a few months. That particular experience was characterized by emotions ranging from discontent to disgust, with not a hint of a wish for this couple of roommates to remain together. Yet he insisted that he longed for marriage to the right woman, and he hoped that analysis would realize that possibility.

I shall not detail the conduct of this analysis, save to say that somewhere along the line, he did marry, but long after he had dropped that issue as crucial to his life as an analysand. What memories he did recover seemed minimal, and as Alexander long ago suggested (1940, p. 146), these were more confirmatory than revealing. I believe that the patient and I would be hard pressed to recount a detailed new version of his life as well. Indeed, most of his analysis had to do with his father, and concentrated not surprisingly on the minutiae of the transference reflective of this.

Toward the end of his analysis, there was no doubt that the patient saw himself differently; thereafter, almost everything problematic in his life, from a telephone call to his mother, to the loss of money on an apparently promising stock, led to his subjecting himself to self-scrutiny. His psychic life was of two parts: the first was composed of a relative ease of events and relationships with others, the second of an intense self-reflection upon anything that represented conflict or difficulty. (It should not be necessary to underscore that this division is not true of everyone, inasmuch as many of us are frequently carefree, whereas others seem never to be free of concern and worry.) My patient regularly reviewed and reflected upon the puzzle of everyday life, and he did so in a manner and with a method that was clearly a miniaturized version of his analytic experience.

I think it safe to conclude that the self-understanding which was facilitated in this analysis was a product of the personalities of both of us, and that it could be characterized by using a variety of theoretical lexicons. That I spoke a certain language, which my patient over time made his own, should not be seen as mere brainwashing. His way of thinking about himself during the analysis would often begin with his announcing: "I know that you would say ...." I took this both as a form of identification and of differentiation. Indeed, one might well say that my patient began by understanding me, and then moved on to an understanding of himself. I take this feature as essential—i.e., the gradual dissolution of the transference should over time reveal the analyst to the patient.

The greatest obstacle to this hoped-for sequence is often the unwitting or unnecessary self-revelation of the analyst. The discovery of what the world, any world, is like may follow the guidelines or map of another, but is not to be equated with a carbon copy of the other. This analysis ended with each of us changing and yet remaining quite different persons. The outstanding feature for the patient was his newfound capacity to puzzle over his life's ups and downs, i.e., his personal form of self-reflection.

RELIEF OF SYMPTOMS

Another patient reported to me after a year of analysis that she felt much better in comparison to how she had felt a year earlier, but could in no way say just what her analysis had accomplished. This feature of feeling better is a happy companion to psychotherapy, psychopharmacology, and even the ordinary occurrences of everyday life. Everything from a good night's sleep to winning the lottery can be capable of eliciting this sort of self-report of contentment, but only a few persons seem able to sustain this desired endpoint. No doubt, a certain amount of ongoing maintenance in the form of the above-mentioned self-analytic or self-reflective work is essential for the sustaining of this feeling of being better, but that seems not to be the whole story. Just as I might give credit to one or more of my teachers who studied and wrote about post-termination self-analysis (Robbins and Schlessinger 1983), I owe my debt for knowledge about the more lasting effect of analytic improvement to Kohut.

Kohut was often at odds with those who emphasized the role of self-analysis following one's work in a therapeutic analysis. He felt that the establishment of meaningful selfobject relationships, or the opening of empathic connections between persons, was the foundation of analytic cure (Kohut 1984). Therefore, one need not be concerned with self-analytic work, save for moments of disruptive breaks in these empathic connections. The availability and deployment of selfobjects were the essentials for navigating through life, and psychic health was equivalent to this dual capacity. Thus, Kohut looked upon self-analysis as evidence more of an incomplete analysis than of the ongoing maintenance of analytic benefits. If one had established a firm and lasting sense of self-cohesion, then there need be few occasions for the self-reflective work necessary to repair an empathic disruption. Or so the story goes.

My own ecumenical bent was to join the two issues of self-cohesion and self-reflection, inasmuch as I remained ever short of perfection, and given that most of my patients were wedded to regular self-reflection. No one in my caseload had achieved the sought-for ideal state of persistent selfobject sustenance alone. Although this was a desirable point of personal achievement, such an ideal state was equally often elusive. For some patients, it was overwhelmingly elusive, while for others, self-reflection was an equal rarity. Once again, the mix of goals among my patients reflected the complexity of an interaction between two complex entities: the patient and the analyst, along with these two elements— self-cohesion and self-reflection—of supposed cure. The patient who reported feeling better after a year of therapy had no doubt made the necessary connection to allow for a firm sense of self-solidity with her selfobjects. But would it last?

THE LASTING VALUE

The lasting value of feeling better is the product of an underlying change which is attributable to something called *psychic structure*. Although this may be described and developed in a variety of ways, it underscores a way of talking about one's stability over time. This stability may be thought of as an enabler of both self-reflection and the relief of symptoms. Although it may seem intangible and even tautological, it is the theoretical convenience that we employ to characterize the improvement associated with analytic goals.

This gain or growth in psychic structure is often claimed to be equivalent to the ordinary processes of normal development. More properly, however, it may be thought of as analogous to development. Normal persons are not analyzed persons. Achieving a solid sense of connection with one's selfobjects, like gaining insight into the contents of one's unconscious, cannot be readily equated with the process of a normal child's development. For the former—i.e., achieving enduring connections—there is an ease of selfobject relationships in development that is rarely the case in analyzed adults, who are at best able to cautiously and carefully choose particular others to whom they can connect. For the latter, that of knowing one's unconscious, it is a failure of repression that reveals the unconscious to an adult who is most successful if his or her drives are neutralized or sublimated. Such non-neurotics claim not insight, but ignorance.

But any psychoanalytic theory can be used to distinguish and describe the analyzed person as different from the unanalyzed but non-neurotic one, and all such theories ultimately point to a crucial distinction of some sort. In a nutshell, analysis *adds* something to the person who is analyzed, and this addition, no matter how one speaks of it, becomes a lasting and distinguishing characteristic. Psychic structure is the catchword for what is added. It is by way of this concept that one is able to consider the significance of the time axis in the achievements of analysis. Change that lasts, or enduring function, reflects this underlying something that offers stability and sustenance. Now perhaps we are able to weld together and join the three measures of analytic accomplishment.

Always Analyzing

My now-married patient described earlier, who is presently gripped by the sheer curiosity of living, once complained to me that he was jealous of those friends and acquaintances who seemed to be happy—or even unhappy—but who had no concern as to the origins of their psychic status. Indeed, they seemed to move through life without really thinking about it. In a way, he was envious of their unconcern, and he often wished that more things did *not* matter so much to him. It was not that he worried—although he would readily admit to that—but rather that he was ever curious.

And he was convinced that his analysis had given him this affliction of persistent puzzling. As glad as he might be about his ability to better see himself, it was also very much as though a chronic illness had been bestowed upon him. What a burden to have—as if life were some sort of continuing mystery story whose clues were unending. However, as any lover of mysteries will tell you, following clues is a lovely addiction.

To borrow a phrase from the eminent French philosopher Ricoeur (1992), we are able to, and we should, see "oneself as another." This perception, which takes place as we step to one side of where we are usually situated, is distorted by all of the prejudices and preconceptions of subjectivity. We may, however, gain a modicum of objectivity with the aid of psychoanalysis. We do so not by sharing another's, i.e., the analyst's, subjectivity, which, although to be valued in part, is possibly merely another person's opinion. The whole point of analysis must lie in the fact that it is a body of knowledge based upon fundamental principles and ideas about transference and the unconscious.

So my patient must see him- or herself through this lens, regardless of whether he or she is more or less successful as an autobiographer. Since this autobiography is coauthored, its credibility rests upon a faithfulness to analysis, rather than to personal clarity or concealment. As a patient, one explains one's self to oneself by way of psychoanalytic understanding, while perhaps failing, more or less, as a writer of fiction, omitting something which might be more interesting and/or fascinating but less faithful to our field. The roteness of analytic lore may make for dullness of revelation, inasmuch as self-scrutiny returns again and again to situations highlighted in the treatment and faithful to our theory.

IMMUNIZATION

The return of a patient who has completed a course of analysis, now with either a concomitant return of symptoms and problems or a whole new set of difficulties, seems to happen often enough for it to be claimed as an inevitability in the life of every analyst. With this return, there is often an implicit registering of a complaint, one that suggests a disappointment that the analysis did not quite work, did not protect the patient from further difficulties, did not bestow a sort of lifelong immunity. It is as if to say that all future troubles are essentially a return of the old ones, either in the same or in a different form, for at heart, the expected solution turned out to be nothing but a Band-Aid. This implicit complaint seeks a voice, despite the fact that time has passed, circumstances have changed, events that no one could have foreseen have occurred, and, quite likely, self-scrutiny has diminished and faded.

While we may embrace the concept of structural change as underlying analytic effectiveness, we may have to strain to account for the continued frailty of our discharged patients. We rationalize our limitations with portentous statements about the limits of analytic treatment, citing problems inherent in libidinal stickiness, or making irrelevant references to biological givens—all the while aiming to remove ourselves and the analytic method from the equation. Perhaps it is our own sales pitch, the one offered to me by one of my teachers, about the very special status of analysis that has led us into this illusion of a perfect psychic paradise. Analytic treatment, like politics, is local. It can make no claim to permanently insulate a person from the unexpected, innumerable vicissitudes of life, because, as much as one would hope, the neuroses of childhood are not complete explanations for the trials of adulthood. The above-discussed two-part explanation for the successful ending of an analysis, that of self-analysis and of open empathic connections, leads us into a clearer picture of the incompleteness of the theory of infantile neurosis and the resulting potential for analyzed patients to encounter continuing problems.

FORM VERSUS CONTENT

By advocating the making conscious of the unconscious, Freud's axiom mentioned earlier implied that psychic health was inextricably tied to insight, that knowledge was empowering, and that this new power was curative. Simply put, this is a "content cure," wherein the exposure of the contents of the unconscious enables a change which, although later elaborated with various forms of energic variations, is fundamentally based upon knowing. The reexperience of the conflicts of infancy and childhood, classically thought of as infantile neurosis, should allow one as an adult to see things differently. To be sure, this reexperience re-quires a full affective charge to qualify as a valid one, but the original foundation was that of revisiting an earlier trauma with later *adult* competence. The transparency of the analyst, even in its guise of a neutral position (Baker 2000), insists that an earlier situation is and must be reenacted in treatment, and that this can only be effected by allowing history to repeat itself within the analysis.. Such repetition involves the analyst not interfering with the emergence of unconscious material, since this material remains the root cause of the neurosis.

This is not the case with the explanation derived from "form" rather than content. Here it is not the "what" that is the problem, but the "how." For this type of patient, we shift our explanation from conflict over unfortunate discord to deficits resulting from faulty development. To be sure, one can readily see that every conflict somehow implies some sort of a deficit, either in repression, neutralization of drives, ego weakness, o: r any variant of alternative theoretical explanations. No matter the theory, one may still comprehend a difference between the patient who needs insight and the one who needs more, regardless of how one chooses to characterize or pathologize the latter. This second patient is the one who seems to gain relief from the regularity of visits, the listening of the analyst, the feeling of being understood—all those ingredients that are lumped together under the unhappy wastebasket term *the relationship*. This is the patient who may, upon recalling his or her analysis, speak of the analyst's tone of voice, the feelings aroused upon entering the room, the long and difficult termination punctuated by an occasional revisit, and the very expected Christmas card exchange. Often, this is also the patient about whom we may feel a bit guilty or embarrassed: the one for whom some administrative boundary had been breached.

The thesis that I wish to offer flows from my earlier conviction that one size does not fit all, that analysis means and does different things for and to different people, and that the straitjacket-like nature of our rules leads to a rigidity in the determination of our goals. Every patient has an individual mix of self-reflection coupled with empathic connections, and one is not to be prized over the other. Indeed, this variability of needs carries over to different patients at different times, and is certainly true of one patient with different analysts. So it is only in the most general sense that we can meld together the activity of self-reflection and meaningful connections with others to fashion an endpoint applicable to any single patient. It is, however, advisable to keep in mind that we can never precisely divide an analysis into the convenient categories that we may sketch out. It is not true that we can determine exactly when we will deal with transference configurations and when with new development, or that at a particular time, we have a real relationship, and at another time, a visitor from the past. We are never so lucky.

DISCUSSION

If one were to ask a primary care physician, a college teacher, and an auto mechanic what the goals of their occupations are, they would probably all preface their responses with "it all depends." In a way, those are dreaded and dreadful words, hiding the fact that the respondents first require some input from the questioner in order to shape and determine the answer. Not so with the plumber called in to unplug your sink, the teacher of first-year French, and the internist treating a specific patient with pneumonia. The easy answers involve focused efforts at fixing a specific problem; the hard ones relate to general aims of amelioration.

Psychoanalysis does not enjoy focused fixes. As much as we would like it to be otherwise, we are haunted by vagueness. Yet this atmosphere of uncertainty makes analysis the rich field that it is, inasmuch as, if every patient has an oedipal problem, then we are too much the plumber. "Never knowing for sure" is the proper place for our own "it all depends" and our own insistence on the individual patient finding his or her own goals.

CONCLUSION

The supposed grammatical error of my tide comes from a linguistic choice. It is meant to state itself in the accusative case, i.e., as the object of a verb. It is intended to convey what the goals of psychoanalysis mean to me and to Max, since Max and I continue to think quite differently, just as I continue to live with uncertainty. The vibrancy of analysis derives from both its fundamental thesis of transference and the unconscious, and from the indeterminate shape of each of these fundamentals. To combine the two—i.e., fundamentals plus change—results in our being able to specify the goals of psychoanalysis with the addendum of some phrase like "as of now" or "for the time being," alongside "for this particular person." In this way, we can and should embrace the vagueness of our work. Max was a great teacher because he was so sure of himself—and, paradoxically, could produce a student who could live happily with a multitude of opinions.

REFERENCES

Alexander, F. (1940). Psychoanalysis revised. In *The Scope of Psychoanalysis*. New York: Basic Books, 1964.

Baker, R. (2000). Finding the neutral position. *Journal American Psychoanalytic Association* 48(1):129–153.

Fonagy, P. (1999). Memory and the therapeutic action of psychoanalysis. *International Journal Psycho-Analysis* 80:614–616.

Freud, S. (1933). New introductory lectures on psychoanalysis. *Standard Edition* 22.

Kohut, H. (1984). *How Does Analysis Cure?*, ed. A. Goldberg. Chicago/London: University of Chicago Press.

Ricoeur, P. (1992). *Oneself as Another*. Chicago/London: University of Chicago Press.

Robbins, F. & Schlessinger, N. (1983). *Developmental View of the Psychoanalytic Process: Follow-up Studies and Their Consequences*. New York: International Universities Press.

Schafer, R. (1992). *Retelling a Life: Narration and Dialogue in Psychoanalysis*. New York: Basic Books.

Deutsch's Discontent (2007)

Goldberg begins his paper, *Deutsch's Discontent* (2007) with this improbable image: "I think I was a little boy when I heard Helene Deutsch speak for the first and only time. Of course it may have been that I merely felt like a little boy." Such was the absolute authority that Deutsch pronounced her discontent "about what others were doing with her concept of the as-if personality." In this paper Goldberg differentiates between Deutsch's concepts of the as-if personality and narcissistic disorders and wonders if there are differences between the two.

Deutsch portrays her patients as "lacking in genuineness and warmth" among other unfavorable descriptors. One might wonder if these are simply unlikable people rather than the troubled souls that they are. It is this insistence on value judgment that Goldberg calls to our attention, as well as our need to overcome judgments about how "patients should be and how they ought to end up." Once Deutsch has made up her mind about how patients should be, it effectively cuts off inquiry—thus creating an impasse.

Is there a solution? Yes, and while Goldberg credits Deutsch with being "brilliant enough" to observe her patients, their conditions and presentations, she was unable to recognize the transference configurations that are well known in the psychoanalytic treatment of narcissistic disorders. Had Deutsch recognized her patient's self-object transference that was expressed in her idealization of Deutsch, then her patient's collapse following a traumatic disillusionment may have been less perplexing. And if, following that disillusionment, she had responded to the patient's cry of "I am so empty" with an interpretation of empathic rupture, then together, they may have realized the crucial therapeutic task of phase-specific, non-traumatic de-idealization.

One might imagine that it was Deutsch's absolute authority, her mind made up about how patients should be, that led to Goldberg's discontent.

—GM

INTRODUCTION

I think I was a little boy when I heard Helene Deutsch speak for the first and only time. Of course, it may have been that I merely felt like a little boy, but the image that I conjure up is that of my looking up at her as she complained (honestly) about what others were doing with her concept of the *as-if personality*. She compared this process of alteration of her concept to changes in an umbrella that had first its handle, then its materials, then its spokes all replaced, until one had to wonder if it was really the same umbrella.

My memory is pretty confident that she used this umbrella metaphor, although nowadays umbrellas are more often replaced than repaired. But the analogy might be a pertinent one. Is the as-if personality a relatively intact concept, or has it been transmogrified into nothing like it originally was? Is it a relic or still a serviceable tool? As a little boy, I could not possibly ask that or even consider the question. I am not sure I can do it even now, but I will try.

With her essay on the as-if personality, Deutsch felt that she was presenting a pathological collection that had not heretofore been considered and categorized. Although she initially wondered if her collection had something to do with schizophrenia, she seemed by the end of her article to have dismissed that possibility—a possibility that presented itself because of the quality that she considered "lacking in genuineness" (p. 326).[1] She later elaborated this supposed symptom with the claim that the relationships of these individuals are "devoid of any trace of warmth, that all expressions of emotion are formal, that all inner experience is completely excluded" (p. 327).

It is sometimes a fruitful exercise to compare psychological maladies to physical ones, as well as to other psychological ones. The person who has hypertension, for instance, may well feel fine, but his or her illness is revealed by reading a sphygmomano meter. The numbers point to and determine the disease. If a person has a depression, complaints are

---

[1] *Editor's Note:* In this article, page numbers from Deutsch 1942 refer to the numbering in the republication in this issue, not to the original Quarterly publication of 1942.

usually verbalized and sadness is sometimes visible. However, this category introduced by Deutsch seems to elicit primarily a reaction of dislike, or even to echo a certain moral failure; these people sound more like unlikable individuals than troubled souls. The value system of the observer seems to carry the day for the diagnosis. No numbers. Few complaints. Mainly judgments.

Deutsch was a careful observer of what was before her eyes, and, furthermore, she was brilliant enough to *see* it, but her allegiance to a specific theoretical way of thinking, one still quite prominent today, forced her to judge these individuals in a particular manner, and this judgment led her inevitably to conclude that psychoanalysis was not of much help in the fortunes of her patients. She so wanted them to have warm relationships, to be capable of intense object love, to have what for her were genuine feelings that she seems to have resigned to settling merely for a new classification. Alas, our present-day diagnostic categories often do not do much better than that, as when one wag said that a patient has a borderline personality disorder when the analyst really and truly does not like them at all.

Perhaps the reason that the original conceptualization of the as if personality was so modified and altered by succeeding generations of analysts was that each of us has allowed our own set of likes and dislikes to determine what is the essential problem of these patients. But one of Deutsch's patients does tell us this problem in the most dramatic way possible. It happens at the moment when the patient seems denied a certain form of lasting relationship with her analyst, a relationship that today is fairly well known and described, and that will be detailed below. The patient (in Deutsch's words) "complained, 'I am so empty! My God, I am so empty!'" (p. 336).

Perhaps that is the key to the diagnosis. The patient, in Deutsch's description, moves from participation in what is said to be an unusually successful analysis to uttering a cry of despair. Here Deutsch illustrates that classic and not uncommon moment in the treatment of an idealized selfobject transference that today, happily, is eminently treatable, once we overcome our judgments about what patients *should be* and how they ought to end up in order to live their lives according to our prescription.

The Cases

One cannot attempt, of course, a detailed reconsideration of the cases that Deutsch wrote about. There are no process notes, no dreams to speak of, and not much evidence of transference configurations. There are, however, loads of striking phrases, such as lacking in "real warmth," "automaton-like identification," "wholly unprincipled," and "lacking in affect." There are very few positive comments, so one would suppose that the Deutsch descriptions do qualify as countertransferences. This may offer a worthwhile clue to our better understanding of this patient population, especially if we couple these negative appellations with a word that also seems to appear regularly in this article, as well as in the many similar redescriptions of as-if personalities: the word is *narcissism,* and the associated emotion is a negative one.

This is not the occasion to review the study of psychoanalytic treatment of the narcissistic personality and behavior disorders. It may be, however, one on which to highlight a few of the familiar transference configurations that are encountered, as well as to examine some of the profound resistances embraced by those analysts who are doggedly antagonistic to these new ideas.

The third patient described by Deutsch (p. 336) begins her analysis with an interest in the analyst per se, and is soon said to have been unusually successful in the treatment. Such early idealizations are nowadays quite familiar in the analysis of those narcissistic disorders that are characterized by a traumatic disillusionment in the parent chosen as an early idealized selfobject. Indeed, this is exactly what is described in the brief summary of this patient's development, and this is more or less what was recapitulated in the analysis with Deutsch. These selfobject idealizations can take the form of intense, merger-like experiences or of more mature connections to the idealized parental imago. The crucial therapeutic task is that of phase-specific, nontraumatic deidealization occasioned by interpretation of empathic breaks. By informing the reader that she somehow told the patient that her determination to be an analyst was not to be—which was followed by the patient's collapse (p. 336)—Deutsch demonstrates the familiar failure that results when this task is not carried out.

Along with the somewhat exasperated tone that one reads in Deutsch's tale of this and other analyses, there is a regular drumbeat of the patient's lack of reality. Once again, this feature is well explained in the literature on the vertical split (Goldberg 1999). The therapeutic resolution of this supposed failure of competent reality testing is often successfully accomplished. Anyone who has lived through similar feelings of exasperation before recognition of the proper analytic technique can only sympathize with Deutsch. Her later explanation of the patient's lack of libidinal object cathexis is on target, but unfortunately is waylaid by what might be described as a moral impasse. Indeed, it may not be too far afield to consider many resistances in our science to be moral rather than intellectual failures.

DEUTSCH'S DILEMMA

In line with the *Oxford English Dictionary* definition of *moral* as pertaining to human character or to behavior as good or bad, or to the distinction between right and wrong (Brown 1993, p. 1827), it is not unusual to see evaluations of patients' psychopathology based largely upon moral considerations. We routinely think ill of the selfish, the self-centered, those who are thoughtless of others and so unable or unwilling to emotionally invest meaningfully in them. As analysts, we have something of a definitive set of principles or standards that allow us to determine psychological health, and accordingly to orient ourselves as to what should be treated in terms of these guidelines.

For years, for example, we insisted on heterosexuality as a sine qua non of normal behavior, until a good deal of evidence to the contrary allowed homosexual behavior to be seen on a par with heterosexual behavior, in terms of both the normal and the abnormal (Goldberg 2001). That these supposedly scientific stances become imbued with moral dimensions should come as no surprise, and much the same is the case with disorders of narcissism. In a sense, we become prisoners of our standards.

Empty depressions are a common if not universal symptom in the psychoanalytic treatment of narcissistic disorders (Kohut 1971). They are seen at moments of significant empathic failure and constitute a reaction to a lost selfobject relationship. Overwhelming fantasies of grandiosity and idealization are repressed or disavowed, and a subjective feeling of emptiness ensues. The analyst's reaction to this is often reflective of a theoretical and moral position—i.e., one can analyze the underlying fantasy, or one can judge the sad and forlorn state of the patient as bedrock (e.g., "This is a truly empty individual").

In one sense, there is some truth in both positions, inasmuch as the latter assumes meaningful object relations that may indeed be lacking. I believe Deutsch was committed to this way of thinking, and I think it fair to say that this is fundamentally a value judgment. As such, it effectively cuts off inquiry. It may well lead to sympathy, but that unfortunately excludes empathy. Such sympathy may arise more out of a perception of the misfortune of that empty soul, with the tacit implication that truly mature and healthy individuals have no such deficiency.

Deutsch tells us that the coldness seen in her categorization of as-if personalities differs from that seen in her description of repressed individuals, for whom a highly differentiated emotional life is hidden behind a wall (p. 328). She here makes a crucial distinction between the lines of development of object love and narcissism, but seems stymied as to how to expand upon this. I would suggest that this failure is a countertransference based upon a moral judgment.

My own case example comes from an analytic patient who was experienced as overwhelmingly boring, until one day the analyst felt a tinge of excitement and interest as the patient began describing the transformation of his law office into a completely paperless institution. The voluminous amount of required electronic and computer equipment seemed to represent an excited and especially valued self that had no room, of course, for other human beings. For this patient, this was a healthy accomplishment in spite of the lack of a so-called object libidinal cathexis. Once free of his moral and theoretical prejudices, the analyst was able to likewise be free of his boredom, and so to mirror the patient's grandiose self presentation.

DISCUSSION

I prefer to read "Some Forms of Emotional Disturbance and Their Relation-ship to Schizophrenia" as a struggle: one of allegiance to an established way of thinking in conflict with a vision that did not conform to it. Deutsch was situated squarely in the midst of this struggle, but her loyalty to a particular theoretical stance did not enable her to go much beyond a descriptive com-promise. Kohut (1971) took an additional step by putting aside these theoretical constrictions and posing the question of the possible modifica-tions in the narcissistic investment of these individuals. This required an inquiry and investigation of the maturation of the narcissistic developmental line, so that extremely self-centered individuals might indeed change, say, from a situation of hypochondriasis to one of creativity, or from the presenta-tion of a cold and aloof character to that of an excited and involved champion of some cause or movement. It is quite rewarding to analyze such individuals who do indeed improve markedly, but who may not ever become the "warm and loving" persons required of our theory.

A few years ago, I attended a conference of the International Psycho-analytical Association and listened to an eminent clinician describe his analysis of someone who was quite narcissistic. The analysis was a heroic effort to get beyond these narcissistic defenses to the hypothetical ob-jects that would eventually be libidinally invested. Despite the obvious failure of this effort, the analyst seemed to make some sort of claim of success for his effort. I turned to my friend and asked why this presenter could not avail himself of the newer ideas about selfobject transferences, and received only a shrug. But I think I know the answer.

Narcissism has a bad reputation. It often carries the unspecified modifier of *pathological.* It is regularly employed to describe someone unlikable, hardly ever to elaborate a positive portrayal. Overall, it has occupied, in psychoanalysis especially, a moral position. Rather than being granted the status of inquiry, it has been given one of opprobrium. As with so many other concepts and conditions, our moral precepts have taken precedence over our scientific objectivity (Goldberg 2007).

So now I know why Helene Deutsch was so unhappy with what oth-ers had been doing to her concept of the as-if personality. It was not that the metaphor of an umbrella's being changed piecemeal—first the handle, then the materials, then the spokes, ending with one's wondering if it was really the same umbrella—was not a valid one. No. It was that it was never an umbrella in the first place.

REFERENCES

Brown, L., ed. (1993). *The New Shorter Oxford English Dictionary.* Oxford, England: Clarendon Press.

Deutsch, H. (1942). Some forms of emotional disturbance and their relationship to schizophrenia. *Psychoanalytic Quarterly* 11:301–321.

Goldberg, A. (1999). *Being of Two Minds.* Hillsdale, NJ: Analytic Press.

—— (2001). Depathologizing homosexuality. *Journal of the American Psychoanalytic Association* 49:1109–1114.

—— (2007). *Moral Stealth: How Correct Behavior Insinuates Itself into Psychotherapeutic Practice.* Chicago, IL/London: University of Chicago Press.

Kohut, H. (1971). *The Analysis of the Self.* New York: International Universities Press.

Sexualization

In his paper, *Sexualization and Desexualization* (1993) Goldberg explores the shifts in the psychoanalytic formulations on sexuality from Freud, to Hartman, to Kohut, and addresses the distinction between sexuality and sexualization. Sexuality is considered the act of a strong and stable self. Sexualization is a "manifestation of a structural deficiency which is handled, because of special developmental circumstances, by way of sexual fantasies and/or behavior. Such actions serve defensive purposes in forestalling further regression, as well as the purpose of mastery, along with sexual pleasure in its own right." In other words, feelings that might be experienced are not, and instead they are sexualized.

How and when is psychoanalytic treatment effective in patients who cope with certain affect states, self-states and psychic deficits by way of sexualization? The efficacy lies in the analyst and his functions participating in and filling in the structural deficit in the psychological makeup of the patient, thus restoring the damaged psychic structure. This occurs by repairing empathic ruptures, allowing for the developing psyche to assume the functions provided by the self-objects. According to Goldberg, sexualized responses are associated with the fluctuations in the presence and availability of sustaining self-objects, which become capable of being used in a more flexible and adaptive way in the course of treatment.

Sexualization and Desexualization also reconsiders the position of homosexuality as both normal and perverse, and Goldberg reflects further on this topic in *Depathologizing Homosexuality* (2001). Goldberg reminds us that psychoanalysis, in contrast to psychiatric or DSM diagnosis, derives its data from the analytic situation and is "confined to manifestations of transference and countertransference. The meaning of one's sexuality, whether perverse or not, is discovered in the transference. In other words, symptoms are not our guide in determining perversions. The proper consideration of sexuality of any orientation must await its participation in the transference."

—GM

Sexualization and De-Sexualization (1993)

ABSTRACT

This paper is a reconsideration of the role of sexualization in psychoanaly-sis. After a review of the accepted definitions of sexualization as defense and/or part of normal sexuality, a new explanation is offered. This posits sexualization as a psychological manifestation of a structural deficit and suggests analytic treatment as a process of structuralization. These terms are defined and illustrated. A case example demonstrates the thesis, and some implications of this concept are discussed.

It seems a paradox that psychoanalysis, which so often has been considered as having been founded and fostered upon the recognition of sexuality, should itself struggle with a concept of sexualization that, at its simplest, is misplaced sexuality. Freud (1926) said that an organ which is sexualized behaves like a cook who no longer wants to work in the kitchen when she and the master of the house are having a love affair (pp. 89–90). The sexuality has taken over. This was the essential sexualization of a nonsexual activity (Fenichel, 1945): the intrusion of the sexual drive into an arena where it did not belong. Implicit in this characterization of sexualization is the notion that the sexual impulse is ever active in seeking expression and so it aims to capture some other activity or function in order to express or assert itself. Once sexualized, that otherwise nonsexual or neutral activity is rendered unable to pursue its ordinary path, just as though an extra weight or burden were to be added to the simplest of tasks.

This neat version of sexualization has over the years become more com-plicated, and the complexity arises from two sources. The first was initiated by Heinz Hartmann's (1950) consideration of the instinctualization of ego functions. This is seen as indicative of a regressive move of the ego—a break-down of the ego's intactness. Hartmann's concepts of instinctualization and its corollary, neutralization, were an elaboration of Freud's ideas, but they necessarily expanded the ideas of sexualization so that a mere "disturbance of function" could be a sign of sexualization. And so we now may have sexualization without the sex. The second source for confusion arose from the use of the term, sexualization as a defense; here the word more clearly was linked with the activity of or fantasies about sexuality, either normal or pathological, employed for defensive purposes. Something more than regression is needed to complete the picture, since the ego now employs and deploys sexual activity for all sorts of defensive purposes ranging from the handling of anxiety to the warding off of fantasies of homosexuality (Blum, 1973). So just as we now allow for sexualization with no manifestation of sex, so too do we have multiple forms of sexual activity without any true sexual meaning. Though the latter is often termed pseudosexuality, it serves to emphasize how we have lost our moorings away from Freud's original formulation. Surely there is little hope for understanding the clinical management of sexualization until we have a better comprehension of its meaning.

The classical or orthodox clinical management of the phenomena of sexualization has to do with its dissolution or transformation by the alchemy of sublimation (Alpert, 1949). The movement of a sexually charged fantasy that would ordinarily be repressed into the preconscious calls for a variety of defensive maneuvers, or else for a redirection of that sexual material into acceptable and desirable nonsexual areas. The sadist becomes the surgeon. Hartmann modified this concept of sublimation by introducing a new one of neutralization or de-instinctualization, i.e., a stripping of the fantasy of its sexual or aggressive charge, an energic transformation. Kohut further elaborated this theory of neutralization in his model of progressive neutralization (Kohut and Seitz, 1963), wherein these archaic fantasies are slowly moved into the manageable and predictably nonsexual arenas of the psyche. How this is all accomplished in a psychoanalytic treatment is considered to be part and parcel of all therapeutic intervention and no different than the management of any and all repressed psychic material. But true sexualization does seem to be different. It is sometimes pleasurable, often habitual, and rarely capable of this shift of category, i.e., although the scientist may be a sublimated voyeur, it is a rare voyeur who is transformed into a scientist by way of psychoanalysis.

In a shift of emphasis from these formulations of Hartmann and this early one of Kohut, I should like to offer an elaboration of the later

Kohut positing structuralization as the crucial component to the clinical management of sexualization. This leads not to sublimation but rather to desexualization. This suggestion rests upon a number of premises which I wish to propose and illustrate. The first is that the occurrence of sexualization is a manifestation of a structural deficiency which may or may not be lifelong but is handled in individual cases, because of special developmental circumstances, by way of sexual fantasies and/or behavior. Such action serves defensive purposes in forestalling further regression (Kohut, 1971), as well as the purpose of pleasure in mastery, along with sexual pleasure in its own right. The defect, however, is often temporarily filled by other persons, and so sexualization is forestalled until the temporary answer is lost. The second premise is that psychoanalytic treatment is effective in patients who do sexualize when and if the analyst can fill the structural deficit in the psychological makeup of the patient and, over time, restore the damaged psychic structure. Such a position of and for the analyst is to be clearly distinguished from the analyst as the target of the patient's drives, or the analyst as a participant in an intersubjective or interpersonal field of the patient, or the analyst as a superego component which controls the drives, or the analyst as an educator who trains the apraxic patient to develop certain psychological competences which were lacking until the analytic encounter. The filling in of psychological structure is indeed an accomplishment of psychoanalytic treatment, but the process of structuralization follows the course of normal development, i.e., it is based upon phase-specific, nontraumatic opportunities to take over functions rather than upon any form of educational exercise imposed from outside. Structure in this definition is enduring function, and structuralization is the process by which the developing psyche assumes the functions offered by the caretakers (Goldberg, 1988p. 130).

The presence of sexualization in a predominant form in certain patients must be distinguished from its almost universal occurrence in the general population, as well as from the theoretical but essentially nonsexual form as proposed by Hartmann. Moving away from the energic concepts allows us to concentrate on a pure form of sexualization reflective of certain sorts of structural defects in certain patients. It also allows us to see that sporadic or occasional sexualization can be more clearly delineated from the usual or normal forms of sexual activity. In fact, the statement (Coen, 1981) that sexualization is an aspect of all sexual activity, offered as evidence of the defensive nature of sexual behavior and fantasy, is a truth that may obscure more than it clarifies. Rather, we need a more clear-cut delineation of sexualization from otherwise normal sexual activity. Such a delineation can serve to explain, for example, why certain forms of homosexual activity are best seen as pathological while other forms may defy that label. This distinction of one manifestation of sexual fantasy or behavior from another, i.e., the pathological from the normal, is rarely one that can be made either casually or descriptively. Rather, one needs the perspective of the psychoanalyst and especially of one who can utilize a theory of structure and structuralization. The following material will also employ basic concepts from self psychology, which considers the self as the studied structure and the selfobject as a constituent of that structure. The analyst as selfobject fills in a defect of the self. He or she is not a coparticipant in a mutual structure, inasmuch as the structural needs of the patient fix the unfolding program of the analysis. The outbreaks of sexualization occur in and around that function and position of the analyst, a position that serves to complete a deficiency and which, in its presence, allows for a variety of self-experiences which may otherwise have been unavailable to the individual.

LITERATURE REVIEW

There is little to add to the excellent review of the subject by Coen (1981), who, after summarizing the literature, came down on a solution that would restrict the concept of sexualization to sexual behavior and fantasy whose goals and functions are those of defense. The relevant literature covers a discussion of the erotized transference (Blum, 1973), the concept of selfobject and the sexualization of that structure (Kohut, 1971), along with the issue of the reparative efforts that sexualization offers to the narcissistically vulnerable individual (Stolorow, 1975).

The lack of consensus about evaluating just what sexual behavior is normal and what is pathological is reviewed by Socarides (1992) in his discussion of homosexuality. His viewpoint considers the homosexual as severely handicapped (p. 317) and, in some sense, as necessarily manifesting a psychological disorder. Socarides bemoans the fact that political pressures have allowed homosexuality to become free of diagnostic labeling. It remains to be seen whether both homosexuality and heterosexuality share in what is essentially a division of purpose, i.e., sometimes an act of sexuality is to be considered as sexualization, while at other times it may be ranked as normal sexuality.

Stoller (1991) extends the political implications of sexual activity to include the moral dimension by insisting on the inclusion of psychoanalytic ideas in any evaluation of sexuality. He does not note the morality implicit in our field's own decisions about normality and normal development. Sexual behavior seems unable to escape a consideration of either illness or correctness.

Otto Kernberg (1991) joins with Coen in the inclusion of some perverse activity within the framework of normal sexual functioning. Thus, sexualization includes any and all sexual activity. Kernberg feels that sadomasochism, for example, is an essential part of sexual excitement. He constructs a continuum from normality to psychopathic perversions which depend upon the nature of ego and superego organization. An integrated tripartite structure would yield normal sexuality with predominant libidinal components, an intermediate realm would reflect borderline and narcissistic personality structure, while an extreme one would conform with the syndromes of malignant narcissism, antisocial personality structures, and psychosis. This particular article of Kernberg's is based largely on the work of Chasseguet-Smirgel (1986), who has developed some specific thoughts about the archaic aspects of the oedipus complex. For Chasseguet-Smirgel, all perversions develop against an anal sadomasochistic backdrop, and their aim is to destroy reality. She also considers homosexuality to be a range of disorders from those close to neurosis to those bordering on psychosis. It is not clear if she would consider some homosexuality as normal and if she would incorporate some aspect of perversion into normal sexuality, as does Kernberg. The continuum may go just so far.

CLINICAL CONSIDERATIONS

We shall here follow the definition of Anna Freud (1965), who said that it is considered a rule that the diagnosis of perversion in an adult signifies that the primacy of the genitals has never been established or has not been maintained. Perversions or sexualizations range from rare and sporadic episodes of behavior, which may or may not be accompanied by feelings of pleasure, to long-lasting, habitual forms of fantasy and action with an equally variable incidence of pleasure. To attribute a certain set of psychodynamics to the operation of sexualization and/or perversion would seem at best to be only a partial explanation. To further complicate the problem, the co-existence of seemingly normal heterosexual behavior alongside of the most intricate and bizarre forms of sexual activity hardly seems to support the existence of a "schema … [that] does apply to all forms of perversion"(Chasseguet-Smirgel, 1991p. 414). Nor could one possibly explain a patient who is a prominent professional man, happily married and capable of full and completely pleasurable sexual intercourse, having to dress in women's clothing, put on rouge and lipstick, and masturbate in front of a mirror solely on the basis of his level of personality organization (Kernberg, 1991p. 334), unless that organization manifests a type of fluidity that strains our usual diagnostic categories. A pure psychodynamic explanation of perverse sexuality and/or of sexualization is inadequate, since there exists for the most part a significant temporal dimension to the appearance of the phenomenon of either perverse sexuality or sexualization. The variability of sexualization remains to be explained.

CLINICAL CASE

The case that follows is illustrative of a patient who would probably be characterized by any diagnostician as employing sexualization. The case is not meant to exemplify a particular technique, and there is no doubt that it would be handled differently by different therapists and conceptualized differently under differing theoretical outlooks. What is hoped for is an altering perspective on how to evaluate sexualization and thus a beginning of an effort to realign our diagnostic evaluations of all manner of sexual disorders. It is presented as the single case example (Edelson, 1986), but clinical experience does allow for a generalization beyond this instance. Indeed, the positive findings of many analyses of such cases can be seen to follow the proposed theory and perhaps explain the outcomes better, or at least differently.

CASE ILLUSTRATION

Following visits to two other mental health professionals, a twenty-seven-year-old lawyer came for a psychiatric consultation for an opinion about his recent decision to come out of the closet as a homosexual. In fact, he was unusually and uniquely unsettled about this decision, inasmuch as he had never had any homosexual experiences whatsoever. Indeed, his entire sexual history consisted of masturbation and one or two furtive and unsuccessful attempts at intercourse with a woman acquaintance. It is of some note to consider that his other consultations encouraged his entrance into the homosexual world and also advised his being counseled in this new endeavor. This last referral was considered by him to be totally different since I, the consultant, asked about the nature and content of his masturbatory fantasies. He said that they consisted exclusively of sexual activity with older men, and that this was usually fellatio. He spent lots of time during an average day searching out this kind of man, and he immediately stated that he knew he must have a "father fixation." His parents had divorced when he was ten years old, and he was quick to say that the divorce affected him not a whit, since he had no use for his father either before or after the divorce, or even until this day. His school performance had deteriorated after the divorce, but he attributed this to a need to transfer schools. Mainly, however, he wanted my opinion about his decision to declare himself as a homosexual, quit his job, and move to San Francisco. I told him that I could not begin to wholly understand his sexual uncertainty, but that I did feel he had problems that seemed not to have much to do with sex, either homosexual or heterosexual. His being intrigued by this response led to several more visits and a decision to undergo analysis. However, the overwhelming note of each and every visit, as well as the dominant theme of the beginning stage of the analysis, was the question of whether or not he was truly homosexual. Alongside of this query was a deep shame about that possible state of affairs, yet a certain fatalistic view that as long as he remained so interested in middle-aged men, his fate seemed certain. My own position was primarily one of uncertainty and curiosity, since his story seemed so much that of a troubled and unhappy person with few close relationships that his sexual preoccupation did not appear to matter very much. At the beginning, he never let up for long on his insistence on knowing for sure just what he was, as if there were an inner fixed reading that could be offered to him once and for all. If anything, his intense focus on a clear decision about his sexuality made me suspect that it was a blanket that had been thrown over his entire life, obscuring what was much more essential about him. He did indeed carry over his focused sexual thinking to all of his life in terms of what co-workers, friends, and casual acquaintances thought about him sexually, i.e., did he look effeminate?, did they suspect?, did they secretly make fun of him?, etc., etc. He decided to begin analysis ostensibly to learn the truth, but also with a wish for some relief from these painful preoccupations.

The patient began his analysis with a rare (for me) eagerness and enthusiasm accompanied, in time, by a new relationship with a woman colleague to whom he confided most of what he told me in a sort of co-conspiratorial vein. Later on, he became sexually intimate with this woman, to the point of intercourse. He had no difficulty performing sexually and seemed to find it pleasurable and fulfilling. I considered this action of the patient to be an example of a defense against the transference. His dreams seemed to confirm that his newfound paramour was being used as confessor and analyst, and that his sexual activity was in the service of avoiding the relationship to me. The interesting point about this rather common form of early resistance was that it was the patient's very first sexual experience, and seemed to qualify for a form of sexualization that might be considered a bit unusual based upon this patient's initial concerns about his homosexual orientation.

Shortly after the onset of his analysis, the patient began to discuss his homosexual fantasies in detail; concomitant with this, he found himself thinking about another analyst with a nearby office. His sexual fantasies about this man consisted of having anal intercourse, with the analyst penetrating from the rear. This sexualized displacement of the transference took place when the patient had to argue a case before a jury and judge. The initial interpretation was that some of his anxious feelings were being transposed to the sexual arena. The fantasy continued on to include this analyst explaining the mechanisms of sex to the patient. This was followed by a fantasy of the patient watching an actor on television having intercourse with a woman while the patient concentrated on the actor's penis penetrating the woman's vagina. The patient's associations were to his upcoming work effort, wherein he would ask an older associate for guidance and instruction. This older man was "a whiz" at this sort of work, and the patient felt very anxious about doing it without help. I interpreted this as a sexualization of his anxiety, along with a beginning dependence on getting help from his analyst. His further association dealt with yet another masturbatory fantasy of his performing fellatio on the TV actor, while very carefully studying his face, his breathing, etc. His concentration was on what the man was doing and what the man was experiencing. This, too, was interpreted as referring to his curiosity about the analyst. The patient said: "There's this big emptiness in me, and it's right in the middle of my chest. There is this longing for a man, but it's not sexual with you [the analyst] as it is with other men. If it were sexual with you, it would be horrible and that would end the analysis."

As the analysis proceeded, more and more material came out which fairly regularly represented a sexual display of events which might ordinarily have given rise to a series of emotions, but these were seemingly lost in the scenarios of sex. The transition to a more open experience of these affect states followed an hour of alternating fantasies of heterosexual and homosexual activity. He told of feeling that he is a "geek," that he looks foolish, hates his body, worries about his skin and hair, and constantly suspects that people poke fun at him. I felt that he was now more able to commit himself to me, and shortly thereafter, the sexualization disappeared.

AS IF BY MAGIC

The cessation of sexualization during the course of an analysis is not unusual. It may, however, be either a dramatic or a gradual event, and it should, of course, always be differentiated from whatever normal sexual activity is proceeding in the life of the patient. This lifting of the sexualization material that takes place is occasion for its consideration and study in the developing transference. Certainly, in some patients, a good deal of analytic work must be done to allow the transference to be realized, but it may be rightfully claimed that sometimes, as Kohut (19710 said, it merely clicks into place.

With this patient, one hour stands out as a turning point. It began with his commenting upon how much he liked to just come in and talk. He then reported a dream of playing with two dachshunds, and one seemed to hold on to him. In a second dream he was sitting between his father and his brother-in-law, and after a moment his father began to put his hands on him in a sexual way. The patient did not know how to respond. He next noted that he was feeling threatened by opening up. He recalled the previous hour when he brought up his irritation at being charged for missed hours, and how startled he was when I agreed to discuss the matter without merely insisting that this was an agreed-upon rule. He thereupon saw the connection to the dream and asked himself why he turned anxiety into sexual things. There then followed the portrait of the father as an enigma, someone who never revealed any-thing. The two dogs and the two men were the father who never talked and a heretofore unmentioned uncle who talked to the patient all the time, which the patient loved.

After this, the patient noted that he no longer had to masturbate and no longer had the sexual fantasies, especially of the other analyst, who he now felt was really me. As the hours progressed, he connected more to me, to missing me when I was gone, to wanting to be my favorite, to wanting a gift from me, etc. The father who was both missing and a mystery began to live and to be discovered in the analysis.

An example of the return or reappearance of sexualization, which is a regular and expectable feature of this and similar treatments, occurred around a point that some might consider equivalent to a disruption or an empathic break or a discontinuity. The patient had anticipated a schedule conflict and called to alert me to the date and to inquire about a different time. I was unable to accommodate him. He did, however, manage to keep the appointment, and he reported dreaming of a baby being held by its hair, and an earlier incident of masturbation. The latter was accompanied by a fantasy of his undressing the aforementioned male TV actor and examining him as though he, the patient, were the doctor. He was primarily intent on studying this man's face and immediately connected this to his own curiosity about me and what I thought of him, along with the usual sexual litany. But now it went further, to his feeling that the baby of the dream was he himself being mistreated by my ungracious reception of his request. However, in the fantasy, he was now the doctor in charge. The next step was to his own conviction of himself as bad or disgusting, both because of his sexual proclivities, but also because he is demanding and needy. He is a bother. And, in short order, together we see him wanting to intrude upon his preoccupied father with his unspoken but unmistakable message, "Don't bother me."

DISCUSSION

The concept of structural deficiency is sort of a grab bag of unpacked ideas that is usually opened to say that patients are unable to feel certain ways or do certain things or think certain thoughts because of a lack in their psyche. That missing feature

is not, however, merely marked by a vacancy but has other forms of exposure that display its presence. Following Kohut's explication of selfobjects and his suggestion that some perverse activity is a sexualization of a selfobject to forestall regression (i.e., an active move to overcome the passive experience of losing the selfobject), a beginning conceptualization to indicate just what function the selfobject is serving was offered in *Models of the Mind* (Gedo and Goldberg, 1973). It came in the form of positing the role of object as that of unification and its gradual loss as one of optimal disillusion. An additional and important elaboration was given by Basch (1988) in his discussion of affect attunement, which described the need to have a shared affective experience to allow for an interaction that forms a healthy self which, in turn, acknowledges the need for other persons' participation in one's life. We soon began to be able to chart a map of a psyche that handled a developmental defect in a certain way, that compensated for it in a sometimes effective manner, that struggled in treatment to participate in the repair of that developmental mishap, and that ultimately reorganized itself in a changed structure.

The map of the patient's psyche is a system that extends into the world of selfobjects that serve to constitute the patient's self. For some individuals, the continued presence of these constituent selfobjects allows for a psychic equilibrium which seems unshakable. Yet the absence of one or more of them may lead to a beginning disintegration. In the sexual sphere, we may see this as the sudden outbreak of homosexual or other perverse behavior in the life of an otherwise heterosexual man, commonly in a midlife crisis. For many other patients, there is never a stable or semistable set of selfobjects in their world, and so sexualization may dominate their lives and soon become so habitual as to need long periods of analytic treatment to allow a semblance of a workable transference. Perhaps the majority of patients that we see have periods of stability along with periods of instability. And so we can observe and explain the coexistence of sexualization with normal sexual activity. The latter requires a stable and cohesive self and can only be achieved at the behest of that structure. Sexualization temporarily shores up the self. Sexuality is the act of a strong and stable self. Sexualization occurs when one or another of the deployed selfobjects is endangered. Sexuality results from the vigor of a consolidated self.

We can now return to an examination of disturbed sexuality seen in the light of a disturbance of structuralization. For one, we can indeed explain the coexistence of perverse sexuality with normal sexuality as due to the fluctuations in the presence and availability of sustaining selfobjects. The transition from archaic to mature selfobjects is thus never a movement from outer to inner, but rather a change in the self's capacity to use selfobjects in a flexible and adaptive way (Goldberg, 1990). Thus persons are not either totally with or without selfobjects, but have a variable repertoire of selfobjects. Treatment increases one's capacity to utilize and to hold them.

One result of this perspective is a possible reconsideration of homosexuality. It may truly be either normal or perverse. There may be one form: a manifestation of a choice of a sexual object which is satisfying and fulfilling regardless of some set of particular psychodynamics. As such, it is not amenable to (i.e., changeable by way of) psychoanalytic intervention. As an example of this, at another time I hope to outline the particulars of some homosexual behavior as a form of compensatory structure which can never be analyzed to yield an altered sexual preference, but which can still benefit from analysis. But other forms of homosexual behavior are indicative of a sexualization to gain and maintain a selfobject linkage. These more troubled individuals are helped by analytic treatment, but the resulting more stable self may still yet yield a homosexual choice. The natural extension of this viewpoint is to offer a view of any sexual behavior, including heterosexuality, as a possible expression of a vulnerable self given to sexualization. There are thus two problems in assessing the sexual behavior of any individual, and this is nicely presented in the above patient, whose presenting bisexuality could yield no certain clues as to the eventual resultant sexuality.

It is not the case that certain forms of sexual activity, such as sadomasochism, are a necessary precursor to or companion of sexual activity considered to be the norm. Rather, it is more likely true that all sexual activity is an admixture of sexualization and sexuality, with the former shoring up the self in order to more fully participate in the latter. My own experience in the analytic treatment of some perversions makes for another category of those patients who, after the resolution of their sexualized fantasies and behavior, show relatively little interest in sexual activity. This seems to be a more striking indicator of the pseudosexual quality of this behavior. Although one may view this as sublimation, it is equally likely that a restituted self has a number of options to pursue, and the usual anxieties associated with sexual behavior preclude that pursuit.

Thus we must be ever more alert to the dual problem of politicalization and moralization. Our field is no different from others in this regard, since we have adopted standards for the determination of normal behavior, and complete sexual fulfillment certainly is one of them. It requires a radical shift in our usual criteria of health to consider someone as normal who has a paucity or absence of efforts at fulfillment in the sexual realm. But just as we may relieve a person of the frantic sexualizations of survival, we should be equally eager to see that some people do without it altogether.

CONCLUSIONS

Sexualization is demonstrated in certain individuals who employ it to avoid painful affects (Blos, 1991), to shore up a vulnerable self, to ward off a regressive movement following the loss of a sustaining relationship, and for a variety of other defensive uses (Coen, 1981). It is seen in psychoanalysis as a resistance to the development of the transference, as an indicator of a beginning but not well-established transference, and as a sign of a disruption in the transference. It regularly diminishes and disappears in psychoanalytic treatment as the transference is stabilized, and it often becomes a barometer of the vicissitudes of the transference.

Desexualization bespeaks a structural modification that demonstrates the tolerance of certain otherwise disavowed and/or unexperienced affects, a more solid and cohesive self, a progressive developmental step, and an entrance into possible new emotional experiences. It is seen in psychoanalysis during moments of transference stability wherein both new information and reactivated points in the past become the currency of analytic work. Its loss in analysis is a sign of a movement of either the patient or the analyst that destroys the connection. Its reestablishment often marks progression in the analysis.

Rather than sublimation, which is a redirection of a libidinal drive, or neutralization, which is a de-instinctualization of a drive, the concept of structuralization is offered as explanatory of desexualization. Structuralization is defined as the entrance of a stable selfobject into the psychological field of the patient. The linkage is demonstrative of a stable transference, and psychoanalytic work aims for increasing the stability and competence of the self, composed as it is of its selfobjects.

Differentiating sexualization from sexuality might offer an opportunity to distinguish forms of sexual behavior that may be manifestly
similar but psychologically distinct. We may then be able to realign our
diagnostic considerations as to the feasibility and advisability of altering
or modifying such sexual behavior.

REFERENCES

Alpert, A. (1949). Sublimation and sexualization. A case report. *Psychoanalytic Study of the Child* 3/4 271–278.

Basch, M.F. (1988). *Understanding Psychotherapy. The Science Behind the
Art.* New York: Basic Books.

Blos, Jr., P. (1991). Sadomasochism and the defense against recall of
painful affect. *Journal of the American Psychoanalytic Association*
39:417–430.

Blum, H.P. (1973). The concept of erotized transference. *Journal of the
American Psychoanalytic Association* 21:61–76.

Chasseguet-Smirgel, J. (1986). *Sexuality and Mind: The Role of the
Father and the Mother in the Psyche.* New York/London: New York
Universities Press.

—— (1991). Sadomasochism in the perversions: Some thoughts on the
destruction of reality. *Journal of the American Psychoanalytic Association* 39:399–415.

Coen, S.J. (1981). Sexualization as a predominant mode of defense,
Journal of the American Psychoanalytic Association 29:893–920.

Edelson, M. (1986). The hermeneutic turn and the single case study in
psychoanalysis *Psychoanalytic Contemporary Thought* 8:567–614.

Fenichel, O. (1945). *The Psychoanalytic Theory of Neurosis* New York:
Norton.

Freud, A. (1965). *Normality and Pathology in Childhood. Assessments of
Development.* New York: International Universities Press.

Freud, S. (1926). Inhibitions, symptoms and anxiety *Standard Edition*
20.

Gedo, J.E. & Goldberg, A. (1973). *Models of the Mind. A Psychoanalytic
Theory.* Chicago/London: University of Chicago Press.

Goldberg, A. (1988). *A Fresh Look at Psychoanalysis. The View from Self Psychology.* Hillsdale, NJ: Analytic Press.

—— (1990). *The Prisonhouse of Psychoanalysis* Hillsdale, NJ/London: Analytic Press.

Hartmann, H. (1950). Comments on the psychoanalytic theory of the ego In *Essays on Ego Psychology. Selected Problems in Psychoanalytic Theory.* New York: International Universities Press, 1964 pp. 113–140.

Kernberg, O.F. (1991). Sadomasochism, sexual excitement, and perversion defense. *Journal of the American Psychoanalytic Association* 39:333–362.

Kohut, H. (1971). *The Analysis of the Self. A Systematic Approach to the Psychoanalytic Treatment of Narcissistic Personality Disorders.* New York: International Universities Press.

—— & Seitz, P.F.D. (1963). Concepts and theories of psychoanalysis. In: *Concepts of Personality: A Comprehensive Survey of Contemporary and Classical Approaches to Personality Including Theories, Clinical Problems and Measurement and Assessment* ed., J.M. Wepman & R.W. Heine. Chicago: Aldine Publications, pp. 113–141.

Socarides, C.W. (1992). Sexual politics and scientific logic: the issue of homosexuality. *Journal of Psychohistory* 10:307–329.

Stoller, R.J. (1991). Eros and polis: what is this thing called love? *Journal of the American Psychoanalytic Association* 39:1065–1102.

Stolorow, R.D. (1975). The narcissistic function of masochism (and sadism). *International Journal of Psycho-Analysis* 56:441–448.

Depathologizing Homosexuality (2001)

Pick up any textbook on pathology and more likely than not it will begin with a definition of the field. Routinely this is presented as the study of the nature of disease. The textbook I used in medical school proceeds then to define disease as "an abstraction" that cannot itself be observed; rather, it is established by extracting and totaling the characteristics of the sick that differ from those of the norm or the healthy. As we move from pathology to disease to sickness, little else is learned until we approach the idea of symptoms, which are regarded as evidence of disease. Symptoms are represented as alterations from the norm. These may be either subjective, such as pain, or objective, such as a rash. As long as we maintain that disease is manifested as an alteration of form or function, we are regularly thrown back to (1) a statistical standard for normality, which may be common enough for quantitative factors such as weight and blood pressure; (2) a purely subjective standard such as unhappiness; or (3) a cultural one that is more vague and depends on factors such as group acceptance. The last of these standards is typically resorted to in instances of behavior disorders involving such outward manifestations as thievery or anorexia. Clearly we cannot rely on statistical norms alone, inasmuch as some conditions (e.g., dental caries) are common but are correctly regarded as pathological. Neither, however, can we rely on group agreement alone, since everything from riots by mobs to hysterical reactions in the susceptible may be supported by one's immediate peers but outside the group be considered an alteration of function. Sometimes personal opinion carries the day. The move from physical disease to psychopathology is a fragile and treacherous one.

DEPATHOLOGIZING

What does it mean to depathologize something? It is a declaration of health or freedom from illness. Is it possible that the very idea of sickness in psychiatry and psychology derives from a decision that lacks clarity, even to the point of saying, as Robert Michels (personal communication) does, that present-day psychoanalysis has no position of its own regarding psycho-pathology? If we see a patient with a blood pressure say of 180/100, we have little hesitation in labeling that as pathological. For blood pressure we insist on norms and standards, and have developed them. In depression we rely on the patient's internal standards of happiness and contentment. If we interview a patient who is homosexual, however, we can make no such claim; indeed, we are constrained from any such comparable decision based on norms and standards. Yet as we move from one or another form of sexual activity, we seem to depend on societal norms of some sort to direct us to a proper label of pathology. Does psychoanalysis need to aban-don its theoretical base and look to psychiatry and DSM-IV for a proper pathology? And in doing so does it become a field with no say in decisions regarding sickness and health? Our psychiatric brethren have catalogued numerous phenomena by which to sort and identify disease entities, but they never claim to know a disease in its essence, apart from citing a con-stellation of signs and symptoms. Thus, there is no tight fit between etiology and pathology, as in, say, tuberculosis, which can routinely be linked to a bacillus. Intermediate cases include hypertension, which can be linked loosely to angiotension and depression, which may be on the verge of such a linkage. By contrast, any factors underlying sexual differences, deemed pathological or not, remain in the terra incognita of research yet to be done.

PSYCHOANALYSIS

Freud surely added to the uncertainty surrounding sickness and health when he seemed to say that neuroses are universal, and that all of them derive from an infantile neurosis. The complexities and varied forms of neurosis may connect to moments of development and degrees of trauma, but for him there was never a complete absence of neurosis; it was just that some neuroses were worse than others. Indeed, Freud's focus on one simple and essential conflict in the origin of neuroses made differentiation even more difficult, inasmuch as, since everyone had an oedipal conflict, the variety of its manifestations were but varia-tions on a theme. Preoedipal conflicts increased both the myriad of manifestations and the degree of complexity, but such considerations merely added to the universality of pathology. This egalitarian approach to neurosis was to be disrupted only by a therapeutic psychoanalysis which, by making the unconscious conscious ("Where id was, there ego shall be"), allowed some to be less neurotic by virtue of the personal insight it afforded them.

Dissatisfaction with Freud's single-minded fixation on the infantile neurosis and the oedipus complex led other analysts to focus on adaptation as the measure of health and disease. One was less neurotic to the degree that one successfully got along or, at a minimum, was able to fit into one's environment. The ego was now the executive aspect of the psyche, and health was now equated with an ego that managed, in Freud's words, to love and work. However, it could not be denied that one could adapt well and yet be symptomatic, just as one could love and work in various states of emotional distress and discomfort. The subjective side of disease need not fit well with the objective side of adequate functioning. Symptoms and adaptation can well coexist, and regularly do.

PSYCHIATRY

Outside psychoanalysis per se, there was a very clear dividing line in general psychiatry regarding health and disease, inasmuch as one could readily rank behavior and subjective states on the basis of deviation from a norm. The collection and cataloguing of such deviations allowed the formulations of syndromes while certain pharmacological agents served to relieve, with varying degrees of surprise, many such constellations. The surprise stemmed from the fact that some drugs seemed to affect some syndromes but not others, so that diagnoses and pathology came increasingly to rest not on observation of a well-delineated syndrome but on inferences drawn from drug-specific responses in the patient. In this situation, with neither clearly established biological causal links nor agreed-on psychodynamic correlations to rely on, psychiatry becomes vulnerable to diagnosis according to social or political criteria. This vulnerability leaves the field subject to trends and fashions, to referendums on pathology.

I recently witnessed a discussion about racism and whether it should be included in DSM-IV as a psychiatric disorder. There was not much real debate about whether racism is to be despised, but the issue of its being a psychiatric illness seemed loaded with confusion. I myself could well imagine an analysis in which a patient's racism might never become evident. I could equally well see how a patient's racism might

take up a good deal of the analysis. Is it not often the case that issues of a patient's life that might well be subsumed under the umbrella of taste and preference are never brought to the fore? Although we may feel strongly about political, religious, or moral attitudes expressed by our patients, it is usually incumbent on us to remain as neutral and objective as possible in order to understand what if anything has given rise to such expressions. And it is not at all unusual that positions may be felt quite intensely but show little evidence of being caught up in psychic conflict. In such cases we strive to remain clear of our own perhaps equally intense feelings about the issue. However, in this psychiatric debate it became clear that the very existence of severe racism in an individual could well cause the person to be labeled as sick, thereby revealing the judgment of pathology as based on opinion rather than truth. We will remain in our uncertainty as long as we allow personal prejudice pro or con to be the arbiter of health or sickness. A somewhat similar situation came about with regard to homosexuality, though unlike racism, which was almost universally deplored, it was on its way to rehabilitation in popular and scientific opinion.

HOMOSEXUALITY AS ILLNESS OR NORMALITY

Ultimately, and surely quite properly in most instances, homosexuality lost its tag of disease and so became depathologized. No longer a symptom, it entered the ranks of the normal.

Psychoanalysis was late to reconsider and depathologize homosexuality, and for a period there was no consensus. Some claimed that it makes no sense to regard homosexuality as pathological (Isay 1989); others considered psychoanalysis ignorant of homosexuality in its entirety (Stoller 1985); still others insisted that diverse psychobiological factors, especially those involving prenatal influences, lead to homosexuality (Friedman 1986). A few continued to insist on the pathology of homosexuality (Socarides 1991), but ultimately psychoanalysis joined psychiatry in declaring homosexuality in both men and women to fall outside the category of disease.

Lacking any claim to a better understanding of homosexual behavior, we might wonder how it can be classified at all. Although we do at times put behavior and characteristics into groups without knowing their causes or origins, we do require some underlying rationale for assigning something as an A rather than a B. The larger question is whether we can determine if A or B is a sign of sickness or of health. And here we encounter what may well be a fundamental flaw in the psychoanalytic consideration of psychopathology—a failure to distinguish the database of psychoanalysis from that of other disciplines, primarily psychiatry. Psychoanalytic data are derived from the analytic situation and are necessarily confined to manifestations of transference and countertransference. What happens outside that situation is of interest only as it becomes relevant to those particulars. As counterintuitive as that may seem, psychoanalysis cannot regard phenomena as symptoms of illness save as they may or may not correlate with certain transference manifestations. Sometimes they do and sometimes they do not.

There are homosexual patients whose sexual concerns and fantasies dominate the content of their analyses; others seem never to pose their sexuality as an issue. The particular transference configuration in either case is the salient factor, and psychoanalysis has norms and standards for evaluating any pathology in the transference. Though transference is indeed universal, its categories of specific pathology include such labels as resolved or unresolved, positive or negative, anxious, depressed, and the like. That these transferences may be played out in a heterosexual or homosexual manner, or in any other arena of meaningful affective concerns, should be seen as important but secondary to the label of pathology. Indeed, one must wonder how the issue of homosexuality, which Freud and other analysts throughout the history of the profession have tried to correlate with health or sickness, could have been allowed to replace the essentials of psychoanalytic data collection and so to stand on its own. Indeed, the proper consideration of sexuality of any orientation must await its participation in the transference. Until then it is a matter of guesswork.

REPRISE

Listening to the history of the treatment of homosexuals in our society, as well as within the specialized fields of psychiatry and psychoanalysis, should cause us to wonder why we have forgotten what we know. There seems to be a disconnect between the proper place of analytic knowledge and its function in the world. We cannot take a stand on moral or political or artistic issues merely because of what we are. We can only attend to the data with which we are familiar by virtue of our training, data confined to the emerging transference configurations of our patients. Similarly, applied analysis demands data from which we choose to make inferences, but these educated guesses often founder on the shoals of verification. If psychoanalysis can find its way back to the study of individual patients, it can readily offer an answer to the question of whether in a given case homosexuality is a manifestation of pathology. The fact of being homosexual is not, properly speaking, a psychoanalytic datum. Homosexuality cannot in itself be a province of pathology, anymore than can any trait. Only in an individual person can we determine its meaning.

REFERENCES

Friedman, R. (1986). Toward a further understanding of homosexual men. *Journal of the American Psychoanalytic Association* 34:193–206.

Isay, R. (1989). *Being Homosexual*. Farrar, Straus & Giroux.

Socarides, C. (1991). The specific tasks in the psychoanalytic treatment of well-structured deviations. In *The Homosexual and the Therapeutic Process*, ed. C. Socarides & V.D. Volkan. Madison, CT; International Universities Press, pp. 287–289.

Stoller, R. (1985). *Presentations of Gender.* New Haven: Yale University Press.

CHAPTER TEN

Mostly Clinical

In his paper, *The Place of Apology in Psychoanalysis and Psychotherapy* (1987), Goldberg introduces the story of a little girl who was hospitalized for mutism. In a meeting, most likely a clinical case conference, the little girl says to a room of doctors and nurses and other specialists, "Say you are sorry." A refrain begins, "I am sorry" and the little girl brightens up and begins to talk.

The place of apology in psychoanalysis is somewhat more complex and in his 1987 paper, Goldberg unpacks the complicated components of apology, mistakes, errors and countertransference experiences. In addition, he endeavors to provide a model of therapeutic action, distinguish between psychoanalysis and psychotherapy, as well as explain the differences between theoretical schools: one placing drives at the center of our inquiry and another that emphasizes failures in development. Finally, one's need to apologize is considered a measure of grandiosity—the therapist's apologies reflect his own need to be better, smarter or more empathic than he is able to be.

According to Goldberg, Kohut has made the problem of mistakes and errors into a solution: "by considering the tenet that meaningful interpretations occur around points of empathic breaks or misunderstandings by the analyst. These inevitable disruptions are, of course, failures on the analyst's part and are to be treated as the sine qua non of effective analytic intervention."

Within a stable transference configuration, patient and analyst move from a position of misunderstanding to understanding by way of a negotiating process. In this exchange, "transferences are to be studied and interpreted in order to correct them or to make the patient understand the analyst's view of the world." We share the patient's experience by way of empathy, but we do not become that patient. The suspension of the analyst's own beliefs and judgments allows access to the patient's inner world but there is always a gap, and that is where the need to apologize arises. "The gap that is never erased by our merger efforts, by our empathic posture, is the source of our wish to apologize."

—GM

The Place of Apology in
Psychoanalysis and Psychotherapy (1987)

What must count as a minor classic in the psychoanalytic literature is the 'Say You're Sorry' article of Lawrence Kubie & Hyman Israel (1955). It is there that the power of apology is seen in what may be considered a pure form. In that clinical presentation a child of 5, who was hospitalized for an acute syndrome of mutism, anorexia and other signs of severe regression, is inadvertently heard to be making a sound that a nurse interprets as 'Say you're sorry'. In a meeting room filled with many people, the examiner of the child begins a refrain with the apology: 'I am sorry, I am very, very sorry', and this is taken up by a series of participants in the conference room. The child brightens up, begins to talk and a week later is recovered.

This case is presented as illustration of the magic of unlocking unconscious processes with precision; and the reaction of instantaneous cure is likened to that gained from hypnosis. The article fills out the history of the child's illness with some speculations about her recovery, but one should read on to a follow-up presentation of this very same girl who is hospitalized again some six years later and followed as an outpatient for several years thereafter (Ravich & Dunton, 1965). Her initial improvement was maintained for a while, but over time she deteriorated and needed to be re-admitted: this time with symptoms of multiple school phobias and hypochondriacal complaints. Her second hospital course focused on the use of the word 'enema', and the reporters of the second article present the case as one of a core conflict over the forcible administration of enemas from the age of 1½ to 4½. Her treatment was suspended at puberty (at age 12) with the note that she was not communicative in the sessions. Not much more can be said about the case, but it is striking and memorable more in terms of the technique employed by Kubie than it is revealing about this particular child's malady and recovery. It seems to make something magic of an apology.

Of course apologizing *per se* is not treated as a normal part of psychotherapeutic or psychoanalytic technique. The above case is that of an apology offered by a non-offender; and in order to move into the realm of the use of apology in the normal conduct of treatment, we must better define the term and survey the literature to see if it is at all applicable to such an inquiry.

Definition of and Some Literature about Apologizing

Apologizing has two components: acknowledging a mistake or error and expressing regret for it. If we confine our inquiry for the moment to the acts of analysts or therapists rather than to those of patients, we will probably note that only the first half of the definition is met, i.e. some therapists or analysts do, on occasion, admit that they have made an error. They seem more apt to make an explicit acknowledgement of a mistake but allow the second half involving regret to remain implicit. By merely recognizing the validity of a patient's grievance, they sometimes embrace the further legitimacy of the entire scope of an apology. As in every case of human communication, a set of unspoken rules can be seen to govern what is allowable and what is taken for granted; and so for one person a simple acknowledgement may equal a very eloquent apology.

The inclusion of both psychotherapy and psychoanalysis in this review is made necessary, because some of the writers in this area claim that the distinction between the two is not based on technique (Goldberg, 1981), while others (Gill, 1984) seem to say that something akin to a therapist's acknowledgement or apology allows for the differentiation between therapy and analysis to be made. For the moment we shall lump together the therapist and analyst and put to one side whether one or the other is more relevant to the subject.

At one end of the spectrum of therapeutic misdeeds is the position of Langs (1982) who seems to feel that much treatment is in error because it avoids the therapist's unconscious needs and wishes. He says:

> In the psychotherapeutic conspiracy between patients and therapists, it is the therapist who is the main perpetrator of harm and distortion. The patient is the willing victim. The conspiracy is largely unconscious, outside of the awareness of both participants. Adorned with sincere wishes by therapists to help their patients, the cure—if it does

occur— is by collusion and victimization or traumatic stimulation for growth.

Newman (1985) examines in detail those analytic failures that do not allow the treatment to progress. He feels that the countertransference reactions of the analyst can be used to facilitate treatment and overcome stalemates if these analytic 'failures' are employed in the service of making 'a new object' available to the patient. He says: 'Having entered into the patient's inner world of objects and *accepting responsibility* (my italics) for repeating an aspect of the failed primary relationship, the analyst now can function as a potential new selfobject'. He later emphasizes: 'We are asked to try and see our failures through our patients' eyes and bear what certainly may feel like considerable distortions arising from these often internal encounters. Much depends on how well we are able to take responsibility and even acknowledge how our own injured self-esteem influences our negative attitudes toward the patient'. Essentially Newman seems to carve out a special group of patients who require a sharing of blame for their patholo-gy. He calls for a re-enactment in the transference to allow it to deepen, and he so suggests that we, as the parents, visit our problem, albeit inevitably, upon the patient.

Such a heavy burden to be borne by therapists is seemingly relieved by Langs when he urges a stance that allows one to be truthful and honest and so to escape this conspiracy. Part of that effort does seem to lie in the use of apology. Often this takes place following grievous errors such as overcharging (Langs, p. 266), but there seems no inherent limi-tation on the use of 'admitting one's mistakes'. No doubt most therapists do entertain a concept that separates real mistakes from unacknowl-edged ones. If we discharge a patient fifteen minutes early, we probably would apologize. If we make a mistake on a bill, the same may be true. The dividing line gets blurred if we, for example, forget the name of an important member of the patient's family or allow our own emotions to be inappropriately expressed. Merely to consider 'mistakes' as examples of countertransference still leave us with the dilemma of dealing with it in treatment. Racker (1968) holds that the telling of one's countertrans-ference is an entirely undecided issue, but we know that one can still apologize without explaining. Indeed one of the foremost proponents of alerting the analyst to his or her contribution to the transference (Hoffman, 1983) insists that the analyst need not 'admit' actual countertransference experiences. Rather he or she should allow the patient to realize the 'plausibility' of certain reactions.

Gill (1982) has developed a strong thesis for considering the here and now transference to be most significant and so to raise the claims that the patient's view of the analyst always has a core of reasonableness to it. The differentiation of treatment into psychoanalysis as a technical pursuit versus psychotherapy is said by Gill to depend on how rigorously one analyses the witting and unwitting suggestions offered by the analyst. He claims that the situation is eased for the analyst who is disabused of the idea that an uncontaminated transference can develop. He skirts the issue of self-disclosure, but says that an atmosphere must exist that allows for the patient's point of view to be acknowledged. He says that this is in contrast to one that argues that, in effect, to acknowledge the rationality of the patient is to confirm his belief that his experience is fully due to the behaviour of the analyst (Gill, 1984). In his book we are also told:

> If the analyst has given the patient cause to be angry, for example, and the patient is angry, at least some aspect of the anger is neither a transference or cooperation ... We do conceptualize inappropriate behavior on the analyst's part as countertransference, but what is our name for the analysand's realistic response to countertransference.

This seems to recreate the burden of determining what is expectable and what is regrettable. We are cautioned not to say *why* we feel the way we do. We should accept the patient's perception of something as true to some degree, and sometimes we are even chastised for doing or saying the wrong thing or even for remaining silent (Gill, 1982, Vol. II, p.4).

Kohut has made the problem into a solution by considering the tenet that meaningful interpretations occur around points of empathic breaks or misunderstandings by the analyst. These inevitable disruptions are, of course, failures on the analyst's part and are to be treated as the *sine qua non* of effective analytic intervention. He says:

In a properly conducted analysis, the analyst takes note of the analysand's retreat, searches for any mistake he might have made, nondefensively acknowledges them after he has recognized them (often with the help of the analysand) and this gives the analysand a noncensorious interpretation of the dynamics of his retreat (Kohut, 1984).

Now this is clearly written as an objective appraisal of the normal analytic process, but one cannot help but see that it is a mistake that ushers in a retreat and an acknowledgement that halts it. The mistakes are those of the analyst and would (probably) range from the inadvertent and inevitable ones of everyday life to the gross mistreatments that a more sensitive and/or seasoned analyst could avoid. From the analyst's transference or countertransference or innocence, a failure seems still to rank as such and is hardly less forgivable if it carries an explanation with it; unless the explanation likewise comes with a plea for forgiveness.

If we choose these several contributors as points in the field of scrutiny, we see that they espouse a position that relieves the patient of the burden of error and shifts it to the analyst. This is much like that of the move that places the seed of psychopathology first in the child's drives and fantasies and later in the parents' mistreatment of the child. We reenact our theories of psychopathology by moving from patient blame to therapist blame, and we redress the error by saying we are sorry for our witting or unwitting folly.

INTERPERSONAL ASPECTS OF APOLOGIZING

In considering a communicative exchange between two persons one may utilize a variety of theoretical constructs to map the field in order to realize some data. These range from fields as diverse as information theory to speech act theory. The theories are devised to explain how one person manages to influence the other, to inform the other, to move the other, etc. In an ordinary conversation a multitude of phenomena present themselves for consideration, but in a psychoanalytic exchange we single out an appropriate pattern in terms of some stable transference configuration. The latter may be familial or otherwise, object-libidinal or narcissistic. Interventions of any sort tend to disrupt the transference. They especially do so if they are designed to alter the explicit and implicit roles that are assumed. Thus when two people are dancing and one complains that his or her toes are being stepped on, the dance becomes something different from what it was before. So too, if a patient is pouring out a tale of woe and a therapist interprets this as a childhood reenactment, there is a momentary bracketing of the content as it is subject to a different level of scrutiny. Apologizing does the same: it resets the nature of the ongoing relationship and forces it to become a different sort of relationship. It is a form of action that allows us to consider it as acting-in in an analysis or treatment, and thus forces us to consider a necessary alteration in the transference. It is not true that it is always what it may seem to be, since apologizing can be employed for a variety of motives. In the most general sense it does seem to lend an advantage to the apologizer who is able to redirect the communication to his or her own ends. Thus there is nothing inherently worthwhile or ameliorative about apologizing, any more than there is about not doing so.

CLINICAL ILLUSTRATION

This patient, a middle-aged man, who had had a long and successful analysis, was once again in treatment for a recurrence of symptomatology. In one hour he told of a relationship with a woman who wanted him to behave in a certain way which he could not accommodate: something like agreeing with her about the worth of a movie. I said that perhaps he wanted to be free of the woman, but the patient protested that I was wrong, that it was not that. Soon after, he began talking of Christmas and wishing to have a tree. He and his childhood family had celebrated Christmas in Germany even though they were Jewish. He could not enjoy such a celebration here in America. I asked 'why not?' since they were not particularly religious Jews. He became quite angry and told me that I simply did not understand what it was like for him as a child. I responded to this with what I felt was a neutral comment about how this sort of effort at understanding, which I had seemingly failed to achieve, was what makes for the effectiveness of the treatment process, i.e. that I was trying to comprehend. He told me that it was just stupid of me to suggest that he have a tree, and it probably related to my own shaky ground as a Jew who probably did now have a tree, but that was nothing like the Jews of Germany who had trees. I responded in a louder voice that that may well be true, but it did not make me stupid. He became contrite and said that he felt horrible that he had made me angry, and that it was very much like the relationship with his wife and brother who would make him angry and then attack him in turn. He felt loathsome and awful. I asked more about this turn of events of people being mad at him. I felt bad and wanted to apologize for raising my voice. He had been right about my reacting to being called stupid, but I allowed him to continue. He told me that, on the rare occasions that his father had yelled at him, he had, indeed, apologized. I asked how he felt about this, and he said that it was wrong of him: he had a right to blow off steam, he did not do it that often and apologizing diminished him in his eyes. I asked that we talk more about the apologizing and whether he would want it of me. He said it was different; that my apologizing would help with his own sense of reality, i.e. that he was not such an awful person who managed to enrage others. I felt like apologizing but did not. Rather I began to wonder about the nature of our interaction.

To begin with, there had clearly been a misunderstanding. One could say that of itself it was of minor significance, but another one followed it rapidly. The patient had also sensed something in me that lent plausibility to his perception of the scene, i.e. that I did not know what Christmas meant to him because of my own defensiveness or perhaps even naivete about the event. Once he felt the second, a more severe or intense misunderstanding, he was even more distraught and by calling me stupid managed to get me to respond angrily, i.e. that is what he experienced, and it was certainly equally plausible. The reactions thereafter were typical of an old masochistic posture that was a part of his first analysis but had long been away and, we had hoped, lost forever. It did dissipate in the next few hours as we talked more about his feeling bound to people who are difficult or self-absorbed or crazy and having to placate them; since he cannot cut himself off completely from those few souls who are so much a part of his life history. He needs to work out an accommodation between submission and independence, and much of his first analysis was connected to this point of reluctantly accepting the reality of his life without despair or depression, i.e. the judgmental condemnation that Freud espoused (1923).

We see several points that apology arouses in this illustration: as a specific transference reference to the father, as a countertransference reaction of the therapist and as an interpersonal transaction in the treatment. To unpack this clinical vignette in order better to examine the problem of apologizing we can follow it sequentially:

1. The first discussion about the woman who wanted the patient to agree with her could be a transference allusion to the patient wanting to differentiate from the therapist (as was suggested) or could be an example of the therapist's failure to understand *per se*. Either way it sets the stage for 'the effort to understand' that should follow.

2. The Christmas tree material was begun by the patient with a tone of regret and sadness that evoked a sense of loneliness and that reinforced the therapist's idea that the patient was telling himself that he could not ever separate from the people who were also so burdensome to him. The therapist probably wanted to challenge this idea with his question but it underscored the gap of misunderstanding. He then tried to make a comment about what they were doing. The strength of his response is significant because he felt misunderstood on both levels, i.e. in the transference as well as in terms of the particular content of his communication.

3. The therapist's anger and the patient's retreat from him may be less significant than it might appear. It did evoke an old characterological response in the patient but that was short-lived. More importantly it was impetus for the therapist's wish to apologize. The reference to similar childhood situations did allow him to delay his wish. The final wish for an apology leads back to the original theme of two people seeing the world differently (e.g. the movie), but neither having to submit to the other in order for the relationship to be sustained.

The following hours showed a shift in the content of discussion in that the patient began to see a pattern of interaction in a number of his relationships. The sequence was that of an intense involvement with someone who expected him to behave in a particular way, a refusal or reluctance of him to so conform, then a withdrawal by that person from him. The time of such withdrawal or alienation was experienced as very painful by the patient who would manage to effect a rapprochement by some sort of apology of his own. With the review and overview of such occurrences the patient connected it all to a familiar childhood experience of being 'frozen out'. This phrase described the mother's way of punishing the patient for anything and everything. Mother would stop speaking to the child for one or more hours in order to let him know how angry or disappointed she was. The patient would feel a desperate pain and would do anything to win back the mother in the form of her attention and communication. This always necessitated some form of apology and forgiveness; and as an adult, he could readily see that the wrong person was doing the apologizing. Thus a deeper transference issue of apologizing was elucidated.

Once the above material was examined and discussed, the patient felt relieved and free and determined to work out relationships that allowed him to feel connected without feeling controlled. The alternative solution of leaving behind the people who interacted with him in this manner seemed untenable to him; just as his analysis had ended with him putting up with his wife rather than contemplating divorce. But first he felt that he had to get someone to apologize to him. He did this in the next few days in a very acceptable manner, but immediately after the wrongdoer (who was easy to find) told him how sorry he was, he felt depressed and frightened. He knew that he had only succeeded in making that person guilty, and he would soon avenge himself for that discomfort. And so he completed the circle of injury, apology and a repeated cycle of injustice.

Apologizing, for the patient, made him feel abused and enraged, much as he felt while enduring his mother's perverse form of punishment. Being apologized to made him feel guilty and frightened, because he recognized the rage behind such social proprieties. In parallel fashion the analyst or therapist at times wishes the patient would apologize for his mistreatment of him, and, in turn, apologizes and then must endure his own feeling of mistreatment.

DISCUSSION

The range of evaluation of a patient's productions and associations covers the spectrum from everything emerging in pure form and seeking a blank screen for its realization to that of an innocent patient having to cope with the unconscious intrusiveness of the therapist. The first position allows interpretation of the patient's drives and fantasies as they are developed and expressed in the transference. The second encourages a view of a traumatized person forced to live in a crazy world and forever seeking redress. Certainly psychoanalysis has always embraced the first and has segregated the second into the lesser class of psychotherapy, and, more particularly, into a therapy of nurturance and support. Apologizing would appear to be non-analytic.

It would seem easy to approach the problem by eliminating the extremes. Are there not a host of egregious mishaps in therapy for which an apology is due? And do these not correspond to the position of the victimized patient that can be readily dismissed? If we let a patient out very early, or overcharge on a bill, or completely mix up one patient's life with that of another it would seem obvious that we are wrong and should apologize. Or should we? There certainly are patients for whom this would be uncalled for or unnecessary. If the patient does not care, should we? Is there any generalizable rule to follow that clarifies what is to be considered as an apologizable error of the analyst, or is it to be evaluated against the backdrop of each patient?

On the other hand there are the seemingly trivial errors of everyday life that for some people may be momentous. Forgetting the name of a favourite uncle, ending the hour some 30 seconds early, not understanding what something meant to a patient and feeling certain that no one else would possibly do better: these are all events that could beg for apologizing from a certain set of patients but would feel forced and unreal from the side of the therapist.

Now one conclusion that can be offered for the dilemma is that of letting the patient determine the rule. The categorization could be that sicker patients get apologies whilst the healthier ones do without. Or the differentiation could be that an apology is called for if it allows the treatment to proceed, while is to be suspended if it does not serve the resistance. Unfortunately, as our clinical case hoped to show, one cannot tell what an apology will do or what it means until long after the fact.

Another escape from the problem would consist of conjuring up something like the 'average expectable analyst or therapist'. This would allow for a community standard of propriety, and the borders of this would determine what is and what is not a mistake. Thus, we apologize for deviations from an expectable therapeutic performance and turn it back to the patient if the feeling of mistreatment prevails in spite of our conviction that we did what everyone might do. Indeed we often operate this way in the sense of our patients learning just what to expect from treatment from just about anyone.

The extremes of patient as victim to patient as provocateur is sometimes handled as merely a problem of an appropriate match. Rather than blame the child or the parent, we say that this child could not be appropriately raised by these parents. But they need not be seen as evil or malevolent. They merely could not fit the needs of this particular child. This posture allows us entry into a possible solution to the problem of apologizing.

THE TWO WORLDS OF TREATMENT

The patient and the analyst live in different worlds. Patients arrive with a life history and a perception of life that the analyst tries to comprehend. He does so by some sort of gathering of data that perhaps can be subsumed under the umbrella of 'prolonged empathic immersion'. In this manner he may attain a state of intersubjective agreement or an ability to see the patient's world as he or she does. If this is successful, then the analyst can be said to understand the patient and, in this sense, every patient can claim a right to be so understood. If one is capable of maintaining such a level of intersubjective agreement by resolving whatever discord may emerge, then the patient and the analyst are truly of one mind. If it is further the case that the analyst assumes the major burden of achieving and maintaining this state, it would follow that the failures of intersubjectivity become the responsibility of the analyst. It takes no great leap of logic to see that an apology might well be forthcoming from such a failure. This is not to say that one should or must utilize apology to repair discordance, but it does make a case for the logic of this response. To the degree that one feels that understanding is essential for any given patient, then that logic becomes more forceful and determinant of your response.

The reverse side of the two worlds of analyst and patient holds the analyst to be the carrier of a more informed reality. Although one is encouraged to see the development of a workable transference, this is always considered, by definition, to be a distortion regardless of the 'plausibility' of its content. Such transferences are studied and interpreted in order ultimately to correct them or to make the patient understand the analyst's view of the world. With all the tact and sensitivity that may be called upon as a prerequisite to this effort, the work of analysis is to dissolve the transference and to have the patient disabused of his view of the world. Thus the differences in perception of patient and analyst never call for apology from the analyst. Rather apology is an indicator of the fact of the analyst's not being faithful to his own world view, much like the analyst who overcharges the patient and so sees a discrepancy between what he sees of himself and what he would like to see. These 'errors' of analytic practice do, of course, lead to an occasional act of apology, but they are not a part of the normal conduct of treatment. To admit them as such is equal to making countertransference the essence of treatment. Certainly errors and countertransference are significant guides to doing treatment, but most practitioners are not ready to make them the whole of treatment. Thus, in this view, the logic carries us to the conclusion that there is no routine place for apology in analysis.

Between the viewpoint of the major task of analysis being that of understanding the patient versus the stance that it is that of the patient renouncing his fantasies and accepting reality, there should be a possible compromise or resolution. Such a resolution is made possible only if one sees these polar positions as basically untenable in and of themselves.

The first position, that of seeing the patient's world as it exists for the patient, demands of us that we put aside our own preconceptions and convictions for the time being. To understand someone means that we forego pre-judgment and put ourselves in the other's shoes. Although this is an admirable goal, one should be aware that it is also an impossible one. We cannot effectively merge with another person in a total way. Rather we move from misunderstanding to understanding by way of a negotiating process. No matter how much we may be able to see what it was and is like to be that child and that patient, we are also simultaneously aware that we are not that other person. We share the patient's experience by way of empathy, but we do not become that patient. As in the clinical example, it is necessary that I understand what having a Christmas tree means to that patient, but it never reaches the point that it means the same to me. My suspension of my own beliefs and judgments allows access to the patient's inner world but there always is a gap that exists between us. No matter how intensely I may persevere in my effort to understand, I have the knowledge that I can leave and return to my own norms and standards and reality. The gap that is never erased by our merger efforts, by our empathic posture, is the source of our wish to apologize. It is the failure of understanding that reflects our mistakes, and it is our own grandiose fantasy that we can completely understand someone else that evokes an apology for our failure fully to do so.

The other position that eschews apology has the implicit assumption that the patient work through the distortions of the transference to a reality that the analyst possesses. This is not something that occurs *after* we understand the patient, since understanding is always operant and transference interpretations are seen as evidence that we understand the patient. There is no place for apology in this transaction, since there are no natural or expectable errors: only accidents of technique. The analyst who is expected to apologize sees this as transference and treats it as such. The analyst who appropriately apologizes can only do so if he has made a move that is deviant from community standards. For the most part he would not apologize, because for the most part the world that he sees is more attuned to reality. Such a posture is equally in error. We are simply not possessed of right ways to consider things, since our norms are likewise negotiated issues. It takes work on my part to see what that Christmas tree means to the patient, just as every bit of knowing a patient demands some alteration in our judgements and convictions. Analytic work does not deal with fixed and unalterable facts and truths as much as it does with agreed-upon states of affairs. To refuse to admit a mistake and apologize is to refuse to acknowledge that we can be more than we are. Just as our grandiosity forces us to apologize, our defects do not allow us to do so. In an abbreviated and perhaps unsatisfactory solution of the problem we may say that we apologize when we try to be more than we can be, and we fail to apologize when we insist on being less.

CONCLUSIONS

Psychoanalysis considers psychopathology to derive from developmental problems. They range in concept from a Kleinian viewpoint which sees the child's intense drives to be the primary source of difficulty, to one espoused by Kohut and/or Winnicott which tends to attribute the problems to parental failures. Freud posed a complementary series for the combination of mismatches that lead to neuroses, but over the years the tendency has been to align oneself in one or another of these camps. Allegiance to a theory of psychopathology forces a posture of treatment that corresponds. Thus if one feels that the drives need to be tamed, interventions are directed to aiding the ego better to control the id and superego with insight that effects neutralization. If, on the other hand, one blames childhood traumatic experiences at the core of adult disorders, this treatment tends to be directed at experiences that correct or undo or, at a minimum, allow normal development to proceed.

If an analyst believes that the patient's wishes and fantasies wreck havoc with his psyche, then the role of interpretation is that of transforming these unconscious products to conscious control. In a sense this is a limited ambition, since such intervention is in itself limited to repressed psychic contents. Of course most analysts are felt to consist of much more in the way of gains achieved in the analytic relationship, but as a model of treatment this form of analysis is confined to a small set of neurotic disorders.

If an analyst believes that the patient suffers because of childhood traumas that have not allowed normal development to proceed, then the interpretations that are made are felt to be ameliorative of the trauma. This can readily be seen to be a much more ambitious approach, since we need only be constrained by our capacity to understand that patient and so to prepare the groundwork that the thwarted development can now utilize and so prosper. There need therefore be no inherent limitation to helping severely disturbed patients save that of our own personal failings. Such an approach tends to promote rescue fantasies and to foster a therapeutic megalomania.

Its counterpart is the humble and narrow stance of one who can only deal with certain circumscribed disorders that lend themselves to cure by insight. That tends to promote a profound therapeutic pessimism as well as an elitist approach to treatment. These therapists hardly ever apologize, because they expect so little of themselves; while the ambitious ones tend readily to apologize, because they expect so much of themselves.

The clinical example that was described, aimed to show that apologies can be of several sorts. For one they can have a special transference meaning that must be elucidated, as in this patient's experience of his father's inappropriate apology. A second point is that the therapist's wish to apologize probably reflects his own need to be better or smarter or more empathic than he is able to be. A third point is that the act of apologizing is always an action that resets the relationship and is experienced by the patient as a reparative effort that may or may not be appropriate. It does seem to delay or forestall a more comprehensive meaning of the transference, as noted in the patient's recall of the mother's mistreatment of him. There is no doubt, however, that this does have a place at certain times in certain treatments. But this is not to be taken as saying that one cannot form a general rule about the place of apology in treatment. To the degree that our own narcissistic therapeutic zeal determines our attitude to a patient, we will be a party to embracing our mistakes. Thus every impetus to admit our errors is a potential indulgence of our grandiosity. But lest we, on the contrary, never expect to help anyone very much or to expand our capacity to help more people, then we can never readily say that we are sorry.

SUMMARY

This paper focuses upon the issues that arise when an analyst or therapist feels called upon to apologize to a patient. The pertinent literature which espouses or suggests such an act is reviewed. It is also noted that the participation of the analyst in acknowledging his or her misdeeds is felt to be a differentiating factor between psychoanalysis and psychotherapy by some authors. A clinical vignette is used to illustrate some issues that arise over the problem of apology. It is suggested that a theoretical school that considers the child's intense drives to be the source of difficulty will yield a certain perspective toward apologizing as opposed to another that attributes problems to parental failures. A position for apology in analysis and treatment is offered that hopes to bridge these differing postures.

REFERENCES

Freud, S. (1923). The ego and the id. *Standard Edition* 19.

Gill, M. (1982). Analysis of Transference I. *Theory and Technique. II. Studies of Nine Audio-Recorded Psychoanalytic Sessions.* New York: International Universities Press.

—— (1984). Psychoanalysis and psychotherapy: A revision. *International Journal of Psychoanalysis* 11:161–179.

Goldberg, A. (1981). Self psychology and the distinctiveness of psychotherapy. *International Journal of Psychoanalytic Psychotherapy* 8:57–70.

Hoffman, I. (1983). The patient as interpreter of the analyst's experience *Contemporary Psychoanalysis* 19:389–422.

Kohut, H. (1984). *How Does Analysis Cure?* Chicago and London: University of Chicago Press.

Kubie, L. S. & Israel, H. A. (1955). "Say you're sorry." *Psychoanalytic Study of the Child* 10:289–299.

Langs, R. (1982). *The Psychotherapeutic Conspiracy* New York and London: Jason Aronson.

Newman, K. (1985). Countertransference—Its Role in Facilitating the

Use of the Object Presented at the monthly meeting of the Chicago Psychoanalytic Society, November 1985 Chicago, Illinois.

Racker, H. (1968). *Transference and Countertransference.* New York: International Universities Press.

Ravich, R. A. & Dunton, H. D. (1965). "Say you're sorry": A ten-year follow-up *American Journal of Psychotherapy* 20 615–623.

I Wish the Hour Were Over:
Elements of a Moral Dilemma (2005)

While principally a clinical paper, Goldberg's *I Wish the Hour Were Over: Elements of a Moral Dilemma* (2005) emphasizes the various views on conflict. On the one hand, he discusses the issue of conflict as internal, as opposing and as unconscious and on the other, conflicts as external for all to see and wholly conscious. These latter conflicts are represented by the narcissistic behavior disorders. "They are conflicts that seem to defy the neatness of internal, unconscious opposition of mental agencies. Many of these patients are completely aware of what they do and are not at all in conflict about it while they are doing it. Yet these behaviors are despised on retrospect, presenting them on those occasions as conflicts." These Jekyll and Hyde behaviors that divide the self into two unequal, parallel sectors are kept separate by the mechanism of disavowal, which maintains the vertical split in the psyche. These parallel selves are in a struggle to dominate and gain control of the psyche and are revealed in a variety of behavioral maladies. These behaviors might include sexual perversions, substance abuse, stealing, or perhaps more subtle expressions in everyday moral conflicts.

The psychoanalytic treatment of such disorders, with the aim of integrating the disparate selves, is likely to involve recognition of a parallel split in the analyst and it may be essential that the analyst experience the patient's conflict as well. The analyst living in uncertainty, as the patient lives in alternating periods of uncertainty, may be the first step in integrating the separate selves. Analytic work involves living for a time in the uncomfortable limbo of a dilemma. It is the interpretation of the dual sectors and the underlying depression that might make things better for the patient. And to live for a while with our patient's uncertainty, conflicts, struggles and dilemmas might be a necessary element on the way to understanding.

—GM

*   *   *

In contrast to the viewpoint that sees conflict as deriving from defense against instinctual drives and thus as an intrapsychic phenomenon, this essay presents conflict as some-times being an external opposition between disparate con-figurations of the self. These parallel sectors with different goals and ambitions can be seen in a continuum from the dramatic narcissistic behavior disorders to more subtle in-stances of moral dilemmas. A clinical illustration is offered to demonstrate its occurrence and management in psychoanalysis.

INTRODUCTION

A patient in psychoanalysis, shortly after contemplating and then voic-ing agreement with an interpretation that had been offered, announced an intense urge to get up and leave, i.e., wishing the not-yet-terminated analytic hour were at an end. Yet no sooner had this thought been uttered than there followed another wish of possibly equal intensity: that the hour not soon end. One might readily say that this patient was ambivalent about staying versus leaving, and, surely, it could also be said that he was in conflict about these two impulses or feelings.

The interpretation that had just been offered had to do with a some-what corresponding set of issues in conflict, these having to do with the patient's father. Although initially, this patient voiced only negative and disdainful memories and feelings about his father, over time, he had recalled more and more positive emotions about this parent, and, even-tually, he had been able to contemplate how much the loss of his father meant to him. This traumatic loss had occurred when the patient was ten years old, resulting from an acrimonious separation and divorce. Although this had first been presented by the patient as an episode of relief to all (i.e., to the patient, his mother, his older sister, and a younger brother), it now served as the carrier of memories of both sadness and longing for the absent man.

The aforementioned relief of the household over the father's depar-ture had been accompanied by an assignment to the patient of the role of man of the house—an assignment made by his mother, and one he had fulfilled with much satisfaction and pride. And so the conflict about

departing the analytic hour early seemed to serve as a miniature enactment of that childhood event, in that getting up to leave allowed him to
feel independent and no longer in need of his analyst, while remaining a
patient for the rest of the hour became associated with the never-
relieved sadness and yearning of the forlorn little boy. We seemed to be
present at a paradigmatic illustration of conflict.

MULTIPLE PERSPECTIVES ON AMBIVALENCE AND CONFLICT

In "Inhibitions, Symptoms, and Anxiety" (1926), Freud presents his
prototypical version of a conflict due to ambivalence, positing the case
of Little Hans as demonstrating a "well-grounded love along with a no
less justifiable hatred" (p. 102). Freud states that although this conflict
may well lead to a symptom such as the phobia in Little Hans, it may
also be resolved by way of an intensification of one of the two feelings
and the vanishing of the other. Although the conflict arises from ambivalence, there may be no evident trace of either of the forces of
opposition. The two feelings are no longer experienced consciously, and
the conflict has now moved to another arena.

That move and disappearance of conscious conflict has been described in modern psychoanalysis as one existing between posited
agencies of the mind. Thus, as the loving feelings of the little boy toward
the father remain conscious, the hostile ones are kept at bay by the
strength and opposition of the superego. Of course, the loving ones may
also be repressed and vanish as well.

The simple formula of ambivalence is now a complicated complex,
with some ambivalence being conscious and remaining so; some leading
to conflict that in turn may give rise to a symptom, such as a phobia, or
to a reaction formation in which overwhelming love drives away the
hostility, or vice versa; and some simply seeming to vanish altogether.
Indeed, the universality of both ambivalence and conflict gives one
license almost to dispense with the specific meanings of the words. We
can be ambivalent about the choice of a dessert, in conflict about a
particular career decision, and seemingly free of either issue while the
struggle remains an unconscious one.

It may be prudent to recognize that much ambivalence lies outside the usual meaning of conflict, as when one goes back and forth in choosing a particular piece of clothing for an ensemble; while some conflict may seem to be without ambivalence, as when we rid ourselves of an annoying fly or mosquito. The significance of Freud's presentation was to underscore the presence of opposition in the form of love versus hate. And the further import of his illustration was to position this opposition within the psyche, thus identifying it as an internal and constant struggle.

Keeping these simple perspectives in mind—internal, oppositional, and unconscious—I would like to offer a puzzle: a form of conflict that appears at times to satisfy none of these requirements, yet, paradoxically, also qualifies as conflict. This form of conflict is represented by the narcissistic behavior disorders, which range from cross-dressing to thievery to all manner of substance abuse. They are external for all to see. They exist, sometimes though not always without a sense of opposition, and they are conscious without exception. For sure, one sees a variety of qualifications to these points, but for the most part, they are conflicts that seem to defy the neatness of an internal, unconscious opposition of mental agencies. Many of these patients are completely aware of what they do and are not at all in conflict about it while they are doing it. Yet they unhesitatingly insist that they dislike or even despise these behaviors in retrospect, presenting them on those occasions as a conflict. They are miniaturizations of Jekyll and Hyde, and as Robert Louis Stevenson (1886) wrote, "Henry Jekyll stood *at times* aghast at the acts of Edward Hyde" (p. 87, italics added).

SOME THEORETICAL WAYS OF CONCEPTUALIZING BEHAVIOR DISORDERS

The theoretical underpinnings of narcissistic behavior disorders have been presented in detail elsewhere (Goldberg 1999), with reference to a variety of clinical case studies (Goldberg 2001). The crucial distinction offered to explain this form of disorder is that of a focus on the mechanism of disavowal, utilizing the concept of the vertical split. This configuration presents a psyche that is divided into two usually unequal, parallel sectors. These sectors are separated from one another and are initially characterized by having different and often opposing sets of goals and values. Thus, a seemingly proper and mature heterosexual man might coexist with one having a periodically active involvement in some sexual perversion. The activation of the perverse sector, of whatever form it takes, is episodic, yet that sector is capable of a complete domination of this man's personality. After the perverse activity subsides, there may be remorse and regret, and so these parallel sectors qualify as being in conflict and oppositional, yet the one or the other regularly submits to the control of its counterpart, and the opposition disappears.

What has become apparent in further studies of such behavior disorders is the lack of their confinement to the usual outstanding and dramatic forms of misbehaviors, such as the sexual perversions, and the recognition of similar configurations present in more subtle and common examples of conflict. Due either to our alertness to the existence of the phenomenon or to our reorientation in the ways of conceptualizing clinical material, we can now recognize the operation of disavowal and the existence of the vertical split in a wider variety of maladies. Thus, we can revisit an analytic patient and his or her presumed conscious conflict with an eye to ascertaining the likelihood of the patient's possession of parallel selves in a struggle (a conflict) to dominate and gain control of the psyche and the motoric mechanisms of behavior.

THE MORAL CONFLICT

To return to the patient of mine whom I described earlier, the initial examination of his battle between leaving and staying in the analytic hour, between independence and dependence, turned out rather surprisingly to me to be a moral conflict as well. We should all be familiar with what may be considered everyday and common (to therapists at least) moral conflicts. These range from our billing insurance companies for missed appointments, to changing diagnostic codes in order to ensure the payment of claims, to not declaring cash payments as income subject to income tax, to employing family members in mock positions in order to claim deductions, to moonlighting on top of salaried jobs that forbid outside employment, to claiming deductions that are personal forms of dining and entertainment as business related, and on and on. It is a rare professional who has not at one time or another been forced to consider and even to struggle with one or another of these issues, and it is probably an equally rare one who has not in some manner rationalized the embrace of one or more items on this very abbreviated list. The active involvement in such an activity that might be considered immoral or illegal is felt by some to be a game of getting away with as much as possible, and by others as an indicator of conforming to a strict code of propriety. Regardless of where one stands, the differentiation between saints and sinners is not an easy one.

CLINICAL CASE ELABORATION

In order to maintain confidentiality, I shall offer only that a particular psychoanalytic patient of mine, the one referred to above, was an active participant in one of these immoral ventures, and this fact became clear at the very start of the analysis. When I first learned of it, I had not a whit of personal condemnation, feeling it to be both *justified*—in that it was a perfectly proper thing to do, and *justifiable*—in that I and my patient could readily explain and support this sort of behavior. Thus, the supposed moral dilemma was initially without a voice.

My patient's peccadillo was not unfamiliar to me, and it seemed further legitimized by his having been given a form of a "don't ask, don't tell" injunction by a superior when he first inquired about it. Thus, the two of us conspired in an agreement that seemed to highlight the peculiar bind that is practiced and indeed forced upon so many people who continue to live by necessity in areas of moral and ethical discomfort. Of course, I do not offer this as anything more than a further bit of armor in the defense of one's ultimately unacceptable behavior.

Indeed, this behavior *did* become openly unacceptable when the patient announced one day that a particularly stupid act of his had led to the exposure of his heretofore secret misdeeds. As he described to me the foolish bit of behavior that led to his exposure, and as he asked me if it were possible that he himself had unwittingly and unconsciously brought about his own state of shame and embarrassment at being "caught in the act," I was unable to do much more than offer the opinion that I felt it unlikely that he wanted to get caught. Thus, we became further joined, now in stupidity.

Much of this patient's treatment after the disclosure of his misdeed seemed focused upon my championing his efforts to feel righteous and vindicated in what he had done, and there can be no doubt that I was quite unable to reach some midpoint of neutrality, or at least of analytic detachment, for quite some time. I cannot now be certain as to the moment at which I finally man-aged that feat, but it was certainly after our analytic work revealed the father as a man who was himself wrapped in corruption and double-dealing, primarily with members of his own family. I am convinced that my own recognition of a personal and private moral dilemma did not arrive as a bolt from the blue, but instead grew out of a succession of uncomfortable feelings that were triggered by my efforts to see the situation from the point of view of my patient's protagonist. I think it is vitally important that one live for a while in this gray area of conflict. Although any psychoanalyst must or should have at least a touch of larceny in order to really help a thief, it is an equal requirement that a period of uncertainty be allowed to have its day.

I vividly recall presenting some of these ideas to a group of psycho-analysts in Philadelphia, when one analyst responded by recounting a vignette of a patient who had stolen a dress in a department store, and who then asked her analyst what he thought of her. He proudly told the audience that he had informed his patient she was a thief, after which he triumphantly sat down. My private thought was that she, of course, knew that she was a thief and hardly needed him to tell her that. What she needed, and what he could not supply, was for *him* to experience *her* conflict.

Living in uncertainty is not as easy as it sounds, since we know that most of our patients with behavior disorders do instead live in alternating periods of certainty. Surviving in the limbo of a dilemma is necessarily uncomfortable, and one is tempted to come down vigorously with a definitive pronouncement, just as did that unhelpful man in Philadelphia. However, the capacity to sustain the parallel state of supposed opposition is the first step in the achievement of a hoped-for integration of what has previously been split apart.

Integration does not by any means gain victory by favoring good over evil. Just as we all know or should know that forensic psychiatry has no room to breathe, with the prevalent McNaughton rule of only knowing and acting upon right from wrong, we should also know that mere cognitive certainty is a poor guide to emotional conviction. It is especially difficult in our efforts to comprehend misbehavior for us to realize that what seems to be wrong beyond a shadow of a doubt is not to be simply judged according to the dimensions of right and wrong. Indeed, I finally succeeded in seeing that what my particular patient had done could have relatively equal support on both sides of the question. And so I was left with the proper stance for any analyst: a state of puzzlement, a condition that must necessarily precede that of understanding and the promise of resolution.

Analysts are not good moral barometers, despite their wish to be so. Our primary tool of interpretation represents but one way of looking at things amid a myriad of such ways. When we offer an interpretation, it is an invitation to the patient to appreciate a new and different perspective, but it cannot completely erase the point of view that the patient has lived by up until now. As much as we might like to feel that we know best, it is best to know that we but know differently.

The difficult task of integrating disparate points of view is no more one of reaching a compromise than it is of choosing one over the other. It is here that psychoanalysis offers a unique perspective by its claim of being a depth psychology: we must attend to what lies beneath this duality of purpose—a hint of which was offered to me by my patient in his announced struggle to leave or to stay.

A Dual Transference

The vision of the father retained by this patient was realized by his seeing me as a bright and competent figure on one hand, and as a corrupt and somewhat doddering fool on the other. Statements that I had made in one hour came back as deliveries by the patient in a much transmogrified form several days later, sounding like the mutterings of an idiot. My much-sought-after and happy neutrality was continually on the edge of being destroyed by a vigorous defense of mine—one aimed at clarification and a restoration of me as possessing unappreciated wisdom. Yet at times, I was convinced that I was indeed a fool, and so I made a silent resolve to keep my mouth shut. (Perhaps some of the long silences commonly attributed to analysts derive from a similar sort of resolution.)

My patient seemed different from Little Hans not so much in his possession of "well-grounded love along with no less justifiable hatred" (Freud 1926, p. 102)—both of which were quite apparent—as much as in his failure to reconcile these emotions by way of identification with both aspects of his father. It became clear to me that he had suffered a traumatic de-idealization of a father who, in one sense, remained always outside of him and for whom he had conducted a relentless search. And what lay beneath this oscillation between the great and the belittled, the good and the bad, and all the other possible dualities was the depression that wrapped itself around him when he admitted to wanting to stay in the hour. The very recognition and articulation of that wish introduced him once again to an empty sadness that he now recalled had enveloped him when his father left home. He could try with limited success and urging from his mother to replace his father, thereby covering this inner feeling of emptiness, or he could vent his rage at the departed and disappointing father in a different but equally unsuccessful effort to obliterate his depression. Interestingly enough, one psychiatrist had earlier diagnosed him as bipolar.

The patient's split of the representative hour and those that followed could be said to nicely mesh with that of the analyst in his parallel, complementary split. We both knew right from wrong, yet had chosen a course based on a set of rationalizations that drowned out the legal issues. While never blind to the sector that we had chosen to disavow, we gave it little heed—until it slowly began to make a claim to recognition. At some undetermined point, we became locked in a moral dilemma and remained there until further psychoanalytic work revealed some of its origins.

I have here presented my main points about this analysis by focusing on the father, with little reference to the patient's mother. I do so in the interest of brevity, as well as out of my wish to pursue the line of inquiry introduced by Freud in regard to Little Hans. Surely, no study of depression can be considered complete without an examination of the early maternal relationship. Nevertheless, this patient's life story did seem to founder on the rocks of some core depression that had telescoped into the time of the loss of his father, and it was there that the work of analysis came to be concentrated. And so it is there that one answer to the connection between psychoanalysis and morality can be focused. This is not to say that all moral conundrums are fundamentally psychological problems, but it is to suggest that psychoanalysis may have a contribution to make to issues of morality. Moral principles are not to be seen as either exclusively God given or intrinsic to humanity, but as solutions to psychic discontent as well.

THE CONTRIBUTION OF DISAVOWAL TO SUPEREGO EXPLANATIONS

The classical explanations for moral lapses have to do with the power and position of the superego as presented in the tripartite model of the mind. Failures in the strength and integrity of the superego allow for the escape of immoral or amoral action. Sometimes this has been conceptualized in the form of superego lacunae (Gedo and Goldberg 1973, p. 14), and at other times, as an identification with a criminal sort of superego (Benedek 1973, p. 246). The predominant feeling that dominates this oppositional scene is that of guilt, and the predominant defense that is operable or absent is that of repression.

A different model of the mind was first presented by Freud (1927) in his discussion of fetishism, where the predominant defense was that of disavowal. This was further elaborated by Kohut as a disorder of narcissism, illustrated by the positing of separate self configurations split off from one another. Neither model can or should claim exclusivity, since

427

models should be viewed as conveniences or tools of explanation rather than as factual representations.

Disavowal, again according to Freud, has to do with perception of the reality of castration: either one has a penis or one does not. In its more familiar usage as denial, once again, we see it in the denial of bereavement over a lost one, as well as in all sorts of common ways that the real world is not allowed to exist. When we move to moral issues, it becomes a case of the forbidden being allowed because of that absence of reality. From the commandments of religion to the injunctions of law, one is confronted with choices and options, to do or not to do, and the denial of the one allows the other. All of the "thou shalt nots" become abandoned or erased by the process of denial following the law of two negatives that yield a positive. All the boundaries vanish through the employment of disavowal.

If we return to the more obvious standards of the allowable, the study of behavior disorders enables us to better study the vertical split in individuals who are grossly aberrant. We are now able to see this split as operant in much more subtle kinds of struggles over what is proper and what is improper. And the inevitable conclusion is that there is no clear and unmistakable point at which a moral conflict moves from the minor to the significant, and so any and all such differences become a proper arena for psychological study.

The model of the superego in conflict with forbidden impulses arises in psychoanalysis by a transference displacement from patient to analyst—i.e., the analyst becomes the bearer of superego prohibitions, and the struggle takes place between analyst and patient. Thus, Little Hans might see his analyst as the embodiment of the superego, as one who would condemn and punish him for erotic feelings toward his mother and hostile ones toward his father. Agencies of the mind become realized in transference interactions. However, conflicts in these forms of narcissistic disorders often take a different form—they become realized within the person of the analyst who matches the patient's personal split. Thus, the patient's misdeed is not enacted and condemned in the interaction between patient and analyst, but rather, it is recognized as a conflict that is then experienced by the analyst. I do not tell my patient that he is wrong, so that together we can analyze the origins of his struggle, with its possible ensuing guilt. I feel that his misdeed is justified at the same time that I feel it is wrong, and so I share his split. Unless I can do so, I may as well sit in mutual triumph with my colleague in Philadelphia as but a mere bearer of correctness.

Discussion

Pluralism seems to predominate in today's psychoanalysis, but it runs the risk of engendering a certain laxity in the clarity and coherence of our thinking—while it also provides an opportunity to try out various perspectives in the effort to explain mental operations. It is certainly no radical move for us to consider a more central role for disavowal, and it is reasonable to suggest that the transference configurations relevant to disavowal will have a corresponding distinction from those witnessed in the mental model underscoring repression. Disavowal invites a scrutiny of reality. The objective analyst is able to form a realistic appraisal of the position or perception offered by a patient, and may respond accordingly—e.g., "you are wrong in seeing the world that way." We see this in the work of mourning, wherein the patient has to accept the fact of his or her loss. The empathic analyst is able to be realistic, but needs to share the disavowed sector as well—e.g., "You are correct to want the world to be different." My point is that the analyst, like the patient, can be both objective and empathic, thereby living simultaneously in what are essentially two visions of the world—visions in conflict.

One other unremarkable but often forgotten contribution to the conviction that one is correct and one is doing right is a feeling of pride and righteousness. The corresponding or complementary feeling attributable to uncertainty and error is often depression. This can be related, of course, to the vicissitudes of the operations of the superego, but, as in my patient described earlier, it can also represent the underlying depression found in many instances of disavowal. I suspect that further study of the types of transferences that present themselves in more subtle forms of behavior in conflict will lead to a deeper understanding of the qualities and treatment of various forms of depression.

SUMMARY AND CONCLUSIONS

The preeminent position of intrapsychic conflict in psychoanalysis merits rethinking with an eye to seeing it as but one way of examining and explaining a variety of oppositional struggles, ranging from indecision to ambivalence to reaction formation to all manner of symptomatology. The battle between instinctual drives and their control is an oversimplified truism that has failed to fully explicate the complex and different forms of transferences that emerge in psychoanalytic encounters.

The best available evidence for confirmation of a different way to think about a wide range of oppositional phenomena is gained by examining different forms of transference manifestations. Viewing disavowal as not only a defense offers us an opportunity to expand our theoretical vision. The particular form of transference seen in those who employ disavowal is a correlation of the vertical split in the patient to one that develops and emerges in the therapist or analyst. The split-apart sectors are often seen in opposition to one another, with one corresponding to reality (the reality ego) and one demonstrating a disregard of reality (the "misbehaving" sector). Psychoanalytic phenomena encourage a matched split in the analyst, reflective of the psychic makeup of the patient.

Analytic work involves the integration of these divided sectors, with particular attention to the underlying depression that seems to regularly characterize these patients. Interpretations of the drive-defense model may be more disabling than helpful, while interpretations of the dual sectors are experienced as ameliorative. As always, the best principle to follow in psychoanalysis is that of the interpretation of the transference, with the added recognition that transference takes many different forms.

REFERENCES

Benedek, I. (1973). *The Emotional Structure of the Family in Psychoanalytic Investigations.* New York: Quadrangle.

Freud, S. (1926). Inhibitions, symptoms, and anxiety. *Standard Edition* 20.

——— (1927). Fetishism. *Standard Edition* 21.

Gedo, J. & Goldberg, A. (1973). *Models of the Mind.* Chicago, IL: University of Chicago Press.

Goldberg, A. (1999). *Being of Two Minds.* Hillsdale, NJ: Analytic Press.

——— (2001). *Errant Selves.* Hillsdale, NJ: Analytic Press.

Stevenson, R. L. (1886). *The Strange Case of Dr. Jekyll and Mr. Hyde.* London: Penguin, 1979.

www.ingramcontent.com/pod-product-compliance
Lightning Source LLC
Chambersburg PA
CBHW060304030426
42336CB00011B/934